To Gayle King,

I have been a big fan of yours for many years. I hope you enjoy my holoholo Diary, as it is a "sabbatical year" that I took between being a Mother and a grandmother.

It is also a tribute book to two wise Hawaiian Kahuna women (a mother and a daughter). These aunties mentored me "as a receiver." Knowing how you have always empowered women, I want to share this book with you.

With Aloha
Nancy Clemens

AKA AND ME

# MY
# *HOLOHOLO*
# DIARY

*One Year on the Big Island of Hawai'i*

*Holoholo:*
*a "walk about," traveling around with no plan,*
*not knowing the destination . . .*

## Nancy Clemens

BLUE DOLPHIN PUBLISHING

Published by Blue Dolphin Publishing
   an imprint of Pelican Pond Publishing
P. O. Box 1255, Nevada City, CA 95959

ISBN: 978-1-57733-507-8   paperback with b/w photos
ISBN: 978-1-57733-509-2   paperback with color photos
ISBN: 978-1-57733-508-5   e-book, with color photos

See also:
www.bluedolphinpublishing.com
www.pelicanpondpublishing.com
www.dolphindivinations.com

Library of Congress Control Number: 2023932958

First edition: June, 2023

Cover art: "Aka" by Mayumi Oda

Printed simultaneously in the United States of America,
the United Kingdom and Australia

       5        4        3        2        1

## *Dedication*

THESE WRITINGS ARE DEDICATED TO Auntie Aka's mother, Fern, Kalehuamakanoe Prim Pule, who passed from this world on October 11, 2009, and to Auntie Aka herself (Haleaka Iolani Pule), who passed from this world, five years later on August 11, 2014.

Even before her birth, Aka was recognized as a *Kapu* (sacred) child. Both Auntie Fern and Aka were ceremonial and spiritual caretakers of the ancient Hawai'ian temple, Hikiau Heiau, at Kealakekua Bay on the Big Island of Hawai'i . . . and much more.

Both of them originally inspired, and then directed me to keep a diary to publish at a later date. Without their continuous support and encouragement over the years, this book would not exist.

During their lifetimes, Auntie Fern and Aka touched and inspired thousands of people from all over the world, both in Hawai'i and, for Aka, on her many trips to Japan and Europe. Auntie Fern, as an iconic figure at her shop next to Kealakekua Bay, greeted and talked to literally thousands of visitors over the years. Emanating that special spirit of Aloha, Auntie Fern sold her hand-made Hawai'ian clothing and crafts, and entertained everyone by strumming her ukulele while she sang an endless playlist of Hawai'ian songs. Under the surface, both of these women were powerful spiritual beings and seers, whose knowledge harked back to royal ancestors, the Kahuna line of Heva Heva Nui, and the ancient wisdom of old Hawai'i. I was honored and blessed to be their friend. Such precious and rare beings should always be remembered and treasured.

I also dedicate this *Diary* to Aka's brothers and sisters: Wanda, Kalehua, Kapali, Kela, Lisa, Mahoe, and Lehua, and to her children, Lilinoe Reed, Nolan Keolaonaali'i Reed (Ola), Suzy Kalehuamakenoe Reed, and to their extended families – and future descendants, who may someday read these memoirs of their ancestors.

And a big Mahalo to all my other heart-friends in Hawai'i, who make up a *lei* – a flower necklace – of the beautiful beings who nourished, guided, and blessed me, like fragrant flowers, during what I call "my Hawai'ian *holoholo* adventures."

AUNTIE FERN -- KALEHUAMAKANOE PRIM PULE

## Table of Contents

## Map of the Big Island
### From Hawai'i National Parks

*Preface*

ALOHA! Finally, after many years, I feel led to put pen to paper and recount some of the experiences and stories from the "diary" I kept from the time when I moved to and lived on the Big Island of Hawai'i for a year during 2001-2002.

These stories and observations are a heartfelt tribute to both Auntie Fern Pule and her daughter, Aka (Haleaka Iolani Pule), their families, and other special local friends who mentored me and shared their Aloha.

The memories that I share are told through my eyes as a visitor, but also as someone who has come to the Big Island for over thirty years. I love the Hawai'ian culture and people. Bruddah IZ (Kamakawiwo'ole) reflects my feelings when he said on one of his music CDs, "Some are Hawai'ian at heart, and support all things Hawai'ian." I am not a historian or a scholar, but I do support all things Hawai'ian.

During this special year, I learned as much as I could about the history, culture, and local customs of the people on the Big Island. The rich Hawai'ian culture and its profound spirituality contains gifts within it that I have found to be universally life-giving and healing. As the true meaning of Aloha unveils itself in its multiple layers, an ever-increasing blessing waits within . . . to be discovered.

***Opening quotes from Aka (Haleaka Iolani Pule):***

*"ALOHA ! In ancient Hawai'ian traditional beliefs, everything in the universe is inter-related. And it is through our relationship with the natural world, the spirit world, the creator, each other, and ourselves, that balance and harmony must be maintained, in order to truly assist each other and be of service to the DIVINE...."*

*"True Ho'oponopono, when you work its principles within yourself, is like finding the voice that God gave to you in the beginning and learning to distinguish it from the other voices that you picked up along the way."*

AUNTIE AKA, HALEAKA IOLANI PULE

# Introduction

MY *HOLOHOLO* DIARY IS BASED upon the very personal diary I kept when I left my home in California to live on the Big Island of Hawai'i for one year in 2001-2002. I call it my "sabbatical year," a time between being a mother and a grandmother. The memories and reflections told here come through the mind of a frequent "visitor" from the mainland, and one who loves and supports the traditional Hawai'ian culture.

The writing of this *Diary* is mainly intended to be a tribute to, and honoring of, Auntie Aka (Haleaka Iolani Pule) and her mother, Auntie Fern (Kalehuamakanoe Prim Pule), and their Ohana (family). They have all shared valuable spiritual and cultural teaching with me that I feel will benefit others. And, they have given me their permission and blessings to share them. Living these ancient covenants can make each of us a happier, well balanced person.

We had been coming to the Big Island as a family almost every year since the mid-1980s, and while we had met Auntie Fern, it was only years later that I met her daughter, Aka. Aka was instrumental to my spiritual growth and understanding of the Hawai'ian culture, both when I first met her in the year 2000, the next year during my one-year return to the Big Island, and in the following years thereafter. She taught me, inspired me, and changed my life forever. And, we continued our relationship for the next fourteen years, both in Hawaii and during her visits to our home in the Sierra Nevada foothills of California.

There are many stories about Auntie Aka, her mother, Auntie Fern, and their *ohana* (family) within this diary. The spiritual and cultural teachings that they imparted to me have been like time-released capsules. They have opened and grown in my heart and mind over the last twenty years in such a way that I never felt I really lost these friends. They strongly urged me to record our shared experiences that were to open my eyes and heart to the original

Hawai'ian culture and the multi-layered meaning of Aloha. This diary also contains stories about other local teachers and heart-friends, who opened for me a window to the original culture. Each, in their unique way, demonstrated to me the true meaning of Aloha.

In this *Diary* I share my growing pains, doubts, and fears, and also my awe and wonder of the island, the people, the ancient culture, as well as some "paranormal," "mystical," and visionary experiences I had while I was there. I imagine holding the reader's hand and taking them along with me on some spontaneous adventures with newfound friends who share their wisdom that I was so blessed to receive.

After various meetings and teachings with Aka, she would often remind me to go home and record in my diary an inspiring conversation about Hawai'ian spiritual teachings, or an adventure we shared as friends – before I forgot it!

There are many times when I feel reluctant and vulnerable about publishing portions of my *Diary* because it is so deeply personal. But because both Aka and Auntie Fern urged me to keep a diary during my time in Hawai'i, I finally decided to follow their advice "to share it with anyone who wishes to read it." Because of their continuous encouragement and my love for them, I have compiled and written these recollections, and hope they touch the hearts of readers as well.

Aka often "talked story" to me about the book she herself planned to write, entitled "Through Hawai'ian Eyes." Years later, while teaching in Europe, she changed her proposed title to "Somewhere Over the Rainbow." But Aka was so busy teaching, traveling, and raising a family, that there was little time to write a book.

One late night in 2012, while Aka was staying with us here in California for a few weeks, we sat outside in the dark, looking at the stars. Out of the blue, Aka said to me, "Sistah, if I don't get my book written, will you please write it for me? You have a great memory, and I already talked it to you, right? And you have your diary, right?" As she said this to me, I felt those tingles, that Aka calls "chicken skin," ripple through my whole body. Yet I protested, saying, "I would never presume to write your book." I knew that it would be impossible to bring forth the *mana* (spiritual power), beauty, and grace that were in her words and spiritual transmissions. It is only now, as this book is about to go to press, that I have had the realization that Aka and her mother, Auntie Fern, assigned me a *kuleana* (spiritual duty). Besides my own experiences, *My Holoholo Diary* includes many stories about Aka and her mother, Auntie Fern, that contain the wisdom and Aloha that they shared with me, and with so many other people from all around the world.

Auntie Fern also wanted me to write these stories as well. Coming from generations of gifted Hawai'ian people, she had been a spiritual mentor to me for many years, helping me to better understand myself as a "receiver," a person with intuitive gifts. One day in 2002, I said to Auntie Fern, "If I write about you, I will send what I have written to you so you can review and approve it." She replied, "That will not be necessary. I trust you. Write whatever you want, because I read your book and I know who you are." Auntie Fern was referring to my recently published book and cards, *The Dolphin Divination Cards* and *A Guide to the Dolphin Divination Cards*.

Aka also read the *Dolphin* book and used the cards as a part of her private counseling sessions. She gave me explicit permission to include in my book her teachings and anything that I wanted to say about her. "Don't you remember, I *told* you to write a diary, and thah's why!" she said enthusiastically.

This diary is so deeply personal that, over the last twenty years, I debated sharing it. But because both Aka and her mother, Auntie Fern, urged me to keep this diary, and to share it with others someday, I have decided to share it now, as a tribute and in memory of their special lives.

By opening this very intimate *Diary*, I hope that you and others will receive their blessing and be inspired by what has been shared here. As Aka always said to me, "If you receive a blessing, the way of Aloha is to share it, in some way, shape, or form."

Nancy Clemens

September 2022, Nevada City, California

*And a note to the Kanaka Maoli — What I have written in my diary is from the perspective of a visitor. After coming to the islands for many years and meeting many "locals," I happen to love the musical and colorful patois called "pidgin English." From time to time I use a little pidgin English in the conversations that I record because that's what was said, and I am trying to give the flavor of how so many Hawai'ians salt and pepper their spoken language. I hope and pray that I have not made too many mistakes, and have not intended to be disrespectful to anyone or anything, in any way, shape, or form. — N.C.*

# My Holoholo Diary

*One Year on the Big Island of Hawai'i*

AUNTIE IOLANI LUAHINE, THE LEGENDARY HULA DANCER

# PROLOGUE

## *Auntie Iolani Luahine, the Legendary Hula Dancer*

MANY YEARS AGO, Auntie Iolani Luahine was seen dancing on the top of a lava stone wall. People said she was supernatural in the way she moved . . . she even seemed to float. At times, people saw fire coming from her eyes, like the volcano goddess Kupuna Pele herself. Her dancing brought the old myths and legends alive. Such dances mesmerized her audiences, and it was as if she floated and moved like the fire of the volcano itself . . . ever changing, undulating, steamy and hot.

And then she could dance like the soft rain that falls on the wild orchids and jungle vines on the Hilo side, moist, dewy-eyed, fluid and wet. All the elements danced through her and she was like no other. Her facial expressions were as fluid as her body, sometimes looking soft and demure, and other times fierce, with wide-eyed wrathfulness. She will never be forgotten and is a legendary Hawai'ian treasure, because in modern times she manifested the old ones and their ancient chants and dances.

When she chanted, her voice seemed to come from everywhere, the trees, the mountains, the ocean. A wail, a cry, a melodious and haunting chant, fiery and then wet, like dewdrops on the plumeria and hibiscus flowers. She was like the *mauka* high lands of the Island, full of jungle vines and flowers and healing plants. She was fragrant with herb, blossoms, and spice, and some said they saw her floating a few inches above the lava stone wall she danced upon, her black hair flying behind her.

She was Iolani Luahine . . . an old one come back. Sometimes she clicked *ili ili* (small) stones between her fingers, tapping out rhythms. Other times she sat (*hula noho*) with her legs folded behind

3

her and danced with her arms and hands and eyes. She had *kala au* (sticks) for rhythms, and she had her drummer with the *ipu heke* (gourd) drum.

On September 7, 1964 Iōlani Luahine was seen dancing down the hallways of a hospital on Oahu with a *maile lei* in her hands, and chanting an ancient song of welcome. Her niece, Auntie Fern Makekau Pule, had just given birth to a baby girl. When Iolani Luahine came into the room, she continued her chant, blessing the new baby. Then she asked the baby's mother, Auntie Fern, if the baby girl had already been named? Auntie Fern told her that the baby's father had already chosen the name Haleaka. Ironically, Haleaka means Harriet in English, identical to Iolani Luahine's English name. So Auntie Io added her own name, Iolani, which means heavenly hawk, to Haleaka. And now this baby was named "Haleaka Iolani." Many years later, she would be known, all over the world, simply as "Auntie Aka."

Many years later, Aka gave me the words to this chant that was sung to her by her Great Auntie Io in the Hawai'ian language:

"*Kapu Child, you bring light into the darkness and you shine like the sun. You bring life to the deeper meanings of Aloha. Haleaka Iolani Pule, you bring forth this powerful energy called mana, embedded with benevolent gifts, bright light, Aloha, and beautiful flowers of love.*"

## MY ARRIVAL

My PLANE TOUCHED DOWN on the Big Island of Hawai'i on September 6, 2001. I had flown to Honolulu from Sacramento, California, and then from Honolulu to Hilo, Hawai'i. I was greeted by the soft and fragrant air, and by that special elevated energy that is unique to the Big Island. This is the newest island in the Hawai'ian island chain where new land from a live volcano is constantly being formed. The island of Hawai'i, also known as the "Big Island," has the Hawai'ian name of *Moku o Keawe*, in honor of an ancient chief. Here I was in the middle of the Pacific Ocean on a tropical island with many diverse eco-systems. There were jungles and waterfalls, high grassy plateaus, relatively recent lava flows, hardened lava deserts, high snow-capped mountain tops, and many beautiful beaches and shorelines. There are ancient stone platform temples, called *heiaus*, and remnants of villages from the old culture that existed here before colonization. And there are tanned-skinned local people with smiling eyes and their warm, welcoming Aloha spirit. I was brimming over with excitement to be here for a long stay.

My white Jeep Cherokee was shipped on a Matson Lines ship and arrived a few days later. Shipping my jeep was far less expensive than buying a car on the island or renting an island "rent ah wreck." I moved into a cottage on the Hilo side that was arranged for me by my friend Carol. The cottage adjoined my landlord and landlady's home in Hawai'ian Paradise Park. H.P.P. was a large subdivision populated mainly by locals and situated between the towns of Kea'au and Pahoa. This was the wet side of the island, the home of orchids and rainbows and downpours that sometimes drown out an ordinary phone conversation.

My landlady, Debra, worked at home. She was a slim, attractive lady with a graceful walk and blond hair that was tightly pulled back. Her light skin told me that she didn't spend very much time at the beach. Her husband, James, was a congenial, good-looking man who worked away from the island for a few months at a time.

The cottage adjoined their home and was partially screened. The bedroom, living room, and kitchen were all in one large room. There was a bathroom, and a nice screened-in porch where I could set up my massage table. Our arrangement was for me to pay them a monthly rent. In addition, I was to trade some massages for Debra as well.

There were dozens of varieties of palm trees all over the large property, as well as a patch of white Maui pineapples at different stages of ripeness. When one pineapple was eaten, the top leafy part would be re-planted which would grow another pineapple. There were papaya and citrus trees, passion fruit vines, a banana tree, and star fruit trees.

A very large, old avocado tree stood tall outside of my screened porch, and seemed to drop one large avocado each night. I would vaguely hear the "plop" as the avocado hit the ground during my sleep. In the morning it would be on the ground, un-bruised, perfectly ripe and velvety green inside. These specimens were so perfect that it seemed as if the tree was giving me a gift every night. I ate these delicious avocados in so many different ways, but my favorites were with tamari and wasabi and of course, guacamole.

Many species of tropical plants and flowers splashed the land with color and fragrance. There were red and yellow hibiscus flowers that looked like trumpets, and Bougainvillea hedges in shades of crimson, purple and white. There were Birds of Paradise and Heliconia and Torch Ginger which looked like they were topped with red feathers. Plumeria trees were filled with the fragrant flowers that were often strung to make *lei* necklaces. The most fragrant and intoxicating flowers were the Pikake, the Pua Kenikeni, and the Tahitian Tiare flower with its five white petals whose fragrance reminded me of Gardenias. With all the fruit trees, palms, and flowers, I certainly felt like I was living in a beautiful arboretum.

Leaning up against my large living room window was a banana tree. Over a short time, I would watch the purple flower and stem transform into a small bunch of bananas that would gradually grow into a large bunch of bananas. When they were still green, the bunch could be cut and hung in the garage to finish ripening. I was encouraged to eat the fruit. But there was no way that I could even begin to eat all this fruit that surrounded me. I sliced the abundant star fruit into cross sections and put the pieces in zip-lock bags to freeze. When frozen, they were like golden, star-shaped popsicles. Surely this red-earthed land was a tropical paradise. If the first people on earth ate only fruit, then this was surely a Garden of Eden.

In the banana tree lived a green gecko, and in the evening he crawled onto the window to stare at me. I could hear his chirp as a "Hello, I'm back." He most definitely was interested in watching me. He did some runs up and down the large plate glass window and seemed to become still, as if screening my reaction. This gecko became my friend and we had a happy connection. Every evening he crawled out of the leaves of the banana tree to visit on the window. Banana leaves are very beautiful and graceful and I loved watching this natural display. When the breezes came up, the palms swayed and whispered, and the banana leaves scratched back and forth on the glass with an interesting rhythm. Often these gentle sounds and watchful eyes would put me to sleep at night.

### The Witness Protection Program

WHEN I FIRST ARRIVED, Debra and James picked me up at the Hilo airport. They wanted to show me around a little. It was a Sunday. They went to get the *New York Times*, and then we went to the large outdoor market in Pahoa for something to eat. After this we went to the "warm pond" at Ahalanui Beach Park, which is fed by volcanic heated springs that come up from under the ground. This large pond is surrounded by black lava walls and trees, and a shaded park with green grass. The water was not too deep, coming up just to my neck when standing. The water was so comfortably warm and relaxing, I floated around, enjoying this setting with quiet excitement. Outside a sea wall were ocean waves that crashed up, sometimes spilling their overflow into the warm pond.

Debra and James set up their folding chairs, put on their sun visors, and settled into reading their big Sunday newspaper. Who would get the funnies first, I wondered? On the way home they told me that living in this part of Hawai'i was like being in the "witness protection program." Somehow that struck all of us as very funny and we all laughed. It was especially funny to me, as it seemed that I was so far away from my family that no one would be able to find me here. Seriously, I thought, this would be a good location for someone in the witness protection program. We were "smack dab" in the middle of the Pacific Ocean. No swimming home if I got homesick.

### A Witness, as a Visitor

THE JOKE ABOUT THIS WITNESS PROTECTION PROGRAM became a part of a repertoire of odd, assorted things that could make me burst out laughing. I told myself that I was living deep in the jungle, in the witness protection program. I imagined that I was a witness, but not the kind that testifies in court. I was a witness of everything around me. I was going to become a witness of the Hawai'ian culture that I had come to love so much in the past. Orchids bloomed in almost every empty lot and alongside many of the roads. Clouds scudded across the sky and it rained a lot. In fact, I heard that the average rainfall on the Hilo side could be up to three hundred inches a year. But clear, sparkling blue skies appeared after the rains, as the dark clouds migrated across the ocean. Everything here was warm, humid and moist. Rain and soft sunshine often intermingled with each other, creating arching rainbows in soft pastels.

I felt so grateful to have this time to "just be" without any of my usual props: familiar and dearly loved family, friends and pets, and the cozy old farmhouse on ten acres of land back in California. I had stripped myself of everything that created my self-image. The familiar "security blankets" were now gone.

This was Tutu Pele's realm, where deep in the bowels of the Earth there was primal shaking and rumbling in this live volcano called Kilawea. Red hot molten lava and steam emanated from her crater and sometimes her vents. I felt she had invited me here, through repetitive dreams, but how the journey would unfold was a complete mystery. No props or supports were here to hold me up. It was left up to me and my wits to figure out how to live here and support myself. And to top it all off, I felt like a lone *haole* (white person) in a land of beautiful, tan-skinned people with soft brown eyes, big hearts and beautiful families.

Even though our family had vacationed in Hawai'i for many years, everything felt new this time, and this was to be the very first time in my life of living alone. I went from my own original family to roommates at college, and then to an early marriage and children. The children were babies when their father was killed in an accident. Then my children and I lived together for a few years until I married again. My husband Paul and I had two more children. So in all we had five children to raise. And so it went. Over the years I was extremely busy and never alone for long. Like many other busy mothers, the bathtub or shower was about the only refuge. Now all the children were grown up and the grandchildren were babies.

How would I do on my own, I wondered? What would I manifest with just my own energy, not enmeshed with anyone else's? Would I ever return home or would I choose to stay here? Would the family follow me to live together on the Big Island? All these questions went through my mind. I certainly was not looking for any romantic involvements here in Hawai'i, as I already had a loving partner. I felt strongly that I needed to learn to be happy by myself and I had never lived alone. I spread my quilt out on the bed, as I got ready for bed. "Alone is the way we are born, and surely, the way we die," I thought. One needed to be prepared for anything in life, even the solitary journey that we call death. As Aka was to tell me later, "We never know how or when we will get our ticket."

### Feeling the Aina (Earth) and the Lani (Sky)

THAT FIRST NIGHT, settling into my cottage, I sat out on my screened porch. It was a balmy night and the stars were out. Everything felt so fresh and alive. The *mana* (life force) was strong and felt like it penetrated my every cell. It was life-giving and enlivening. I began to meditate. I was so full of gratitude to have this time to myself. As I gazed at the stars, I said a little prayer of thanks for having a chance to be here in this sacred place, this beautiful *aina* (land). Before long I realized that something quite unusual was starting to happen. I

9

sensed being lifted up out of my body and into the sky. There was an older Hawai'ian woman on each side of me, guiding me up into the stars. It is very hard to describe, but there was a feeling of exquisite freedom and bliss. I will never forget the smiles and love that these two *tutus* gave me, as they escorted me up into the stars.

After all, I was following the directions that I had received in repetitive dreams of Kupuna Pele, the volcano goddess. In the dreams she was dancing in an orange fiery cloud as she invited me to come here to this island . . . for purification. They were such strong and vivid dreams that I eventually decided to be bold enough to act upon them. My family was open to me having this time in Hawai'i. They even told me that eventually they would follow me and we would find a new island home. It never worked out that way. But this lifting up into the sky was not a dream at all. It was a vision with the full sensation of being lifted and guided through the heavens by these two beautiful *tutus*. It was blissful being amongst the stars and feeling complete joy. When I had been full of doubts and insecurity, it gave me the confidence that I had done the right thing after all, and I felt welcomed.


## The Jeep Arrives


DEBRA, JAMES, AND I WENT to the port of Hilo to pick up my Jeep from Matson shipping lines. These large ships come into two ports on the Big Island: Kawaihae on the western, leeward side and Hilo on the eastern, windward side. These ships supply the island with endless imported goods. In the ports, huge cranes lift cars off the ship, which look like tiny toys dangling in mid-air as they are lowered onto the dock. The people of the islands had gotten used to the groceries and goods that Matson Lines delivers regularly from the mainland. Gone are the days, before colonization, when the islands were totally self-sustaining. I didn't have a horse, a canoe or a mule, so I was happy to have my jeep. Now I would be free to go exploring, to actually go *holoholo*!!

Little did I know then that my landlady wouldn't like me going out to explore. Her husband had left for three months for a job off island. Why would she think that I would come all this way to just stay home, I wondered? Although my car was parked away from her house and windows, she began complaining that I had driven out twice on a particular day and wondered why I didn't just stay home. Debra was able to work from home, and she didn't leave the house very often. Somehow the sound of my tires driving slowly on gravel annoyed her. But I could not comply with her wish, as I did pay rent and was here to explore and enjoy this beautiful

island. Wanting to be respectful, I offered to park out along the street, which was at a good distance from the house. But she said, "No," that she wanted me to keep my parking place in the driveway. This was only "small time" or "small kine," as the Hawai'ians say, compared to other things in life, and it never diminished my enjoyment of being here. And I wasn't upset with her. I was just really puzzled.

### Six Days after Arriving: 9-11-2001 / New York, Twin Towers

JOB HUNTING WAS ON THE HORIZON SOON, and I was open to whatever I could find. At home, finances were very tight, so I was going to need a job. My jeep was my only large prop from home that provided a "security blanket." I had been here five days. As I went to bed the night of September 10th, I was consumed with great anxiety! It was the type I feel before something bad is going to happen. I couldn't figure out what was wrong. It was not loneliness. It was something else. I had already hooked up a land-line phone, so I called home. Everyone at home was fine. A fitful sleep ensued, and this anxiety woke me up again and again, throughout the night. In the early morning I felt led to turn on the T.V. Hawai'i is about six hours behind New York and, when I got up, right in front of my eyes I watched the twin towers of the World Trade Center in New York

City topple to the ground . . . bodies and papers were flying through the air. And then it was played over and over again, with footage of planes flying into the buildings and people screaming as they ran down the streets, closely followed by plumes of smoke and debris from the collapsed skyscrapers.

Many people had died a sudden death! Over three hundred heroic firefighters and first responders, making every effort to save people, lost their lives too. It was such a shocking and horrendously tragic event! It reminded me of the rapid death and destruction in the ancient city of Pompeii, Italy centuries ago. The people were gassed and then covered with lava from the volcanic eruption of Mt. Vesuvius. I could hardly believe what I was seeing. The news reporters shouted out their panic, as they gave each new development of this horrific news. Sirens blared in the background and I NOW knew what I had been feeling anxious about the night before.

I called my landlady Debra, who had not gotten up yet, and told her what had happened. She was just as shocked as I was. I called home. It was 9-11-2001, and it was going to change life in America, and it would also change life here in Hawai'i! About the fourth time this scene was broadcast, the T.V., which had been furnished with the cottage, blew up with a flash of light and smoke! I quickly unplugged it, but it would never work again. As they say in Hawai'i, it was *pau* (done for, finished). It was as if an energetic ripple from the event in New York City had reached Hawai'i. From that moment on, I did not watch T.V. Instead I read the newspapers and listened to the news on the car radio. In a short amount of time I stopped engaging with the news.

On this memorable and terribly tragic day there was a tangible feeling of mourning in the air. I could imagine that there was a similar feeling when Pearl Harbor was bombed, back in 1941. In the days and weeks that followed there was a great deal of panic all over the country. No one knew what might happen next. Terrorists might attack anywhere. Possibilities of more, huge attacks and sabotage were discussed and feared. Planes stopped flying for a while. People did not want to travel, imagining that terrorists might hijack their plane and crash them to their deaths. Worldwide, people canceled vacations.

Hawai'i, largely dependent on the visitor industry, was suddenly in deep economic trouble. Planes were not flying in or out. The hotels were almost empty. The car rental agencies, restaurants and other visitor-related businesses were seriously hurting. Employers had to let go of their employees. With so many job losses, locals had to "tighten their belts." More local people would go back to or expand their traditional way of life: go fishing, plant a big garden, hunt wild pigs, and park the car, ride a bike, paddle a canoe, and share with their friends and family. The *kanaka* (people) are resourceful, generous, and happy people. Even with a national disaster the Hawai'ian people were going to be okay. I felt sure of it.

### The Home Front

PAUL AND I HAD RAISED five children and had run a printing and publishing business for twenty-five years. It had been a huge energy output, trying our best to give enough love, care and energy to each child and a busy business! There were seven of us sitting at the dinner table. After the dishes were cleared, the table became a makeshift study hall. Even with desks, the children liked doing their homework at the dining room table. Some needed help with their homework, others didn't. We remember many science projects and each year there was the inevitable diorama of a California Mission.

We had chickens, peacocks, ducks, goats, a lamb, cats and dogs. We had brown eggs, white eggs and blue eggs. Our oldest two, James and Stacy, milked the goats and have never forgiven us for giving them that job. They said they were avoided on the school bus for smelling like goats. Our oldest son, James, was fifteen when the last little brother, Michael, was born in

1980. James was ecstatic exploring the woods, creeks and river nearby, and panning for gold. The second son, Sean, with his kind heart and love for animals, rescued a number of wounded birds. When he was five, he had to wear his cowboy boots and red Superman cape to the grocery store. His musical career started when he was very young. His first song was composed when he was four. "I am a Fireman" had many, many verses. There was a large span of ages and there was endless cooking, laundry, and housework.

Stacy was eleven years old when her little sister Christina was born in 1977. She sometimes held her little sister on her lap while she practiced the piano and, as a voracious reader, she retreated to her room to read at least one book a day. Christina, who was the sign of Cancer like me, loved helping me cook and bake. She was my travel buddy at age eleven, when we backpacked across China on our way to Tibet. She was sixteen when we went to Moorea, in French Polynesia for three months. Almost every year we had a family vacation in Hawai'i. We all looked forward to papayas for breakfast, swimming in the ocean, and that undefinable beautiful energy called *mana*.

We had a lot of family gatherings with friends and relatives, festivities on holidays, and spiritual retreats that were held on our

 ten-acre land. Our old barn was converted into a rustic meditation hall and chapel. For many years we hosted revered Tibetan Lamas, Native American medicine people, Sufi and Christian teachers, as well as authors from our publishing company. We even had Auntie Angeline, from the island of Kauai, come and teach a class on Lomilomi massage. The children grew up knowing all these wonderful teachers that lived with us during their two-to-three week visits and summer retreats. They participated in sweat lodge ceremonies and heard precious teachings from teachers of many

traditions. I can still visualize Lama Gonpo Tsetan Rinpoche, who was undoubtedly a living saint, feeding part of his breakfast to our visually impaired son, Michael, when he was three years old.

Many people came and went. Some people stayed on our land over the years. During their short or sometimes longer visits, they stayed in a re-modeled school bus, a tipi and a trailer. In the summer there were tents and porta-potties. That time was before we had an influx of bears. The guests helped with gardening, and sometimes helped prepare for retreats. We couldn't take five children to retreats, so in order to attend retreats we decided to invite and host the groups on our ten acres. Except for utilities, all funds went to the visiting teacher. Teenage girls had art and play camps for the children of attending parents. Everyone camped in tents. Our neighbors, Rosetta, Dio, and John Neff, made their eight acres and bathhouse available as well. It was a rustic lifestyle, living in our 1880s farmhouse built in the gold mining days with two wood-burning stoves.

Over the years I had done a lot of cooking, cleaning, gardening, and event coordination. I grew flowers and herbs and made herbal salves, cosmetics, teas and tinctures. I had a part-time therapeutic massage clientele. At times I helped review manuscripts for the publishing business. The years went by like a whirlwind. We had large gardens and an orchard, and all the kids helped with weeding and harvesting vegetables, nuts and fruit. Everyone helped with splitting and stacking firewood for the woodstoves that we used every winter. I became an expert at getting the fire in the woodstove going, early in the morning before light. When burning oak, there are still coals at five-thirty A.M. Then in the early fall there was the apple picking, canning and drying. We competed with the bears for the apples and the squirrel families for the walnuts from our century-old trees.

Paul was busy with our printing and publishing business all week, and on weekends he had to morph into a car repair man and a fixer of the well and broken pipes. He was rototiller and tractor man, and firewood man, as well as having been ordained a Catholic priest, and later a Bishop, in the Eastern Catholic Apostolic Church of Antioch – Malabar Rite. We had Sunday morning Eucharist services in our chapel /meditation barn/hall. He officiated at weddings, baptisms and funerals, and all of his services were inspiring and universal in nature. I continued to study herbology

CHAPEL OF ST. FRANCIS

and natural healing, and planted many medicinal herbs in our gardens. I also helped in the publishing business by doing some writing and design. At times I reviewed the many manuscript submissions and connected with potential authors. Our son Sean, through innate talent and persistent practice, blossomed into a fabulous lead guitar player. He would make Santana, Stevie Ray Vaughn and Jimmy proud. James got into the concrete and building trades. Stacy and Christina became R.N.s, and Michael became a very good gardener and drummer.

From 4 o'clock clockwise: JAMES, STACY, SEAN, CHRISTINA, MIKE

As I reached midlife in my fifties, I felt a strong longing to have a rest and retreat from everything. I was terribly tired in body and soul. Although we still loved each other, frustration had set in for both of us. I was sure that it was caused by having almost no time alone together. Paul needed a change too. I needed a retreat and rest from this busy life. Most of all I felt I had become mired in my own repetitive patterns and small view. I knew I needed to change. I longed for the ocean and to be in the water and close to the dolphins, the whales, and Kupuna Pele. Coming to Hawai'i was to become a mid-life sabbatical between being a mother and a grandmother, and I had no idea how it would all turn out.

In the very early days of being on the Big Island, I reflected on all these years and activities that seemed to have flown by so fast. I re-visited in memory many events from the past. I re-visited happy times as well as regrets. I wondered if having so many children deprived each one of them from getting enough individual attention. They were living their own lives now. Our ideals about publishing spiritual and self-help books did not create a financial reward beyond supporting the families of our twelve employees. Somehow, through grace I believe, little miracles always seemed to save us and make payroll at the last minute. Always living on the edge was stressful. But here, I was in this sweet little cottage in Hawai'ian Paradise Park wondering how the following months would unfold in this new post 9/11 era.

Since all of our windows were open, I could hear heavy sighs early in the morning, emanating from Debra's bedroom. They were the kind of loud, heavy sighs that people make when they are really stressed or have just finished a big cry. I imagined that she was feeling blue and missing her husband. He had left for his job off-island just a few days after I arrived. I made attempts to spend time with her, thinking that what might be loneliness could be somewhat eased. But after her husband left, she didn't seem to want to socialize with me. I wondered if she felt resentful of, what could have seemed to her, my being on a perpetual and frivolous holiday.

# The Dirty Laundry Island

THE BIG ISLAND IS SOMETIMES CALLED "the dirty laundry island." Some visitors cannot handle the high energy which is quite tangibly felt on this island with a live volcano. They may have to leave for home or go to another island. In the high vibration of an island with a Goddess like *Kupuna Pele*, our own shadow side can arise for cleansing and purification. Our blockages, blind spots, and negativity can loosen and rise to the surface, for us to feel or others to see. It is an opportunity to be cleansed and transmuted. Sometimes after feeling the pain of recognition, we can release and let go of irritations and issues. We might even laugh and feel somewhat relieved after an "aha" moment. Insight is the first step to positive changes. I was here to see my blind spots, lighten up, and make these changes. The first thing I realized was that I had never been grateful enough. I also carried too much worry and stress, and absorbed the problems of others, like a sponge. I lacked confidence in myself. There would be many more limitations to come to grips with over the coming weeks and months. However dirty laundry, once laundered, can potentially become clean laundry.

## Kupuna Pele

SOME SAY IT IS *KUPUNA PELE*, the volcano Goddess, and the great energy of that shaking, trembling spectacle of nature, that can lead to the arising of our shadow nature. A live volcano with a Goddess that can be harsh or compassionate makes us want to be *pono* (good). Vents on the side of the volcano can open at any time and burn and eat the landscape with flowing, steaming lava that covers anything in its path on the way to the ocean. Trees and shrubs can burn. If houses are in the way, they burn too. I have seen cars half covered in lava, which becomes so solidified that the cars can never be extracted.

I had met Haleaka Iolani (Aka) the year before, in the year 2000. We had become fast friends and kindred spirits. Then, to my surprise, I became aware that I had been friends with her mother, Auntie Fern Pule, for many years. Aka was a magical woman and so was her mother. Rich in the Aloha spirit, they would never claim to be *kahunas*, but many locals said that they were. I did learn in later years that in their genealogy they were descended from the great Kahuna lineage of Heva Heva Nui. Aka had his carved wooden staff. Humble in all ways, gifted people on this island often conceal their power and insights, but just quietly help others in numerous ways. They both knew I had arrived and I was eager to drive over to the other side of the island to see them.

The Volcano Goddess is often called *"Tutu Pele,"* but Aka's family usually call her *"Kupuna Pele,"* so that is why I am also calling her that. If one's *ohana* (family) is in great favor with Kupuna Pele, her lava flows may split and go around both sides of their *hale* (house), leaving their *hale* untouched. This has happened in the past, especially to the homes of certain *Kahuna Nui* (spiritual specialists / priests) and other special people who pray in sacred ways. Western people may see these things as superstitions, but in Hawai'i the forces of nature and the Gods and Goddesses are revered by many people as real. The people have seen things with their own eyes. They have no need to convince scientists or skeptics. In this land myth can become reality and reality can become myth.

### *Living on a Live Volcano*

THE LIVE VOLCANO ON THE BIG ISLAND of Hawai'i is a force of nature that the Hawai'ian people live with and respect. A Goddess, who

exacts a certain level of *pono* (goodness) and respect from the people who dare to visit her realm, is a Goddess to respect. And if a person is not *pono* (good), or if she feels a person is not *pono,* that person may be blown off the island, or "spit out," as some like to say. There is a protocol for visitors not to take home any lava rocks or black sand from the island. It is said to bring them bad luck. Whether it is true or not, who knows?  But why tempt fate?  Some people bring lava rocks back to the island thinking their bad luck will turn to good luck. Some visitors have even mailed lava rocks back to Hawai'ian post offices trying to improve their luck.

When people get "blown off" the island, by any number of circumstances, they may be welcome to come back at a later date, but also may be banned forever.  It depends just how *pilikia* (trouble making or disrespectful) one has been.  If someone has been spit out forever, then no effort will bring the person back to the island. They will be mysteriously blocked.

But often, this living being called Tutu Pele, or Kupuna Pele, and the island itself can show a softer side that is more like a lover

who showers you with the most exquisite fragrances, soft rains, warm sun rays, caressing breezes, and the soothing and rhythmic sounds of waves lapping the shoreline. The swish and sway of palm fronds moving like hula dancers merge with the cooing sounds of the little gray doves, and there may be no other place on earth that has this very unique type of healing vibration or *mana* (spiritual power and energy).

## FIRST WEEKS

THE FIRST WEEKS AFTER MY ARRIVAL were very busy. I had to get the jeep inspected and registered. Then I went shopping in Hilo and got some beautiful sheets for my bed. I had brought a light patchwork quilt from home. It never got cold enough to need anything heavier. Several times I visited the warm pond for a relaxing float and signed up for water aerobics at the big Hilo outdoor pool.

I walked around Hilo soaking up the ambiance of this old harbor town and shopped for vegetables at the outdoor market. There were so many things to see in Hilo. I attended a play at the historic Palace Theater. At the end of the play, there was a roar in the audience of *"Hana hou, Hana hou, Hana hou."* That is the Hawai'ian version of "encore." I visited the famous "Naha" stone in front of the Hilo library, as well as the Liliuokalani Gardens, the Japanese Gardens, and the Wailuku River State Park and Rainbow Falls. To see the rainbows at Rainbow Falls, you have to go very, very early on a sunny day.

I attended several weekly meetings and potlucks in Hawai'ian Paradise Park of a group called "The Intenders for the Highest Good." This group of people focused on positive thinking and positive manifestations. There was another group that did "Shamanic Journeying" that met in a house by the shoreline of H.P.P. I enjoyed attending a few of their drumming and journeying sessions. Twice a month I gave Debra a massage as a partial trade for rent. Her gardens were so beautiful that I sometimes did a little weeding and raking, which reminded me of gardening back home.

During this period of time I often felt terribly lonely and missed Paul, my children and friends. I questioned the wisdom of coming here in the first place. One rainy day I went to the Hilo Pana'ewa Rainforest Zoo and enjoyed the company of the animals and birds. It was the first time I got to see the Ne'ne goose, which is an endangered species and the state bird of Hawai'i. This zoo included a beautiful botanical garden as well, including over one hundred varieties of palm trees, orchids, bamboo, and water gardens.

Richardson's Beach Park, near Hilo, had calm water that was great for snorkeling and it also had some of the olivine crystals mixed with the black sand, making it almost a green sand beach. Weekends at Richardson's were incredibly crowded, so I only visited it and other nearby beaches on weekdays. One particularly lonely, rainy evening I went to the indoor Hilo mall. Seeing happy Hawai'ian families shopping together deepened my loneliness and a feeling that I didn't belong here. What had I done, I wondered? I had made a move that was beginning to feel more and more like a big mistake. Many doubts arose about coming to Hawai'i for this long stay.

I was also very disturbed over the 9/11 events with the twin towers in New York City, and the threats of terrorism to our country. There was a heavy feeling in the "collective energy field" about terrorism and what might be next. Many local Hawai'ian people had lost their jobs because so many jobs are connected to tourism. Visitors had stopped coming, as planes were not flying. I didn't really know anyone, so I was trying to make some new friends. I had met Kumu Dane on a previous visit, but I hadn't connected with him yet. All of my friends were over on the Kona side, and I was particularly missing Aka and her mother, Auntie Fern, Carol, Barbara and Rika. I decided I would drive over there to visit them soon. That thought pulled me out of the doldrums.


## Remembering Meeting Kumu Dane Silva, Luther and Desmon Haumea in Hana, Maui

I ORIGINALLY MET KUMU DANE Kaohelani Silva in the town of Hana on the island of Maui. He had been on an inter-island sail on the Makali'i, the double-hulled voyaging canoe that was built on the Big Island. Often while sunbathing or swimming at "Two Step" or at

Ho'okena beach, I would see the Makali'i sailing up and down the coast of the Big Island. I couldn't understand why it tugged at my heart every time it sailed by. *Makali'i* literally means "little eyes," which is the Pleiades star cluster. This training canoe is for the Hawai'ian youth to learn about their ancient culture, and to understand voyaging from first-hand experience. I was intrigued with the art and science of sailing ancient voyaging canoes.

When my son Mike and I were in Maui in the late '90s, Mike insisted that I drive us to Hana on the infamously windy road. It was the windiest road I had ever driven, but ever so very beautiful. With most inland switchbacks there were streams and often a waterfall. Little wooden stands were here and there with children selling fresh coconuts. Much to my surprise, when we arrived in Hana, we saw the Makali'i anchored in the bay. I wondered what the voyaging canoe was doing here on Mau'i, as I knew its home was in Kawaihae harbor, on the Big Island.

Mike went to the beach to play his drum and I began to walk to a cafe next to the beach to have a coffee. As I walked by some outdoor tables, two Hawai'ian men gave me an Aloha and a *"shaka,"* a shake or flick of the hand, with thumb and pinky finger extended, that says, "hello." They waved me over to their table.

I began telling them that I noticed that the Makali'i was in the bay. At first the two tanned men, with salt and pepper hair, were wearing sunglasses. But soon after we began to talk, they both took their glasses off. One of them had more silver in his hair than the other, and was a little rounder. This was Luther, one of the voyagers. The other man was Dane Silva, who was wearing a white shirt. He was slim and muscular and had wavy hair. I guessed them to be in their mid-fifties. I told them how fascinated I was with the voyaging canoes and the pan-oceanic travel that had taken place in the Pacific in recent years.

These replicas of ancient, double-hulled voyaging canoes had two crab-claw sails. In ancient times they had sailed throughout the Pacific with no instruments. Now the replica voyaging canoes were sailed in the same ancient way. The ocean sea roads *(kealaikahki)* of ancient times were being re-discovered by modern wayfarers.

The men laughed and said they were part of the crew that sailed the Makali'i over here to Maui from the Big Island. The rest of the crew had gone off somewhere to eat and had left Dane and Luther to keep an eye on the canoe. I was left facing Dane, who then asked me if I was from Nevada City, California. I said, yes, I was. I asked him if we had met before, if he knew me. He said very cryptically, in a slightly hushed tone, that maybe we had ... somewhere, sometime.

We went on to speak about voyaging, and then he asked me if I was a massage therapist, and I said, "Yes, I am." By now I realized that this man was quite intuitive, as we had never met before. He then told me that he lived on the Big Island. I told him that that's where my son and I were staying too, but that we had had a chance to come over to Maui for a week. Pretty soon Luther got up and told us that he was going to find the others. They planned to sail the Makali'i back to the Big Island in the next day or two. Even though Mike and I could not hitch a ride on the canoe, we were invited to a dinner near Pahoa, when we were all back on the Big Island. We exchanged email addresses and phone numbers. We never did have that visit, as the Makali'i lost one of its sails in the rough and windy channel on the way back to the Big Island. They had to turn back to

NEW SAILS FOR THE MAKALI'I
An Ancient Hawai'ian Voyaging Canoe

Maui until they could get a new sail. By the time Dane returned home after this delay, Mike and I had flown back home to Nevada City. We kept in touch by email, from time to time, and discussed voyaging and the healing arts. I discovered that he was quite a reputable *Kumu* (teacher) of *lomilomi* massage and the healing arts. I seriously considered taking some training with Kumu Dane Silva, sometime in the future.

### A Healing with Kumu Dane and Yuki San

NOW, LESS THAN TWO YEARS LATER, I was back on the Big Island, for what turned out to be a stay of almost a year. I had developed a seriously stiff neck soon after arriving, and needed some healing myself. I called Dane and he said to come over to his house and he would see what could be done to *kokua* (help). All the changes in my life, leaving home, the 9/11 attack, and not having a job yet, had created the stress that locked up the muscles of the neck and upper back, resulting in something called torticollis, or wry neck. It makes it very difficult to drive, as it is painful and you cannot freely turn your head.

My friend Liz, in Idaho, worked at a power tool store and had been able to get me a Dremel and a set of diamond bits for Dane at a great discount. We had discussed this by email, so he was pleased when I presented this gift to him. When I first arrived at his house, Dane and his friend Yuki were in the middle of practicing the Hawai'ian art of *Lua* (a traditional fighting art, for warriors). They continued on for a while, and afterwards I was introduced to Yuki. He was a Japanese/Hawai'ian man with a round smiling face, and his ever present ukulele was nearby. Then Dane and Yuki tried some *Lua* moves on me, and of course, I couldn't return the moves and got trapped.

Dane told me that *Lua* is an ancient Hawai'ian art that was only taught to Native Hawai'ian men, *Ali'i* (chiefs) and royalty in the past. Lua incorporates movements that are the same or similar to many of the *hula* and *lomilomi* massage movements. He went on to say that all three ancient arts are related to each other. The movements are similar but are adapted differently to each individual art. He gave us a brief demonstration of all three. He had a *lava lava* (sarong) wrapped around his waist and a bare chest, and I had to smile at his rendition of the *hula*.

Kumu Dane looked like he stepped right out of an Herb Kane painting, as he was sleekly muscular and had the tan skin and strong, good-looking features of the old Hawai'ians. Herb Kane was a Hawai'ian artist, writer, and historian, who wrote and illustrated several books and is famous on the islands for painting ancient Hawai'ians in their cultural settings. He helped to research, design and build the first Hawai'ian replica voyaging canoe–the Hokule'a. He was her first captain when it took its maiden voyage to Tahiti. He wrote and illustrated *Pele: Goddess of Hawai'i's Volcanoes*, *Ancient Hawai'i*, and *Voyagers*. Herb Kawainui Kane was given the great honor of being elected a Living Treasure of Hawai'i in 1984. Now, like so many treasured elders, he has passed away, leaving an unfading impression on the next generation.

Kumu Dane had grown up on the Hilo side of the Big Island. He later told me that his mother was born and lived on the grassy plateau above the Waipio Valley. He descends from a traditional *Ali'i* (chiefs or royals) family of Hawai'ians. He carries a great deal

of knowledge of the old ways, including *Lomilomi* healing massage, *lau' lapa' au* (herbal medicine), and *Lua* (fighting arts). He also knew a great deal about the canoe culture, dance, chants and many of the crafts. Like many Hawai'ian men, he is a surfer and a great chef. Over the years he has become a favorite of the Japanese, many of whom have a love affair with Hawai'ian culture. He's made many trips to Japan to teach Lomilomi massage and healing methods. And, many Japanese people have come to his workshops on the Hilo side of Hawai'i as well.

After the *Lua* demonstration, Kumu Dane's friend Yuki sat down on a stool and began to play the ukulele. Earlier in the day he had given Dane a ukulele lesson. Yuki was a good musician! He told me that he often played aboard cruise ships around the islands as an entertainer. I felt lucky to have him here today. He strummed out one melody after another, which lent a beautiful atmosphere to the room while I was having a healing treatment on my neck and upper back.

Kumu Dane had me get up on his massage table and began to assess the body. He placed a fresh protective Ti leaf on the end of the table and said a prayer in Hawai'ian. It was so soothing lying there, having long, deep strokes up and down my back and up into my neck and occipital area. The sweet sounds of Hawai'ian songs on Yuki's ukulele, accompanying the massage, made me feel as if I were about to melt. I drifted off into a reverie. I could imagine laying on woven pandanus leaf mats in a *hale* (house) made of bamboo, pandanus leaves and pili grass. A large *Ipu* (gourd) calabash, containing hot rocks which had been heated in a fire pit, was cooking herbs. They were fragrant and medicinal. I was drifting in imagination, into the past.

Yuki never missed a strum and Kumu Dane never missed a stroke, as they quietly joked back and forth with each other. Being included in the light banter, I found them both amusing. "Better to be laid back like Hawai'ians than 'up-tight' like mainland *kine*," one said. "Not everyone gets serenaded when they're getting a treatment," another said. It was all slow and easy, a few chuckles here and there. The trapezius muscles in my neck and back were beginning to relax and loosen, and once again faith in this *holoholo* adventure was being slowly restored.

Kumu Dane surely had great *mana* (spiritual energy) and healing energy in his hands. I could feel the warm radiance penetrating deep into the muscles. He felt like a big brother, a warrior, a protector. I was glad that I had met him on that previous trip in Maui, as later he was to become my *Kumu* (teacher) of Lomilomi massage. As I was getting ready to leave his house, Dane gave me a little thin twisted black root and told me that I could chew on it, on the way home. It was *Awa* (also called Kava), a root that is used to relax the muscles. Kava is also used in a traditional drink by chiefs and *kahunas* in their ceremonies. It is slightly mind altering, I had heard. He told me that it would help the muscles to relax, and not to be concerned when it made my mouth slightly numb. He went on to tell me that he had been given some top quality *Awa* ... and this was a piece of this most excellent "stash." "One last word," he said, "take the Red Road home. It is very beautiful and it will relax you even more." I thanked Kumu Dane and Yuki and headed out for the Red Road.

Well, yes, it did relax me, just as he said. The red road is actually red, paved with reddish colored dirt, and there are lush trees overhanging the road and a thick surrounding jungle of bushes and vine-wrapped trees that go off to both sides. It felt as if gnomes, elves and *menehunes* (mythic Hawai'ian "little people") might pop out from behind a tree at any moment. Suddenly I realized that the *Awa* root that I was chewing was not only making my mouth a little numb, but was making my mind feel light and somewhat altered. Everything did take on a kind of surreal appearance and feeling. I did feel grateful that my neck was so much better. I would not need a second treatment. *Mahalo nui loa* (Thank you), Kumu Dane!!!

## *Rika-San*

I WAS SO EXCITED TODAY as I found out that my Japanese friend, Rika, had moved over from the Kona side to the Hilo side. She and I had originally met at Paleaku Peace Gardens and worked together there with the owner, Barbara DeFranco. Previously, after I returned from one trip back from Hawai'i, I told her about meeting Kumu Dane in Maui and about his school of Lomilomi massage in the Pahoa area. She decided to move to the Hilo side so she could take his training. She also acted as translator for his Japanese students. Now she had already completed the classes and was ready to start her own practice. And, she was going to demonstrate what she had learned on me. I was excited and happy to hear this. I had become a certified massage therapist years earlier, but in the Western traditions. I had not yet learned Hawai'ian Lomilomi, although Paul and I had experienced a wonderful tandem massage from the famous Auntie Angeline and her healing partner, in Kauai, a few years earlier.

Living over here in the Puna district, we were close to Kupuna Pele and the volcano. There were days when the acrid, sulfuric smell of vog (volcanic fog) wafted through the air, depending upon the winds and the amount of volcanic eruption at any given time. Nobody liked the vog very much, as it created respiratory problems for some people. Aka always said *Mamaki* tea helped vog problems. Her grandmother had taught her how to gather it and make a tea from it. Aka always gave me a new supply of it every time I saw her. Years later, her sisters Wanda and Kalehua continued the tradition of gifting me with Mamaki tea.

Some people inhaled Noni juice from a nebulizer. Some people just lived with the occasional wafting smells of vog and paid no attention to it. Other people moved to other islands to avoid vog, but even Maui sometimes got some residual vog that drifted on the air currents from the Big Island. The islands of Molokai and Kauai are pretty much vog free, and the island of Oahu has very little problem. *Haoles* seem to be more susceptible to vog problems than locals, I noticed. Some *haoles* even moved back to the mainland, finding they couldn't live with it. A very few developed asthma or C.O.P.D. Certain zones had more and certain zones had less. The north end of the Big Island, at Havi, was often very windy and seemed to blow the vog away. It always depended on the moods of the volcano and the winds, both of which were always changing. Mamaki tea, nebulizers and herbal extracts, *lau' lapa' au* (herbal medicine) are helping everyone today.

Rika and I had met at Paleaku Peace Gardens, on the Kona side, in previous years, when we were care-taking the retreat center during Barbara DeFranco's absence of several weeks. Rika was one

of the staff as well, and we had already become good friends. We worked well together managing the retreat center, making sure all the assignments were being done by those who lived on the ten-acre grounds. We had a good rapport with everyone, and we all took pride in keeping this beautifully groomed shrine and meditation garden in perfect order.

Rika is a very pretty, soft spoken, Japanese woman. She looked much younger than her forty years. She, like so many Japanese women, was thin, petite and graceful. When she laughed, she would cover her mouth, and spoke softly with a Japanese accent. Some-times I had to ask her to speak up. She was raised in a traditional Japanese household and grew up in Germany with her parents. Her parents would have liked her to stay in Japan, but Rika loved Hawai'i. Here she had become an excellent hula dancer and chanter of ancient Hawai'ian chants. She felt she had been Hawai'ian in a previous life, and it wasn't surprising to me, as she mastered the Hawai'ian cultural arts with ease. She also loved dolphins, as I do, and she swam easily and strongly in the ocean with these wonderful mammals, who were our beloved friends.

From previous visits to the Big Island, I knew quite a few people on the Kona side, like Auntie Fern and Auntie Aka, Mayumi Oda, Barbara DeFranco, Kauila and Danny, Uncle Lanakila Brandt, Carol, Dixon and Barbara Enos and others, but it was a long day's drive to Kona and back. I was grateful to have an old friend nearby now. Rika and I would surely go *holoholo* together, as we both love an adventure and exploring.

Rika followed my directions and found my cottage. We greeted each other with a big Aloha hug. Neither of us had very much money, so we became accustomed to making budget dinners together. She would bring tofu and Japanese pickles. We had fruit and avocados from the garden that surrounded us. I always had poi. I made different versions of Ramen, with mushrooms, scallions, cilantro, fish, shrimp and vegetables. At other times we made stir fry and rice, or *poki* (raw, marinated fish). We both loved fried breadfruit, called *ulu* in Hawai'ian.

Rika sliced the tofu and blotted the water out of it onto a clean cloth. Then she dredged the slices in rice flour and fried it. We dipped the fried tofu into a delicious sweet and sour sauce that Rika made. This was delicious! "So Onozzzz broke dah mouf," as the Hawai'ians say in pidgin English (so delicious it broke the mouth!). We always had fun cooking together. Afterward we traded massages and I learned some of the lomilomi methods that she had learned from Kumu Dane. She was just as good at massage as she was at Hula and chanting.

### Green Lake and Meeting Douglas

GREEN LAKE, OR LAKE KAPOHO, was reputed to be one of the most sacred locations on the Big Island. Its Hawai'ian name was *Ka Wai o Pele* meaning Pele's lake. People said it was Old Kapoho's Cinder Cone of Green Mountain. It was located near Pahoa, here in the Puna district, but I had no idea where. I had heard that it was on fenced private property. It was said that at one time Jacques Cousteau took a little "one man" submarine down in the depths of this lake and could not find the bottom. I am not sure whether this is true or not. Some legends say that *mo'o* live in the lake, and I only heard about this long after I had a personal experience of the *mo'o*. A Mo'o is a legendary giant lizard or dragon that lived on this island in ancient times. Even on the island of Moorea in French Polynesia, the name "Moorea" means "yellow lizard." Some of the Hawai'ian people believe that the Big Island and other Hawai'ian islands are the mountain tops of the continent of ancient Lemuria or Mu. In this civilization it is said that beings could shape-shift in and out of physical manifestation, into a light body, and then back to the physical. Stories tell of this large ancient continent sinking from a series of gigantic volcanic explosions. Often place names, ancient history, and legends of the island have *mo'o* embedded in them. Residual mysteries are left behind by the ancestors to be decoded.

Some Hawai'ians understand that current historical theories, claiming that Polynesians from Tahiti and the Marquesas settled the Hawai'ian islands, are only part of the truth. It is said that continental soil was found at South Point when geologists drilled deep core samples. This fact was confirmed by geological surveys. This could point to the Big Island being a remnant of an ancient continent. Stories like this are passed down through families who have astounding memories for transmitting stories and genealogies in the oral tradition. Our family had been coming to Hawai'i each year for over thirty years, but Green Lake had always eluded us. Now I was on a mission to find it.

So one day I went to the health food store in Pahoa and thought I would ask someone for directions to Green Lake. While walking up and down the aisles of the store, I spotted a very tall, thin man who looked like a good person to ask. Even though he was part *haole*, there was something else in his looks that looked Native American. He had high cheekbones, long sun-bleached brown hair with blond streaks, and glasses. He had a pleasant demeanor and was barefoot. I went up to him and asked him if he could give me directions to Green Lake. He smiled and looked rather excited. He told me that, actually that was where he planned to go today, and if I would give him a ride, he would take me there too. So feeling warm and safe in his presence, I shopped for a picnic and we headed out in my jeep.

Douglas guided me to a road with a fence alongside it and suggested I park there. From there we crawled through an opening in the fence. He explained that he knew the caretaker of this private property and had been told that he was welcome to come here any time. He began to explain the sacredness of Green Lake and told me the story of Jacques Cousteau. He said that some *haole* people swim in the lake, but that Hawai'ians do not, as it was supposed to be *kapu*. He said he always followed the local traditions. He had lived in Hawai'i all of his adult life. I guessed him to be somewhere between fifty and sixty. We chatted as we walked by a huge banana grove.

Seeing so many banana trees in a large grove is a beautiful experience. Wild guava and *lilikoe* (passion fruit) vines were in abundance, and again, it felt like a much wilder version of the Garden of Eden. There surely was a strong and lovely energy in this place. Vines wound and twisted up the large trees amid groves of bamboo. This large bamboo was the type used for the ancient *hales* as their framework. It felt pristine here, as if this little piece of the *aina* (land) retained the energy and *mana* of old Hawai'i, the Hawai'i before colonization.

Douglas's name somehow didn't fit him. He started to introduce himself a bit to me. While he had lived on the island most of his life, he was raised in the Midwest by a white mother and a Native American Alaskan father. His father had an *avant garde* newspaper, in which he shared his activist views on indigenous rights. How interesting, I thought. I now knew why his facial features reflected a Native American face. It was easy to be fooled by the blue eyes and honey-colored hair.

Douglas told me that he eats very little food and mainly forages wild fruits, macadamia nuts, avocados, coconuts, and eats Ezekiel bread. He went on to explain that he lives in a tree house, has no post office box, no car, no driver's license, no bank, no money, no debts, no girlfriend, and loves his life: simple and uncomplicated. He said he had been married when he was young and that they had lived on the island of Kauai. He said they split up simply because he was too eccentric for her. There had been no bad feelings.

I asked him how he shops at the health food store if he has no money. He then told me that he is a tree man, and that he is spiritually connected to trees. He said he never cuts them down to get the wood that he needs. He went on say that he always finds the right wood, somewhere on the ground, when he is ready to carve and craft his homemade guitars, ukuleles, and wooden spoons. He trades instruments and spoons at the health food store for store credit. He also told me about his morning ritual that I was welcome to attend any morning. I wondered what he meant. But he answered without my asking. He harvests coffee beans from wild coffee plants on the hillsides, and then roasts them in a big black iron skillet over an outdoor campfire. He has a hand coffee-grinder to grind the roasted beans. Then he makes several pots of coffee in old-fashioned percolators over a wood fire with a grill, right below his tree house. The bee man in Honaka'a donated jars of honey to him, and he serves sunrise coffee and honey to the people who live in the bushes around Pahoa. *Kahikina* is the Hawai'ian word for the place where the sun rises in the east. As Douglas's place was high on the hillside, it was a perfect place to watch the sunrise and drink coffee, blessed by his time-consuming, old-fashioned methods, and his Aloha.

Wow, once again, I heard a mention of the people who lived in the bushes. Douglas spoke of them with much compassion, telling me some of their stories and what brought them to homelessness in Hawai'i. Yes, some of the women had babies, too, just as Debra had said. However, she told me about them with distaste, and he told me about them with compassion. Well, what an interesting fellow, I thought. He reminded me more and more of an Indian sadhu, a yogi, or a St. Francis of Assisi. He had a very sweet and gentle nature. It seemed as if he had transcended the usual desires and needs of most human beings. He did not boast about his lifestyle. He just simply stated it. I told him that I worried about not being able to survive on the island financially, now that 9/11 had happened, and local people were losing their jobs.

He asked about my living situation. I told him about my expenses . . . food, rent, gas for the car etc. He looked pensive for a moment and said, "You know, you could live the way I do. You really don't need money." Wow, I thought. I just couldn't imagine myself going out on a limb . . . so to speak . . . with a tree house of my own, or a tent, and the radical leap of faith that he had taken.

He didn't seem to think it was a radical leap of faith. To him it was just natural and easy. He was very, very relaxed. I felt very safe and comfortable with him. As there was no attraction between us, I just felt I had a new friend that I could trust. There was nothing quirky or weird about him either. As we talked, I found him to be very educated and intelligent and able to discuss many subjects. His talk was never controlling or extreme. He just seemed to be very comfortable in his own skin.

As we walked through the lushness of the Green Lake property, we stopped in front of a large tree. He told me that this particular tree was the shaman of all the trees around us . . . that this one was very special. Now this started to sound a bit strange to me . . . a tree being a shaman. Well . . . okaaaay, I thought. He said he wanted to show me something. "Okay," I said. He asked me if I could pick up any scents or aromas. I said, "No, nothing in particular. It just smells good here, but it's just a general smell of jungle and plants."

He told me he was going to communicate with the tree. He stood very tall and still, and just looked as if he was meditating with this large tree as his focus. After a few moments I noticed a most distinctive and deliciously spicy scent emanating from the tree. It was unmistakably strong and most enticing. "I smell it!" I told him with excitement. It smells delicious and kind of spicy." He said, "The tree just gave us a gift. The tree knew it was being appreciated and it gave up a gift for us."

Okay, I thought, I guess he really does have a connection to trees. Native Americans and indigenous people do have gifts that connect them to nature in many different ways that are not a part of the belief system of the dominant society. In this native world, on a large island, in the middle of the Pacific Ocean, the extraordinary is ordinary.

So after the communion with the tree, we stepped up our pace and proceeded up to the crest of the hill which overlooked the beautiful Green Lake. Oh my, how beautiful it was, round and green and surrounded by trees and lush vines, and oh so tropical. "There are no snakes here," he said. "There is nothing to fear. Just enjoy the energy here. It is a sacred place." He picked some guavas from a bush and stacked them up next to the lake. "It is our *ho'o kupu* . . . our offering to the spirits of the lake. It is always good to make an offering." We sat beside the lake and ate our picnic. Douglas ate fruit from the trees and his Ezekiel bread. I had cheese and bread and fruit. The water was clear and still. I wouldn't have been surprised if a mermaid had appeared, as this place seemed like places I had visited in my dreams. Dreams can concoct anything at all from our deep imagination, but nothing happened. It was just all very still and very peaceful.

*P.S. Green Lake: in 2018 there was a volcanic eruption from Kiluaea crater. For more than three months, lava flowing from an eastern vent inundated two ocean communities. It also filled in Kapoho Bay, which was known for its colorful reef fish and tidal pools. The southeast coast of the island was once again changed by the action of the volcano and many homes were lost. Toxic, acidic steam coming from hot lava creates "laze" (tiny particles of glass) when the steam contacts the salt water of the ocean. It was all over the ground near the coast. On June 2, 2018 lava entered Green Lake, Hawai'i's largest lake. Within five hours all the water in the lake had evaporated, sending a huge plume of steam into the sky that could be seen from space. The lake was filled in with lava and the land around it was covered in lava.*

### Community Ohana Convenes

PLANES STILL WERE NOT FLYING. The visitor industry had come to a halt. Many people were out of work. Community discussions about sustainability continued. Ideas were shared. Inter-island travel once took place on boats and ferries. Double-hulled sailing canoes had been used in the distant past. In relatively recent times inter-island ferry boats were being considered. A ferry boat was built that made a maiden voyage from Oahu to Kauai. Aka's sisters, Wanda and Kalehua and their husbands, Jerry and Pancho, were on this voyage and told me about it. Locals were happy to have the ferry. Now they would be able to transport their own vehicle to a neighbor island and have no need to rent a car. But the car rental and airline industries didn't like this new competition. "Somehow" the proposed ferry boat travel got shut down, almost before it got started. There was a lot of community disappointment. Almost every Hawai'ian family, the *kama aina*, has relatives living on neighbor islands. I remember taking my friend Tea's *camionette* (pick-up truck) on the ferry boat that connects the island of Tahiti to the island of Moorea. It is such a great service, and it would be wonderful to have inter-island ferry boats in Hawai'i.

The very basics of life and survival were being examined by everyone. It was a time of re-evaluation and the spawning of creative new ideas. It seemed as if parts of the old culture were being brought back to life and renewed. There had already been a cultural renaissance that began in the nineteen seventies, but now further ideas were being explored. *"Malama the aina"* rang out from people's lips. "Take care of and love the land, and the land will take care of you."

Community programs sprang up to help people. Quite suddenly people were out of work. Grass root projects and new businesses were encouraged. People were discussing grant writing to seek funds from foundations. Food banks were being set up. This was NOT the time for me to find a job. Local people deserved the few jobs that were still available first. This 9/11 event had ripple effects everywhere. Many discussions took place in little towns all over the islands. The local people showed their Aloha spirit, based upon tender loving kindness, sharing, generosity, understanding, humility, and *kokua* (helping). It was a beautiful thing to witness. I, too, started attending the community meetings. Everyone was asking the question: How could they survive and be self-sustaining in the very middle of the Pacific Ocean? The ancient Hawai'ians had a very organized, disciplined, and self-sustaining society, but things had changed so much. Colonization, when it permeates an indigenous culture, brings about an irreversible change. And for every bit of "progress" brought in from the colonizing society, there is also great damage to the indigenous culture.


### The Coqui Frogs and the Mongoose


INVASIVE SPECIES HAVE WRACKED HAVOC on the Hawai'ian islands. Somehow the tiny Coqui frogs, with very big voices, found their way to these islands. Some think they were imported accidentally on nursery plants from Puerto Rico. They sing at night with high-pitched voices that can go up to ninety decibels. They have no predators in Hawai'i, so by now they have invaded almost all parts of the island. Some people can't sleep with their shrill night-time songs, and others can. Many discussions take place about how to get rid of these tiny frogs that seem to migrate and multiply with record speed. During 2001 and 2002, they were just getting started on the Hilo side, but they hadn't quite gotten to Hawai'ian Paradise Park yet. Thankfully I was able to have a peaceful sleep at night. The mongoose was introduced to Hawai'i with the idea that they would rid the island of rats in the cane fields. But the plan didn't work, and the mongoose population has become huge. They destroy native bird populations, including the endangered *Nene* goose, by eating their eggs. The wild *Alala*, the raven-sized Hawai'ian crow, has become extinct in the wild due to predators, but is being preserved in a captive breeding program. Even the number of turtle eggs has declined, as the mongoose eats both bird and turtle eggs. Often while driving, I saw them scampering across the road, just as squirrels do on our Nevada City roads.

### Housekeeping in a Moist Climate

I WAS ADVISED TO TAKE ALL MY LAUNDRY to the laundromat once a week to dry them to prevent mildew. I was also warned against having leather shoes, purses or belts as they would be ruined by mold. Books too were at risk of mildew. People living on this wet side of the island had any number of devices in their closets to ward off the mildew. Some had lights. Others had bags of rock salt that would wick the moisture out of the air. Some people went to dry their clothes at the laundromat. Others had dryers at home. This was part of "housekeeping" on the Hilo side, especially if you lived in an open screen house like mine.

### Flashback: How I Met Aka the Previous Year, The Iwis, and the Burial Grounds

THE YEAR BEFORE I CAME to the Big Island for a year's stay, I had stayed at Paleaku Peace Gardens on Painted Church Road for several weeks, while the owner, Barbara DeFranco, went to visit family in

California. Paleaku Peace Gardens, like our home in California, was comprised of about ten acres of land.

That year, 2000, is the year I first met Aka. As Rika Soeda and I were caretaking and managing this land and retreat center for several weeks, Barbara had left us with several assignments: one of which was landscaping and clearing a particular area of the property. Through Auntie Fern, Aka, and Auntie Mona Kahele, I had heard about the desecration of burial grounds and the *iwis* (bones) of their ancestors. (In the Hawai'ian langage, 'w' is pronounced as 'v', so 'iwi' sounds like 'ivi'.) In the Hawai'ian tradition the *iwis* are sacred and are never to be dug up, separated from each other, or disturbed in any way. The bones are thought to contain *mana*, or spiritual power.

Strange and disturbing things have often happened to those who disturbed a burial ground or burial caves. The unseen forces – the *aumakua* (ancestral spirits) and protectors of these people – can exact payment in some form. I heard of the horrible things that happened to construction workers and tractor drivers who bulldozed burial grounds and graves in preparation for a large building project nearby. This was to be a large complex of expensive condominiums and a golf course near the town of Kealakekua. Those who drove the bulldozers and tractors were heard to say that they would see bones tumbling down the lava fields, disturbed by their earth moving and grading work. One mentioned a skull rolling down the hill like a soccer ball. Other burials were being massively disturbed, and it was abundantly clear that this was a large burial ground.

The *IWI* (bone) Committee of the Island, chaired by traditional elders, had already warned them and told them . . . to stop! So far their protests were to no avail. Auntie Mona Kahele told me that she was on the "*Iwi* Committee." There are usually several elders from each island on this committee. These *kupunas* (elders) were a true force of nature. When desecrations of burial grounds were taking place, the *kupunas* would spring into action in every way possible.

From Auntie Mona and others, I heard the following stories of those who were doing the work: A few went crazy. At least one committed suicide. One heard the screaming voices of an elderly couple, who were not physically there . . . but at that very moment two skeletons were being dismembered by a bulldozer. Other workers had serious accidents, with resulting disabilities and other serious misfortunes. Most local Hawai'ian people in the construction business would not work there. They were spooked, and soon others became spooked, too. I was told that at times the uncanny misfortunes occurred to the equipment operators or to those in their family. It was dark and serious business and altogether *KAPU* (forbidden, sacred). In this case *Kapu* meant, "Do not disturb!" *Kapu* can also mean that a place is sacred and should not be trespassed upon, but in this case it meant both sacred and forbidden.

## Kapu

HIKIAU HEIAU SITS AT THE HEAD of Kealakekua Bay and this ancient Hawai'ian temple has been there for centuries. Stone steps lead up to the flat top of the *heiau* and there is a rope across the steps saying, "*KAPU* – Stay Off, Sacred, Forbidden." If tourists ignore the rope and sign, Auntie Fern, in the shop next to the *heiau*, would come over to scold them. "Can you read? Did you see this sign and this rope? It means what it says, "*Kapu*, keep off." In other contexts, *kapu* can mean "sacred," as in a *Kapu* child. Sometimes there are crossed *Kapu* sticks topped with white *tapa* cloth in front of a cave or sacred site, meaning that it is not to be entered. *Kapu* signs are important to respect.

This is the realm of the Gods and Goddesses, and of powerful ancestral forces. The four main Gods in the Hawai'ian pantheon are: Ku, Kane, Lono and Kanaloa. Briefly, Ku is the God of war. Kanaloa is the God of fisherman, long distance sailing, the ocean and darkness. Kane is the God who is thought to be the creator of all human beings, and is connected to procreation, the sun and sunshine. He is considered the highest God of all. Lono is the God of agriculture, rain, nature, music and peace. Ku rules over eight months of the year and Lono rules over the other four, which is called the *Mahahiki* season. There are many minor Gods and Goddesses as well. Each oversees and is associated with some aspect of nature, as the ancient Hawai'ians were completely attuned to, respectful of, and at the mercy of Nature. *Pele* is the Goddess of the Volcano. *Laka* is the Goddess of the Hula. No dance was done in the old *Kahiko* style without inviting the Gods and Goddesses to attend. The dancer and *Laka* were to become one. Sacred Ti leaves were placed upon the altar before the dance began. Cultural experts have already written books exploring the realm of Gods and Goddesses and all the legends and stories that accompany them.

To many Hawai'ians, the old Gods of the ancient religion are still very real. Some Hawai'ians still honor and practice the old religion. It is a polytheistic, animistic religion that believes in Gods and Goddesses, and spirits that are able to inhabit many objects. Certain *pohaku* (stones and rocks) were considered sacred and able to

communicate with gifted persons who could hear their messages. In the 1800s, the *Kapu* system and the old religious practices were outlawed. In 1819, shortly after the death of King Kamehameha I, the *Kapu* system was overturned by his son and two of his wives. Symbolically, the end of the *Kapu* system was celebrated by men and women being able to eat together. The royal family had been influenced to end the *Kapu* system by the staunch New England Christian missionaries who built churches and baptized Hawai'ians on all of the Hawai'ian islands. The Tiki statues and other ceremonial objects were destroyed.

In 1830, Queen Ka'ahumanu, who had become a Christian convert, banned *hula* being practiced in public, as she had been convinced by the missionaries that it was an immoral dance. On June 17th, 1839 Liholiho – King Kamehameha III, and Ka'ahumanu and Keopuolani (two of King Kamehameha I'st wives) issued an Edict of Toleration. This allowed the establishment of the Hawai'ian Catholic Church.

Although the religion of Gods and Goddesses was made illegal, I was certainly convinced of the reality of the Volcano Goddess, *Kupuna Pele*. The veil between worlds here on the island of Hawai'i is very thin, and the spirits are around, sometimes seen at night as tiny, flickering white lights, or orbs . . . larger floating balls of transparent or jewel-toned luminous light.

It is very disrespectful to ignore *Kapu* signs at Heiaus, petroglyphs areas, or the many burial caves on the island. It is said that there are burial caves along the ocean's edge near Puako and Kawaihae. They exist in other places as well. Some of them have already been  disturbed, and bones and artifacts have been stolen from them. People who disturb *ivi* (bones) remains can also risk disturbances or dangers to themselves. In more recent years there has been a return and "repatriation" of some of the bones that were stolen from the Hawai'ian islands and kept in the Smithsonian Museum in Washington, D.C.

During the 1800s there were grave robbers of both Native American and Hawai'ian burials. Many small museums in the United States as well as the Smithsonian Museum acquired and displayed them. This of course was a great trespass to these native peoples. In recent years it became known that the Smithsonian Museum held many thousands of skeletons and skulls from Native peoples of Hawai'i, Alaska and North America. During the time I was visiting Hawai'i, the *ivis* (bones) of some of the Hawai'ian royalty and *Ali'i* (chiefs) were returned. Traditional Hawai'ian *Kahunas* (priests, specialists) did a number of reburials with ceremonies that accompanied them. Some were repatriated to traditional burial caves in the dark of night.

### *Landscaping at Paleaku Peace Gardens*

PALEAKU PEACE GARDENS is approximately ten acres of land that is beautifully landscaped with shrines to all the major religions of the world. The lawns are immaculately mowed and there are beautiful flowers everywhere. I had stayed here before on several short visits and had become friends with Barbara DeFranco, the owner and  creator of the gardens. While Barbara was away on her mainland visit, I worked on refreshing the landscaping of all the beautiful plants and flowering bushes which were in a more or less circular garden, surrounded by lawns. There were pink, yellow, and red hibiscus, and the jewel-toned colors of fuchsia, and purple and red bougainvillea. There were *lauhala* (pandanus) trees, and trees that shed tiny bright-orange waxy seeds that looked like beads resting on the black lava paving stones or ground-lava gravel. These seeds were coveted by the local people for jewelry making. I collected the ones that had fallen to the ground in a little film can and gave them to a local lady, who was happy to receive them for her crafting. There were ferns, palm trees, bushes, and a knotty vine that covered the flat, smooth stepping stones of lava rock that wound and curved through this garden. Without making it "look" landscaped, I carefully trimmed and cut away the excess, revealing the natural beauty of each one of the plants, like a hair stylist. With clippers and pruners in hand, I uncovered the carefully laid pavers and soon I could hear, in my inner imagination, all the plants singing in unison, happy to be cared for (*malama'*ed).

42

In these gardens at Paleaku there was an occasional Io hawk that we could see flying overhead, as if interested in what was going on below. As I watched it circling above, I felt a lovely tingling on the top of my head that I had come to recognize as a blessing. There was also a red cardinal who perched himself in one of the trees, as if curious to watch what was going on. I have found that when in the Polynesias, whether in the Hawai'ian islands or in the islands of Tahiti and Moorea, that having good intentions, a good heart, humility, and respect go a long way with the spirits and guardians of sacred places. The opposite of *pono* is *pilikia* . . . and that means "trouble." When dealing with the spirit world and the *Aumakua* (ancestor spirits), you never want to be or create anything *pilikia* (bad, trouble).

Finally, after several weeks, I felt the landscaping was complete. I sat out on the lawn under the palm trees and watched the sunset. The large red-orange orb sunk into the water of Kealakekua Bay and beyond, into the most distant ocean, to the edge of the

world. Another night the sun had been put to bed, and *Hina*, the Moon Goddess, would appear in her various stages of dress. As it became dark, I continued to sit and admire the beauties of nature. The transition from day, to the golden hour, to dusk and then to night, was a magical time. The new moon appeared and the stars shone brightly. It was a soft and balmy night with that slight breeze that kisses the skin, like a lover, and the palm fronds swished back and forth, and danced, in the breeze, ever so lightly.

I looked at the round, almost oblong shape of the garden that I had just finished landscaping. Behind it and a little lower on the hillside was a large and magnificent Tibetan Stupa that had been built for the garden. The golden hour had cast a beautiful light upon it, which kept changing as dusk approached. Now that it was dark, I noticed something unusual. In between the leaves of bushes and trees in the garden I had just completed, there were dozens of tiny, little glowing twinkle lights, moving around like fireflies. I had seen these lights before, in Native American sweat lodges, and had come to recognize them as spirits. I felt that they were happy.

## CIRCLING THE ISLAND HOLOHOLO

BARBARA HAD A GOOD TRIP and was glad to get back home. In a few days we would have the blessing ceremony of the land, so I had time to take a day off and go *holoholo* to make a pilgrimage all around the island, honoring the *kupunas* (elders) of old and thanking them for the opportunity to be here . . . because every time I visited the Big Island, I felt like it was a tremendous privilege to be able to visit here. I had a CD of old Hawai'ian chants recorded back in the nineteen twenties that I would play in the car, all day long, as I circled the island. I was going *holoholo*. In Hawai'i I have always sensed that there is a thin membrane or veil between this physical world and the spirit world. The ancient warriors, royal families, and *kanaka* (common people) of old don't feel very far away. It feels as if they are living, side by side, with us more dense-bodied beings, but occupying the same space.

The next day I left Paleaku Peace Gardens early in the jeep, and drove from the Kona Coast and the coffee fields up to Kailua Kona and then up to Waimea, in the upcountry of green grass, ranches of cattle and horses, and eucalyptus trees planted by the Japanese . . . then down the hills to the Hamakua coastline . . . and all the little towns on the north eastern side of the island.

Up *mauka* on the Hamakua coastline, there were a lot of farms. Citrus grew well here, as well as other fruit trees, like dragon fruit and *lilikoe* vines. *Lilikoe* butter was my favorite treat for putting on toast. This wet rainforest side of the island had filtered sunlight coming through the trees, occasional little showers, with sunlight breaking through the clouds, even as it still rained, creating rainbows. On this auspicious day I saw six rainbows! As the old

45

saying goes, the rainbow is the reminder of God's promise and heavenly realms. Local people told me that seeing a rainbow meant that the Gods and Goddesses were near.

I drove along the high coast road looking down at the ocean as the waves broke white with spray upon the rough and rocky shoreline. I wanted to stop and visit the old railroad museum in Lapahoehoe, but it was closed. I have heard it has a good historical exhibit about the railroad that served the sugar cane fields and mills up and down the Hamakua coastline. On April 1st, 1946 there was a surprise *tsunami* (large tidal wave) which came to be called the April Fools' *Tsunami*. I believe it was this particular *tsunami* that destroyed the railroad tracks beyond repair. That same *tsunami* washed away a school house in that town, and most of the students and the teacher were drowned. Today sirens are placed all around the island to warn people to get to higher ground when there is a *tsunami* threat.


### *Malama the Aina: Take Care of the Land and the Land Will Take Care of You*


I WAS FILLED WITH SUCH HAPPINESS this day, and I was reflecting on the Hawai'ian culture. All day long I listened to the musical soundtrack of elders on my CD, singing old Hawai'ian *oli's* (chants) and *meles* (songs). Their voices made me think of what the old days in Hawai'i had been like, before colonization. This culture is inextricably bound to nature, agriculture, fishing, and ceremony. Instead of selling or bartering, it was mainly a culture of sharing. An island culture is a village, even if it is a big island made up of many villages and eco-systems, as on the Big Island. Everyone was connected and dependent on the land and ocean for their food and shelter. Everything was constructed of rock, wood or plants. Iron and metals were not a part of this culture. Grass huts were made of *pili* grass, coconut tree fronds, pandanus leaves, and had frames made of large bamboo.

Someone once showed me *pili* grass, on the Hilo side, but there wasn't too much left now. After colonization, so much of the land which grew this grass was converted into sugar cane and pineapple fields. By 1887 about twenty-six thousand Chinese people were working in the sugar cane fields. I wondered how many *hales* could be made today with the little remaining *pili* grass? I heard recently that in Tahiti and Moorea they have fake thatch to put on their roofs. Hawai'i was an ancient canoe culture, with songs, dances and ceremonies. There had been cross-oceanic travel in double-hulled voyaging canoes that sailed vast expanses of ocean, using star navigation. I could only imagine what it was like.

## *Finding a Navigator*

THE NAVIGATOR OF THE VOYAGING CANOES went through an extensive training. This training used star navigation, the knowledge and appearance of waves and swells, birds, and something called "dead reckoning" to take him or her to their destination. If they were going to Tahiti, which was more than a thousand miles away, they would visualize themselves sailing into a Tahitian bay. It was amazing that a skilled navigator could steer the canoe "right into the box."

Dead reckoning is an intuitive knowing of where you are located within time and space. It is a knowing that not everyone has developed. I was thinking about dead reckoning today as I drove my car around the island. I longed to meet one of these wise people who might share more of the culture with me. I wanted to find a navigator to guide and help me sail into my own bay of destiny. Even as a *haole* (white person), I felt that I was coming home, as an island spirited person . . . to a home that was familiar from another lifetime. Could this be true? One never knows for sure, but it can be a gut feeling that feels convincing. Later I would learn about the *na'au*, which is the energy center where there is a unification of the mind and heart, and is often called the "gut instinct" that feels and knows things. It is what we might call that gut-level guidance that informs our inner voice.

WHEN COMING TO VOLANOES NATIONAL PARK, I turned off the road and headed to a ledge that overlooks the *Halema'uma'u* crater. It looked like a barren moonscape. Parts of the crater had steam arising, and I had been told that it can change suddenly, with new eruptions

or explosions. I had been here to Kilauea's summit quite a few times before, and I could not drive by the volcano without making an offering to Kupuna Pele. Again, I was astounded by the energy that I always experienced here. It seemed like this was the place where worlds come together and intersect. It was the home of the Volcano goddess, Pele. I threw my bouquet of flowers over the ledge and sang a song, which Rika had taught me, and offered a sincere prayer, thanking her for her blessing and invitation that was sent into my own "dreamscape."

After leaving Volcanoes National Park, I drove through the Kau desert. I noticed hikers out and about, taking trails which I had never explored. The Big Island is a hiker's paradise, as there are so many trails and so many ecosystems. I passed by the famous Punalu'u black sand beach and the town of Na'alehu and other little towns, without stopping, wanting to finish my island tour before dark. A blessing I had heard came to mind. "May there always be *poi* in your bowl. May there always be warmth in your *Hale* (home). May there always be fish in your net. And may there always be *Aloha* in your heart." This little blessing song, that someone once shared, was like a "post-it note" in my mind all day long.

## Aka and I First Meet in the Ocean View Grocery Store

As I PULLED INTO THE GROCERY STORE in Ocean View, I could already imagine the taste of the fresh raw *Ahi Poke* (raw Ahi tuna) that was marinated with sesame seeds, toasted sesame oil, and tamari sauce. I had better pick up some "Ramen" too. I made dozens of variations of the noodle dish. There was still plenty of time to get back to Paleaku Peace Gardens before dark. Cruising around the grocery store, I became acutely aware of my lone status. Beautiful, golden brown-skinned, happy locals, with children in tow, were shopping for families, as could be seen by the full carts that they pushed up to the checkout counter.

I had gotten used to the patois or pidgin English that so many local people spoke. It had a lilting sound that was almost like laughter or singing and was playful and fun. But as a visitor, I dared not use it myself, as local people might think that I was poking fun at them.

I had been quite content being alone this month at Paleaku Peace Gardens until this visit to the grocery store. Suddenly I deeply missed my family in California and the missing tugged at my heart. I was reminded of all the full carts of groceries and full bags that I had brought home to our family over the years. With five children, a large garden wasn't enough. There were still many trips to the store. "A woman's hunting trip" was what our daughter, Stacy, called grocery shopping. And for the vegetarians out there, I always say that if we buy meat in store packages, we are on a hunting trip with our credit cards or wallets. I have always had great ambivalence about eating meat and admired my friends who had become vegetarians or vegans. There were months at a time that I followed the vegetarian diet, but I had not been able to sustain it for long. No matter what we eat, I feel it is important to give thanks and bless our food before taking it in.

There is something very lonely about a "shopping cart for one" when surrounded by many happy, local families. I pulled my cart up behind a large Hawai'ian woman wearing a black sports bra, a *lava lava* (sarong) of bright red design, a shell necklace, and slippahs

49

(what we mainland people call "flip flops"), and a large black and white purse flung over her shoulder. She had a full cart and the checker was picking up one thing at a time and ringing it up. She turned around suddenly and faced me, "full on," with such force that I almost fell over. Her smile was full of vibrancy and warmth as she said, "Aloha, sistah! That's a beautiful necklace you are wearing." She was admiring a friendship necklace that my Pueblo friend, Maria from Santa Domingo Pueblo, had made for me. I told the woman what Maria always said, "A prayer in every bead."

Without any physical contact at all, I felt I had just been hugged with big love and big *mana*. All lonely feelings evaporated. She looked and felt like the "cosmic mother of man." Tall, strong and big-breasted, she had a soft feminine face, with full sensuous lips and wild salt and pepper hair that seemed electrified. Her large beautiful eyes sparkled with fun and love, but also spoke of hidden powers, prayerful invocations and *kahuna* (priestess) magic. She looked like

she was very Hawai'ian, and I thought that she just had to be a *Kahuna*. Her eyes were penetrating as well as kind. I could tell that she could see clearly, with great discernment, and I knew she would do no harm.

Then she asked me, "Why do women think they have to be thin, rich, young and beautiful to be marketable?" I don't remember my answer but I thought, Well, she's getting right into it with me, as if we were old friends. She continued on, "Well I'm not thin, rich, young or beautiful, but I'm hella marketable." At this she gave out a robust laugh! "I can feesh, grow gardens, make temple instruments, craft, dance and sing and collect healing herbs, and I think that makes me hella marketable!" Again she laughed with a laugh that shook her body, and I could tell she was totally enjoying herself. She asked me what I was doing here and where my family was. We went back and forth a few times and then her groceries were bagged and she had to pay and leave. She bid me a big *"Ah hui hou* (see you later) sistah" when she left, and before I could ask her name, she was gone, in a cloud of dust, driving down the road, with gusto, in a green Forest Service truck.

Who is this woman in the red *lava lava* (sarong)? I wondered. I wanted to know who she was and where I could find her again. This encounter felt like destiny and certainly like soul recognition. It is odd how it happened, after a full day of circling the island, and praying for a navigator. Now I felt that I had found my navigator and I wanted to see her again. But she was gone. If she lived here in Ocean View, it was at least an hour away from where I was staying. What were my chances of encountering her again? I wondered.

Little did I know, at the time, that I had already known and had the highest regard for her mother, Auntie Fern Pule, for many years.

### *Celebration and Blessing Ceremony of Paleaku Peace Garden*

IT WAS A BEAUTIFUL MORNING. Looking from the top of Paleaku Peace Garden downhill, I could see the coastline with white caps on the ocean. The sun was in the east and glinted on the ocean like little golden jewels, and the palm trees were swaying overhead, in the South Kona breeze. Down far below, almost out of sight, was the one-lane road that ran from the village of Napo'opo'o, the Hikiau Heiau and Kealakekua Bay to Honaunau Bay. And just there was the City of Refuge, Pu'uhonua o Honaunau, a place where ancient Hawai'ians who had broken *Kapus* (laws) could find refuge, "rehabilitation," forgiveness, and Ho'o'ponopono. Sometimes warriors who were defeated in battle were lucky to save their lives by making their way to a place of refuge. There were several large Heiaus there. This place was such a sacred area, brimming with the ancient events of history which hung in the air like pendulous fruits on a tree, just waiting to be picked . . . and to come back to life as little vignettes of living history.

51

Paleaku Peace Garden is dedicated to all the religious traditions in the world and was the inspiration of Barbara DeFranco. She had worked hard over the years to make it a thriving and beautiful retreat center. There were tasteful shrines to all the major world religions which dotted the immaculately groomed gardens. Each building was landscaped with local fauna and flora. Flowers were everywhere, filling the air with sweet aromas, like so much of Hawai'i. The ever present sound-track of the little doves, cooing, is the comforting sound that tells me, even when coming out of a dream, that I am in Hawai'i, and not in California. This area, or vortex, was already powerful from ancient days. Today it seemed to form the pinnacle of a large triangle above and between the City of Refuge and Kealakekua Bay.

### Preparations for the Luau

THE PREVIOUS DAY WE HAD BEEN BUSY as a colony of ants, cooking for the event that was to take place today. The *Kahuna* (priest), Kumu Lanakila Brandt, was coming to conduct the ceremony. During his life he taught as a Kumu Hula, taught Hawai'ian spirituality, did

Lomilomi massage, played the guitar, and conducted spiritual ceremonies as one of the priests of Lono, for the Place of Refuge. He was highly honored and respected, and everything needed to be done with the most exact protocol. I found out later that both Kumu Dane and Aka had studied with him earlier in their lives.

We, as sous chefs, were under the direction of head chef Kauila, who had had a career as head chef for large hotels. I always think of him as a cheerful man with a smile and a twinkle in his eye. With a soft voice, he was gentle in his way of delegating jobs and instructing us. When he wasn't cooking or mowing lawns, he was doing Hawai'ian Lomilomi massage for regular clients and guests of Paleaku Peace Gardens. He was a close student of Auntie Margaret Machado, the famous *lomilomi* teacher. He was a real man of the land, a healer of the people through his hands, his cooking, and his Aloha. His name, *Kauila*, means "lightning" and that is how he cooked: quickly and with precision. He knew exactly what he was doing, and his *wahine* (lady friend) Dannie and other helpers worked together with him like a well-oiled machine.

The men had dug the *Imu* earth-pit oven, and the hot lava rocks that were put inside reminded me of a sweat lodge. Over a period of hours, the hot rocks would roast all the food inside of the *imu* oven. The *imu* pig, turkeys and fish had been wrapped in large banana and Ti leaves. Then these large offerings were accompanied with wrapped blue sweet potatoes, taro roots, plaintain, bananas and *ulu* (breadfruit). Burlap bags went over the top. Some metal scraps from an old tin roof protected it from the top layer of dirt. Then it was all left to cook, for hours, inside of Mother Earth.

The large greenhouses had been set up as provisional kitchens. There were several gigantic woks cooking different dishes. Large rice makers were cooking up huge pots of rice. Spices and sauces were laid out, and Kauila would come by and add this and that, a sprinkle of Hawai'ian salt, more ginger, macadamia nut oil. Everything sizzled aromatically. In the retreat center kitchen, women were making *haupia*, a delicious jelled coconut dessert. On the tables in the huge screen room, fresh fruit platters with every kind of tropical fruit were being sliced and arranged in *mandala* designs . . . pineapple, mango, papaya, fresh coconut slices, and citrus. Beautiful bouquets of flowers and greenery from the land adorned several long banquet tables. Before the arrival of Kumu Lanakila, the *imu* oven was opened. Steam filled the air with the fragrant aroma of Imu-cooked, *kalua* pig.

### The Ceremony with Kumu Lanakila Brandt and Auntie Aka

THE MOMENT HAD COME! Kumu Lanakila Brandt arrived dressed in full Kahuna regalia with a beautiful conch-shell trumpet in one hand and a long bamboo instrument in the other. Much to my surprise, the mystery woman was with him! This was the woman who had worn the red *lava lava* (sarong) in the Ocean View grocery store a few days earlier. There she was, looking like an apparition! I did not have to search for her after all. She was here with Kupuna Lanakila. She was wearing full regalia herself, dressed in a cantaloupe peachy-colored

long dress that tied over one shoulder. She was adorned with fresh flower *leis* and a *haku po'o lei* (crown of flowers and leaves) for her head, made of red Ohia flowers and foliage from the forest. She too carried a long bamboo instrument. She had braided Ti leaves around her wrists and ankles. Later, she told me these were for spiritual protection. The Hawai'ian people had always believed that the Ti plant is imbued with mystical and protective qualities. Hedges of sacred Ti leaf plants were grown around the homes of old, and the tradition continues today.

People called her "Auntie Aka." She was to become my navigator and good friend. How surprising and auspicious it was to have my wish fulfilled in this way. It was as if puzzle pieces were coming together . . . orchestrated from above. Somehow each visit to the Big Island seemed to be guided by the ancestors. Living a walking prayer was how I wished to walk upon this *aina* (land), just as Aka did. Later, Aka told me that it was destiny that we met, that we were *Ohana* (family) from long, long ago. Later, I would learn more about our connection long ago.

When we see everything and everyone as alive and sacred, we ourselves become beings filled with humility, light and unconditional love. I had seen this in Aka and other Hawai'ian people who helped and inspired others. How long would it take to see everyone and everything in this way? Being able to do it in fits and starts was not enough. I wanted to be able to sustain it. Sustaining that state of sacred vision and Aloha was my intention and prayer.

We all formed a circle holding hands around the whole garden. This ceremony was a blessing of the land and the gardens and shrines, celebrating the unity and common goals of all religions

and spiritual traditions. My contribution to the ceremony was the beautification of this garden, and it was looking particularly beautiful on this day. Now we were gathered in prayer with the two ceremonial leaders chanting and uttering prayers in Hawai'ian. Kumu Lanakila blew his conch and delivered a powerful *mele oli* (a

chant by one person) and then they both blew their long bamboo instruments. It was very quiet, except for the long deep tones that came from these *pus*. Then both celebrants chanted together and said many prayers. When the ceremony was complete, we all made our way over to the large screen rooms where the tables were laid out with a beautiful and fragrant *luau* (feast).

### A Second Encounter with Auntie Aka

I WENT UP TO AUNTIE AKA and she immediately recognized me from the grocery store. "Hey, Aloha, sistah!" she said! She grabbed me and hugged me. She smelled sweet from the flowers in her *leis*. "Do you live here?" she asked. I said "Yes, for now." She said, "This is a powerful zone. I knew we would meet again soon. What do you do here?" she asked. I told her about gardening and helping run the retreat center when Barbara was gone to the mainland for a while. She asked where home was and who was in my "*Ohana*" . . . husband? keeds?" She put her head back and laughed a deep belly laugh. She said, "Well bring it on." I told her that each trip to Hawai'i always turned out to be a pilgrimage for me. She looked deeply at me and was serious, pondering what I had said. And then a moment later she said, "Well, come on sistah, let's grind (eat). This is some *ono* food."

So we both went back to the food tables and took more of everything. I noticed she loved the *poi* (the fermented pudding of the Taro roots), the lomilomi salmon, the *poki* (marinaded raw fish), and all the offerings from the *imu* oven. She called it "Onolicious" and I had to agree. *Ono* means delicious in Hawai'ian. It was an unforgettable ceremonial meal. Barbara always did everything to perfection, and I so admired her for all she shared.

Yes, everything was so *ono* (delicious). Aka said, "Come down and see me at the shop, and we'll talk story." "What shop and where?" I asked. "Down at K bay. My Ma and I run the shop down there." I said, "Is your mother Auntie Fern?" She laughed and said, "You know my muddah?" "Yes, I said, I've known her for many years. She always tells me to get in the water and wash those buggahs off, before I can come over to talk story with her." "That would be Ma," she said. "Sistah, you must be a "receiver," or she wouldn't say that to you every time."

Then other people came up to us who wanted to talk to Auntie Aka, and the day wound down to an end. And then we did the clean-up, and even though there was a lot to do, it felt effortless. Barbara was the perfect hostess, bidding everyone a big thank you for coming and adding their beauty and prayers to the ceremony. Her eyes were always warm and had a smile in them. I deeply appreciated Barbara's *Aloha* and graciousness and her continuous support of the Hawai'ian community. Her daughter had married a Hawai'ian man, so her grandchildren were Hawai'ian. Everyone was happy and the land sparkled with the renewal of blessings.

## The Shop at Kealakekua Bay

I ALREADY KNEW THE SHOP at Kealakekua Bay. It was a small rustic wooden structure that sat between the *Heiau* and the park. Auntie Fern had been a friend of mine for many years, and I always liked to spend time with her and talk story. Now I had discovered, much to my surprise, that she was Aka's mother! Her name was Auntie Fern Pule. She was the spiritual ceremonial leader and keeper of Hikiau Heiau at Kealakekua Bay on the Big Island of Hawai'i. This honored

position had been passed on to her from the famous legendary hula dancer, her Aunt Iolani Luahine. Auntie Iolani was the youngest of five children and was born a Makekau. Auntie Iolani and Auntie Fern's mother, Matilda Makekau, were sisters. But Auntie Io (as she was called) was *hanai'ed* (a Hawai'ian informal adoption, usually to other family members) by a great aunt who was an accomplished *hula* dancer. There was never any stigma to the *hanai* tradition in Hawai'i, and it was very commonly practiced. Auntie Fern was also a musician, a cook, a seamstress, a police officer and warden, a genealogist, a dedicated member of the Church of the Latter Day Saints, and . . . a very wise woman.

When Auntie Fern became pregnant with her youngest daughter (Aka), she knew she was carrying a blessed child . . . a sacred child, known in Hawai'i as a *Kapu* child. Embracing both the Heiau temple traditions of old, and the temple traditions of the Mormon Church, Auntie Fern found them to be compatible. She had told me about this *Kapu* child a few years earlier and had expressed a lot of concern about her. She didn't like her smoking and was critical of her in other ways too. She wanted her daughter to fulfill her sacred destiny. She told me that often a *Kapu* child could become "distracted" by things that were not "life giving." All these former conversations came back to me now that I had actually met this daughter of hers.

Auntie Fern and her husband, Mahoe (William) Pule, and her former husband, had a large family. Each of the children was gifted, as many gifts were carried in the blood line, or the DNA, of this family, which traced its roots to the Kahuna Heva Heva Nui. But this *Kapu* child would be different. Auntie Fern told me that she, in her own way, had the potential to bring this world a little closer to becoming heaven on earth. Aka later told me that when missionaries first arrived, it was a Hawai'ian woman who told her fellow Hawai'ians that the Mormon church had beliefs much like their own cultural and spiritual traditions. Many of the *Kahuna nui* families became Mormons without the need to give up all of their traditional, cultural practices.

This *kapu* child came to dance upon the Earth . . . and she would be named Haleaka Iolani Pule. After she grew up, she would be known by people from all over the world as "Auntie Aka."

Auntie Fern always asked me if I traveled with the "man in white," as she pointed upwards towards the sky. I always told her that I did. Aka's sister, Kalehua, later told me that when Aka was a baby that she saw visions of Jesus, and as soon as she could talk, she called him "the man in white." Yes, we all traveled with him.

## The Family Heiau at Kealakekua Bay

THE BEACH OF KEALAKEKUA BAY was filled with large lava rocks and boulders, and it took some nimble footwork to walk over them before getting into the water. But when Aka was a child, it was a beach of white sand. This beach was in front of and facing the side of Hikiau Heiau. These large, rectangular stone platform temples harked back to the days of the old Hawai'ian religion. This religion of Gods and Goddesses was a religion which honored every part of nature as sacred. Hikiau Heiau is a tall, rectangular platform of carefully placed lava rocks. Some feel that this temple of stone is at least one thousand years old. There are differing opinions about the heiau's age. It is possible that it was re-built in the seventeen-hundreds. This Heiau is dedicated to the God, Lono. He is the God of nature, agriculture, music, peace, and fertility.

For forty-four generations this temple was in the care of Aka's family. Auntie Iolani Luahine was the ceremonial *kahuna* (priestess) of this temple before she passed it on to Aka's mother, Auntie Fern Pule. Before her death, Auntie Fern passed the *kuleana* (responsibility) on to Aka. Their ancestors were buried here in the surrounding area. Some of them were placed in high, inaccessible caves. Aka told me that there is a *heiau* on the side of the cliff above Kealakekua Bay. It no longer can be seen as it is covered with foliage. Today, wild goat families live along the steep cliff walls above the shoreline.

When Captain Cook first aimed his white-sailed schooner into Kealakekua Bay in 1779, the *Kanaka Maoli* (Native Hawai'ians) thought that he was the God Lono, as his arrival coincided with the season of Lono. They welcomed Captain Cook and his crew, prepared feasts for them, and provided provisions for their ships. But before long they realized he was not a God, as his crew got sick, and Gods and their retinues were not supposed to get sick. Later, when his ship returned, needing repair, it was the season of the war God, Ku. The *Kanaka Maoli* became disillusioned with these Englishmen when Captain Cook and his crew mistreated them. The last straw occurred when Captain Cook and his crew tried to kidnap the Hawai'ian king and his daughter. This would not be tolerated and, to make a long story short, the Hawai'ians killed Captain Cook.

Over the years the family did the seasonal ceremonies up on the top of Hikiau Heiau, which renewed the traditions of old Hawai'i – to pray for the people, to pray for the land, and for the forces of nature to either remain in balance or return to balance. There were also ceremonies for sending off the spirit of a family member who has passed from this world.

Through chanting of special sacred chants, "calling" forces could be summoned and invoked, protection could be given, and healing and balance could be accomplished. Here, Aka and her sisters and brothers developed and learned from their grandmother, their great grandmother, their aunties and uncles, their mother, and other spiritual teachers.

### *Genealogy*

AUNTIE FERN BEGAN TO TELL ME a little about the history of Kealakekua Bay and Captain Cook. "When Captain Cook arrived in Kealakekua Bay, the Hawai'ian chief requested him to recite his genealogy. He only knew about four generations of his family. Hawai'ians know dozens of generations by heart, and can recite or chant them when they introduce themselves. Some Hawai'ians can chant the names of their ancestors for hours," she said. "They have an amazing memory to recount all the names, going very far back."

Auntie Fern explained to me, "The Mormon belief in genealogy is similar to that of the Hawai'ian people. It made becoming a Mormon easy for us, and especially easy for the families of the *kahuna nui* (priest class). The Hawai'ian healing tradition included the 'laying on of hands' and the Mormons practice this type of healing also.

"Most large, traditional families have a number of cultural specialists. They may include a *lomilomi* practitioner of healing massage. And they may have a practitioner of *lau'lapa' au* (herbal medicine). A very gifted child would be mentored by their *kupuna* (elders) to eventually become a practitioner of *Ho'o'ponopono* (conflict resolution and bringing things back to goodness and harmony). Aka said to me, "We have a relative named Auntie Morrnah Simeona who became a famous practitioner and teacher of *Ho'o'ponopono*. She traveled all over the world sharing her gift. She actually passed away while she was teaching in Poland in the 1990s. When she introduced this teaching, she adapted it to Christianity. Of course, it is a universal teaching," she said. I had heard Aka speak of her great Aunt Morrnah Simeona (on her mother's side) with great admiration, and wondered if Uncle Abel Simeona was related to her as well.

One day, Auntie Fern said to me, "A person has the potential of becoming a vehicle of divine forces, to help another. We say, 'to kokua', which means 'to help'." Her usual eagle-sharp eyes suddenly became soft. She looked at me intently and suddenly sent out a waft of blessing energy that surrounded and infused me. I felt light and airy with a blissful feeling running up and down my spine. The top of my head felt tingly and showered with sparkles. So this was what it is to kokua, as a vehicle of divine forces, I thought. I closed my eyes to savor the feeling, and both of us were silent. This was a rare occasion, as Auntie was often quite stern with me. I thought, never try to describe Auntie Fern as a kahuna or priestess. She would deny it vehemently.

As I told Aka at the Paleaku Peace Garden ceremony, "I always had to head into the water to wash before I could go to talk to your mother. I guess she felt I was contaminated, as she always said, 'Go get in the watah and wash dos buggahs off. Den come and talk to me.'"

Aka laughed loudly and said, "That would be Ma." Auntie Fern's talk morphed into pidgin English sometimes, like Aka and so many locals. This admonition, to wash in the ocean before talking to her, caused me to feel like there was something innately wrong with me, or certainly, with my energy. She said this to me almost every time I came down to the Bay. It worried me, as I knew Auntie Fern was a largely incognito, powerful seer and posed as a shopkeeper, under the guise of selling colorful lava lavas, clothing, jewelry, and other Hawai'ian arts and crafts.

I knew that she was the 44th generational spiritual guardian and mistress of ceremonies of the Hikiau Heiau, which stood right next to her shop. She was also monitoring the tourists that came to Kealakekua Bay to swim with the dolphins. She really would prefer to have "no one" out there swimming with the dolphins, to put it mildly. Too many humans were disrespectful, chasing the dolphins, grabbing for their fins, and basically harassing them while they were trying to rest and sleep. She didn't mind telling people either.

Auntie Fern is a very powerful woman, disguised by selling her traditional hand-sewn clothing and jewelry, as well as sodas, chips and water. A lot of tourists came through here to see Kealakekua Bay. Many of them just came and looked, took pictures, walked over the lava rocks and boulders on the beach, maybe bought something from her, walked around, used the rest room in the park, and left in their generic rental cars. The locals often laughed about the rental cars. They all looked pretty much the same. Tourists came to the bay wearing shorts and socks and tennis shoes, and a brand new brightly bold Hawai'ian shirt, that hadn't faded out yet. The ladies may have dresses or shorts exposing their white legs, and maybe a brand new colorful Aloha shirt. They wore sunglasses and hats, and the "locals" kind of laughed at them, as their legs were either white as snow or sunburned from their first sun exposure at the beach. I was a visitor too, and probably looked the same way when I first arrived. There were plenty of visitors from Japan and other Asian countries as well. As Hawai'i is almost equidistant between the United States' mainland and Japan, it has become an international hub and favorite vacation destination.

Sometimes Auntie Fern would tell me a little of the history of this area from back in the early years of the 1900s. "You know, steamer ships would come in here to deliver the mail back in my mother's time. And cattle from our nearby ranches got shipped over to Oahu from here too. There was once a large village here. Even King Kamehameha the Great had a *hale* here. There used to be an *Ali'i* fish pond here too, which grew beautiful fish for the *Ali'i*. The bottom of the pond was fitted with carefully collected smooth stone pavers. Little by little it went to ruin. At one point the Greenwells used it to water their cattle before the cattle were boarded on to the steamers. Later a Japanese family cleaned it up enough to grow and sell *opae* (shrimp). The steamers would also come into Kailua Kona." Things had changed so much in the twentieth century. Now multi-storied cruise ships carrying international visitors dock in both Kailua Kona and Hilo harbors.

## "Ask Me Any Song, Any Hawai'ian Song"

AUNTIE FERN WOULD PULL OUT HER UKULELE, when she didn't have customers, and would sing from a long internal play list of Hawai'ian songs. She would say, "Ask me any song, any Hawai'ian song, and I will sing it for you." I loved listening to her songs. She was a really good, soulful musician. She could "ad lib" anytime she wanted to, seamlessly fitting in a greeting to a passer-by as she sang. Or she could insert a funny comment into her song, as one of her friends or relatives walked by. They would laugh, give her *shaka*, and keep going . . . or come over to sit down to listen. Or you might hear, "Love you Auntie. Alohaaa!" Everyone seemed to be a tutu, an auntie, an uncle, a cuz, or a braddah or sistah. And that's the truth, as many of the local people are related to each other by blood.

Auntie Fern wore glasses and had short-cropped, wavy hair, which was an attractive salt and pepper mix. She was "lit up" with zest, energy and enthusiasm. She also had high standards and expected everyone else to have them too. However, every now and then she would surprise us and laugh at a rowdy joke. It was easy to see that she had been stunning in her youth. Even now, she was very attractive and had a lot of charisma, or *mana*, as the islanders call it.

## Auntie Fern Directs Me to Manini Beach

ONE DAY SOON AFTER THE BLESSING CEREMONY at Paleaku Gardens, I went down to Kealakekua Bay to see if Aka was there. But she wasn't. Her mother, Auntie Fern was there, and she was showing me her Blue Green Algae and gave me a convincing sales pitch. She was into multi-level marketing, and she was good at it. Later she would introduce me to "Zango," a Mangosteen health juice. She was so good at this that I signed up to get both of these products.

On this day I mentioned that I had met her daughter, Aka. She said, "Oh, you met my daughtah, Aka? All this time you never met her? I think she is over at Manini Beach right now." *Manini* is the Hawai'ian name for the Convict or Tiger fish, which is one of the reef fish that swims in these waters. I think they have black and white stripes like the old-time jail suit. This made me think of one of Auntie's prayers when she was rebuking evil spirits: "*Ke Akua* (creator), *okie* (cut) the forces that would seek to diminish the light, bind 'em, and lock 'em up, and *Ke Akua*, you do with 'em, what you deem fit."

Auntie Fern asked me how many of her keeds I had met. I said, "Only Aka and Kalehua so far." She said, "Aka is our baybay, our *Kapu* child." She then went on to tell me about how Aka was born with very strong *mana* . . . as she was blowing all the lights out! – the toaster, and almost any piece of electronic or electrical equipment, without even trying. She told me that, after the first few years, Aka was trained by the *kapunas* and brought over here to Napo'opo'o village to live with her grandmother and aunties in the family home, which was just a short walk from the bay and Hikiau Heiau.

## Auntie Fern's Children

ONE DAY, AUNTIE FERN TOLD ME ABOUT all of her children. Wanda was the oldest and in charge of the younger children while Auntie Fern worked. Next was Kalehua, who shared the names of both Fern and Kalehua with her mother. Kapali was the first son. She told me that her first husband, John Nawai Kamauu, had been a merchant marine and had been lost at sea. Her second husband, Mahoe (William) Pule, was the father of Kela, Lisa, Aka and William, who was also called Boogee. Lehua, also called Wanda, was *hanai'd* (adopted) and was the youngest. Initially she was raised by Auntie Fern and then later by Wanda and her husband Jerry Iokia. We had talked about many things over the years but never about all of her children. I did not meet Lisa, Lehua, Kapali or Boogie, until some years later.

I asked Auntie Fern about the *hanai* children in the family. "The *hanai* adoption system may seem very foreign to mainland or European societies, but it was, and still is, commonly practiced by traditional Hawai'ian families. There was no stigma to being *hanai'd*. The *hanai* is a kind of informal adoption that is agreed upon within a family. The child will know who their birth parents are and will see them often at family gatherings. Even today a family may have a *hanai* son or daughter. Often times a grandparent might suggest that the birth parents give a child to another family member. Since large Hawai'ian families gather together often, the *hanai* child is always educated and loved by everyone. Sometimes the *hanai* may take place to provide a son or daughter who could help work for older relatives. Sometimes it was to give a child to a sister who was unable to conceive. There were many reasons, but it was, and still is, an accepted practice. Most often it is done informally within a family. Historically *hanai*, which seems natural to Hawaiian people, was used to create alliances within royal families."

I was glad that Auntie Fern explained this adoption system to me because I often heard local people talking about a *hanai* son or daughter. It was inconceivable to me to think that I could have given one of my children to a relative. But I suppose it is all about what we are raised with that feels comfortable and normal.

Auntie Fern continued, "We lived in Oahu, in Alewa Heights, and we had a shop over there and made plenty of lau laus!" she said. "Wanda and her husband Jerry live on Oahu, where they raised their children, as well as dogs, geese, ducks and chickens. The beach was right across the street." Wanda was a very good hula dancer. Before she married, she traveled to Tahiti to perform with her *halau*. Wanda's husband, Uncle Jerry, is a well-respected *kumu* of *lomilomi* massage and a true body mechanic who can fix long-standing physical problems. In my opinion, he is a miraculous healer. But I always knew that Wanda's own intuitive and healing gifts supported and added to Uncle Jerry's healing work. In later years Paul and I received many healings through Jerry's *lomilomi*.

The second oldest, Kalehua, also known as Fern, sometimes worked at the shop at Kealakekua Bay, and that is where I first met her. Her gentle nature and wide, friendly smile covered the powerful warrior woman who lived inside of her. She and her husband Pancho had raised their family on Oahu and, being an industrious person, she had numerous businesses. The ones I remember are, she was a limousine driver, and had a balloon and party business. She, too, had the intuitive gifts of the family line.

Later, I would meet Aka's sister, Kela, who looked a lot like her mother and was also a very talented singer and guitar player. Kela's English name is Sarah, as she was named after her grandmother, Sarah Pule. Kela is hilarious and her facial expressions even funnier. She could make you double-up with laughter as she ad-libbed or changed the words of "old standard" songs into risque lyrics. What a lovely, free spirit she is. And, she is really good at hugs, too. In fact, this whole family is good at hugs. As a rather large woman, Kela always said, "Grab my love handles and hang on for the ride." Making fun of her own size, she claimed to be "two queens in one." She also said she "didn't have a weight problem . . . only a height problem."

It was so easy to like Aka's three sisters (and later five sisters), as the humor, love, and *mana* that they emanate is magnetic. And, according to Aka, they all danced in a *hula* line as children, when their musical parents were entertaining. And, for the greatest of belly shaking laughs, the sisters performed, in a line, with their backs to us, singing, "If it's not jam, it must be jelly, cuz jam don't shake like that." Then they would look over their shoulder with giant grins and shake their booties like you wouldn't believe. Tahitian dancers might be envious of the fast shake and sway of the *okoles* (behinds) of these beautiful and fun loving *wahines* (women).

## Super J's and the Famous Lau Laus

LAU LAUS WERE MY FAVORITE, and from time to time I went by Super J's, a small shop up on the highway, and picked up two plate lunches "to go" for Auntie Fern and I. Auntie Janice at Super J's made *lau laus* of pork and chicken, taro leaves chopped and cooked and inserted into the mix with the meat, and then wrapped with taro leaf and tied with string. The cooked taro leaf was soft and green and was reminiscent of cooked spinach, but even better. They were cooked by  steaming, and the plate lunch had macaroni salad, a scoop of steamed rice, *lomi lomi* salmon and a small cup of *poi*.

What I didn't know until much later was that Auntie Fern had been the one who, many years before, had taught Janice some of her own *lau lau* making techniques. Fern and the *ohana* had a *lau lau* shop in Oahu, when Fern's "keeds" were young . . . and they all made *lau laus*, "an'plenee of 'em!"

Auntie Fern was always happy to see me bringing a boxed lunch for her, as she was watching the shop all day at the bay, and selling her crafts and hand-sewn clothing to visitors. Her little dog, Pule, was always with her, and he darted around playing with the children and greeting everyone. He was always part of the scenery. When Pule started running around the rental cars, Auntie would call him back. "Tourist drivers...!"

Auntie Fern went on to tell me more about her job as a police matron in Honolulu at the women's prison, and then later Aka told me that her Mom had helped find missing people and solve crimes, incognito of course, as this was her style. After all, she was a

Kalehuamakanoe, and that was a powerful Hawai'ian name. Years later I would tease Aka's sister Fern, also a Kalehua, asking her, "Am I speaking with Fern today, or Kalehua?" We had our jokes about the English name versus the Hawai'ian name, and the kind of power that manifested with the name "Kalehua."

In her younger years, Aka's mother, Auntie Fern, would fly over to the Big Island with her husband to play gigs for weddings, luaus, and parties in the hotels. Often all the children would be in a *Hula* line performing with their parents. After all, they had Auntie Iolani Luahine as their great Aunt. Auntie Fern was an accomplished musician and played the big stand-up bass. Later, Aka told me that her mother would slap the bass and spin it around, and her dad would play the slack key guitar . . . and they both sang. It was a household full of music and dancing.

When did Fern fit in the time to teach piano and other music lessons, I wondered? I do not know. But I know she was a power-house, didn't need much sleep, and was a "go getter." Both Aka and her sister, Kalehua told me about going to sleep at night to the whirring sound of the sewing machine. "Ma was hemming *lava lavas* and sewing clothes for the shop and the family, late into the night."

Locals came up to Auntie Fern all day long . . . to talk story, to ask for advice, or to give her the local gossip. She was a very discrete clearing-house for the coconut telegraph. No need for a newspaper. Auntie got all the news before it ever hit the paper – and lots of things that would never make the paper . . . lots of things that she kept to herself. Her lips were sealed.


### Ferocious Love


AUNTIE FERN HAD A KIND OF FEROCIOUS LOVE for her children and grandchildren. I knew this from stories she told me. She was a lady warrior, and she had a tough, protective love for her *ohana.* As a way of training her children, she was strict. Never too generous with direct compliments to her children, she felt free to brag to me about them. She also had quite an inventory of "qualities" that she felt could be improved.

This included me, so I felt honored to improve in all the ways she thought I should improve. She had given me a lot of advice, and she constantly chided me with, "Don't waste the wisdom of your elders by not paying heed." Auntie Fern's constructive criticism was surely a part of my purification program. One time when she was

Fern "Kalehuamakanoe" Pule

being fierce, I saw fire come out of her eyes. When I saw this, I blurted out, without thinking, "Oh, I know who you really are!" Ooopps, I thought, I am not being respectful. She shot back at me, looking at me fiercely over the top of her glasses, "Well, I know who you really are too!" But she suddenly became as serene as a lotus pond, picked up her ukulele, and started singing a soft, sweet song in Hawai'ian. She could change as fast as the wind. She never seemed to hold that remark against me.

Auntie Fern clearly saw the potential of each one of her children and was impatient for each one to come up to one hundred percent of their potential. Her blood line, and those of her husband's, were filled with gifted and royal people. I believe that Fern's second husband, Mahoe William Pule, who came from Kohala, was descended from King Kamehameha the Great. Aka told me that the family was also related to Prince Kuhio. In the early 1900s he was the first Hawai'ian to be elected to the United States Congress. It was important to Auntie Fern to see this gifted blood line carried on through her descendants. In spite of colonization, there were pockets of the old culture and spirituality being carried on throughout this island nation. And her *ohana* was one of these pockets. Auntie Fern's name was Kalehuamakanoe, and she passed it on to her daughter Fern, who often went by Kalehua. It is a powerful name, given to powerful females in this family. Aka's daughter Suzy was given this name, and her daughter Lauae also has this name.

## *Pidgin English*

ONE OF THE LOVELY THINGS ABOUT LOCAL PEOPLE on the Big Island is their wonderful use of Pidgin English. They salt and pepper their speech with this sing-song local Hawai'ian "patois," which is typically sprinkled with many Hawai'ian words and phrases as well. After a while one develops quite a large vocabulary of Hawai'ian words because of hearing them so often and in context. Not many people are completely fluent in the Hawai'ian language any more, but phrases and words continue to be used. I always enjoyed the pidgin! There are times that I use it in this diary when Aka or other people are talking, to give a flavor of authenticity to their voice. There is never any disrespect meant when I put a little pidgin into my stories.

Aka and her mother Auntie Fern can quickly switch into the most eloquent King's English whenever they feel like it, especially when talking with *haoles*. Many local people go back and forth between pidgin and standard English quite seamlessly. "Howzit Brah" is a popular phrase meaning, "How are you, brother?" One phrase that I didn't understand at first was "brok da mouf." When a meal is really delicious, people often say, "it brok da mouf." So it translates to "broke the mouth," and sometimes in today's computer posts people abbreviate it to BTM. "Onolicious" is another one. *Ono* in Hawai'ian means "good or delicious," so here is a fusion of Hawai'ian and English. I really laughed when I saw the Bible in Pidgin in a Kailua Kona bookstore. It is called *Da Jesus Book: Hawaii Pidgin New Testament* by Wycliffe Bible Translators.

"Da kine" is another expression that can mean almost anything but is similar to "whatever." While visiting Tahiti and Moorea for a few months, I saw the Tahitians speaking Tahitian with their friends for a while and then, for no particular reason, they would switch over to French. Sometimes their language was a blended smattering of both French and Tahitian.

## Cleansing with the Pu

THE NEXT TIME I WENT TO K. BAY, Aka was there manning the shop, and Auntie Fern was gone. "Ma had something to do today, so you got 'me,' sistah. Did you wash dos buggahs off yet?" she said, laughing. "No, not yet," I said. She laughed and said, "Go get into the water and wash . . . *kapu wai* . . . dunk yourself five times, completely under." Kalehua told me much later that they always did this purification before they did a ceremony on top of the heiau. So over to the beach I went, negotiated the rocks, and got into the silky smooth water that was daily blessed by the dolphins.

The water wasn't too cold. It was just pleasantly crisp, the perfect temperature for me. I just floated at first, bobbing up and down on the waves, which were gentle. It felt good to feel the sun on my wet body. I had worn my bathing suit under my clothes, so I was ready, at all times, for getting rid of buggahs. I had a few layers of tan, so I looked more like a local *haole*, rather than a tourist *haole*. When I got out of the water, I was dripping salt water all over the boulder-sized lava rocks that lined the edge of the bay. Wrapping up in my beach towel, I walked back over to Aka and sat down on one of the folding chairs that Auntie Fern kept for family and visitors.

Aka was already talking with a customer and she was demonstrating how to use the Pu, by blowing the long, deep tone that didn't break apart, sputter or fizzle out. She was blowing it on the energy centers of this woman (energy centers that correspond to the endocrine system) . . . starting at the root chakra and then gradually raising it to each chakra on the way up to the crown of the head. The lady made a shivery movement as if she had what Aka and most Hawai'ians call "chicken skin," and what most mainlanders call "goose bumps." She loved it, throwing her arms back and out to her sides. She tilted her head way back with her eyes closed and a blissful smile on her face.

Aka was explaining to her that there were many ways to use the *pu* (bamboo instrument) and that what she had just done was an energy clearing and healing . . . a balancing of her energy. The *pu* could be used to honor the directions, or they could be used for "calling," or for opening or closing a prayer or a ceremony . . . for starters. Then Aka showed us a small coconut instrument, called a *pu'eo* that had been carefully crafted into a unique type of nose flute. *Pu'eo* means "owl" in the Hawai'ian language, and this coconut flute is called that because its tones sound like the hoot of an owl. The owl was especially important to the ancient people that lived in South Kona.

This lady bought a *pu* after Aka had her try several different ones. The first try squeaked, the second try sputtered and the third try was almost a short tone. Aka said, "I make the mouthpieces all different sizes so they fit all kinds of lips." She smiled one of her big smiles and made a rather fast series of gymnastic movements of her own lips. "The fit is very important for getting the right tone. Each *pu* has a different tone. So it is like finding the one that belongs with you . . . the one that calls to you."

Around the hole that had been drilled for a mouthpiece was a little line drawing of a whale, dolphin, or heart. There were no finger holes, just a long and wide piece of hollow bamboo, open on one end and with the mouthpiece hole on the other end. The lady went away, *Pu* under her arm. Then Aka placed her full attention on me and told me that this was one of the ancient temple instruments that she had learned to make – one of the things that makes her "so marketable."

## "Sistah, You're Dah Bomb!"

AKA ASKED ME IF I WOULD LIKE an energy clearing. I said, "Yes, you never know, there still may be some buggahs left on me, like sticky barnacles, that didn't come off in the water." She laughed at that and started blowing her *Pu* from the bottom of my feet to the top of my head. I was standing up and she did both sides of me. She had me lift my feet so she could do the bottoms of them too. She could sustain the deep, full tone for a long, long time, with a steady breath. It felt good. I could feel the *mana* opening, clearing, and flowing. Wow, I thought . . . this is amazing! I feel so good! She said, "Sistah, what you are feeling right now is your own energy . . . the way it feels when it is totally clear. There were some entangled 'Aka cords' hooked into you that were not serving you well." Well, I thought, I had better learn to clear my energy completely because my own "clear" energy felt excellent . . . ecstatic . . . wonderful!!! I felt fabulous! She looked at me with a big smile and said, "Sistah, you're dah bomb!" And she didn't mean the kind of bomb that blows up.

### Being a "Receiver," Ti Leaf Protection and Salt Water Cleanse

"AS MA TOLD YOU," Aka said, "you are a 'receiver', meaning that with a high level of intuition and sensitivity all the spirits want to come and feast on your *mana*. And there are plenty of wandering spirits here on this island. You can feel 'em, especially at night. They find you yummy and want to cling onto you. It also means that you have the wiring of a clairvoyant and medium. Being a receiver also means that you are super sensitive and feel the feelings of others as your own. And you know whether people are lying to you or not. In your case I am sure Ma has been helping you to be better at your own protection. Getting into the ocean takes all the hooks, lines, and sinkahs off of you," she said with a laugh. "*Pule* and *mele* (prayer and song) clear our energy too. Spirits are all around us, in the other realms, but they can see us, feel us, and know us. And most of us can't see them. The hungry, confused, or negative spirits can really suck your energy and feed on you and make you feel bad. We rebuke these kine. The good ones, like our family *tutus* and *Aumakua*, bless

73

and help us and give us a "heads up" when we need it. And never forget the man in white. So you have to keep clearing yourself off in the ocean on a daily basis. The salt in the ocean water really washes dos buggahs off.

"For us salt is a sacred substance. We clear our houses and land, with both salt and salt water, too. We splash the salt water around the ceiling and over all the doors and windows. And then we do the outside of the house." She told me that the Kauai salt was the best. "We grow hedges of sacred Ti plants around our homes too, and carry a Ti leaf in our car and have one by our bed. Remember, you have seen me with them braided around my ankles and wrists.

"Keep one Ti leaf in your jeep. Keep one by your bed. You see," she said, "I don't have that problem as much as some receivers, because, from the time of my birth, my 'grandmudder and dem' and our *ohanas* blanketed me with their prayers and their protection. Our *tutus*, on the other side, are always protecting me.

"You didn't have anyone like that when you were young. If you had been born into our family, things would have been different. Your gifts would have blossomed at a younger age. Sometimes we have a blind spot and one of our *ohanas* has to give us counsel, or sometimes even an important warning. But if we are too stubborn or too blind, we may hunker down like a mule and not listen."

### Aka Cords and the Web of Life

I HAD HEARD PEOPLE DISCUSSING "Aka cords" and asked Aka if she could explain them to me. She said, "My name is Haleaka, but for short, I am called Aka. When we are very sensitive, we may pick up on events or people at a distance and even in other parts of the world. These cords, or filaments of light, connect everything and everyone. They are invisible to most people. We can send Aloha and healing energy through these Aka cords, too. When negativity is sent, consciously or unconsciously, it can be painful and even harmful to the receiver. These filaments of light and energy connect everything to each other. This is what I mean when I refer to the web of life. We are especially connected to our friends and family. It is because of these cords going between us that we sometimes pick up on the events in their lives or feel their feelings of happiness or distress. We may even dream about things that are going on with our friends far away. Telepathic communication travels on these Aka cords too. When we collect *lau* (herbs) for healing, we communicate with the plant. It happens through these invisible strands, or Aka cords, between us and the plant. They, too, respond to our voices and our intentions and our appreciation. You just gotta love 'em, all of 'em."

This made sense to me.

## The Blessing of Grandmothers

"MY GRANDMOTHER'S NAME WAS Matilda Ku'upua'ainahau Makekau (Prim) and she was born in 1903," Aka said. "Local people's names are very, very long and mainlanders can't usually pronounce them. But our Hawai'ian names are very important to who we are and empower us. We are related to all the Makekaus. Auntie Io was a Makekau too. When ma married my father, William Mahoe Pule, her last name became Pule, which means 'prayer' in our language. Ma's first husband was lost at sea and he was a Kamauu. He was Wanda's, Kalehua's, and Kapali's father. One of our homes was on Oahu, but another was here in Napo'opo'o, very close to the bay and the Heiau. The Napo'opo'o house had no electricity, so there was no problem for tutu having me there with her, being the child that could turn lights on and off, or burn out electrical equipment without ever touching anything. Oh *kala mai* (I'm sorry), I nevah mean to, Ma!

"Here, living with my grandmother in the Napo'opo'o village, I was protected from the *pilikia* (troubles) of everyday life. My tutu wove a web of protection around me, so that my natural sensitivity and *mana* could be protected and grown. She was a mighty protector. Too bad today, most "born receivers" often have no one to recognize them, teach them, or protect them. It is really sad how many troubles they can have, going around with thin skin and open auras. And they wonder why they feel overwhelmed, sick, or drained, and don't know why or what to do about it.

"They often pick up the feelings of others and don't realize that these feelings may not be their own. If they're with sad people, they will feel sad, until they learn to protect themselves and find ways to clear their energy. Our traditional culture helps gifted people like this to learn how to protect themselves from energy that is not their own. But it also teaches these people how to cultivate and use their gifts. The greatest protection of all is a heart flowing with so much love for others. But no matter what culture, grandmothers are wonderful people. They love their grandchildren. Then you can never underestimate the power of a grandmother's prayers for their grandchildren. And this is true, no matter what culture.

"*Tutu* is what we called our grandmother. My *tutu* took me to the Kilauea crater at the volcano to commune with Kupuna Pele and to make offerings, and of course to introduce me to the volcano Goddess herself. Auntie Io went with us sometimes. She was able to open herself to receive direct messages from Kupuna Pele, who would sometimes speak through her. Some people might call Auntie Io a trance medium, but she was much more than that. She was in a category all her own. The Goddess infiltrated her inner channels and spoke through her. That is how I first met Kupuna Pele. And when Auntie Io danced *hula*, there were times that Kupuna Pele danced through her. It was so awesome to watch her dance. Laka, the Goddess of the Hula, danced through her too. She was magical. Our Tutu and 'them' made the offerings and chanted the chants that had been passed down from one generation to another. And that is how I learned.

"We never offered food at the Kilauea crater. Some people offer pork or gin to Kupuna Pele, but in our *ohana* we are taught not to feed them, as they might come to expect food all the time. And they might get upset if they weren't being fed often enough. So we offer beautiful flowers to her, instead of food. I was also taught how to make temple instruments. We made nose flutes, earth drums, Pu's and Pue'os. Temple instruments are used for "calling" and temple work. We wove mats of *lauhala* (pandanus) leaves and made coconut flutes, called *Pueo's* that are played by blowing air through the nostril of the nose. Crafting, gathering medicinal plants and flowers, praying and chanting was all a part of our way of life. We also visited sick people and treated them with prayer and herbal medicine (*lau lapa' au*)."

"MY GRANDMOTHER WAS CALLED UPON to conduct healing sessions of *Ho'o'ponopono*. This was the ability to restore harmony, goodness, and balance back into our lives and relationships in both the physical and spiritual worlds. *Ho'o* means to bring about an effect or produce a result, or to make. *Pono* means right, harmony, and balance. There were times when this ceremony went on for days. It is the most profound method of returning to our covenants and reclaiming the magic that we were all placed here to experience, to share, assist with, and to fulfill our positions and destiny.

"To put it in Western terms, it is a type of conflict resolution, but it is spiritual in nature, and requires prayers and tracking to the source or origin of the problem by the practitioner. My *tutu* took me along with her from childhood, as a way of teaching me. We can all use the principles of Ho'o'ponopono in our lives, but people should not set themselves up as practitioners."

I asked Aka about the changed and shortened versions that are being taught by non-Hawai'ians and called "Ho'o'ponopono." Aka answered, "Some people are teaching something they call Ho'o'ponopono, but it is not authentic, and our traditional Kupunas do not approve of self-styled teachings. Auntie Morrnah Simeona was a great, great Aunt of ours on ma's side. She had beautiful teachings of Ho'o'ponopono. She traveled the world sharing this teaching and her Aloha with the rest of the world. But there are some people who have their own versions of Ho'o'ponopono that are not really authentic." I thought to myself, 'Yes, there are "self-styled" instant coffee *kahunas*, just like the *haole* people who try to become instant coffee Native American medicine men.'

"A person needs to be trained for a long time by a traditional Hawai'ian practitioner or 'specialist', as they are sometimes called. Secondly, the specialist should be a person gifted with a special kind of intuition to be able to do the deep and far reaching 'tracking'. This kind of trained and gifted person is able to see more deeply into the souls and psyches of the participants.

"Part of Ho'o'ponopono is the art of 'tracking'. It is an intuitive skill of tracing back to the root of a problem, sickness, or situation. We find the source of the problem … the origin. At times the problem goes back a number of generations. If someone in one's ancestral lineage has never been forgiven for some misdeed, then that guilt can be carried into the psyches of descendants in his or her bloodline. Ancestral healing and clearing is another skill connected to Ho'o'ponopono and tracking."

Aka continued, "In the ancient Hawai'ian traditional beliefs, everything in the universe is interrelated, and it is through our relationship with the natural world, the spirit world, the Creator, each other, and ourselves, that balance and harmony must be maintained, in order to truly assist and be of service to humanity, nature, and the divine."

### Having Mana and Ho'omana

"IN OUR TRADITION *mana* means spiritual power and *ho'omana* is to empower or use spiritual power to heal or to manifest," Aka said. "Often a person is born with *mana*, as it comes through our blood lines. Other times *mana* is developed and earned by many positive actions and brave deeds. Sometimes *mana* is gained by learning from a *kahuna* or *kahu*, who has strong *mana*, and who can guide us in purifying ourself and developing higher consciousness.

"*Ho'omana* is a word that means to 'draw upon, carry, and give spiritual power.' It is the ability to recognize, open to, and direct the flow of true spiritual power. It is walking a path that honors the power of the creator that flows through all of us and all of nature. The Hawai'ians did not have a word for their religion, but *Ho'omana* would be a word that closely describes it. We are living in a most powerfully magical time today. There is a lot of releasing in the spirit world, as we need to clear things up, in some way, shape, or form. Triggers and blocks can come up from the past. We need to ask ourselves, 'What's inside of me? What do I need to clear? What do I need to purify before strong, healing *mana* can flow through me?'

"During earlier times in Hawai'i, when someone got sick or was disturbed mentally, the *kahuna* would be the first person they would consult. The practitioner could track back through a person's bloodline and find the triggers and blocks that are causing the problems. Sometimes emotional or physical trouble comes from the bloodline and can manifest in genetic ailments. But we can change the way we perceive it, make prayers, and often heal the condition. Hawai'ians use consultation with a *kahuna* and tracking to maintain the correct flow of *mana*. This *mana* flows through the web of life, which is the life force or the juice within us. Then after we track the source of the problem, we patch what has been broken and what has been frayed. This is the secret to opening to the magic that is always swirling around us, which can lead us to being able to direct its flow. As we do this, either on our own, or with help, we become more successful in manifesting all that we choose to do and create."

Aka knew how to be self-sufficient on this island and from my observations she was a keen manifester. She could survive without money, if she needed to, and she had, at various times. Later, after knowing Aka for a while, I truly came to understood what she meant, when we first met, when she said to me, "Sistah, I'm hella marketable!" She never claims to have powerful *mana*, but I know that she does.

She and I had been raised so differently. I had been raised in a middle-class home on the mainland, in four different states as well as France as a young teenager. Growing up I did not learn to fish in the ocean, harvest wild foods and healing herbs, grow a large garden, or paddle an outrigger canoe. I did not learn to dance the *hula*, make leis or crafts for temple work, or practice the ancient art of conflict resolution and restoring harmony, called *Ho'o'ponopono*.

It was fascinating for me to hear about the upbringing of a Hawai'ian *kapu* child. Hearing so much about Aka's grandmother made me think of my own grandmothers. They were both kind and naturally spiritual women, but they didn't know the spiritual arts that Aka's great grandmother, grandmother, aunts, mother, and Auntie Io knew.

### *My Grandmothers*

MY PATERNAL GRANDMOTHER ZDENKA, was a famous Bohemian cellist, painted in 1913 by the Art Nouveau artist, Alfons Mucha. She taught me how beautiful all races of people are, and how we must all come together as one. She had Native American friends and harvested wild rice with them from a canoe in Wisconsin. She had

beaded moccasins made for her by friends who lived in the Taos Pueblo in New Mexico, and she wore them daily. Her clothes were of Mexican fabrics and made by a Mexican seamstress. She had an "Indian" room in her house. It was my favorite place to sleep. There were kachinas, portraits of Native Americans, Navajo rugs and pillows, other Southwest paintings, and turquoise jewelry. She thought it was tragic how the Native American people were treated both today and in the past. She taught me to love and respect all races and to always want to learn more about diverse cultures.

My other grandmother, Ellen Philips Grove, grew up on a farm in Illinois. Her father farmed, and also raised and trained carriage horses. Some of her ancestors from Scotland, Ireland, and Wales settled in Maryland and Pennsylvania during the colonial days. She was very religious and did Bible study with me. She taught me to clean and bake and embroider. She took me to church, the zoo, museums and libraries. She encouraged reading. Her attic was full of antique treasures, and I would dress up in clothing, including pantaloons, from the 1800s that I found in a trunk. My apple pie is her special recipe which came down through many generations. Both grandmothers took me on wonderful excursions and taught me how to cook, bake, garden and grow herbs. They mesmerized me with compelling family stories. But what was most important . . . was that they loved me dearly and prayed for me! Perhaps it was their prayers that opened the way for me to meet Auntie Fern, Aka, their *ohana*, and many other special people on the Big Island.

With such a large *ohana*, I learned from Aka's sister, Kalehua, that each child in the family had special, one-on-one stays with Tutu in Napo'opo'o village. Wanda spent three years with her. The children also loved visiting their Pule father's parents, who lived up north in Kohala. These grandparents were the famous Akoni Pule and his wife Sarah. The children were all blessed to receive their grandparents' love, wisdom, and cultural knowledge.

Hearing this story of Aka's grandparents, I thought back to a very special summer when I was eleven. I traveled from California to visit my two grandmothers and my one grandfather in Berwyn, Illinois, a suburb of Chicago. Every week I changed houses. My grandmothers, Zdenka Cerny Vasak and Ellen Philips Grove were both loving and wise. I am deeply grateful to have had this nourishing time with both of them, as well as my father's father, Otto Vasak, my Bohemian grandfather, that I affectionately called "Mompa."

## Aka's Father

I ASKED AKA HOW SHE WAS ABLE to hold her breath for so long and to keep the tone of the *Pu* so rich, even and strong. She told me that her father, William Mahoe Pule, had worked on a sea-going research vessel and that they traveled all over the ocean tracking the schools of fish. Her "Faddah" was an amazing free diver who could go down to deep depths without an air tank. He knew how to come up slowly so he wouldn't get the bends. Later, Aka gave me a necklace she had made that incorporated some black coral which her father had gathered in some remote free dive.

"I guess I inherited his lung capacity. With practice you can increase your lung capacity too. But you have to work with the *Pu* and your *Ha* (breath). You will find that it gets easier every day. And you will be forced to do deep, deep breathing. It will open up all your energy, and will oxygenate and relax your whole body. Most people forget to breathe, or they breathe very shallowly. Many people lack enough oxygen. The deep breath is the HA in the word Aloha . . . it is the breath of life. The Ha is intertwined with the life force. Without the Ha . . . we leave our body. Life cannot be sustained."

### The True Meaning of Haole

"In old chants and stories and later in books and newspapers in the Hawai'ian language, Hawai'ians understood the word *'haole'* to mean 'foreign or unusual'. When the fist white men came to Hawai'i, they were called *haoles* as they were foreign and not common to Hawai'ians. However, in more recent years the popular meaning of haole came to be understood as white people.

Literally, *haole* can also mean 'those without breath.' Ha-ole. The traditional way of greeting in the old days was to put your foreheads together and breathe together . . . with the *HA breath*. This is called *honi*," Aka said. And sometimes I heard it called *honi honi*.

After this visit with Aka, I pondered what had been said about the breath and the buggahs. This information was put in such a way that it stood out in my mind boldly! This was something I really needed to work with. The importance of deeply understanding this could mean life or death, or good or bad health, at some point in the future. What kind of spirits had I unknowingly come in contact with in the past? Were certain misfortunes due to influences of bad spirits?" I wondered. Which ones were "life giving" as Aka had said, and which ones sought to "diminish the light?"

My being a "sponge-like" empath was more apparent to me now more than ever. In the past, friends had called me a cosmic AAA or a "cellular empath." But Aka and Auntie Fern put it in terms of "being a receiver." And now it really made me want to pay attention and act vigilantly on their advice. How many times had I wasted the advice of my elders? Youthful ignorance and a "know it all" attitude had created problems in my youth. I now see how important it is to constantly watch my breathing and to continue to be vigilant about clearing my energy. Auntie Fern had taught me about the importance of swimming in the salt water. Without the ocean, a bathtub would have to suffice in the long winters at home. In the summer time there was the Yuba River and nearby lakes.

Aka's continuous prayers and songs, throughout the day, were the way she maintained her happy and high energy. Sometimes she broke into a few *hula* moves or just laughed a long and joyful laugh. When I echoed these methods back to her, she laughed and said, "Don't forget that getting a good grind on (eating) is another way to uplift your spirit and clear your energy." These were new tools that I totally enjoyed using, as gifts from Auntie Fern and her daughter Aka. However, I already knew how to get "a good grind on."

### Prayer, Breath and Salt Water

I NOW HAD MY OWN *PU* and I could practice making a long, deep tone to deepen and sustain my breath. The ocean was ten minutes from where I was living, and I would keep clearing my energy in the salty, buoyant birthing waters of the dolphins.

Sometimes we hear really good advice from a wise person and we just "shine it on" and don't do anything about it. Why is human nature like this? I wondered. Now I wanted to be *akamai* (smart). I thought "It is not a good thing to let someone's wisdom go to waste. It is important to *see* it and *use* it, as the gift that it is.

I now echoed Aka's prayer in my own mind – "*Mahalo lui noa Ke Akua* for the blessings that we so abundantly receive. *Mahalo* for bringing my sistah home again, and may she remember what she has known before. May she awaken to the light inside of her."

Before I left for the Hilo side of the island, Aka said that prayer over me. I echoed her prayer. "*Mahalo lui noa*! Thank you, Creator, for the blessings that you blanket us with, and that we so abundantly receive. Thank you for bringing me home, *Ke Akua* (creator). Thank you for bringing me home Kupuna Pele. *Ke Akua*, please bless and protect my loved ones' back home in California."

### Diminishing Numbers of Dolphins in Kealakekua Bay

KEALAKEKUA BAY IS THE BIRTHING GROUND, or nursery, of the spinner dolphins, the *nai'a*. It is their bedroom, as dolphins sleep one hemisphere of the brain at a time. Often they can be seen swimming in a circle, in pods of about thirty, coming up for air every few minutes, and sometimes leaping and spinning. To observers, they may not look like they're sleeping, as they keep swimming and breathing, but most of the dolphins' sleep takes place in the daytime. At night, they go out into the ocean to hunt fish.

Aka told me that, due to the harassment by too many kayaks in the bay, and some "dolphin swimmers" who try to chase and grab them, the population of the dolphins had seriously diminished. When a dolphin does not have the peace to sleep, they can get tired when fishing out in the open ocean at night. A tired dolphin is more vulnerable to shark attacks. When Aka was a child, there were hundreds and hundreds of dolphins in the Bay, and there was a sandy beach next to the Heiau. This is where they birthed their young and rested in the daytime.

*As of September 2021, a regulation was passed prohibiting people from swimming with Hawai'i's spinner dolphins.*

# A Swim in Honau'nau Bay

SWIMMERS AND SNORKELERS were taking turns jumping or softly gliding into the gentle waves of the wide blue bay. The waves and white foamy swells washed up on the two lava stone steps which were the best entry point into Honau'nau Bay. The locals call it "Two Step." People would wait on a lava rock, above the steps, as they waited for swimmers down below, to put on their fins, snorkel and mask, or scuba gear. They would await an outgoing wave or swell, and then, slip or jump into the water. I waited for my turn and before long I was off the shelf and into the magical waters of the bay.

On one side of the bay was a national park, the City of Refuge, Pu'uhonua o Honau'nau. On the other side of the bay were a few houses: one in particular that flew the Hawai'ian sovereignty flag

which was always dancing and waving in the soft Kona breezes. Once in the water I adjusted my mask and snorkel while treading water, then set out to become a part of this amazing underwater aquarium. Close to the shore the water was about ten feet deep, so the coral and many fish were well illuminated for wonderful snorkeling. An array of brightly colored tropical fish swam beside me and below me, and skittered in and out of coral hiding places on the ocean floor.

There were yellow and lavender Convict Tangs darting about or gliding in groups around the coral. Parrot fish, dressed in rainbow colors, could be seen here and there, and the brown and white spotted Puffer fish added to the many varieties of this real life sea aquarium. There were Trigger fish, Sharpnose Mullets, File fish, Oval Butterfly fish, Damsel fish and many other varieties of fish cruising around both beside me and below me, in the sparkling, ever changing designs of the moving water.

As I swam in the shallow waters close to the shore, I remembered hearing that there are more than a hundred varieties of tropical fish and sea life in this bay. They are colorful and mesmerizing to the eye. The locals remind the tourists not to feed the fish and not to leave trash on the shoreline. Some tourists carry laminated picture cards with the names of the fish for identifying them. I preferred just to swim amongst them, watching their graceful movements in this underwater world. For me, it was the ultimate meditation, and I felt like a mermaid that could stay in the water forever.

Suddenly a long, thick Moray eel swam up beside me, with long, undulating, snake-like movements. It was such a big one that I felt alarmed at first, but it was not particularly interested in me. Nevertheless, I kept my distance by moving away from its curving zigzagging path. I remembered the warning that parents give to Hawai'ian children and that tourists need to know too: Never put your hands or feet into a *puka* (hole) or small sea cave in the ocean, as you may get badly bitten by the sharp teeth of a frightened eel, who make these *pukas* their homes.

I swam a little farther out into deeper waters to the place where you can see A L O H A written on the ocean floor, in carefully placed rocks (or cinder blocks?) on a place where there is a patch of white sandy bottom. I remembered seeing the free divers practicing their dives here, holding onto a rope held by a person above them in a canoe. They would lower themselves down holding onto the rope, hand-under-hand, holding their breath. Some free divers can hold their breath for a very long time. The world record is about twenty-four minutes, but this is with a huge amount of training and by a remarkable individual. Navy Seals are trained too and can stay under water without breathing for about two to three minutes. The black pearl divers in the Tuamoto islands have trained themselves to stay under water for about seven minutes. But almost all of us need to breathe every thirty seconds or so.

Going farther out, into deeper water of at least one hundred feet in depth, the patches of white sand were interspersed with coral forms, which receded into the depths, becoming faded and pastel as the water became deeper. As light rays from the sun penetrated the ocean's surface, lavender columns of light seemed to emerge from the ocean floor in clusters looking like bouquets of lavender/purple blooms. These lavender flowers of light shifted and swayed with the water, and to me were beautiful beyond belief. As tropical fish swam among them, I could only imagine that I had entered a dream world . . . a reef world full of life and beauty, hidden under the waves, and below a surface that was studded with thousands of golden glinting sparkles, surfing the waves, under the sun.

My legs moved languorously with fins that elongated my feet, giving me more speed while swimming. I breathed through the tube of my snorkel, relaxing deeply, feeling at home in the water. Having spat into my mask before putting it on, it stayed clear and didn't fog up. The fish swimming by me and under me stayed in sharp focus. Locals had shown me how to do this when I was first getting used to using a mask and snorkel. As time went by, I gave up the fins and preferred to swim without them.

With so much salt in the water, it is almost impossible to sink. One is buoyed up, and it is easy to float on the surface, with slight flutters of the hands and feet, using almost no energy at all. Floating was the secret to not getting tired in the ocean. Swim and float, swim and float . . . and a person can stay out in the bay for a long time.

Farther out in the bay, tour boats started coming in from the ocean. After anchoring down, they dropped people into the water with scuba diving gear. As the day went on, this bay became busy, especially because it was a sunny day. The parking places along the edge of the narrow road filled up with cars by ten o'clock.

There were times when the dolphins would enter the bay. When they did, people on the shoreline would become excited and start shouting, "Dolphins, dolphins! The dolphins are here!" People would stand up, shading their eyes with their hands, and watch the deeper waters attentively. Soon they would catch a glimpse of the characteristic fins, dipping and diving in gentle undulations.

Sometimes the dolphins would circle for a while, and then cruise or jet through the bay in formation and then disappear into the ocean beyond the bay. As soon as their arrival was spotted, a bevy of swimmers would head out to the location where the dolphins were circling or cruising. I never joined them, as it felt as if these were aggressive battalions invading the dolphin's habitat. Somehow so many dolphin swimmers failed to understand that when the dolphins come into a bay, they are there to rest and sleep. My

"dolphin swims" occurred spontaneously when I just happened to be out in K Bay, Honaunau Bay or Ho'okena Beach, swimming and floating, when I would be happily surprised by their arrival.

Beyond the boat launch on the south side of the Bay were the *Honu* (large sea turtles), that were grazing on algae which grows on the coral. They were almost always found swimming in a group of four or six, a number of yards out beyond the boat launch. Later in the afternoon the boat launch would be filled with long outrigger canoes entering the water, with racing teams made up of different aged school children. Coaches would be yelling out orders! There were also men's and women's racing teams that would launch their six-person outriggers off the boat ramp, pass the large sea turtles, and pass through a narrow opening between the coral, out to the far reaches of the bay and then disappear into the ocean. This modern canoe culture still loves their canoes and racing events today, just as their ancestors did. When the golden hour approaches, in the late afternoon, it is a pretty sight to see the silhouettes of the canoes and paddlers out on the fringes of the bay, with a sinking sun behind them.

### *Dolphin Ambassadors*

VISITORS FROM ALL OVER THE WORLD come to Hawai'i to swim with the spinner dolphins. I swam with them too, a number of times, with the greatest thrill and delight. However, as time went by, I witnessed some distressing human behavior which appeared to be harassment of the dolphins. Some uninformed tourists come to Hawai'i's bays and try to grab their fins, touch them, or chase them aggressively. The more respectful people just commune near the dolphins, peacefully, on the surface of the water. I felt the distress of the dolphins from the aggressive behavior and later decided that communing with them from the shoreline was no less thrilling. The mind to mind, heart to heart connection that dolphins make with human beings, dogs, or other creatures does not depend on being in close proximity. They respond to thoughts, prayers and dreams and they send out the most exquisite healing energy and love.

Terry Walker took me for my very first "dolphin swim" out in Kealakekua Bay. It was wonderful! Terry spent twelve years swimming with dolphins almost daily. She really came to understand their behavior and has guided many people in the etiquette of swimming with dolphins. Now years later, I am still immensely grateful to Terry and greatly admire her books about dolphins which teach safety tips and respectful protocols when encountering them. I especially like Terry's book, *Life with*  *the Spinners ... Twelve Years Swimming with Wild Dolphins in Hawai'i.* I also met Linda Shay and Yurika Nozaki. I love Linda Shay's book,

*Dolphin Love, from Sea to Land.* Joan Ocean (*Dolphin Connection*, 1989, and *Dolphins into the Future*, 1997) educates her guests and seminar students to be very respectful to dolphins and whales when they swim together in the wild. Her teachings about them include their spiritual and esoteric connections to the heavens, the earth, and to us. I am grateful to these dolphin sisters, and other dolphin-spirited people, as they have done so much to advocate for the protection of dolphins and whales worldwide.

### How the Dolphin Divination Cards Came into Being

MANY PEOPLE HAVE ASKED ME how the *Dolphin Divination Cards* came into being. For a number of years, starting when I was a child, I had very lucid dreams of dolphins and whales. In dream time, I had been invited into their waters. There I would experience the rapture of swimming amongst them with an energy and fearlessness that never tired me out. Through our bonding, I experienced them as highly conscious and intelligent beings. They were compassionate and playful. They cooperated and lived with a synchrony and synergy that we rarely see in the human world. Where we have "flashes" and "seasons" of love and higher consciousness, the dolphins and the whales seem to "live there" and be able to sustain these elevated states.

Their energy and vibration, and the way they live together as a unified community, come closer to an enlightened society than our human society. Our human society still engages in war and out-rageous violence on the streets. One day while visiting Maui, Paul and I went out on a whale watching boat. The captain said that on a one to ten day, it was a twelve day. Whales were close to our boat, spy-glassing and breaching. There were baby whales which swam under our boat and then surfaced, looking at us with their large eyes, right next to our boat. A pod of dolphins played with the whales and zoomed under our boat as a pod many times, and then spun up in the air in swirls of silver. It was thrilling!

When we returned to land, Paul was still a little wobbly and seasick. We went and laid out on the beach to rest from this exciting day. Suddenly I got the strangest sensation that an invisible dolphin was sliding up my back. A stream of words and phrases began pouring through my mind. I grabbed a notebook and pen from my beach bag and began scribbling words and phrases. I had to write so fast that I could hardly read my own handwriting later.

*Words of counsel and affirmation on round cards that fit comfortably in your hand.* Draw a Dolphin card whenever you feel the need for guidance and inspiration. Let synchronicity and your own inner guidance collaborate with these *Divination Cards* inspired by the joy, love, and liberation of our Dolphin brothers and sisters. Use these cards as a focus of meditation or as an affirmation. The *Dolphin Cards* reveal the archetypes underlying our everyday lives, and they hold outer, inner, and secret meanings to explore for fun and guidance.

The whole time I felt like I was in a tremendously altered and blissful state. Much later, at home, I deciphered my handwriting, wrote everything down, and then made little round cut-outs with the words and phrases written on them. I knew they were a gift from the dolphins. Later I was impressed to start playing with them, giving myself divination readings. Our children joined in combining the words and making phrases, songs and stories. Even later, I made better round cut-outs and re-copied them again. Then we started doing readings with them. Our readings led to producing the cards in a printed form and eventually they were published in five languages. And that is the story of the birthing of the *Dolphin Divination Cards*. Even though I never felt it was needed, bookstores started asking for a guidebook. A few years later, I wrote *A Guidebook to the Dolphin Divination Cards*, and again during this process I felt the presence of spirit dolphins guiding the writing.

# BACK TO HILO 2001

## *Massage for Debra*

AFTER REVIEWING THESE MEMORIES of meeting Aka and a few of our first encounters, I focused in on present time, and that meant being here on the Hilo side in Hawai'ian Paradise Park. I had been lucky to find a housecleaning job with a lady who is an archeologist. Jobs were so scarce that we were both feeling lucky to have jobs cleaning houses for wealthy *haoles.* Most of our jobs were in Waimea or the Honaka'a area.

Auntie Fern's and Aka's advice from the previous year had already helped me tremendously. Today was not a housecleaning day. It was my day off and I was looking forward to giving Debra her massage. Debra was very pleasant when she came for her massage, and she seemed to relax and enjoy it. We chatted, as if we were two friends. During the massage she became very soft and her sweet, inner child was right on the surface. She became gentle and was receptive to the love of Lomilomi massage. I hoped the massage would bring a lasting relaxation and gentleness.

She had come from the mainland and seemed to like living in the tropics. She did not seem to engage with too many local Hawai'ian people. One day she told me that there were people who lived in the bushes around Pahoa. "They're hippies, and some of them even have babies," she said. So besides being in the "Witness Protection Program," we also had hippies living in the bushes nearby.

At home, in the mountains of northern California, we had bears, mountain lions, deer, raccoons and skunks. Hippies never bothered me. They survived on the income from the marijuana that they grew. Later I would get to know a few of these people who lived in the bushes near Pahoa. I was eager to know more about the culture and the people of Hawai'i. For me, being able to be here in Hawai'i for a longer period of time was a rare opportunity.

The entrance to my cottage did not go through Debra's house. We had separate quarters and entrances, but there was a door that went into her house from my studio, which was locked from her side. When I wanted to talk to her or pay rent, I went to her front door and rang the bell. Sometimes when I was gone, she came into my cottage from her side of the locked door and put some of her own things in my freezer. At times my boom box was missing when I got home. When I asked Debra about it, she said she had borrowed it. I felt uncomfortable about her doing this without asking me. However, I was grateful to Debra and James for allowing me to have a place to land. It wasn't easy getting started in Hawai'i, and it wasn't easy to find a sweet place to live.

I had a nice sound system in my car and a lot of good music to listen to. My son Sean had made me some designer CDs of his recordings, and I especially loved listening to his soulful and upbeat compositions. After first arriving, one of my favorite pastimes was driving around the area, sightseeing, exploring and finding my bearings. I had already had my car inspected and I had gone to the Hawai'i Department of Motor Vehicles to register and get Hawai'i license plates and tags. I got two *mu'u' mu'u's* (dresses) at Hilo Hatties, and years later, after many washings, these cotton Hawai'ian style dresses are still not worn out.

My computer sometimes had problems at this location. I preferred listening to music and didn't miss T.V. Time that I would have watched T.V., I spent meditating. It gave me great depth of relaxation and insight. There were however, some very lonely nights, and I can remember crying at times and missing my family. Hawai'i is a place for families and lovers. There were doubts that arose in my mind about the wisdom of coming here. I was on the Hilo side because that is where my friends had been able to locate a rental. I was also here to be closer to Kupuna Pele. Hawai'i is not so welcoming for a single person who has no friends nearby . . . YET. I had such rich times over in Kona with Barbara, Carol, and Aka and her mother and other friends. Maybe I should be living over there, I often thought. When I felt lonely, I took Aka's advice and swam, prayed, and sang . . . and got a good "grind on."

### *The Sovereignty Movement / Flying the Hawai'ian Flag*

THE SOVEREIGNTY MOVEMENT ACTIVISTS made an example of this current 9/11 crisis, saying that Hawai'i was "once" self-sustaining and could be again. They felt this was the perfect time to . . . "throw off the yoke of the U.S. government." After all, it had been an illegal seizure of Hawai'i by the United States government in the first place. Hawai'i didn't need the United States! It didn't need a bunch of *haoles* buying up the land, which had once belonged to everyone in common! It didn't need Matson Lines to deliver food and material goods. It didn't need a 'visitor industry' to survive, and it didn't need the U.S. military making bases and artillery ranges on sites and mountain tops that were sacred to the Hawai'ian people."

These were some of the points that the Sovereignty Movement activists made. Mauna Kea, the mountain which is profoundly sacred to the Hawai'ian people, already had a large observatory/research complex on top of it with huge telescopes. Most local people felt it was a desecration of their sacred mountain. They were thinking that now might be the perfect time to take back the islands and turn back to large scale agriculture, aquaculture fish ponds, and ocean fishing, like in the days of old. After all, with a mild tropical climate, agriculture can thrive twelve months a year. Some people were proponents of bringing back the *alapu'a'a* (ancient land divisions) as a system of wedges of land that went from ocean to mountain top. The complication was, of course, "private property," in that it already existed and prevailed in this present time, which prevented implementing the ancient system.

The sovereignty movement here in Hawai'i was still strong. Those involved were very passionate about getting their country back from – and what they can prove was an illegal seizure by – the United States government. In the hearts of many people with

Hawai'ian blood there is a deep desire to have their sovereignty returned to them. And the movement lives on today. I wish the Islands could be returned to the Hawai'ian people. I am on their side.

Deep in the hearts of many Hawai'ians is either sadness or anger that their islands have been colonized by the white society. The history of the takeover is sad, and once again indigenous peoples were not understood, honored, or treated with justice. Certainly the Hawai'ian culture, spirituality, and well-organized society was not understood or respected by the early explorers and missionaries. Through their eyes, the white explorers, settlers, missionaries and business men saw great opportunities for their own wealth here on this island chain. One could say that they had dollar signs in their eyes. Here again was an incoming world view of imperialism and manifest destiny imposing itself on another culture. This seems to happen to all the world's indigenous peoples.

I was intimately aware of this, having spent so much time with the Native American and Tibetan peoples. They, too, had their lands stolen and had experienced genocides. Missionaries found fertile ground in Hawai'i with people who were already deeply spiritual. Business men planted fields of sugar cane and pineapple to exploit this land for their own profit. Local Hawai'ian people were paid a small pittance to work in the fields and later the mills and canneries. Their former life of self-sustainability was compromised, and then later, almost gone.

The arrival of Captain Cook on his sailing vessel was the beginning of this sad history. There is even a town in up-country Kona named Captain Cook. Auntie Mona Kehele cringes at this name, as she knew the original place names before there was a big influx of "haoles," who changed the names of villages, towns and bays. Across from Kealakekua Bay is a white monument with a small obelisk top, close to the area where Captain Cook was killed by the native people. This marks the spot, which was the beginning of the loss of Hawai'ian sovereignty.

## The Alapua'a, Way of Life

HISTORICALLY, THE ALAPUA'AS were wedge-shaped regions that went from *mauka* to *makai*, from the top of the mountain to the edge of the ocean. The people did not use money or live on a sales system, but depended on a system of sharing with occasional bartering. Each *Alapua'a* had their chiefs and leaders, and each region had resources to share from the various elevations of the *Alapua'a*. The people on the ocean shore brought fish, shellfish, seaweeds, coconuts, and shell and bone tools. In the middle regions were terraces and fields of sweet potatoes, pumpkins, squash, taro, the *ulu* trees of the breadfruit belt, and other agricultural products. *Ipus* (gourds) were a very important crop and were grown and used for the *Ipu heke* hula drum, and for calabashes for cooking and water storage. Big *Pahu* drums were made out of cut sections of the trunk of the coconut palm tree and covered with shark skin for the drum head. Higher in the mountains were the Koa and Sandlewood tree forests used for making canoes, surf boards, and carving household objects. A vast array of medicinal plants grew at these higher elevations and were used in the very highly sophisticated herbal medicine called *La'au lapa'au*. *Hales* (houses) were made of large bamboo for timbers and were thatched with *lauhala* (pandanus leaves) and *pili* grass. Mats were woven of pandanus leaves for floor coverings, and several mats were stacked for soft beds.

What an interesting and advanced society lived here on the islands. These people, without the wheel or tools of steel, made everything from rock, trees, shell, bone, and plants. They made trans-Pacific voyages in their double-hulled canoes with tightly woven sails of pandanus leaves. Much of the cordage for ropes came from coconut fiber or tightly braided *ti* leaves. Their skills as navigators, using the stars, the position of the sun, swells, waves, birds and "dead reckoning" gave them the freedom for pan-oceanic travel. Today, replica voyaging canoes have been made, navigators have been trained, and Hawai'ians are once again successfully voyaging thousands of miles across the oceans, without motors, compasses, radios or instruments of any kind.

I KEPT THINKING ABOUT THE LUCID DREAMS of Kupuna Pele that had inspired me to come to the Big Island in the first place. I prayed for a chance to drink deeply of the essence of this culture. I prayed to her for guidance. In the dreams Kupuna Pele appeared dancing, in a fiery, volcanic orange cloud, and invited me to come to live on the Island. She told me I needed to come "for purification." I had no idea what that was going to entail in the coming months.

Green Lake, also known as Lake Kapoho, was reputed to be one of the most sacred locations on the Big Island. Its Hawai'ian name was *Ka Wai o Pele* meaning "Pele's Lake." People said it was Old Kapoho's Cinder Cone of Green Mountain. It was located near Pahoa, here in Puna district, but I had no idea where. I had heard that it was on private property that was fenced. It was said that at one time Jacques Cousteau took a little "one man" submarine down in the depths of this lake and could not find the bottom. I am not sure whether this is true or not.

Some legends say that *mo'o* live in the lake, and I only heard about this long after I had a personal experience of the *mo'o*. The *Mo'o* is a legendary (?) giant lizard or dragon that lived on this island in ancient times. *Mo'o* can also refer to this place as a part of ancient Lemuria or Mu. Often, place names on the island include *Mo'o*. In the Tahitian island chain, the island of Moorea means "yellow lizard." The Tahitian language has many similarities to the Hawai'ian language. Legends or ancient history can be embedded in names of places and villages. Residual mysteries are left behind, by the ancestors, to be decoded by present or future peoples.

Some of the Hawai'ian people, including Aka, believe that the Big Island is a part of the continent of ancient Lemuria or Mu. In this civilization it is said that beings could shape-shift in and out of physical manifestation – into a light body and then back to the physical. Such beings are also called "inter-dimensional beings." Some Hawai'ians think that a current historical theory, claiming that Polynesians from Tahiti and the Marquesas settled the Hawai'ian islands, is only part of the truth.

There is continental soil at South Point that was found when geologists drilled core samples. This fact was confirmed by geological surveys and could point to the Big Island being a remnant of an ancient continent. Stories like this are passed down through families who have astounding memories for transmitting stories in the oral tradition. Our family had been coming to the Big Island each year for over thirty years, and Green Lake had always eluded us. Now I was on a mission to find it.

So one day I went to the health food store in Pahoa, thinking that I would ask someone for directions to Green Lake. While walking up and down the aisles of the store, I spotted a very tall, thin man who looked like a good person to ask. Even though he was part *haole*, there was something else in his looks that looked Native American. He had high cheek bones, long sun-bleached brown hair with blond streaks, and glasses. He had a pleasant demeanor and he was barefoot. I went up to him and asked him if he could give me directions to Green Lake. He smiled and looked rather excited.

He told me that actually, that was where he was going today and, if I would give him a ride, he would gladly take me there. So feeling warm and safe in his presence, I shopped for a picnic and we headed out in my jeep.

He guided me to a road next to a fence and suggested I park there. From there we crawled through an opening in the fence. He explained that he knew the caretaker of this private property and was told he was welcome to come here anytime. He began to explain the sacredness of Green Lake and told me the story of Jacques Cousteau. He said that some *haole* people swim in the lake, but that Hawai'ians do not, as it was supposed to be *Kapu*. He said he always followed the local traditions. He had lived in Hawai'i all of his adult life. I guessed him to be somewhere between fifty and sixty.

We chatted as we walked by a huge banana grove. Seeing so many banana trees in a large grove is a beautiful experience. Wild guava and lilicoi bushes and vines were in abundance and, again, it felt like a much wilder version of the Garden of Eden. There surely was a strong and lovely energy in this place. Vines grew up the large trees and there were groves of bamboo. This large bamboo was the type that the ancient *hales* had as their framework. It felt pristine here, as if this little piece of the *aina* retained the energy and *mana* of old Hawai'i, the Hawai'i before colonization.

Douglas was his name. Somehow the name didn't fit him, but that was his name. He started to introduce himself a bit to me. He had lived on the island most of his life, but he was raised in the Midwest by a white mother and a Native American father from Alaska. His father had an *avant garde* newspaper, in which he shared his activist views on indigenous rights. How interesting, I thought. I now knew why his facial features reflected a Native American face. It was easy to be fooled by the blue eyes and honey-colored hair.

Douglas told me that he eats very little food and mainly forages wild fruits, macadamia nuts, avocados, coconuts, and eats Ezekiel bread. He went on to explain that he lives in a tree house, has no post office box, no car, no driver's license, no bank, no money, no debts, no girlfriend, and loves his life: simple and uncomplicated. He said he had been married when he was young and that they had lived on the island of Kauai. He said they split up simply because he was too eccentric for her. There had been no bad feelings. I asked him how he shops at the health food store if he has no money. He then told me that he is a tree man – and that he is spiritually connected to trees. He said he never cuts them or chops them down to get the wood that he needs. He went on say that he always finds the right wood, somewhere on the ground, when he is ready to carve his homemade guitars, ukuleles and wooden spoons. He trades instruments and spoons at the health food store for store credit.

He also told me about his morning ritual that I was welcome to attend any morning. I wondered what he meant. But he answered without my asking. He harvested coffee beans from wild coffee plants on the hillsides and then roasted them in a big black iron skillet over an outdoor campfire. He had a hand

Douglas' tree house

coffee grinder to grind the roasted beans. Then he made several pots of coffee in old-fashioned percolators over a wood fire with a grill, right below his tree house. The bee man in Honaka'a donated jars of honey to him, and thus he served sunrise coffee and honey to the people who lived in the bushes around Pahoa and who walked over to his place, since it was high on the hillside. It was a perfect place to watch the sunrise and drink coffee, blessed by Douglas's old-fashioned methods and his Aloha.

Wow, once again, a mention of the people who lived in the bushes. Douglas spoke of them with much compassion, telling me some of their stories and what brought them to homelessness in Hawai'i. Yes, some of the women had babies, too – just as Debra had said. However, she told me about them with distaste, and he told me about them with compassion. Well, what an interesting fellow, I thought. He reminded me more and more of an Indian sadhu, a yogi, or St. Francis. He had a very sweet and gentle nature. It was as if he had transcended the usual desires and needs of most human beings. He did not boast about his lifestyle. He just simply stated it. I told him that I worried about not being able to survive on the island financially, now that 9/11 had happened, and people were losing their jobs.

He asked about my living situation. I told him about my expenses – food, rent, gas for the car etc. – and a landlady who was annoyed by my going out. He looked pensive for a moment and said, "You know, you could live the way I do. You really don't need money." Wow, I thought. I just couldn't imagine myself going out on a limb . . . so to speak . . . with a tree house of my own, or a tent, and the radical leap of faith that he had taken. He didn't seem to think it was a radical leap of faith. To him it was just natural and easy. He was very, very relaxed. I felt very safe and comfortable with him. There was no attraction whatsoever; I just felt I had met a friend I could trust. There was nothing quirky or weird about him either. As we talked, I found him to be very educated and intelligent and able to discuss many subjects. His talk was never controlling or extreme. He just seemed to be very comfortable in his own skin.

As we walked through the lushness of the Green Lake property, we stopped in front of a large tree. He told me that this particular tree was the shaman of all the trees around us – that this one was very special. Now this started to sound a bit strange to me – a tree being a shaman. Well, okaaaay. He said he wanted to show me something. "Okay," I said. He asked me if I could pick up any scents or aromas. I said, "No, nothing in particular. It just smells good here, but it's just a general smell of jungle and plants."

He told me he was going to communicate with the tree. He stood very tall and still, and just looked as if he was meditating, with this large tree as his focus. After a few moments I noticed a most distinctive and deliciously spicy scent emanating from the tree. It was unmistakably strong and most enticing. "I smell it!" I told him with excitement. "It smells delicious and kind of spicy." He said, "The tree just gave us a gift. The tree knew it was being appreciated, and it gave up a gift for us." Okay, I thought, I guess he does have a connection to trees. Native Americans and indigenous people do have gifts that connect them to nature in many different ways that are not a part of the belief system of the dominant society. In this native world, on a large island, in the middle of the Pacific Ocean, the extraordinary is ordinary.

So, after the communion with the tree, we stepped up our pace and proceeded on to the crest of the hill which overlooked the beautiful Green Lake. Oh my, how beautiful it was, round and green and surrounded by trees and lush vines, and oh, so tropical. "There are no snakes here," he said. "There is nothing to fear. Just enjoy the energy here. It is a sacred place." He picked some guavas from a bush and stacked them up next to the lake. It is our *ho'o kupu* . . . our offering to the spirits of the lake. It is always good to make an offering. We sat beside the lake and ate our picnic. Douglas ate fruit from the trees and his Ezekiel bread. I had cheese and bread and fruit. The water was clear and still. He said sometimes it grows a lot of foliage that covers the surface. I wouldn't have been surprised if a mermaid had appeared, as this place seemed like places I had visited in my dreams. Dreams can concoct anything at all, from our deep imagination, but nothing happened. It was just all very still and very peaceful.

*P.S. Green Lake, in 2018*

*In 2018 there was a volcanic eruption from Kiluaea crater. For more than three months, lava flowing from an eastern vent inundated two ocean communities. It also filled in Kapoho Bay, which was known for its colorful* reef fish and tidal pools. The southeast coast of the island was once again changed by the action of the volcano, and many homes were lost. Toxic, acidic steam coming from hot lava creates "laze" (tiny particles of glass) when the steam contacts the salt water of the ocean. It was all over the ground near the coast. On June 2, 2018 lava entered Green Lake, Hawai'i's largest lake. Within five hours all the water in the lake had evaporated, sending a huge plume of steam into the sky that could be seen from space. The lake was filled in with lava and the land around it was covered in lava.

On June 4, 2018, the Kapoho Tide Pools were covered by the lava flow from fissure 8.

On July 11, 2018, the Ahalanui Hot Pond (referred to as the Warm Pond) and the surrounding park was covered by the lava flow from fissure 8. Three miles of the Red Road were covered with lava about the same time.

## A Job, in a Time When Jobs Were Scarce

THROUGH FRIENDS, I FOUND A JOB. I was told about a woman named Betty, who has Ph.D.s in anthropology and archaeology. She had a house-cleaning business and needed a partner. I drove up the island along the Hamakua coast where Betty was house-sitting a most unique and beautiful home. It sat on a cliff top, overlooking the rugged and beautiful Hamakua coastline below. As I drove through the tall grass to park on the side of her driveway, I saw a house that was fashioned after a Samoan men's house. Wow, I thought, this place is amazing!

There were many French doors exiting, from the inside out, onto a wide lanai that wrapped around the whole building. When I came to the door, she opened it and invited me in. It looked like a ballroom with a beautiful wood floor. Little sitting areas, with comfortable chairs and tables, were placed here and there. In one area of this large open room was a queen-sized bed. A kitchen area was on one side and there was a very tall ribbed ceiling that reminded me of a large boat. The sides of the large room were lined with windows for enjoying the ocean view and sunrises. I was amazed that someone built and owned this huge home, but was not even here to enjoy it.

Betty was the caretaker. I told her it was the perfect ballroom. We talked, had an informal interview over lemonade, and made a plan for me to go to work with her. We would be working in the homes of wealthy people from the mainland. As jobs were terribly scarce in Hawai'i at this time right after 9/11, we were both grateful to have work. She gave me a list of cleaning supplies to get, and we planned to go off to work together in a few days.

We both laughed about having college degrees and having to do cleaning jobs to pay bills. How ironic, we both thought, but humility was the name of the game on the Big Island. We did what we needed to do, but not only that, we didn't complain, as we were so grateful. A few days later I arrived in my jeep with buckets, broom, mop, dustpan, natural cleaning supplies, and lots of rags. I noticed that my supplies filled the back of my car and that the local people were checking me out as I drove by. Without a doubt there is a coconut wireless on the Island, and everyone knows when someone new has arrived. We knew we were being observed. Friendly locals gave us the *shaka* hand-greeting with big smiles as we passed them driving down the highway. They seemed amused at our brooms and mops and may have been thinking, "These *haoles* were cleaning ladies, certainly not *'da kine'* lounging around in hammocks on the grounds of tourist hotels by the beach." These middle-aged ladies (us) were certainly not tourists, and the word got out that we worked for rich, white people in big fancy island homes.

Betty had an open-aired jeep and it was our custom for me to park my Jeep Cherokee at her house, which was about forty minutes north of where I was living, near Pahoa. I would then load my supplies into her jeep, which was already loaded with hers. Then off we would go, with loud Hawai'ian music playing on the radio, and loving the wind and salt air in our faces. We then headed up-country to some elegant plantation homes near Waimea, down to the community of Kawaihae by the shoreline, and later to Honaka'a and some ranches that were perched above the Waipio Valley. These jobs were interesting and we worked very quickly together. I really liked Betty. She was a brilliant woman and had wonderful stories to tell about archaeological sites she worked on in Micronesia, Ponapei, and other places around the world. She was an entertaining story teller and knew many legends and stories about island life, as well as historical and cultural accounts of life on Micronesian islands and islands off of Greece. We both loved history, culture and myth, so we babbled happily together whenever we weren't in the middle of scrubbing, mopping, dusting and vacuuming. She always said, "Work from the inside to the outside and from the top to the bottom."

The ranches, up-country near Waimea, were surrounded by horses and cattle grazing on lush green grass. The owners ate a lot of steak. It was my job to completely clean the stove and kitchen each week. The grease was thick, but I loved that the owners enjoyed their own organic, grass-fed beef. Like some of the other homes, the owners were third- or fourth-generation *haole* ranchers. We changed bed sheets and duvet covers together, hung quilts and pillows out in the sun to air, polished mirrors, cleaned up after parties . . . emptying ash trays and picking up dishes and wine glasses. We vacuumed, dusted, scrubbed bathrooms, did laundry, and polished wooden floors. I actually learned a lot about cleaning from Betty. We cleaned cobwebs, stood on ladders to dust the tops of room fans, and waxed furniture and floors. We left the houses looking immaculate and feeling good. Usually the people would leave so we could do our job quickly. Each place took about three hours, and we had three houses a day, three days a week. I always looked forward to the stories Betty and I shared on our drives to and from our jobs and on our lunch break.

On the outskirts of Kawaiha'e was a home of an attractive middle-aged woman where we cleaned. A local man lived with this lady and looked about twenty-five years younger than her. He was sullen and unfriendly to us, never looking us in the eye or greeting us. This was rare in the land of Aloha. He slept until noon, so we had to be very quiet around his quarters. When he got up, he ate and then went to the pool room and spent time playing pool. Sometimes he would take off with his surfboard strapped on top of one of her fancy cars. Even if you're not a nosy person, you do get a peek into people's lives, when you clean for them.

At an old and well-preserved plantation home, on the outskirts of Honaka'a, lived a very thin, attractive woman. She often talked to us when we first arrived at her house. She was suffering from depression. We prayed for her well-being while we cleaned her house, as house-cleaning is not only about physical dust and dirt but about the energetics and "thought forms" that reside in the home. Often through cleaning, intention, and adding flowers to the rooms, we could change the vibration to a higher and happier atmosphere.

This sad lady was a descendant of one of the Americans that played a part in the overthrow of the Kingdom of Hawai'i back in the 1800s. I didn't know this for some time. One of the large rooms in her home contained a library of old books and "a museum" of artifacts. Some items were displayed under glass domes. There were old photographs hung on the walls with antique frames that pictured a serious and starchy looking man, with a waxed, handlebar mustache and what looked to me like cold, beady eyes. There was a gold pocket watch, with engraved initials, a sextant, a telescope, and old maps, which were also framed and hung on the walls. Old books, in glass cases, lined part of the room. I always felt a little ill at ease when I dusted this particular room, and I kept wondering why?

One day, Betty recounted the history of this ancestor, as she knew his name and historical relevance. He had made his fortune as one of the first American land owners in Hawai'i and had large plantations both before and after the Kingdom was overthrown. I felt sad about this history and again, I wished the Hawai'ians could regain their sovereignty. As his descendant, the lady of the house had indirectly inherited his wealth. I believe karma can be passed down in our DNA. Today it is called "epigenetics." I kept thinking of Aka's teaching about how we carry the deeds, tendencies, talents, traumas, and phobias of our ancestors in our DNA. Aka knew methods of clearing one's entire ancestral line of negative deeds, trauma, and illnesses, so *mana* could flow down to us, from the source of all . . . Ke Akua. She felt it was important to keep the inherited talents and intelligence, but not the negative qualities of genetics or ancestral misdeeds.

On the way home, after retrieving my car at Betty's, I liked to stop at Akaka Falls. I walked down to the overlook, which is about a half-mile loop walk through a beautiful jungle growth of ferns and bamboos. I let the clean mist of this beautiful waterfall cleanse me from any buggahs or "cling-ons" that may have jumped onto me during the work day. I always thought of Auntie Fern, over on the other side of the island, and how she always chided me to "wash those buggahs off." I also thought of Aka, on the other side of the island, giving me the teaching of the breath . . . the HA . . . deep breathing, and using the Pu to develop a greater breathing capacity.

With a smile I remembered a time we drove past a cemetery, and she said, "No riders!" with her palm up, in a stay away, blocking gesture.

Housecleaning was a healthy "work out," and going to the waterfall on the way home was a beautiful way to decompress and re-charge after a long day. As darkness fell in the tropical garden outside my cottage, the gecko, or mo'o, climbed from his large banana leaf, then ran up and down and back and forth on the window and then became still and gazed at me. And I gazed back.

### Manifesting a Future Destiny at the Warm Ponds

ONE DAY, AFTER A LONG DISCUSSION about "soul mates" and love, Rika and I went to the Ahanui warm pond to float around and relax in the warm water. This place is scenically beautiful with a view of the ocean and palm trees, lawns, and picnic tables all around it. It has showers and restrooms and a lifeguard, so it is a place where parents can bring their children. There is no charge either, and it makes for a magical, healing day. It is called Pu'ala'a county park, on highway 137, on the ocean, not far from Pahoa. Locals usually refer to it as the "warm pond." It is a volcanic, geothermal pool containing natural sulfur. The heat of the springs is cooled by ocean waves that spill over a protective wall into the ponds. There is an access to the ocean here too, but it is not a safe spot to swim. The warm pond is relaxing, as the heat is about the same as bath water or a hot-tub. Some people say the temperature varies with the phases of the moon. I never noticed this myself.

Rika showed me a form of water *lomi* that was very similar to Watsu water massage. Because the warm ponds were not very deep, only coming up to my shoulders in most places, I could easily float Rika around, or float her in place with a noodle under her knees by gently holding the two occipital points on the back of the head. There was no fast swirling, but slowly, slowly pulling the person gently through the water, with a few slow, gentle turns here and there, and sometimes just letting her float quietly, as I held her by the back of the head.

I thought, what a perfect way to do manifestation work. It is almost like being in a Samadhi tank. Her eyes were closed and she was completely surrendered to me as her water guide. I told her this was a great place for setting affirmations for the soul mate that she longed for. She was concerned that she was in her forties and had not met a husband or soul mate. I told her that she needed to list all the positive qualities she wanted him to have, to make a "mock up" of the character, the personality, the interests, the habits.

At first she started saying things like: He won't be an alcoholic. He won't cheat on me or be abusive. He won't be someone who prefers to be alone. We corrected our style of wording and eliminated all the negative words. I had heard that the unconscious mind seems to manifest the words it hears. If it hears "won't be an alcoholic," it may not hear "won't be," but it will register and perhaps manifest "alcoholic." So we corrected our wordings. Some people say that whatever your mind focuses on, you will get more of it. So, if this is true. we need to focus on positive qualities. "He will be sober, faithful, and kind. He will be attentive, available, single, fun, loving, gentle, abundant, interested in many things, loving, creative," and so forth.

With her eyes closed and being guided gently through the water, it was almost like being under hypnosis, or more correctly, self-hypnosis. In Lomi there was some very subtle massage on the back of the head and the neck. We actually made a prayer out of this ceremony and gave thanks at the end of it, and then said, "And so be it and so it is." Later when we were out of the water and back home, we wrote down the affirmations for the manifestation of this soul mate on paper, just as we had said it in the warm pond. Within less than two years Rika met Mark and it was "love at first sight." He was the soul mate of her dreams, and soon after they were married and very happy.

### "Do You Believe in 'Love at First Sight'?"

RIKA'S TALK OF LOVE, SOUL MATES, sensual ecstasy, and "love at first sight" must have touched me too, as I awoke from a lovely dream the next morning. I was dancing in movements with my partner, back home, which gracefully merged into oneness, igniting the whole body into flame, and winged hearts. In tandem the winged hearts propelled themselves into the next universe. A fragrance of coconut oil and plumeria teased my senses. The softness of love penetrated my heart, causing it to open from a bud to a bloom, in the quivering elegance of the moment.

I awoke and the dream readily receded, slipping around the corner, out of sight, leaving a mood, and a memory. And the dream of ecstasy and bliss drifted out to sea like "a note in a bottle" looking for love on a foreign shore. Soon the moist, early Puna morning stood tall and wide, like an outline of a dim grey warrior, announcing a dawn that was soon to illuminate the garden outside with color. It had rained hard during the night and in the distance, before first light, the cocks were already crowing. Did these dream caresses cross the ocean like a voyaging canoe, I wondered, without a compass but finding me with dead reckoning?

This dream opened reservoirs of thoughts about relationships and all of the complexity that is entailed when having one. We share our intimacy with cats and dogs and shy away from looking deeply into a lover's eyes, to say with an open heart and shining eyes, "I love you." Yet under the surface of so much isolation lies a deeply embedded genetic desire to be in "twos," as we were designed to be, and to "at times" become merged as one. As a culture many of us run from love. We sabotage it, become too busy, too lazy, too indifferent, or too numb. We tell ourselves that we've already tried it . . . been there, done that. "It's not what it is cracked up to be." It may last six months, and then it erodes into "the dailies," or some outside interference may spook it. Our career may take all our time. We may be afraid to be hurt again or to "take a chance." And why? I wondered. We may even feel ashamed of feeling longing and desire, as if it is some kind of character flaw or an undeveloped Buddhist practice of non-attachment.

When these feelings loom large, they beg for fulfillment. This desire and need to be in love, to search for it and find it, ignites our inner dervish to whirl in ecstasy and to re-open the factory that produces the hormones of bliss! And why would this freedom and joy be something to fear? People scoff, saying that idealization always ends in disillusionment . . . that one must become whole and healed oneself, first. There may be a few too many old partners in our rogue's gallery. A whole lifetime can go by without a union with another, while we're trying so hard to become whole, or by getting derailed in our habitual patterns.

Hearts can become as fossilized as petrified wood, and lips can strain into a tight, unhappy smile, reflecting years of "staying the course." But the smile of joy is expansive and contagious. And there surely are those beings that are joyful no matter what their circumstances, whether alone or partnered. Even though there is every excuse, life can often end up in self-created isolationism, created by an unconscious mind riddled with fears. "I can't meet anyone. I am too old. There is no one for me. My hormones have quit. They drink. They cheat. I am too picky. They are too fat, too thin, too poor, too rich, too lazy, too driven, too nervous, too crazy. They have too much baggage." These negative "affirmations" lock the doors to a relationship and throw away the keys.

Rika's open heart and positive affirmations attracted her soul mate. But not everyone is as adventurous as Rika. Instead we can become single, perhaps even compulsive, wearing our badge of freedom proudly, as we keep our own "order," our own schedule, our own independence. We convince ourselves that this is the best life. And for some people it is. There can be great satisfaction and contentment, but is there joy? For some, there is joy no matter if they're single or partnered.

Lives can fill with jobs, friends, organizations, activism, causes, hobbies and pets. They can take up all the space, crowding out the space reserved for the beloved. A life can be neat and tidy and good, and we need not feel fragile, vulnerable or "unzipped," the way we feel when we fall in love. That crazy, wonderful feeling lights us up. It makes us think of the beloved upon waking in the morning and upon going to sleep at night, and at many moments in between. It is natural to shy away from pain and complications, or a religious vow. We all want to be smart. But in the night when the messenger visits, luring us to take the leap, or giving us a dream to remind us, what do we do? How do we feel? The lover that awaits us visits our bed with a phantom kiss that enlivens our whole being and gazes upon us, with a gaze that we may never forget. A person that we know so well, who may seem ordinary, when seen with a dreamer's eyes, and felt with a dreamer's heart, can suddenly become mythic and magical. And perhaps, that one has yet to come on the stage of our life . . . or they may already be on the stage, unrecognized.

### Going Holoholo with Rika and a Challenge to Kupuna Pele

THERE WERE TIMES THAT I BECAME DISCOURAGED and wondered if I was really doing what I was meant to be doing. I wondered what Kupuna Pele meant with her dream invitation, or did I assign too much meaning to the invitational dreams that I had had. The dreams had instructed me to come to the Big Island – for purification. There were many times of loneliness and missing my family at home, which filled me with doubts. Rika and I had decided to go *holoholo*, as it was not a house cleaning day. We were going to the volcano to make offerings, and to chant and commune with the Volcano Goddess, Kupuna Pele.

As I had been full of doubts and fears for the last few days, I had challenged the Goddess Pele to show me "a sign" that I really was supposed to be here on her island. There were days when I just wanted to go home. This particular day I learned to never challenge her again, as I have come to trust myself and my dreams. Over time I came to dispense with doubts and fears. When I missed my family, I made the prayer, "*Ke Akua*, what would you have me do today to take myself out of my 'self,' to help someone else, or to be of service in some way? Please guide me. *Mahalo nui loa* (thank you)."

An opportunity to help someone else almost always would arise as a result of this prayer. Sometimes I was asked to drive a child to school when the family car was broken down, or another time I gave some clothing to a family in need. Numerous times I helped pick fruit. However, I never had the chance to pick the red coffee berries. Or I drove the neighbor's trash to the transfer station and fed the stray cats that were always there, so hungry, meowing as a chorus as they crowded around my feet.

Rika and I drove south on the two-lane highway to Volcanoes National Park. We entered the park and drove down to the Chain of Craters road and parked. It took us right to the edge of the crater. There was steam coming up out of numerous places on this rugged, treeless landscape that looked like the surface of the moon.

Just as we got out of the car with our *ho'okupu*, (offering) of flowers, the most radiant rainbow instantly appeared and arched from one edge of the crater to the other. We had never before seen such a full spectrum, brilliant and radiant rainbow. It felt like it was surely "the sign" that I had asked for. We both felt such a surge of energy and blessing that we began to chant a Hawai'ian chant together.

Rika and I had made many trips to the cliffs above the ocean near Hawai'ian Paradise Park, where we loved to chant and pray. I played my Native American cedar flute there, too. She had taught me some of the chants she knew. And for a petite and shy Japanese woman, she had a mighty voice when she chanted traditional Hawai'ian chants. We put a gin offering in a little *puka* (hole) near a vent of steam, and offered our *ho'okupa*, a bouquet, which was carefully attached to a bundle wrapped in a Ti leaf. Later we were told that Kupuna Pele does not need gin, and park rangers do not like picking up all the broken glass from bottles of gin left in the park. Other people told us that an offering of pork is what she likes. Others disagreed with that too. I felt that the intention of the offering may be more important than what food or fruit or flower is offered.

The rainbow remained for much longer than most rainbows that illuminate the sky. We just kept chanting to Kupuna Pele to thank her, to honor her . . . for her Mother creation of new land through her lava flows. Traditional Hawai'ians believe that the appearance of a rainbow means the Gods and Goddesses are present. This was the Mother of all Rainbows, and we were inside a mythic moment with the Mother Goddess of the *Aina*.

How many places can a person live where new land is being formed all the time, I wondered? This is the womb of creation, right here, at this crater. New land is being formed out of this crater and nearby lava vents, right now. It was wondrous to think of how so much of the land masses on this earth have been created by volcanoes and lava flows, over eons of time. The Big Island has five volcanoes and one active seamount (underwater volcano). Kohala, Mauna Loa, Kilauea and Mauna Kea are all considered active, and Hualalai is dormant. The Kohala volcano is considered the island's oldest shield volcano. "Blessings, blessings, Kupuna Pele," we both said in unison. We had shivers and chicken skin as we felt the blessing of being here, so close to her crater. Then Rika began to dance the hula . . . a beautiful thing to behold, as she was a superbly graceful dancer. Watching her, I felt that she belonged right here, dancing this honor dance forever. It was a moment when all time stopped and disappeared. This moment was a forever moment and has continued to live inside of us.

Neither of us had ever felt so close to Kupuna Pele before. She may have been invisible as a Goddess to us, but her presence was seen and felt in the rainbow. "Kupuna Pele," I said, out loud, "I will never ask you for a sign again. I stand before you with humility. Now, I really know I am meant to be here. *Kala mai*" (I'm sorry), I said, with tears in my eyes.


### *Going Holoholo with Rika Again*


ONE DAY THAT WAS A DAY OFF from the cleaning job, Rika and I headed out again, *holoholo*, not knowing where we were going. We ended up at the Black Sand Beach of Punalu'u. She had something special she wanted to show me there. We parked the car and walked over to the beach where several sea turtles were sunning themselves, on the warm, black sand, a few feet away from where the white foam of the waves laced the sand. The *honu* (sea turtles) love to sun themselves on black sand beaches, as the sand stays so warm. Some young male tourists were trying to pick up the *honus* to haul them into the water. They were being playful and just trying to have fun with each other, but they were being very careless with these large sea turtles.

Both Rika and I knew we needed to intervene, as it is illegal to harass or touch the sea turtles, and it was not *pono* (correct) or respectful to the *honu*. We went up to the men and told them that they probably were not aware that in Hawai'i there is a law against touching, moving, or picking up the *honu*, the very beloved and rather rare, sea turtles. We were very diplomatic and friendly towards them, so they backed off without an argument and left the turtles alone. They went off in another direction, jabbing, poking at each other, and laughing as they disappeared to a distant picnic area with their cooler of beer. At least they weren't going to hurt these *honu*.

ONE PORTION OF THE HERB KANE MURAL

Then Rika said, "Let's go see the mural that I showed you last year. Not very many people even know about it." "Okay," I said, "you lead the way." We walked by a freshwater pond surrounded by palm trees. Ducks were swimming around on the pond, filled with water lilies, and ducklings were swimming behind their mother, all in a row.

We now entered a building that had been abandoned. It was made of cement and looked like it had been a hotel. Wires were hanging down from the ceiling and lying over the cement floors, and we carefully picked our way over them. There were large cracks and breaks in the walls, and all the windows had long ago been broken out. Rika said that some years back there had been a *tsunami* which had hit this area very hard, and that this hotel and history center had been destroyed and abandoned when the *tsunami* flood rushed in here at Punalu'u.

After weaving our way through the ruins of the building, we went around a corner into a little alcove room. Here was the perfectly preserved mural painting, as perfect as it was last year when I first saw it. It was on a curved wall and was quite large. The mural had been painted by Herb Kane, the famous Hawai'ian artist, who so skillfully recorded life in old Hawai'i with his paintbrush. The mural depicted life in the village that existed here at Punalu'u in the old days, before colonization.

It showed the native huts of the *Kanaka Maoli* (native Hawai'ians), going about their chores, men coming in from their outrigger canoes, children playing, and all aspects of village life. How beautiful it was! Herb Kane's artwork made all the people look so life-like. He was surely a talented artist who had a gift for painting the people and culture of the past, so they would never be forgotten. Strangely enough, with all the damage to the building, the mural was perfectly intact. It wasn't chipped or stained or broken in any way. It was perfect, just as Herb Kane left it when the mural was finished. Rika was right. This was a wonderful surprise that she had shared with me.

Rika had said to me before, "Be very careful about who you bring to see this. The wrong people might damage it or try to steal it. It is kind of a secret." Her comment was rather prophetic, as years later someone did come into the building and cut the mural into sections and stole it. As far as I know, it has never been found. Herb Kane proceeded to re-paint the stolen mural, as a painting.

Before going home, we stopped in a small cafe for coffee. Over this little town of Pahala hovered the tall, empty buildings of an old sugar cane factory, which closed in 1996 when the sugar cane industry moved from Hawai'i to other countries. Now these former sugar cane fields are planted in macadamia nut orchards.

I remembered Aka's sisters telling me about their jobs in the pineapple packing plant on the island of Oahu, when they were young. The sugar and pineapple industries had made some outside individuals and corporations very wealthy, but the Hawai'ians who worked in the fields and canneries made very little. There were many strikes due to such poor pay for the workers. The sugar cane fields and factories gave rise to a railroad that ran up the Hamakua coastline. There were trestles that crossed the three large gulches north of Hilo. Today, the trains and trestles are gone, due to damage by tsunamis, and so are the sugar plantations and factories. I believe the last of the sugar plantations shut down in the late 1980s or early 1990s. There was a tsunami on the Hilo side in 1946 and then one in 1960 which damaged the railroad and the port town of Hilo.

I thought of the photo of the man, with the handlebar mustache, at one of our house cleaning jobs. He was one of them. I thought of all the immigrants that came to Hawai'i to work in the fields and canneries after colonization. They came from Japan, China, Portugal, Spain, and the Philippines. These populations mixed with many of the Native Hawai'ians, and eventually the local culture became diversified.

People from the Philippines and Mexico were employed on the islands too, many as *paniolos* (cowboys) in the new cattle ranching business. Things are always changing, I thought. That's one thing we can always count on, but then, some things never change. The *aina* (land) holds all the bones of the ancestors and the *aina* will be here long after we are gone.

## *A Magical Apparition – The White Dragon*

ONE MORNING I AWOKE TO POUNDING RAIN on the roof and an inner message that came in so clearly that it was almost like someone speaking "out loud" to me. "Go south this morning, to a mountain on the west side of the road, and there you will meet the white dragon." Then a few more specific landmarks were mentioned.

"White dragon! What white dragon?" I thought. And who was talking to me as I lay in bed, still groggy with sleep. Again, I heard the inner voice, saying the same thing again. I argued, "But there is a torrential rain storm going on outside. My windshield wipers can never keep up with this downpour. I won't be able to see. It's too dangerous." The message came through again, but this time it said "we" would be protected. "Well, who is *we*?" I asked.

Just then the phone rang and Douglas was on the line, calling from the Pahoa health food store. "Are you ready to go Holoholo today?" he asked, with a twinkle in his voice. "Well, no," I said. "It's raining too hard. It's dangerous to drive in this kind of a downpour."

Then he asked me, "How is your *kundalini* this morning?" I told him that it actually was running, and vibrating in my tailbone and spine, and that I had received a strange message. He said, "My *kundalini* is roaring today, just like Tutu Pele put hot lava up my spine." He continued on with, "I got a message this morning that we need to head south to meet the white dragon." "What?" I said, astonished! "You have to be kidding me. What's going on here? This is really getting weird, because I got the same message, several times, just as I was waking up. What white dragon?" I asked. He said, "Well let's go find out. Obviously the tutus want to gift us with another adventure."

I told him I just couldn't imagine driving in this rain storm, on the two-lane road that went south to both the volcano and the black sand beach at Punalu'u. "What else did they say to you, Douglas?" I asked. He said, "Well, something about a pyramid shaped hill on the west side of the road and that we are to stop there and watch the white dragon come out of its nest." "No way!" I said. "Have you ever heard of a white dragon before?" I asked. Douglas said, "No, I haven't, just in fairy tales."

Auntie Fern had told me to be careful, but what was the meaning of this? Both Douglas and I got the same message, at the same time, in two different locations. . . . I wondered. He had his mind made up. He was going, even if it meant hitch-hiking down there. He said, "Do you think I would pass up a chance to meet a white dragon? Are you coming or not?" By now I was thinking about the message that "we" would be protected. I was slowly deciding to go, to embrace an adventure. "Okay," I said, "I will get ready and meet you at the health food store."

Douglas was waiting in the front of the store wearing shorts, slippahs, a light jacket over a T-shirt, a hat, and a small backpack. His tall, slender figure was agile as he slid into the passenger seat of the jeep. I knew he would have Ezekiel bread in his pack. We made our way south, slowly and with great difficulty. The rainstorm continued and the rain came down in buckets. It was true that the windshield wipers couldn't quite keep up with this downpour. It was so difficult to see the road that I appreciated Douglas helping me to navigate and watch the road. As always, he was very calm. Nothing ever seemed to ruffle Douglas' feathers. He kept repeating to me that his *kundalini* was really roaring today. Now and then he would give a little shake, and shudder, of his whole body and say, "Down, Rover!" Honestly, I was feeling this way too, and I was a little altered by all the energy that was running up my spine. I kept wondering what was causing this. In India, this "serpent fire" – that ignites the spine and the energy centers – is called Kundalini. Yogis try to cultivate it with meditation and breathing. Why did we have it? But, we both did, from time to time. That was one of the things we had in common, in spite of our life-style differences. And neither one of us had ever tried to cultivate it.

Neither of us used drugs, and we were both experiencing a "natural" high. He told me that his Alaskan Native American father had experienced the *kundalini* too. I hadn't even had coffee today. But so early in the morning, in the middle of a torrential rain, it seemed strange to feel energy radiating up my spine. We drove between forty-five minutes and an hour. As we got closer to the area we were looking for, the rain let up and the sky became a mix of clouds and blue. We finally saw, to the right of us, a small mountain, in the distance, that had a pyramid shape . . . a mountain covered with foliage and trees, making it appear dark.

Douglas said, "This is it! We are supposed to find a place to pull over, remember?" We did find a place to pull over, next to a barb-wired fence and ranch gate, and we immediately turned our eyes to the pyramid-shaped mountain.

As if right "on cue," and much to our amazement, the head of a white dragon began to slowly emerge from behind this mountain. At first we saw the head, which was blowing smoke out of its mouth, just like in a fairy tale. Before long the whole body had risen up and was ascending into the sky! Whenever Douglas was amazed, he shouted, "Grandma!" and for some odd reason "Grandma!" was his version of "Wow," and at this moment, he shouted it loudly! Neither of us could believe our eyes as it slowly emerged. Each scale on the dragon's body was well defined, as were the spikes along the spine. There were wings, moving slowly and rhythmically, and the long tail was whipping back and forth. There was a well-defined face and eyes, and smoke was coming out of the mouth. It was pure white and very beautiful. As it arose and unfurled itself, it began to undulate right above the dark mountain ridges and started moving towards the north. I had the feeling it was heading towards the direction of the sacred mountain, Mauna Kea.

It was not like looking at a cloud and saying, "Oh, doesn't that look like an angel or a bear?" This was a real live white dragon, and it was not made out of clouds or mist. It was huge and mighty and emanated a most sacred feeling. We both felt like it circled the island, every day, giving its blessing. Why were we being allowed to see it? We both wondered. Another thought that came to our minds was that the dragon was ancient and went back to the time when this island was part of ancient Lemuria . . . or Mu. Aka was quite sure that this island was a remnant of the ancient continent. She also told me that in ancient Mu beings could move in and out of manifestation, from a physical body to a plasma body and then to a light body and then back again. Betty had told me tales of the Micronesian islands, especially Ponapei, and she had heard the same thing about ancient Lemuria. Island people have a long oral history that is passed from generation to generation.

This was a stunning and almost unbelievable experience for both of us! But here it was, unfolding right in front of our eyes, just as we had been told, early this morning. I wished that I had brought my camera along. The white dragon kept blowing smoke out of its mouth as it continued to move farther away, towards the north. How could this be? I wondered in amazement. Both of us said at the same time, "No one would EVER believe this. No one . . . absolutely no one . . . would ever believe this." We watched for about ten minutes, as it moved north until it disappeared from sight. We both had the impression that its nest was somewhere behind or under the pyramid-shaped mountain that looked almost black with its covering of trees and foliage.

Well, this was the most amazing thing that had happened so far on this journey, and I was grateful that Douglas was along as a participant and witness. If it had just happened to me, I might start to doubt that I had ever seen it. But later on, he and I discussed it a number of times. We both decided not to tell anyone about it, at least not at that time, and not, for me, until years later. I asked him if he had ever had an experience like this before, and he said, "No! Never!" And with a loud shout he uttered, "Grandma!"

We pulled back onto the road and continued to drive farther south after the white dragon disappeared from sight, and it began to rain again. But this time it was not a downpour, just a light, steady rain. We turned off the road when we saw the sign to Punalu'u Black Sands Beach, and made our way to the parking lot. This was a spot that had fresh water springs arising in the bay. In the old days this was a village site, and the people dove into the water with their gourd calabashes to collect fresh water. It was also a good bay for fishing and launching outrigger canoes. I knew this from seeing Herb Kane's mural with Rika, which was in the ruined building nearby. Not only was Herb Kane an excellent artist, but he was a historian, a cultural expert, and he knew the history of this part of the *aina*.

Douglas said it was time for us to show our gratitude for the blessing that we had just received, and that it was best to be anonymous about our *kokua* (help). *Kala mai* (excuse me), Douglas, for me being a squealer. Douglas pulled some big black trash bags out of his backpack, and we began picking up trash, first on this beach, and then around the huge Kane'ele'ele Heiau complex which is on the east end of the bay. Not a soul was here on this day, due to the rain. Even the *honu* (sea turtles), who are usually sunning themselves on the beach, were in the water instead, poking their heads up from time to time. But it wasn't cold, and we didn't mind getting wet. There was fishing line, hooks and sinkers, old flip flops that were missing their mates, plastic water bottles, and other assorted trash. On the way home, we took our bags of trash to the transfer station. The rain had stopped, and we were silent as we drove back to Pahoa. Both of us were having our own thoughts about what we had seen today. There was really nothing more that we could say about it. The sacred gift that we had been given today was being taken inside of us to a very deep place.

### A P.S. to the Inter-Dimensional White Dragon Story

FOR YEARS I NEVER TOLD ANYONE about seeing the white dragon, as I knew I could lose all credibility as a sane person in one fell swoop. And I was concerned with being seen as a liar, crazy, or at best an exaggerator, who really only saw the movement of thick mist and imagined a dragon, the way people see images in clouds. For a long time, I didn't even tell Aka. Auntie Fern said their family didn't tell much, as they could be "locked up" as mental patients.

Then there was also the thought that one shouldn't reveal sacred experiences, as it could be like giving it away, and possibly having an overlay of scorn or disbelief placed upon it, which in a subtle way could contaminate the original experience. Then there was the thought that I might be insinuating that I thought I was someone special. I am clear that I am not. I have as many afflictions and faults as everyone else.

I struggled with this decision for a number of years and finally came to the conclusion that it was an important part of this year's experience and inner transformation. To leave it out didn't feel authentic. I often prayed that I would learn more about the experience and, most of all, I wanted to know if other people had ever seen it.

The feeling that both Douglas and I had was that it was a sacred and benevolent dragon. We felt that it had been here since the time of Mu, circling the island and blessing it with *mana*. I felt that it was a part of what Aka always called "the unseen world" that is with us, but invisible to most.

Several years after my year on the Big Island, Paul and I came back for a visit, and were with some local friends for dinner. We had also been invited to spend the night. It was one of those nights when the food came out in courses, and Corona's with lime came out with each new course of food. We were having a delicious soup, some tenderly prepared pork meat, a big salad, and a platter of tropical fruits. A local man arrived, halfway through the dinner, who we had never met before. Our hosts told us that he rarely socializes. Like Kumu Dane he looked like one of the ancient Hawai'ian men in the Herb Kane paintings. I noticed, more than anything else, how very tall and muscular he was, his sparkling dark eyes, and quiet charisma.

After dinner the man started telling stories, and as a natural storyteller he had us sitting on the edge of our seats. The stories were about old Hawai'i. He was clearly full-blooded Hawai'ian or very close to it. He had been brought up on the land in a traditional way, with a family of *kahuna* and elders who had given him spiritual instruction. He told tales of being self-sufficient and hunting pigs and fishing in a secret spot near his land. He grew a garden and rarely went to the store for provisions. He told of his elders, and he made a very slight mention that his family's *Aumakua*, or clan, was the dragon. He said it so softly and quickly, under his breath, that I believe others at the table didn't even notice it. The evening went on, and more stories were being told by everyone at the table. There were the clinks of empty Corona bottles going into a recycle box.

I began to feel that he might be just the person I could ask about the White Dragon.

It got late, and the guests started to leave. Our hostess was cleaning up and putting the food away. I offered to help her, but she said, "No, just keep visiting." The man was still there. I decided to tell him the story of seeing the White Dragon. For a few minutes he didn't respond. He was stroking his chin thoughtfully, with his eyes cast down, and said nothing. I felt afraid that I had just broken some kind of protocol.

Then he answered me with, "I know what you're talking about, because I have seen it myself. I am the right person for you to ask, as it is the *Aumakua* (totem) of my family. That dragon exists all the time, circling the island, even though people can't see it. It is an inter-dimensional dragon, existing on another plane. So unless you are tuned into this other plane, it's invisible. It is a blessing dragon that circles the island, and it adds to the healing energy of this island. Its origins go back to the time when the Big Island was part of ancient Lemuria, or what is sometimes called Mu. It is not a huge lizard as some of the Hawai'ian legends refer to as the *Mo'o*. It is truly a dragon. My grandparents, uncles and father first told me about it when they told me that the dragon was our family *Aumakua*."

He asked me if I felt scared when I saw it. I told him "no," that it felt benevolent and wondrous. "That's good," he said. We talked a little more about it, and he told me a few things about his own experiences. I felt such a feeling of relief. I knew that Douglas and I didn't doubt our sanity, but to talk to this man about it answered so many of my questions.

### A Trip to Waimea and Visit to the School of Acupuncture

ONE NIGHT SHORTLY AFTER I ARRIVED, I attended a lecture in Hilo by a man named Arthur Pacheco, who was a trance medium. My eyes were drawn to a couple who were sitting in the audience. After the lecture I was able to talk to them, and it turned out that Edyson Ching, also known as Kapua, had spent a lot of time in Nevada City, my home town in California. He was a local man of both Chinese and Hawai'ian descent and spent his childhood on the island of Oahu. He lived in Hilo now, but he told me that he would be moving soon. He was a big, tall Hawai'ian with long, black hair tied back in a ponytail. His full name is Edyson Kapua'okalani Ching. He reminded me of some of the men of Kham that I had seen on my trip to Tibet. He had the same high cheekbones, and his racial mixture of

 Chinese and Hawai'ian gave him a very exotic appearance. After coming back from military service in Vietnam, he lived with his wife on the Kona side of the Big Island and raised a daughter. During that time, he worked as a fireman at the Kailua Kona airport. But presently, he was working in Waimea as an instructor of Acupuncture and Chinese medicine at the Traditional Chinese Medical College of Hawai'i. This college was founded by Angela Longo and mentored by Dr. Lam Kong, the famous Chinese acupuncturist and herbalist. I told Kapua that I needed some herbs, as I was developing symptoms of mold allergy. We exchanged phone numbers, and I said good night to Kapua and his lady friend.

122

A few days later I drove up-country to Waimea and was able to sit in on an acupuncture class given by Kapua or "Edyson," as he was sometimes called. He liked to say that Edyson stood for son of Eddy, which was his father's name. He was very funny and was cracking jokes in his class which made learning great fun for the students. When the class was over, he went to the herb room and made up some packages of herbs that were geared to help mold allergy. He said that a lot of visitors get mold allergy on the Hilo side. One of the symptoms was white mucous, unlike the yellow or green mucous of a sinus infection. He suggested that I could move to the other side of the island that was drier, and feel "mo bettah."

Kapua told me about an upcoming gathering in Kapoho of different healers that were going to have a kind of a spa day, sharing different healing modalities. "No money kine involved," he said. Because I was a massage therapist and grower of healing herbs back home in Nevada City, California, Kapua thought I would enjoy participating and meeting island healers. Before we said goodbye, he told me that he had been a student of Johnny Moses, the Native American teacher and story teller of the Northwest tribes, north of Seattle, Washington. What an interesting synchronicity, I thought, as I too had listened to the wonderful story telling of Johnny Moses.

### Captain Clay Bertelmann and the Voyaging Canoe

MY SON, MICHAEL, AND I HAD MET Kumu Dane Silva, Luther and Desmon Haumea almost two years earlier in Maui. They had been part of the crew that sailed the Makali'i over to the bay in Hana from the Big Island. They were well aware of my enthusiasm for voyaging canoes, and the Makali'i in particular.

Clay Bertelmann was the captain of the Makali'i and was training hundreds of island youths in voyaging. I had read about him and always wanted to meet him. He was a crew member on the first Hokule'a voyage that went to Tahiti. Later he was the captain of the Hokule'a and sailed the canoe on many long voyages throughout the Pacific. He was thought to be gruff by some people, when first meeting him, but he was a strong and determined man, who would not let go of his dreams. Having been a cowboy and rancher earlier in his life, he was made of true grit and a heart of Aloha. He was the inspiration, builder, and captain of the Makali'i.

*REPLICA MODEL OF HOKULE'A*

This replica canoe project was started after Clay had already been on a number of voyages on the first original replica canoe, the Hokule'a. The Polynesian Voyaging Society was launched on March 8, 1975, and in 1976 the Hokule'a took its maiden voyage to Tahiti. There was no government or state assistance

124

with building the Makali'i, so it became a grass roots project for and by the people of the Big Island. Clay had the motto, "dollar by dollar," and the local people raised the funds and participated in the actual building of the canoe. Voyaging had been a big part of the Hawai'ian renaissance in the 1970s. The local people of the Big Island were very excited about having their own voyaging canoe. They donated, had fundraisers, and some of them even helped to work on it directly. The Makali'i became a symbol for reconnecting the people with the roots of their culture. The name, *Makali'i,* is the name of the cluster of stars called the Pleiades. In the Hawai'ian language it literally means "little eyes."

The Makali'i became a training canoe for hundreds of local youth in canoe culture. Crews from other island nations came for training too. Different youth groups and school classes rotated through the training program. The students were asked to keep a diary of what they learned, how they felt, and their experience in the voyage. They were trained on land at first, but they would all have a chance to sail the Makali'i up and down the coast of the Big Island, too. When one group was finished with their rotation, each one of the youths would become a mentor for someone in the next group. They felt that there is no better way to ingrain learning than by teaching.

The sailing excursions often went from Kawaihae to Miloli'i and back. There were times when I was sunbathing or snorkeling at Honaunau Bay, Ho'okena Beach, or Kealakekua Bay, when I would see the Makali'i sail by. I got shivers of excitement each time I saw it. The Makali'i was docked in the harbor of Kawaihae when it wasn't sailing, and I visited there several times, wishing that I was one of these local children who would sail this canoe out into the ocean.

### *A Day Trip with Kumu Dane*

ONE DAY I GOT A CALL from Kumu Dane who invited me to join him, a few days later, for a visit to Clay and Deedee Bertelmann's home up in Waimea. He knew that I always wanted to meet them. I picked Kumu Dane up in the morning and drove us up to Waimea. Dane told me that his wife, Pam, was visiting California at the moment. I hoped to meet her, too, sometime in the future. We talked about our children for a while. He asked if our visually impaired son, Michael, still did African drumming. I told him that he did. Mike had to wear sunglasses outside due to his light sensitivity. Dane mentioned that his eyes were feeling very sensitive lately, so he kept his sunglasses on and was glad not to be doing the driving.

He told me about the many Lomilomi massage classes that he taught, and how he also incorporated cultural teachings and field trips into his classes. He was planning a field trip for his students, so he told me that he needed a fleet of four-wheel drive vehicles like mine and pick-up trucks to take his next class down to the Waipio Valley. Dane was definitely *Kanaka* . . . the old name for a Hawai'ian, but more exactly he was *Ali'i*, from the royal, chief, and aristocratic class. His mother and her people came from the grassy plateau above the Waipio Valley. He pointed to it as we drove by that area. I didn't mention to him that it was very close to one of the ranches where Betty and I did house-cleaning.

We arrived at the Bertelmann home and Clay and his wife, Deedee, welcomed us at the door. The name, Bertelmann, is misleading, as Clay is definitely a Hawai'ian man . . . big, tall, tan, barrel-chested, with long, white hair tied back in a ponytail. He had the commanding presence of a captain. Clay, like Kapua Ching, was also a Vietnam War veteran. Dane shared with me that he suffered with pain in his body. But Clay was also quick to smile, had a warm heart, and he and his wife greeted me warmly when Dane introduced us.

This little journey was not going *holoholo*, as we knew where we were going. "Holoholo" means that you probably don't know where you're going to end up. Local men often use the expression when leaving home for a fishing trip. A fisherman is often called a "*holoholo* man." There were a lot of people in the house, and it turned out that many of them were voyaging crew members. A group of women were in the kitchen cooking. Deedee invited me into the kitchen to meet the other women, and I joined them and chopped vegetables for a while.

Then Dane called me out to the living room, where he had Clay lying face down on the floor on a big beach towel. Dane said to me, "I want you to help me. I am going to do *Mo'o lomilomi* on Clay and I want you to mirror my movements, on the other side of his body." This was an ancient form of *lomilomi* massage, using the feet. We needed to be barefoot, and Dane showed me how he was pressing the side of his foot into the muscle that went along the spine, avoiding direct contact with the spine. Gradually we pressed down, putting a little more pressure on the muscle. We were both facing Clay's head, so we were each sideways to Clay's body. This reminded me of the four-handed massage that Auntie Angeline gave us in Kauai, but this method was using the feet in tandem. One leg was the anchor to balance oneself, and the other foot was used for the massage.

This made sense to me, as I had often reclined on the couch and given back massages to my family with my two bare feet. Feet could channel energy just like hands, and sometimes there was more strength in leg muscles than arm muscles. The family liked these foot treatments, but always teased me about it, thinking it was a little odd. I found out that Hawai'ians have always used their feet as one of the Lomilomi massage techniques. 'Aha,' I thought, 'I'm not so odd, after all.'

We went up and down Clay's spine with our feet with matching, mirror-like movements. With the one foot, we placed and pressed. We did the same thing on his legs and arms, and then, more delicately, on the back of his neck. We finished with his two feet.

After this treatment, it was time to eat. There were enticing aromas of good Hawai'ian food coming out of the kitchen. Deedee, kids and friends all called us to come to the table. And in any local home, there is always plenty of *ono* food to eat. Hawai'ians are generous people, and they show their Aloha in many different ways, sharing good food being an important one. At the table there was a *pule* (prayer) for the blessings that we so abundantly receive. As the food was being passed around, there was talk about a group of Maori youth who would soon be coming to the Big Island from New Zealand to train with Captain Clay and his crew. They, too, were reviving their traditional culture and wanted to build a voyaging canoe in Atearoa, the original Maori name of New Zealand.

"Papa" Mau Piailog, the famous navigator from the island of Sataval in Micronesia, would be training them too. Clay said, "Without Mau, there would be no navigating in the old way." Mau was willing to travel to Hawai'i upon the invitation of the first Hokule'a crew to teach them navigation. This tradition was still alive in Micronesia, but few skilled navigators were left. Traditional navigating included knowledge of the stars, the swells, the waves, the winds, sea birds, and dead reckoning. No instruments were used . . . no motor, no compass, no radio, sextant or map.

The young people in Micronesia are now becoming influenced by Western ways, and many of them are losing interest in the old traditions. Mau was very concerned and didn't want to see this tradition lost in Micronesia, as it had been in Hawai'i. Even with Hawai'i's long history of voyaging and navigation, this knowledge had been lost for a number of generations, and there was no one left who remembered or had experience. Clay said, "More than twenty years ago Mau brought us to where we are today. During our history in Hawai'i, we lost our ability to navigate. Mau's willingness to help us was truly an honor and a blessing for us, as he gave us the pieces that we lost." I had not yet met Papa Mau Piailog, but I hoped to, as he was already a living wayfaring legend. He deserved the honor and respect that was given to him throughout the Hawai'ian Islands. I admired his mission to help restore this tradition in Hawai'i. I often wondered why I felt so much passion about wayfaring.

Ancient peoples could cross the oceans from one continent to another, using star navigation and other ancient methods. The recent trans-oceanic journeys of the Hokulei'a and Makali'i were successful and had proved that voyaging in double-hulled sailing canoes had been done in ancient times. Such exciting proof has made the world re-think the history of voyaging and trans-oceanic migrations. After this discussion of voyaging, Clay got up from the table and went off to discuss things with a few of his crew members and friends.

A family with twin babies arrived at the house. Dane was asked if he would *lomi* the twin babies, who looked like they were about three months old. Dane called me into a room where the parents had laid the twins on a large bed. Dane again asked me to help him. He would work on one of the twins, and I on the other. They were very sweet. Dane asked me to mirror his movements and keep every movement gentle and loving. Both babies were laying face up. First we touched them gently so they could get used to our touch and "aloha." Then little by little, we began a baby massage.

Clay told Dane that he felt a lot better, and asked him why he didn't come to help him out more often. This seemed to be a friendly chiding, as he knew Dane was really busy with his local classes and travels to Japan. It was easy to see the appreciation and respect that Clay had for Dane and his healing gifts. And it was also easy to understand how much Clay would have liked to have more frequent healing treatments from his good friend. It was now mid-afternoon and time to drive back to Pahoa.

By the time I dropped Dane off at his house, we were having a typical Hilo downpour and the windshield wipers were at full speed. I thanked Dane profusely for giving me this opportunity to meet the Bertelmanns and some of the crew members, and also for the Lomi teaching that he had shared with me. Then he said, "You know, I would like to invite you to come to a class I am having. The diamond drill bits and Dremel you gave me are really great for my carving, so I would like to gift you with the class." "Oh, Mahalo," I said, "I would love to come to learn more about *lomilomi*." I had met a lot of healers in my life, but I could see that Kumu Dane carried a special kind of radiance and blessing *mana* that was the mark of a true healer.

## ANOTHER VISIT TO THE KONA SIDE

### LA 'IKE KONA HEMA
Visioning Day, October 2001, at Paleaku Peace Gardens

BARBARA DEFRANCO HAD CALLED and invited me to come to Paleaku Peace Gardens for an event she had helped to plan and organize. It was to be a "visioning day" about land use in the *makai* region below Paleaku Peace Gardens, which was between Kealakekua Bay and Honaunau Bay. What a beautiful day it was! The sky was a brilliant blue, and the prayer flags in Paleaku Peace Gardens fluttered in the soft Kona breezes. However, the weather could change quickly and we could still have rain later in the day.

So much preparation had gone into this day. I admired Barbara for honoring those Hawai'ian people, who were some of the Big Island *kupunas* (elders), and *kahus* (teachers), and community leaders who helped revive and support the Hawai'ian culture during these renaissance years. The day was called *KONA HEMA*, South Kona (La 'Ike) Visioning Day, October 2001 and was spearheaded by Nona Beamer, the famous musician and matriarch of the talented musical Beamer family. This planning/visioning process was initiated by both Tutu Nona Beamer and Paleaku Peace Gardens and Sanctuary. Kona area *kupuna* (elders) and residents would be relating cherished traditions regarding fishing, agriculture, old place names, and the ancient *alapua'a,* or land division system. Together with officials of the county of Hawai'i and representatives from the Kamehameha Schools, participants would envision a future for South Kona.

Barbara and friends had been preparing for days. A large canopy and chairs were set up in the gardens. A microphone was placed there for speakers, and a feast had been prepared. Many elders had been invited and were slated to speak and share about their lives and contributions to their communities. There would be some "Living Treasures" invited too. Living treasures were living individuals who had made important contributions to the Hawai'ian culture in many diverse ways.

As the elders began to arrive and find their seats under the canopy, I noticed that the ladies were dressed up, and their sweet, tanned faces were adorned with beautiful straw hats wrapped with fresh leaves and flowers. The list of guests featured: Nona Beamer, Moana Kahele, William Paris, Teunisse Rabin, Neil Hannahs, Mayor Harry Kim, Walter Keli'iokekai Paulo, Wayne Leslie, Kepa Maly, Mikahala Roy, Maile Mitchell, Chris Yuen and Lily Kong. Puna Kihoi was the MC for the panel discussion.

Nainoa Thompson would also attend. He had become a master navigator of the voyaging canoe and was trained by Mau Piailug, who was his cherished teacher from Mircronesia. Sustainability of this Earth and the protection of her large oceans and waterways became one of Nainoa's greatest concerns and teachings. Later, all the journeys of the voyaging canoes, in their many sails as they circled the globe, were to bring the love, kindness, and compassion of Aloha to other countries. The children of the world were enthusiastic to see the canoe and seemed to be deeply affected by the Aloha and excitement it brought to them. Nainoa's talk included the contributions that had been made in restoring and implementing the revival of the ancient voyaging culture, first in Hawai'i and then in other islands in the Pacific Triangle. The canoe culture inspired many other islands to build their own sailing canoes. Nainoa's father, Pinky Thompson, passed away shortly after this gathering, on Christmas night, 2001. He had contributed a great deal to the Hawai'ian people as the President of the Polynesian Voyaging Society and through his community outreach as a social worker. He was instrumental in helping to promote canoe culture in the early days and supported the voyagers of the Hokule'a.

Auntie Moana (Mona) Kahele spoke about her practice of Ho'o'ponopono during her life, as well as her cultural expertise in remembering and writing about the early history and culture of the

Hawai'ian people on the Big Island. As a native speaker, she also wrote down and preserved many of the old stories that had been passed to her orally from one generation to another. She was one of the few elders that still knew the original Hawai'ian place names of towns, villages, trails, bays and sacred sites in South Kona.

These Kona area *kupuna* and community leaders were gathered to share their backgrounds, and to help create a vision for the future for some large natural ocean-front areas that stretch up the hillsides. Developers wished to develop this area. It could so easily become crowded with hotels and condominiums, ruining the natural beauty of the area. The elders wanted to have this land preserved and kept natural, as it was the coastal land between Kealakekua Bay and Honaunau Bay and the City of Refuge (Pu'uhonua o Honaunau). It also included the land going *mauka* (uphill) as well. Of greatest importance, it was home to many sacred historical areas.

Many sacred sites and *heiaus* had already been destroyed or disrespected by the rows of hotels and condos that had been developed along the Ali'i Drive shoreline between Kailua Kona and Keauhou. Some hotels along this stretch were reputed to be haunted because of the careless desecration of these sacred sites.

The presenters were honored with leis when everyone sat down. The gathering was started with a *pule* (prayer) and was followed with talks by the various presenters. Auntie Mona had suggestions for the future use of the area that was being discussed. She suggested a youth and elders project, growing traditional medicinal herbs (*lau' lapa' au*), and having elders and youth partnered together on the project. Her idea was that the youth would tend the gardens, and the *kupuna* would be mentors. Also, the *kupuna* would have a chance, in this setting, to share stories important to the culture. I felt extremely lucky to be asked to take Auntie Mona Kahele home, as she no longer drove a car. This was the beginning of a wonderful friendship with her, as we would continue to visit with each other during this year.

## A Visit to Paleaku Peace Gardens and Seeing Barbara

I HAD STAYED WITH BARBARA DEFRANCO many times in the past and knew her land like the back of my hand. I had missed her and wanted to check in with her again, after *La Ike*, on this beautiful *aina*. This is also where I met Aka for the second time, when the re-dedication of the land had taken place the previous year. Barbara came out of her office where she had been working and greeted me with a big hug and a smile. Of Italian descent, she is a very pretty woman with soulful eyes. She is very smart and enterprising, and is one of the best manifesters I had ever met. She was wearing a loose Hawai'ian dress and flip-flops as she descended the steps of her office lanai.

I had called Barbara ahead of time, so she was expecting me. I brought the makings of dinner for both of us. I always loved cooking in Barbara's retreat center kitchen, as it was all screened with a big table and surrounded by beautiful gardens of tropical plants. The warm, moist breeze would come up over the land from the ocean and caress the skin. It was a very powerful land location, and everything about this place delighted the senses.

Barbara keeps this center busy all the time, and she is gracious in her way of working with people and juggling all the events that

go on here. She is also great at delegating various responsibilities to the volunteers who live on the land or in the neighborhood. There was an open-aired yoga room with a roof, and yoga classes took place a little before sunset, as well as a big art room for visiting artists. There were hula classes here too, that Barbara, Cindi Punihaole, Rika and I had taken with Peccolo (Peter) Day, an accomplished Kumu Hula.

A temple room, with a beautiful traditional Tibetan entrance and door, was across from the kitchen. Here Barbara hosted meditations and Buddhist teachings

BARBARA DeFRANCO

133

by Tibetan lamas. There were a few rooms and tents on platforms for guest rentals also. One of Barbara's volunteers lived in an old converted water tank that was actually very quaint, with hobbit-style windows. A number of beautiful shrines were placed all over the land, each dedicated to a major religion.

Looking from outside the kitchen door, I could see down two rows of palm trees above a green lawn that gradually descended to a tall, white Buddhist stupa. Close by was a statue of the Buddhist

master, Padmasambhava, which had been crafted and empowered by two Nyingma lamas, Lama Tharchin Rinpoche and H.H. Dudjom Rinpoche's son, Thinley Norbu Rinpoche. In addition, there was a traditional labyrinth, a Native American medicine wheel, and Jewish, Islam, and Christian shrines . . . as well as a small replica of a Heiau, to represent the spiritual tradition of Hawai'i. Before cooking, I walked around the Peace Gardens, enjoying the golden hour, as the sun sunk lower towards its descent into the ocean. Once again we would enjoy a beautiful Kona sunset. The golden light splashed all over the landscape, as if an artist had gilded the lawns, plants, trees, and shrines.

I walked over to the south end of the land to see how the Noni bushes were doing, which had been planted on one of my previous visits. Their shiny leaves and fist-sized, grenade-shaped fruit looked healthy, and had grown a lot since the last time I was here. These pale yellow medicinal fruits were a kind of "cure all," but they tasted absolutely foul. When they were ripe, they would fall off the bush and be put into a glass jar in the sun to ferment. After a few days, they would end up being a thick, nasty smelling liquid. One very elderly Hawai'ian man told me that he added raspberries to *Noni* to make it palatable. However, this ancient Hawai'ian medicine was supposed to heal all kinds of illnesses. He said that "he" was a living testimony to the healing powers of *Noni*. To be honest, it smelled like barf. But if it healed almost everything, it was worth the bad taste. It must have been called the "Hawai'ian cure all" by many for a reason.

The young lemon and lime trees were doing well too. The macadamia nut trees were doing well and dropping ripe nuts. I had to go by to inspect them, as I had been very invested in taking care of them in the past. One of the lime trees had struggled. Love and care never ceases, when we bond with the natural world, I thought. *"Malama the aina,"* is what is said about taking care of the land here in Hawai'i.

Barbara still had some things to do, so we would have dinner a little later. She had invited me to spend the night in the loft space above her kitchen house. This was right next to her house, adjoined by a roof that covered the outside corridor. I loved it up in that loft, as it was all screen sides, with a roof.

Here you could feel the breezes and smell the blooming flowers all through the night. It was one of the most peaceful and wonderful places I had ever slept. From time to time I could feel a slight earth tremor, a constant reminder that we were living on an island with a live volcano. Not far away was a little house where Danni and Kauila lived. As I fell asleep, I could vaguely hear them talking and laughing together, and their sweet, soft voices put me to sleep.

I DIDN'T WANT TO DRIVE BACK over to the Hilo side in the dark, so I was glad to be invited to spend the night at Paleaku Gardens. Local people had given me plenty of warnings and stories about the possibility of encountering the "Night Marchers," which were sometimes called the "night walkers." I had never seen them. This battalion of ancient ghost warriors was sometimes said to be accompanying the royal family and even Gods and Goddesses. Sometimes people, who were looking from a safe distance, recognized their own "dead" relatives in the procession. People known to be honest and reliable have reported seeing or hearing the night marchers. Some people report seeing torch lights. Others report hearing music, and some experienced both. I wondered if all this was myth-reality. Then again, it might be inter-dimensional phenomena.

The Saddle Road, which was a shorter but rougher road to Hilo, was known for this kind of activity. In more recent years, the Saddle Road has been re-paved and is quite an easy way to get from the west to the east side of the island. However, some people are wary of the night-time drive, and sometimes there is dense fog on this road. I had already discovered that this was an island of unusual phenomena and magic. People had vastly different opinions about whether the night marchers were real or not.

These stories were not just a way to scare tourists either. Some elderly *tutus* warned me about these ghostly apparitions, and other local people did too. I was told that, if anyone was in their way on their path, they could be hurt. Some said to lay face down on the ground if they suddenly appeared and you happened to be in their path. A warning is given to not look at them when they are close. If a person comes upon them unexpectedly, it is important to get out of their way and lay face down on the ground. Some people also say that it is good to strip all your clothes off. I thought to myself, what if you didn't have time? People have been reported to be killed or maimed, when they didn't follow these instructions. Who knows? I have no direct experience.

Before colonization there were many actual processions that took place on all of the Hawai'ian islands. That was how the people traveled from place to place, if they weren't traveling by canoe. On the Big Island there was a yearly procession that circled the island during the Mahahiki season that celebrated the season of the God Lono. The procession began and ended at Hikiau Heiau. There are still remnants today of smooth paving stones that made up this pathway.

In the old days, royalty often traveled at night, accompanied by warriors who carried torch lights that burned kukui nut oil. Night travel avoided the *kapu* of having common people see them or cast their shadow upon them. During these times common people were to prostrate themselves or squat down when a procession passed by. Common people who cast their shadow upon an *Ali'i*, or royal person, could be given a death sentence. Perhaps it was thought that the shadow of a common person could contaminate an *Ali'i* with lower and harmful vibrations. A death penalty seemed extreme to me. However, this was an ancient cultural practice.

There are people who say that they have seen the night marchers from a distance, or from inside of their house. They often report that a ghost herald announces the procession by blowing a conch shell. The music of flutes, chanting, and drums are said to be heard, sounding either beautiful or strange, depending on who is telling the story. The marchers can sometimes be seen with lit torches bobbing up and down as they travel traditional pathways.

I am not sure if this is true or not, but someone told me that when the Waikaloa Hilton Hotel was built, local historians showed the contractors a pathway near the hotel site that was known to be used by the night marchers. Apparently the contractors did not develop this particular area, leaving the old pathway intact.

Some accounts say that the night marchers walk with heavy footsteps, and others say they have seen them floating a few inches off the ground. The squeaking of litters, carrying royal ghosts, have also been said to be heard. Sometimes only a mist is seen, but music, drums, and the blowing of a conch is often reported. One story tells of a Japanese man's horses that would die mysteriously from time to time during the night. A traditional *kanaka* told the owner of the horses that his stable was sitting right on an ancient path used by the night marchers, and advised him to move his stable. After the stable was moved, the horses no longer died mysterious deaths.

I wondered how things from long ago could appear so real, when they were actually ghosts. I wondered if they were all earth-bound spirits, or whether they could go in and out of realms. Or could they go in and out of physicality, the way beings allegedly did on the ancient continent of Lemuria? Aka and many other Hawai'ians with ancient lineages and long oral histories believed that the Hawai'ian islands were a part of the ancient continent of Lemuria.

Here we were in modern day Hawai'i, but many remnants of the ancient culture remain, and some of the laws of the *kapu* system of "taboos" could still affect modern people. It was as if ancient time tracks, like little lava flows, could sometimes wind their way through the islands, penetrating present time. My first thought was that, perhaps a person had moved into a very subtle state of consciousness, opening their clairvoyant perceptions, which could allow a person to see into this level of reality. Could it be that a whole group of people could be inducted into a subtler realm of consciousness and see things that people don't ordinarily see? Then I wondered if masters, spiritual guides, and angelic beings could induct a person into an alternate state of consciousness, in order to see a subtler plane of reality. Aka often talked cryptically about what happens when the veil is lifted.

I remembered how my mother had gone to the Isle of Iona, a sacred place in Scotland. St. Colomba started an abbey there in 563 A.D. The ruins still exist and are said to emanate a very powerful energy. While she spent the night there, she had a vision: a man in white light touched her feet and blessed her. It was very sacred and very real to her. Aka told me that, when she was a child, she had seen the night marchers, and she told her family that there was nothing to worry about because they were all relatives.

I wondered if different time tracks were stacked here and some unknown natural laws brought them up for viewing under certain circumstances. Maybe it was the phase of the moon, or the anniversary of an ancient ceremony or event? Maybe there is no time at all? Maybe everything, in all time tracks, co-exist. If there are different dimensions that exist with different levels of vibration, or frequency, then perhaps, under certain conditions, one realm can penetrate another. I was particularly wondering about all of this in regards to the night marchers, but even more so in regards to the apparition of the White Dragon that Douglas and I had seen. For now, it was our secret.

## Flashback: Memories of Living on the Island of Moorea

TODAY, MEMORIES KEPT FLOODING MY MIND of Moorea, which is an island eleven miles northwest of the main island of Tahiti in French Polynesia. I couldn't help but think that the native house that we were living in was similar to those used in Hawai'i before colonization. During our three-month stay in 1993, we had some experiences that could be called "paranormal." For example, during two rather ferocious storms I saw apparitions of an ancient warrior in our bedroom house.

Our daughter, Christina, was sixteen at the time. We had the good fortune to meet Ma'atea Raisin, better known as Tea (pronounced Tey-ah) at the ranch of our friends, David Warren and Joan Schleicher, in Cambria, California. After we had gotten acquainted during an enjoyable ranch weekend, Tea discovered that we could speak French. To our great surprise she invited us to care-take her house and land in Moorea for the three months that she would be away. The offer came with a Camionette, a canvas-covered pick-up truck, so we could drive around the island and be mobile. It also came with an outrigger canoe to paddle in the lagoon and to the small grocery store nearby.

Soon we had Christina signed up for "home study," and we were off on this adventure. Paul thought it was too good an offer to pass up, so he gave us his blessing to have this experience. He was occupied with his printing and publishing company and was always generous with having others in the family have a chance to get away.

David Warren came with us for the first three weeks. He was a sight to behold with his shorts, cowboy hat and cowboy boots. When we awoke early in the morning, Dave would be sitting on the porch of the kitchen house, peeling skin off his sunburned legs. A cowboy in the tropics was very interesting for the local people, and for Christina and I as well. Dave found the sleeping loft of the kitchen house to be his dream tower, as he said he had so many lucid dreams while sleeping in this powerful vortex. He claimed that the dreams he had here revealed deeper meanings of so many aspects of his life, as well as issues that he has had on his large ranch in Cambria, California. French friends of Tea visited us and went spear fishing with David. He wasn't worried about the sand sharks that lived in the lagoon. Tea had told us that they were harmless.

Tea's land was on the lagoon with a sandy beach, and included an ancient *marae*, very similar to the stacked stone *heiaus* in Hawai'i. The beautiful bedroom house that Christina and I shared

had a lava stone foundation, was framed with large bamboo, and thatched with a pandanus leaf roof. The floors and siding were covered with matting of tightly woven pandanus leaves, called *lauhala* in Hawai'ian. We had one electric light-bulb in the kitchen house, which was run by a solar panel, while the fridge and cook stove ran on gas.

Upstairs above the kitchen house was a large sleeping loft, which Dave had called his dream tower. Dave said his most important dream was of making love to his wife Joan, in mid-air, flying like birds, but joined in union. She was taking care of the ranch at home. Somehow this dream illuminated a realization that he had about their relationship. After those three weeks, Dave was eager to get home to her . . . and back to his ranch with his new insights. We saw him off at the ferry boat that would take him to Papeete, Tahiti and the airport.

The shower house was also constructed of bamboo with siding of woven pandanus mats. It had a thatch roof, with a woven mat siding that came up to our shoulders. While shower water was streaming over us, we could look out on the tropical garden of coconut palms, pandanus trees, hibiscus, and delicate white tiare flowers, ornamented with shiny green leaves. The shower floor was black powdered lava stone mixed with cement and encrusted with beautiful shells, inlaid in the floor, which was surprisingly smooth. I imagined that this lovely setting in Moorea was much like Hawai'i used to be in the old days.

The *marae*, too, was located on Tea's land, only a few yards away from the bedroom house. It was very old, and even though it was built on land of lava stones, it protruded a few feet out into the ocean lagoon. We recognized it as the same kind of ancient, ceremonial stone structure as the *heiaus* of Hawai'i. I never found out to which god or purpose that this *marae* was dedicated. In my imagination I felt it might have something to do with the ocean and canoes. Often, long outrigger canoes had appeared in my dreams. In

waking hours, we often saw long, racing outriggers go by in the lagoon with at least six people paddling, the black silhouettes of the strong paddlers outlined on an azure blue sky. We were going to be staying here for three months, care-taking this exotic piece of land for Tea, our new Tahitian friend.

The land was lush with tall coconut palms, ferns, pandanus trees, a breadfruit tree, and a number of tropical fruit trees. We had an outrigger canoe and could paddle over to the small Chinese grocery store nearby, if we wanted to travel by water. Or we could walk through a dense coconut grove that had, at one time, been a commercial coconut grove that supplied Copra (coconut meat) that was taken to market on freighter ships. We swam every day in the turquoise waters and spent at least two hours a day raking the yard, cleaning the beach, and picking up coconuts. We were warned about the potentially deadly "Stone" fish, so we wore soft water-shoes. There was a sharp metal spike on one of the palm trees for opening coconuts, and a hand-grater that we placed between our legs for grating up the coconut meat. Then the grated coconut was squeezed through a cheese cloth to produce fresh coconut milk. This delicious milk was an essential ingredient for *poisson cru,* the famous Tahitian dish of cubed, raw bonito fish, tomatoes, cucumbers, onions, garlic, lime juice, and coconut milk. We never tired of it.

We washed our clothes by hand and hung them on a clothesline that stretched between two coconut palm trees. Hand tie-dyed *pareaus* (sarongs), halter tops, shorts and swimming suits were all the clothes we ever needed, and they were sure to be wind dried by the afternoon. The *pareaus* were like colorful flags flying in the winds, which always came up in the afternoon. In the morning the lagoon was most often like glass, smooth and silvery blue, with only the ripples of the canoes that clustered close to our shore, with young men hoping to catch a glimpse of *"Madamoiselle la Blanche,"* Christina's new island nickname.

If some article of clothing disappeared, it was sure to have flown off the clothes line in the wind, to be harvested, and taken down a hole, by one of the many land crabs. A pair of my favorite shorts disappeared. One day I saw a tiny remnant of fabric sticking out of a hole. I pulled it out to discover my mostly eaten shorts. But inside of a remaining pocket, were a few bills of French paper money that the crabs hadn't devoured. This was a happy surprise. Poor Dave watched a rat take a hundred-dollar bill out of his money clip and disappear with it into the rafters of his sleeping loft.

When we first arrived, we unlocked and opened the property gate. A lovely scene opened in front of us: coconut palms, fruit trees, a beach, thatched houses, and a very blue lagoon. We had keys from Tea's mother, Purea, to open the kitchen and bedroom houses. Since no one had been there for a while, we swept and cleaned and unpacked. After that we felt that our first job was to pay honor and respect to the *marae* and its spirit caretakers. We first put on our rubber water shoes and walked out into the water at the lagoon end of the *marae*, and started picking up flotsam trash that had washed up on the waves. Then we cleaned our sandy beach of trash. While doing this, we found some exotic shells and Christina started her shell collection.

Not knowing the protocols of an ancient *marae* or temple, we invented our own and hoped the spirits would be happy with us. We placed some of the shells that we found on the top of the *marae*, without going up on top of it ourselves. We filled them with fresh water and flowers as an offering. We hoped that the care-taking spirits would recognize us for having good hearts and respect for old traditions. As we brushed up on our French, we got to know some of the local people in the area, and they told us that it was not good to be living so close to a *marae* . . . that it could upset the spirits. Tea was a modern and good-hearted person who did not worry about things like this, and she had never experienced any disturbances. But, we felt that it was important to honor this ancient place with prayers and offerings.

I can remember two separate occasions when we had violent storms at night. Lightning cracked and thunder rolled. The rain came down in torrents, and the wind blew and howled so loud that we wondered if the house would blow away. Waves from the lagoon grew large and crashed against the lava stone foundation of the bedroom house. The palm trees creaked and swayed in the wind, and we were concerned that they might fall on top of the house. Coconuts fell, with loud thuds, as they hit the lawn below the palm trees. But there was not a single leak in the bedroom house. From that time on I praised the construction genius of this pandanus leaf roof, woven mat siding and floor, and bamboo framing. And not a single palm tree fell over. Christina and I huddled under the quilt in our queen-sized bed. We had the illusory protection of a white mosquito net, which cascaded down from a high hoop, falling on all sides of the bed. Christina could sleep through most of the storms.

It was during these two storms that I saw an apparition of an ancient warrior who stood tall, at the foot of our bed, looking at us, with no expression at all. The stare was not friendly or fierce. He was just simply looking at us. He was Tahitian, with feathers and paint on his face. I immediately associated him with the *marae*. He appeared clearly, as if real. But before I could be afraid, he disappeared. It happened this way during both of these big storms. This made me wonder why he only appeared at night, during a big lightning and thunder storm accompanied by fierce winds. Again my inner questioning began, about what conditions create an apparition. I wondered if it had anything to do with intersecting timelines. Somehow, I had to learn to be content with living with this "mystery." But my mind just didn't want to let go of it. I kept wondering and wondering about a way to explain apparitions and visions. Finally, I surrendered to the mystery and awe of a sacred experience and said, inside, *"Maruru Roa"* – thank you.

Now this reverie, about what had happened a few years earlier in Moorea, gave way to the present time, here in Hawai'i, and my present musings about night marchers. I wondered if the apparition of the warrior from the *marae* was similar to the apparitions of night marchers. This led me to wonder what would have happened to us if we had not made frequent offerings of prayers, shells, water, and flowers on the *marae*? I wondered if there were *kapus* against looking at spirit apparitions in Tahiti, like there were in old Hawai'i? I had looked back at him, and he knew I had seen him. I met people in Hawai'i who had direct experiences of seeing the night marchers from a distance. I did not want to ever be in the way, on their path, so I rarely traveled around at night. The idea of having them appear suddenly and being in harm's way, just because I happened to see them, gave me the shivers.

I had to put these thoughts out of my mind now, before I climbed up to the cozy sleeping loft in Paleaku Peace Gardens. I was not likely to have an encounter like this. I realized that my initial feeling of caution had changed into a feeling of being loved and protected by divine forces. It was good to have peaceful, relaxing thoughts when going to bed. I ended my day with prayers for my family and friends and all beings in the universe. Long ago I had learned that if one wanted to sleep soundly, one had to let go of discursive thoughts and go into emptiness.

As it got light in the morning, the little doves in Paleaku Peace Gardens started cooing. Filtered sunlight spread so beautifully on the flowering bushes and vines all around Barbara's house. It was nice to get up and stretch and walk around the beautiful gardens before breakfast. Barbara and I met in the corridor and shared the mirror, outside the bathroom, as we brushed our hair. We often felt like sisters. We moved on, walking over to the retreat kitchen. The people staying at Paleaku were already in the kitchen making their breakfast. It was always a congenial group, with friendly banter and laughter back and forth. Then Barbara sat down and there was a quick meeting about the chores that needed to be accomplished this day. We had coffee and ripe papaya halves. My favorite way to eat a papaya was to fill the halves with yogurt, sliced bananas, and with lime juice squeezed over the top.

Barbara had told me the night before, over dinner, that there was something she wanted to discuss with me, in the morning. Brimming with energy from a restful sleep and good Kona coffee, we were both excited to visit some more. She began to tell me about a program called H.A.C.B.E.D. This organization, which was established in 1992, stood for Hawai'ian Alliance for Community-Based Economic Development. They were expanding their already existing programs because of the disastrous post-9/11 job crisis throughout the islands. There was still a lack of tourist trade at this time, and people on the islands needed economic help.

Barbara, being a community leader in the Kona district, had been asked to send a representative to the meetings and trainings that were to take place one weekend a month in Honolulu. "Airfare, lodging and the training weekends would be paid for by HACBED," she said. She showed me a packet of information to fill out, and asked me if I would be willing to be a representative. The program would consist of training in how to form a non-profit, create grass roots organizations for sustainable living, grant writing, and working with foundations. Immediately, excitement welled up in me and I said, "Yes, I would love to be a part of this! Thank you!"

Before I left to drive back to the Hilo side, Barbara walked me out to an area of the land where she shared a dream she had. "I am going to make a garden here that represents the constellations that are in the night sky above us. They will be reflected here in flowers and plants." She knew Jon Lomberg, a well-known astronomer and artist who lived nearby. He had agreed to help her map out the Constellation Garden, which later was named the Galaxy Garden. Barbara was always brimming with creative ideas. I told her it would be both educational and beautiful, like everything else in the garden!

## BACK TO THE HILO SIDE

### *The Healing Spa Day*

I WAS NOW BACK ON THE HILO SIDE in my cottage. Work days came and went, and the date arrived for the spa day with Kapua and his healer friends in Puako. Kapua was our Hawai'ian class clown. His comments and original jokes made everyone laugh. In this happy setting he had everyone introduce themselves and talk a little about themselves and the kind of healing work they do. There was a nice group of people. Anne Lemieux was there, and I knew that she had worked closely with Auntie Angeline, the Kumu Lomilomi on Kauai. Other healing arts practitioners were there too, both Hawai'ian and *haole*. We had a wonderful day exchanging massage, using the hotstone treatment, essential oils, meditation and some Qi Gong. We took a break at lunch time and enjoyed the food that everyone had brought to share. Yet another Hawai'ian feast heightened the enjoyment of an already relaxing day. It was a good chance to visit, eat, and get to know each other.

Kapua was also an acupuncturist, so he demonstrated a treatment in which he did *lomilomi* massage first, and then inserted the needles for an acupuncture treatment. He called it "Acu-Lomi." A person could be very relaxed this way, and it was very effective for opening up the energy channels. He said, "You have to align the energy channels of the person and deeply relax them. Their energy has to be flowing correctly before the body can begin to heal itself."

Then Kapua pulled out two smooth stones from the hot water in his turkey roaster pan that was heating his special smooth *lomi* rocks. He anointed the smooth stones with an essential oil. He then showed us how to open the meridians in the legs by massaging upward with the hot stones, from the foot, up the leg. "The heat and the essential oil help open the meridian, too," he said.

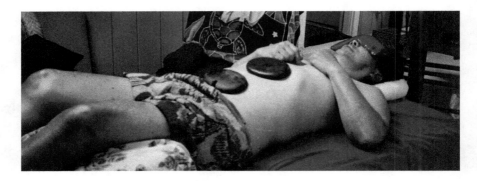

At the end of the day I had made a lot of new friends. We had shared and exchanged healing modalities, and I had given several massages. Everyone had a chance to give and to receive. I had learned many new things. Kapua had been trained in *lomilomi* too, and was also a close friend of Kumu Lomilomi Dane Silva. He demonstrated part of a massage on me. Being such a tall man with very long arms, Kapua was able to make long, deep sweeps down the back, from the shoulders to the hips. With just the right, smooth, deep pressure, the whole body relaxed. The long sweeping motion reflected the movements of the dolphins and whales, the movements of the *hula*, the movements of ocean waves, and even the sway of palm trees in the breeze. It was so relaxing and nourishing that it could almost put you to sleep. No wonder *lomilomi* developed here in Hawai'i. It was a reflection of all the aspects of nature here on these islands.

### New Friends Gather in Waimea

BARRIE ROSE AND JEANNETTE BECAME NEW FRIENDS whom I met when up in the high ranch lands of Waimea. Barrie Rose is a beautiful lady who has a lot of warmth and class, and also loves the Hawai'ian culture. She always made me welcome in her home. Jeannette is a tall, attractive blond who had come to live on the island from

148

Australia. She was the personal assistant to a famous movie director who lived part-time in Waimea. She, like myself, is very interested in the history and culture of Hawai'i, but was on the verge of a divorce.

Suddenly I found myself spending some of my free days up in the cattle and cowboy country of Waimea with these two kindred spirits. Before long, these two ladies, and many of the Hawai'ian friends whom I had met, started having dinner parties at Barrie Rose's home.

JEANNETTE AND NANCY

There was always good food, good music, and interesting conversation. The locals called it, "Grind (eat) and talk story."

Kapua was in transition also. He was already working in Waimea and was in the middle of breaking off a short-lived relationship with a lady in Hilo. It seemed like a lot of us were undergoing changes or life transitions. To cheer Kapua up, I took him up to Barrie's house one day and introduced them. Before you know it, they got together. "Falling in love at first sight?" I wondered. I remembered how Aka said she fell in love at first sight with every "braddah and sistah" that she met. Before long Kapua was moving into Barrie Rose's house. I helped Kapua move boxes and belongings from the house in Hilo to the house in Waimea. Later he helped me make two moves.

Kapua is quite an amazing chef, who could easily be a candidate for a T.V. cooking show. His humorous commentary as he chopped, peeled, and cooked made us laugh and delighted all of us. He even made funny faces and moved his eyebrows around in a style that we had seen in Tahiti. Few restaurants could serve anything as good as the wonderful concoctions he made, which were either inspired by Chinese or Hawai'ian cuisine. I was always glad to be a sous-chef for Kapua, as I learned some wonderful local recipes. He also shared that he had been chef to some generals in Vietnam and that his cooking assignment may have saved his life. However, he had witnessed so many traumatic things in Vietnam that he claimed to be struggling with P.T.S.D.

We had a lot of happy gatherings. Kapua invited several of his local "brahs" (male friends) to join us. I was amazed to find out that most Hawai'ian men like to cook and are excellent chefs. It started to feel like a little "spirit family." Soli, and others who had been strongly involved in the Hawai'ian sovereignty movement, joined us. We had discussions about the history of the sovereignty movement and their involvement.

Soli was a historian and a researcher as well as an activist! He lived on Hawai'ian homeland, in the green hills which were on the slopes of Mauna Kea. He and his family lived quite a traditional life in a Matson Line "container" that he had converted into a home. I was impressed with his calm energy, his solidarity, and his passion for restoring a free Hawai'i. I never tired of listening to his soft but strong voice as he recounted history and various activities. Although he never spoke directly about spiritual things, his demeanor and presence was deeply spiritual. It was just who he was.

Like most Hawai'ians Soli had a very long name. His full name was Henry Papkihei Welokiheiakea'eloa Niheu Jr. A number of years after meeting and knowing Soli, I found out that he passed away November 20th, 2012, at the age of sixty-nine. I was very sad when I heard this, as he took with him tremendous cultural and historical knowledge as well as his very warm Aloha.

### *Turning a Typhoon*

ONE NIGHT WE WERE ALL at Barrie Rose's house for another wonderful dinner. The topic of hurricanes came up. We all discussed the devastating Hurricane Iniki that had hit the island of Kauai some years back. Mike Tomson, who had come for a visit from Nevada City, fit right into this little group. He said certain people had abilities to change the course of a typhoon so that it would stay out to sea and not damage an island. He had learned about this when he was young and living on the islands of Pilau and Saipan. Soli said that this ability had not been lost in the present day. He said that many a hurricane heading for the Big Island had been turned off its course and sent out to sea by strong intention and traditional chants and prayers.

## The La'amaomao Wind Gourd and Controlling the Winds

THE SAME EVENING, WE HEARD a little about the La'amaomao wind gourd, or calabash. In ancient times the people needed to know all about the different winds, especially for fishing and long-distance voyaging in their double-hulled sailing canoes. The wind gourd was supposed to magically hold all of the thirty-two winds. The wind *kahunas* had special powers and were said to have control over the winds. The winds could be summoned by calling their names in chants and prayers. These magical gourds or calabashes would represent the thirty-two winds. One story tells of a wind gourd with as many holes in it as there were winds. When a voyage to a faraway island was being planned, all the holes would be plugged up except for the hole or holes that represented the wind that was needed for the voyage. There were prayers and chants specific to the winds. One of these wind gourds and some of these prayers and chants have been preserved in the Bishop Museum in Honolulu, Oahu.

## Dolphin Card Readings at Douglas' Land

ONE EARLY MORNING I WENT UP to Douglas's tree house for his "free morning coffee" ritual. He had several pots of coffee brewing over the campfire, and it smelled aromatic and inviting. It was like a camping trip and reminded me of the Indian coffee that we had in the Nevada desert camping with the Western Shoshone people.

I have to say that this wild-crafted coffee that Douglas so carefully picked, roasted, and prepared, was delicious! He was warm and friendly to everyone, pouring cups of coffee for the people who were sitting around the campfire. He pulled out the honey too,

151

which had been donated by the bee man in Honaka'a. There was a spectacular view of the sunrise over the ocean, as his land was perched high up above the water. I thought to myself that the people in Kona see the sun go down into the ocean, and the people in Hilo see the sun rise up out of the ocean. People may think that the sun is moving, but when they think again, they remember that the Earth is moving. As Corbin Harney, Western Shoshone spiritual leader, always said, "Remember, we are all rotating together on our Mother Earth."

Here at Douglas' place I finally met some of the people who lived in the bushes that my landlady, Debra, had told me about. That morning I brought a deck of my *Dolphin Divination Cards* with me and, soon after showing them to the group, they asked for readings. So I had each of them pick a card out of the basket. Then I asked them for their own interpretation of the card they drew before I gave them my reading. When you don't know the person you are reading cards for, it is called a "cold read," as you can't be influenced by things you already know about them. I remember one woman had the "birthing" card. She revealed to everyone that she had just found out that she was pregnant. Another person had "Faraway Shores." He said he was really missing family on the mainland and was thinking of going home. This was fun, and the people found their readings relevant. Some of the young women who were there asked me if I would preside over their women's group, as an elder, the following week. They told me the day and the place where we would meet. Since it was not a cleaning day, I said yes, and thought it would be interesting to learn what kind of issues these young women had, who lived such an alternative life-style.

### Billy Mitchell's Church

IN WAIMEA, SOMEONE TOLD ME about Billy Mitchell's church, which was held in his home on the eastern outskirts of Waimea. So one Sunday I decided to go, as I was told they sang songs in Hawai'ian. As I entered the large, white, plantation house, I was greeted by Mrs. Mitchell, who is a pretty, middle-aged woman dressed in a *mu'u mu'u* (long dress). There was a welcoming feeling here for locals and visitors alike. A strong feeling of *mana* and *aloha* flowed and sparkled in the air. Hawai'ian quilts hung on the wall, as well as beautiful wooden canoe paddles of Koa wood. Folding chairs had been set up in the living room, which acted as the provisional church. Guitars, drum and ukuleles were warming up in the front of the room. *Kahu* (preacher) Billy Mitchell came out wrapped in a *lava lava* (sarong) and wearing a *kukui* nut *lei*. He was a Hawai'ian man of middle age with white hair. He flashed a quick smile at everyone as he went to the front of the room. People greeted him as *Kahu*. His smiling wife was welcoming people as they entered the door, which was next to the kitchen. A large coffee urn was heating up for the coffee and cookies that would be served after the service.

This was a home-style church which already felt warm and friendly. Everyone that came in the door seemed so lit up and happy. Most of the people knew each other, and there were lots of *Alohas*, hugs and *honis* going around. A big screen was hung high on the wall in the front of the room, and a man with a projector displayed the song lyrics, which were in Hawai'ian. The print was large enough to read. So, church began with a typically Hawai'ian band of ukulele, guitar, and drums playing, and the beautiful voices of local people singing in their own language. Ahhh, I thought, this is so beautiful and soothing to the soul. Tall, slender, old-fashioned windows opened to a view of a green lawn and tropical plants. Gazing out of the window, I felt embraced by the feel of old Hawai'i, as the soft and gentle songs, sung in the Hawai'ian language, seemed to blanket the church with invisible *mana*.

I attended the church a number of times and loved seeing the beautiful rural scene outside of the window of Ti plants and flowers, in both rain and sunlight. One Sunday a rainbow touched down in the yard. I felt that these beautiful and loving people were the pot of gold at the end of the rainbow. A feeling of expectancy suddenly quieted the room as Kahu Mitchell stepped up to the podium in front. He opened with a Hawai'ian prayer, which was followed by one in English. People bowed their heads and the room was silent, except for his voice. After the opening prayer the band started playing and another song began. The voices were strong and robust, and Billy Mitchell shouted out, "Sing it with more *mana*! Give it soul! Share your *aloha*!" There was a blessing energy that filled the room, and then it was time for another prayer, "*Mahalo nui loa Ke Akua* (Thanks to God)!"

One of the first sermons I remember was one that really moved me. *Kahu* Mitchell told of his past – his wayward youth, and what a bad dude he had been as a young man. He didn't go into details, but I assumed he wasn't exaggerating. He used this as an example to show us that even the greatest sinner could be redeemed by Jesus Christ and the power of the Holy Spirit. He described the turning point in his life before he became a *kahu*, or preacher. One of his children was deathly ill, and the illness appeared to be close to taking the child's life. Billy Mitchell prayed and prayed that his child's life would be saved. He promised God, and he promised Jesus too, that if his child was saved, he would give his life to God and give up his evil ways. He repeatedly asked for forgiveness for his sinful way of life. After these profound, heart-felt petitions, he went through a night of crisis with the sick child. But in the morning the child was well. And from that point on, he redeemed himself and kept his promise to God.

The service ended with a rousing song in English, which seemed to be part of the Sunday ritual – "This is the day, this is the day, that the Lord has made, that the Lord has made." It was a catchy tune, and I loved the Hawai'ian band playing the music. Sometimes I found myself singing this song in my car. "This is the day. This is the day that the Lord has made."

## Mauna Kea, the Sacred Mountain

ONE SUNDAY MORNING AFTER ATTENDING CHURCH, I drove through Waimea and looked up at Mauna Kea, one of the tallest mountains in the world, stretching up over thirteen thousand feet above sea level. This ancient, extinct volcano is extremely sacred to the Hawai'ian people. Culturally, the top of the mountain is home to sacred Lake Waiau, and it is *kapu* (forbidden) to drink the water, or swim or wade in this alpine lake. The summit of the mountain is thought to be the portal or *piko* (umbilical cord) between this earth and the heavens and the cosmos beyond.

154

Mauna Kea is also known as the abode of many heavenly beings, the realm of the Gods. It is the home of *Papa* (Earth Mother) and *Wakea* (Sky Father) and to *Na Akua* (divine deities) and *Na Aumakua* (divine ancestors). For this reason, many Hawai'ian people

are very upset that thirteen telescopes have been installed on top of the mountain. They want it to remain pristine and treated with honor and respect as a sacred site. In Hawai'ian legends it is claimed to be the home of *Poli'ahu*, the beautiful snow goddess that lives on the top of the mountain and who is a sister of *Tutu Pele*. *Lilinoe*, the younger sister of *Poli'ahu*, is the Goddess of the fine mist. Two other snow goddesses are believed to dwell on Mauna Kea as well. While people are in the snow visiting the top of Mauna Kea, not too many miles away people are enjoying swimming and surfing at Hawai'i's many beaches. Often when looking up to the heights of Mauna Kea, part of the mountain is hidden by clouds. Locals say that it is a beautiful *lei* of clouds that wreath the sacred mountain . . . the celestial home of the Gods.

### The Women's Group

THE FOLLOWING WEEK I FOUND MY WAY to the remote beach near Pahoa where the women were gathering. They had invited me as an elder to mentor them. I was not sure what their issues were, or if I could help them. They were all young, appearing to be in their twenties or early thirties, and they had all come from the mainland. They were living in tents in the bushes and in various encampments in the Pahoa area. Here I was, with the very women that my landlady had told me about. Some of them were nursing babies, and all of them were nude from the waist up. They had golden tans and golden sun-bleached highlights in their hair, no matter if they were blondes or brunettes.

At the beginning they all introduced themselves and told me their own unique story of why they were living a homeless lifestyle. Some of them enjoyed this way of life and others didn't. Some of them had partners and others didn't. They discussed men for a while, and the unique challenges of having almost no money and no home. Some of them were on welfare and food stamps. It seemed that they shared food and harvested wild fruit. Finally, they finished, shyly circling around the issue that they wanted to discuss with me.

It seems that their group was involved in a lot of spontaneous concerts, which were called "Raves." Raves, it seems, were wild concerts with a DJ playing music, which usually lasted all night. A place had to be found. People only found out about the rave on the day that it was to happen, as often the location was on the private property of someone who was away from home at the time. From the sounds of it, there was a lot of alcohol and drugs being used at these events.

After beating around the bush for a while, they told me that several of them had been raped by two different men, who lived in their camp. It seems the rapes took place during the raves. A few of the women had it happen more than once. They seemed very distressed about this, and there were tears in the eyes of most of the women. After they finished telling me this story, I asked them a lot of questions. Were they high on drugs and alcohol at the time that the rapes happened? What was the reaction of their male partners? How had it affected their self-esteem and self-empowerment as women? What kind of support were they looking for? Had they sought help from social services or law enforcement? We discussed the actual circumstances of the rapes. I tried to be supportive and neutral, remembering some of Aka's principles of *Ho'o'ponopono*. I listened carefully to each story. I did my best not to judge and to keep love in my heart. All this was part of *Ho'o'ponopono*, but I did not pretend to be a practitioner.

It seems their husbands or male partners didn't want to confront, or do anything to these two men, even though they all lived in community together. I asked them why their male partners didn't have the usual protective instinct of men for their women? They said that the two men were friends of their partners, and their male partners didn't want to upset the two men. I was starting to feel "hot under the collar." Rape was an assault on a woman's body, mind and spirit. I couldn't imagine the women's partners tolerating what these two men were doing to their women.

I asked them how they felt about the lack of support or protection from their partners. They said it was pretty f—ed up. They made it very clear that they didn't want the local police involved. I asked them what they wanted to do about it. They said that, since they were in Hawai'i, they would like to have some support from traditional Hawai'ian men, since their own men were wimpy. Yikes, I thought. So I made a prayer for them to stand up strongly for themselves and suggested that they go, as a group of women, to confront the two offenders. I told them that these two men needed to be banished from their little community. I also suggested to the women that perhaps they should stay away from Raves.

They said that they had already confronted the two men and their response was, "You wanted it." This seemed to be an age-old story. I thought about all the rapes that take place in Africa and the Middle East and on the mainland and other countries. Women have been used and abused in this way throughout history, especially in times of war. Sometimes rape is a racist assault on women. In every woman's heart there is a "soul wound" about this, whether a woman has experienced it directly, or not. Rape is a desecration of the divine feminine.

I told the women that I knew some traditional Hawai'ian men, and I would discuss this situation with them, if they wanted me to. They thought this was a wonderful idea, and I promised to do it and come back to them with the results. I left this meeting feeling sad for their lifestyle, and the children and babies that they were raising in this environment. None of these women or the others in their community were Hawai'ian, and none of them wanted to go back home to the mainland, even though some of them could have gotten help from their families to return home. Trying hard not to judge, I couldn't help but feel that these women and their male partners were acting spineless. I thought that maybe they were acting out of co-dependence and enabling the men's behavior. They certainly didn't seem to understand or enforce boundaries.

## A Private Meeting with the "Braddahs"

BEFORE LONG I MET WITH SOME of the Hawai'ian "brahs." None of them have been mentioned before in this narrative, and due to discretion I never even recorded their names in my diary. I explained to them the situation that these women were facing. "Well, what kine men are dese?" they asked. "If someone tried to do that to my *wahine* (woman) or daughtah, they would be in big *pilikia* (trouble). Whahs' dah mattah wit dese brahs?" they said.

They went on to say that if these *wahines* wanted it handled in the old Hawai'ian way, they would be willing to help them out, and it would be the sweetest deal they could get over here. They went on to describe something called the "net treatment." I asked them to describe the "net treatment" to me. They said that this treatment was a kind one, because it gave the person the chance to have a change in attitude and not get hurt. They went on to describe:

A big, heavy, and strong net would be used. Sometimes the net would be made up of strands of fishing line that would painfully dig into the skin, as the body's weight would sink into it. Some nets were made up of heavier rope or twine. The offender would be put into the net, forcibly, and hung over a cliff, above the water of the north shore, where the sharks hang out. The sharks may even be fed chum, to arouse them below. Then the person would just have to hang there until they decided to have remorse, an attitude adjustment, or change their *pilikia* (trouble) action into a *pono* (good) action.

If and when they would confess and say they would change their ways, and they really meant it, the net would be pulled up and they could get out. They said they wouldn't drop the two men, just get them to be sorry and "change it up." It would not be good to be on the bad side of these local brah's, I thought. But this might change someone's attitude about violating and disrespecting women, really quick!

I took this offer back to the next women's group, and they discussed it in front of me, and ended up saying that they thought it was too harsh. "I did what you asked me do," I said, and I don't think there's anything else I can do to help you." I left feeling disgusted with the passive, lethargic attitude of these women, and even more so with the passive and unprotective attitude of their men. I guess their whole lifestyle was quite passive. Nobody worked. There didn't seem to be any motivation to make a better life for themselves. They lived off the food stamps and welfare checks of the ones that had state aid. I didn't want to be in judgment, but I did feel that they needed some of Kupuna Pele's fire!!!

Later, talking to Aka, she was amazed at how these women, trying so hard to live a life of love and peace, did not understand that there are times in life that strong boundaries need to be set. By being willing to tolerate this abuse, and their unwillingness to take action, sends a message. It tells these men that their behavior was really okay, or at the very least, would be tolerated. Aka held up her fist and said, "*Ikaika Wahine* (strong woman)! If this happened to one of our local sistahs, deez guys would not get off easy. Our local sistahs would gang up on deez guys and give 'em a dirty lickin,' and kick their *okoles* (butts) down the road, if our men didn't get to them first." Now, Aka was a peaceful person, but when it came to abuse, her inner warrior could rise up. They would be blown off the island, like leaves in a hurricane-force wind.

### Pondering the Cycles of a Woman's Life

THE NEXT DAY WAS THE MASSAGE TRADE DAY with my landlady. She really missed her husband. He would be coming home around Christmas time. She was in a jovial mood, thinking about his return. She was also excited about the new harvest of sweet white pineapples that were getting ripe in her pineapple patch. She shared one with me, and I agreed with her that they were the most delicious pineapples on the planet. I told Debra that I would soon be going to Honolulu for a weekend as a new trainee of HACBED. She seemed pleased for me that I was going to do this. I decided not to share with her that I had met with the women that lived in the bushes. And yes, some of them DID have babies, just as she said. This experience had made me sad, and I did not want to hear, "I told you so." I also did not want to feel more judgment placed upon them, as I was already struggling with my own.

Kindness is always the rule that I try to live by, and I've always felt that there is never enough of it in this world. I've often thought of and wondered where the boundaries of real compassion ended and stupid compassion began. Tolerating abuse was obviously "stupid compassion." I started to think of all the cycles in a woman's life, and the lessons learned the hard way by foolish experiences. These women that I had met will get older, mature, move on, and be initiated into another cycle of life. Some day they would live in a house and tell exciting stories about "when they camped out in Hawai'i, foraging on wild fruits and dancing the night away at raves."

I thought to myself that, by mid-life, there usually is a certain amount of wisdom that develops, just from experience, and sometimes from hard knocks. We don't fall into as many pits. We learn about boundaries. We trust our intuition more, and when we sense trouble coming, or a gut level warning, we may go the other way, instead of diving right into something that appears to be an adventure. We may be more philosophical, or even humored, by the times when we are rejected by a relative, friend, lover, or job. We may know that sometimes, "rejection is protection."

We know by now that actions speak louder than words. We also know that "some" of the most handsome, charismatic men are also players. We know how to recognize "a line of B.S." and we know what a "red flag" means. We know that some of the shy, quiet men really have strong and kind dispositions. We learn the difference between judging and discerning. And we know that nobody is perfect, including ourselves. We learn to forgive ourselves and others for our human imperfections, and strive to do better.

By the elder years there is even more experience and wisdom. I thought of Auntie Fern and the wise advice she was always giving to me each time I saw her. I also remembered Grandma Eunice Silva and Grandma Florence Vega. Both of these Western Shoshone medicine women lived to be way over 100 years old. They had powerful advice and they didn't mince words.

I remembered a time when I was sitting with Grandma Eunice at the sacred grounds out in the Nevada desert. She was scanning the people in the camp and was watching a few of the men. She pointed out a certain man, and said, "See that one over there?" I nodded my head. "He thinks he's somethin', but he ain't nothin'!"

There were a few moments of silence. Then she pointed to another man, in another part of the camp. "See that one over there?" I looked over at the man and nodded my head. "Well, he thinks he's nothin', but HE'S . . . somethin'."

I also remembered the humility of these two elder women that went right along with their toughness. When someone referred to Grandma Florence as a medicine woman, she shook her head and said, "No, I'm not a medicine woman. I just pray for the people." Real medicine people

GRANDMA EUNICE

GRANDMA FLORENCE

never claim to be medicine people or shamans. One of the "real" ones said to me one time, "Only the 'fako bakos' claim to be, or announce themselves, as medicine men. There are a lot of 'instant coffee' medicine men out there these days."

In my younger years I didn't pay much attention to the advice of elders, including that of my parents. By not listening I made some painful mistakes. I wasted their wisdom. Now I knew how important it was to NOT waste the gift of wisdom that comes from parents and wise elders.

I thought of my grandmothers and all that they shared . . . one living until ninety-four and the other to one hundred and two. They had given me so much love, and took the time to share advice, wisdom and family stories, both when I was a child and when I was a young woman.

In some ways I used to be like the women in the women's group. I began to realize that they were not frozen in time. They would probably grow into maturity and wisdom as they got older. My frustration with them was that they presented a mirror to me, of an exaggerated version of how I once was. The truth was that I didn't like looking back on my own foolish mistakes that had caused me pain. Once again Aka's words came back to me, "Sometimes the one you need to forgive the most is yourself." *Amene! Mahalo*, Aka. I, too, had been passive and co-dependent at times. I had put up with abuse too, when I had a youthful marriage in my early twenties. But it wasn't rape or beatings that I sought to heal from. It was invalidation, dismissive coldness, and other forms of emotional abuse.

These things had chipped away at my self- esteem. Later, as I got older and matured, I learned that we never need to have validation from another to feel good about ourselves. And we don't need to give someone else the authority to define us. And we can walk away from an abusive situation. And if we don't know how to exit an abusive relationship, there is help available to do so. Throughout my life I have been a part of a large pilgrimage, with many other women by my side, or in front of me or behind me. We have all been seeking self-esteem, worth, equality, dignity, and confidence, in various measures. We have also been seeking respect, appreciation, and fair treatment by others. We want the equality of sitting side by side with our men. Most of all, we have had to root out the oppression or intimidation that lives in the DNA and ancestral lineages of women, who were not honored, but treated as possessions, servants and vehicles of reproduction.

Many women have risen up in themselves to feel strong and independent, self-respecting and honoring. They are holding the lantern, on the path, for others coming up behind them. Through these reflections I was finally able to let go of my judgment of these women.

Our brothers, lovers, husbands, sons, and male friends are also struggling to find new ways to relate to themselves and the women and brothers in their lives. And we cannot undervalue that we, women, must give to the men the same things that we want. We are all together, in a collective shift. Sometimes it seems that the transition is difficult and awkward. Other times we are surprised by delightful breakthroughs.

I used to think that my love for that "certain someone" would heal any dysfunction that the "certain someone" had. What foolish and naive arrogance to think such a thing, I thought. But in actuality it was youthful idealism and lack of life experience. It never really worked, at least, not for me. I have found that we all need to do our own work on our own issues, and we need to clear away victim mentality. No one else can do it for us. And as we become more whole and self-reliant within ourselves, we are more capable of joining with a partner and having a healthy, respectful, and loving relationship.

## HACBED – Hawai'ian Alliance for Community-Based Economic Development

IT WAS A BRIGHT, SUNNY HILO DAY, and I was on the way to the Hilo airport to catch a plane to Honolulu. I would leave my car in overnight parking at the airport. There was a group of us going to the HACBED training that assembled at the gate headed for Honolulu. As a community leader in South Kona, Barbara DeFranco was asked to send a representative and had made this training possible for me. Everyone was excited and happy. Planes were flying again after the 9/11 hiatus, and there had been no big attacks since 9/11. People were starting to relax a little about terrorism. Visitors were starting to come back to the islands, but not in the numbers that sustained jobs for local people.

Once in Honolulu, there were shuttles to take us to the hotel where we would stay and have our training. People were being picked up at the airport from Kauai, Oahu, Maui, Molokai and the Big Island. When we had all gathered in the big hotel conference room, we were given a HACBED notebook. We donned our name tags and began to introduce ourselves, one by one, in front of the whole group, sharing a little bit about our background and interests. As I looked around the room, I saw so many wonderful Hawai'ian

163

faces, and just a very few *haoles*. As we listened to the reports of how 9/11 had impacted the various regions of all the different islands, I realized that the people that were here represented many others who had been severely affected. Each person told about job losses and hardships. But they also shared about the projects that were being initiated, on their island, to create jobs and sustainability during this rough economic crisis. A man from Molokai spoke of solar projects and the re-building of ancient fish ponds for aquaculture. People from all the islands talked about increasing gardens and farms and growing more *Taro* and *Awa*.

The Big Island had a project where teens were helping elders by planting fruit trees and gardens for them, and also building small fish ponds in their yards, where they could cultivate their own fish for eating. There was a lot of vacant land where pineapple plantations and sugar cane fields used to be. Food could be grown in these large tracts.

Agriculture was a big topic of discussion, as the climate is so friendly for growing crops twelve months of the year. Soil and water availability was an issue at times. Some people talked about harnessing more solar and wind energy. The older islands, such as Oahu and Kauai, had less hard lava to contend with, as much of it had broken down into mineral-rich soil.

In the afternoon of the first day we had some special guest speakers. The topic was community development, sustainability, and creating businesses with grant writing and the help of foundations. We were told that we were also going to receive training in how to start a non-profit organization, how to write grants, and how to do the research necessary to find matching foundation money. This was very interesting to everyone.

I was always acutely aware that I was not Hawai'ian, which was just the way I feel when visiting both the Native American and Tibetan communities. But I found that with love in one's heart, respect, and a good sense of humor, a person can be welcomed into any culture, anywhere in the world. During our lunch break I began to talk with a lady that had come on the same plane from the Big Island. Her name was Lovey. We agreed to team up on rides to the airport for future HACBED weekends. She told me that she came from a big Hawai'ian family and she lived in Hawai'ian Paradise Park, just like me.

## *A Transmission . . . a Woman's Mana*

COMING HOME FROM THIS WHIRLWIND WEEKEND of listening, learning, and meeting so many new people, I wanted to relax before returning to work the next day with Betty, when we would be driving together to our cleaning jobs. I went out to my screened porch and sat in the comfortable wicker chair. Since the porch was all screens, with a roof, the outside yard came in, infusing the screen room with a variety of scents and breezes. It felt like being outside. It was dark already, and the stars were out. It reminded me of the night when I first arrived, when I experienced being lifted up to the stars by the two Hawai'ian *tutus*.

There was a soft vibration starting to move through my body, and I felt the tingling at the top of the head. Auntie Fern has told me that this feeling was the one when you recognize that one of the *tutus* is perching on your head with something to share. She scolded me one time for trying to stop it when it was so obviously beginning to happen. "Why do you want to insult or block the *tutus*, when they have something to tell you?" she had asked me, with a very stern look on her face.

When this feeling came, I reached for a pen and tablet of paper and started to scribble down what was being said to me, wordlessly, with pure thought. This feeling reminded me of the time when I scribbled down the words that became the *Dolphin Divination Cards*. I actually felt the slippery body of an invisible dolphin, sliding up my back, as this happened on a Maui beach some years earlier. I was familiar with this feeling.

This could also be called automatic writing, but Auntie Fern kept it simple. She just said that this was part of being a receiver, and I should never think of it as something weird. The *tutus* were perching and sharing. *Tutus* could be a spirit dolphin, or a spirit person or ancestor, but a being in another realm or dimension.

There was a message trying to come through. It was coming to me in pure thought, and I had to find a way to put it into my own words. Pure thought was so much purer than words. When pure thoughts are transmitted, it almost feels insulting to put them into words. They never seem to do the transmission justice.

"It is time to be quiet. Not much needs to be said. Move into the heart space. The Aloha heart just emanates . . . love. Be with it. Let it awaken inside of you. Remember it. Allow yourself to be helped by those who have greater development. Be humble and listen with your heart. What is taught to you will rarely come in words. You can be open to learning, through your heart.

"You can surrender habitual ways of thinking . . . for pure being. Allow the feminine energy of the ancient women to fill you with their feminine *mana.* This is a new but ancient way of being a woman. This is about the simplicity of loving and being loved. Great softness and great strength can be inside of your heart, side by side. The woman just loves and supports . . . and uses her wisdom to know how to best do this.

"This is not subjugation . . . this is truly participating in joy and happiness. When healing, it is *Ke Akua's* energy and *mana* that goes to the person needing healing. You are the vessel. You make an intention for healing, and then follow the guidance. You are only a willing vehicle.

"There are several kinds of *mana* a woman uses. One kind is for her children, family and relatives. One kind, which is a little different, is for the community – caring, service and humor – but does not emanate sensual *mana* or her inner heart *mana.*

"Then there is intimate *mana.* This kind of personal *mana* is the kind a woman gives exclusively to her mate, or it will be diluted and contaminated. This *mana* activates the entire body from head to toe, and is good and delicious. This *mana* is an inseparable combination of deep heart love and full body sensuality that flows in the body from head to toe.

"When this *mana* is given to one's mate, it will help to keep the mate young, healthy, happy, satisfied, fortified, and creative. However, it does not override destiny if it is time for the mate to be called to the heavens. This can include, and usually includes, sensuality, but this sensuality is a vibration, and can be infused either "up close" or "from a distance," if the couple is separated for a time.

"It is by invitation only, and must be mutual in order to offer this great benefit. The woman's entire body will also be completely infused with this pleasurable, happy *mana*, from head to toe, and engenders good health.

"The mate, feeling loved completely, perhaps not with words, but with this infusion, is so filled with this goodness that he, in turn, gives great kindness, protection, love and humor in return. The joy in the body leads to relaxation, laughter, and peaceful living."

When this state of receiving passed, I wondered about this message. Paul was far away in California. We had both decided that this time alone would be good for us. But there were many times that I just felt like getting on a plane to go back home. I missed Paul and I missed our grown children and friends. I thought they would all visit me, but they were immersed in busy lives. At this point I really did love being here in Hawai'i. Paul was bonded to our location in California. His printing and publishing business with employees and equipment was there, and it was deeply rooted. I knew we would reunite. We stayed in touch on the phone and in dream time.

Each of us needed time to more deeply know ourselves. We also felt a need for renewal, as we felt engrained in old, habitual ways of being. I was tired from many years of raising five children, working the land, and having part-time jobs as well. Paul was engulfed in work and had little free time. Finances were always right on the edge.

Conjuring up this state of being that was described in the message, with all these levels of *mana*, seemed idealistic and difficult for me to practice. But the message said that this *mana* could be sent from a distance. This was certainly something that I was going to consider and practice. I thought of Aka, and how her *mana* is always flowing so completely and emanating love to help and to heal everyone that comes into her realm. She had all these levels of *mana* in full operation. She was a living embodiment of a woman that has integrated all these aspects of *mana*, but then again she was born as a *kapu* child.

## House Cleaning in Waimea

IT WAS ANOTHER HOUSE CLEANING DAY in Waimea. On the way we listened to a wonderful CD by slack key guitar virtuoso, Keola Beamer. We had two large houses to clean. When it was lunch time, we decided to go out to lunch at a nice outdoor cafe. On the way to the café, we came upon road work that caused traffic to stop and back up.

A policeman was directing the traffic. As we came up to him, the traffic stopped again, and Betty recognized him as a friend of hers, Reynolds Kamakawiwo'ole. She introduced me to him and we all had a short chat. He was jovial and friendly and said, "Sorry for the delay." When the traffic started moving again, she told me that he was the cousin of Brother IZ (Israel Kamakawiwo'ole), the famous singer and musician. She told me that she and Reynolds had spent some time visiting together and discussing Hawai'ian culture. Many locals attended Kamehameha Schools. Some of them joke that graduates from Kamehameha Schools usually become firemen, policemen or musicians. Actually I had met one of each. You just never know who you're going to meet on the Big Island.

## A Pie Topped with Whipped Cream

ON ONE OF MY TRIPS TO THE KONA SIDE and Kealakekua Bay, I met with Aka. She said she had a surprise for me. When I drove up to the parking area of Kealakekua Bay (K Bay), I could see her talking to some of the locals. She glanced in my direction with a big smile and an exuberant, hand-shaking shaka. She went to her truck, brought out a box, and walked over to me where I was sitting at a picnic table next to the Heiau. The box was sitting on top of her hand, palm up, like a waiter delivering a *flambe* dessert. Her faithful dog, *Pupuka* (Puka), was walking at her side.

"Sistah Nancy, I brought you one very 'Akalicious' treat from this Big Island, and just one of her most bountiful gifts, given to us by *Ke Akua* and this beautiful *aina*," she said, dramatically. She licked her lips and had happy mischief in her eyes. "Sistah, are you ready to grind?" she asked. She pulled out some napkins and two forks.

When she opened the bakery box, I could see that it was a pie topped with mountains of whipped cream. Keeping the air of suspense, she started to cut a slice for each of us. "Can you guess what kinah' pie this is?" she asked. "Well," I said, "whatever kinah' pie it is, it's hiding under all this whipped cream!" She laughed and set a big piece on my napkin, saying, "Ok, now tell me if this isn't just the most 'onolicious' pie you ever tasted?"

First though, she prayed over the pie with a demeanor that suddenly became serious. "*Mahalo nui loa, Ke Akua*, for all the blessings you so abundantly bestow upon us, each and every day. Blanket our loved ones, those connected to us by blood or by heart, with your love and protection, whether they are near or far. *Mahalo nui loa, Ke Akua*, for all our many blessings."

I know there were many more words spoken that I cannot remember now, but prayer was just part of her day . . . many times a day, each and every day. And her prayer was never perfunctory. With Aka, prayer was always spontaneous and joyful, and most of all, sincerely from her heart.

Pupuka was watching a chicken that was strutting around the park, pecking at the ground. He kept looking up at us as we ate the pie, with pleading eyes. I addressed royal Pupuka as "His Majesty." As a handsome small terrier, he was regal. I loved the way he sat in the truck, in the passenger seat, straight and tall,  watching . . . always watching. I came to deeply love *Pupuka,* knowing him for so many years. Aka reached her hand down to *Pupuka* very stealthily. He was waiting eagerly under the table. He actually smiled after his bite of blue, sweet potato, cheesecake pie.

The first bite of the pie was truly like ambrosia, melting in my mouth. The pie was sweetened with local honey. I guess you could call it blue sweet potato cheesecake. The texture was soft and the color a lavender/purple. When we had finished the first piece of pie, she cut another piece of the purple pie for each one of us. While we were eating the second piece of pie, I wondered if the two of us were going to polish off the whole pie. Hawai'ians like to "grind," and in this way I surely was Hawai'ian at heart.

Suddenly I remembered another trip to Hawai'i, years before, with Paul. We were staying with friends on Kaua'i. We stopped at the Green Lantern Restaurant in Hanapepe, and I picked up a lime chiffon pie for dinner. Then our friend proceeded to take us on a tour of numerous cane fields and ocean overlooks for the rest of the afternoon. While alone in the back seat, I quietly got into that pie and, bit by bit, I polished it all off . . . and there was no dessert left for dinner. Aka would be able to relate to this. I told her about it and she put her head back and laughed a rowdy, gutsy, belly shaking laugh. "Now that's a good grind story, Nancy, fer shore!" she said.

### Held Hostage by Pigs

ONE DAY I WENT OVER TO VISIT RIKA, as we had a plan to go to the cliffs and chant and pray. When I arrived, I saw about five wild pigs, with razor sharp tusks, cruising around her front yard. They were right in between the steps that went up to her lanai and the place where I parked my car. I knew that their tusks were so sharp that they could shred me, so I didn't want to take the chance to upset them by invading "their space." I honked the horn, but they didn't move. Rika didn't seem to hear me, so I felt stuck in my car. I opened my car door. The pigs didn't move but just stared at me, grunting. I tried the horn again. Finally, I just drove home and called Rika. She said they had never been there before. I laughed, wondering how many people had a wild boar as an *aumakua* (totem or spirit animal). I laughed again later, thinking that I had been held hostage by pigs. And this reminded me of another pig story . . . but a totally different, pig story.

AKA ASKED ME, "Sistah, please give me an update from the Hilo side." I told her about the HACBED training in Honolulu, the upcoming *lomilomi* training with Kumu Dane, and the way I was held hostage by wild pigs. She was amused by this, and it prompted her to tell me a story of a pet pig that she once had. Aka referred to this pig as a *lomilomi* pig, and named him *Li'ili'i* (small). He was a Norwegian pot-bellied pig who lived in the house, jumped up on the bed and slept with her. She said he was a very clean pig, was potty-trained, and went outside to do his business. Aka loved this pig, as it would jump up on the couch and give her the best massage she had ever had, with his snout. Over the years of knowing Aka she often referred to these wonderful pig massages. Every massage she ever had was somehow compared to her *lomi* pig's massage.

"He would know just where all the sore places were and would go to work on them, in just the perfect way . . . with the perfect pressure," she said. She told me that this pig had to be a reincarnation of an ancient *Kahuna* of Lomilomi, and she and her Ohana were the lucky ones, gifted with this pig. I didn't know if this story of an ancient *kahuna*, reborn as a pig, was true, or if it was Aka taking poetic license. Li'ili'i loved hanging out with Aka's dogs and played with them, and sometimes even played with the neighbors' dogs. Everyone in the neighborhood knew that this was their pet pig . . . a family member, and not a pig that would ever be put in a *imu* (under the earth) oven or eaten in a *luau* feast.

One day, Aka came home and couldn't find her pig. Had he gotten out of his yard? To her great shock and distress she discovered that the man next door had killed her pig! He lamely tried to use the excuse that the pig had gotten out of his own yard and was bothering his dogs. Now everyone knew that this pig just liked playing with the dogs, as he had done this many times before. Aka was grief stricken with this loss in her family, and the mean-spirited attitude of her neighbor, who was hungry for smoked pork.

She heard the inner voice of one of her *tutus*, who was suddenly perching upon her head, telling her, "No one was going to have a chance to eat her pet pig." Aka felt that it was Kupuna Pele, herself. She felt inner fire, as she demanded that the neighbor return the pig's body to her. But he refused to cooperate. When his wife got home, she was horrified to find out that her husband had killed Aka's pet pig. She too knew that the pig was a beloved pet and that it had played with their dogs many times. She was so mad at her husband, and yelled at him to return the body to the family. But on this day, he was determined to go ahead with his plan to smoke *Li'ili'i*.

He had already fired up his smoke house and had the pig inside, ready to be smoked. He had used this smoke house on a regular basis and, as smokehouses go, it had always been safe without any malfunctions. But, this time, suddenly, as the smoke house was fired up, the whole smoke house burst into flames that went high into the sky. "It was a phenomenal fire," Aka said. The smokehouse burned down to the ground, leaving nothing but ash. The *lomilomi* pig, who was truly a member of Aka's *ohana*, had been "cremated." *Tutu's* words had turned out to be true: "No one was ever going to eat this pet pig."

As Aka told me this story, she had tears running down her cheeks. This had truly been one of the saddest stories she had ever told me. What a terrible experience, I thought. In spite of all of Aka's joyful and loving Aloha, she too, had had her share of sad experiences. It was a sad story for me too. I had tears in my eyes as well. I said to her, "I'll bet you had a hard time with this neighbor after this."

She said, "Sistah, remember what I've shared with you about *Ho'o'ponopono*! You track back to what made him do this. With understanding, you finally come to forgive him. Then he is liberated from your sad heart, and you liberate yourself from sadness, by deeply understanding and forgiving. You are both set free. Sometimes it helps to get in the water to cleanse yourself, make an offering to our creator of some flowers, and breathe, and breathe, and breathe, to help yourself to 'get there'. Playing music, singing or blowing the *pu* helps too. It takes time at first, but it gets easier the more you practice forgiveness. Your heart cannot be full of Aloha and love if part of it is occupied with sadness and grief and 'angah'. Remember this, sistah. This will help you, as people will hurt you many times in this life. This is one of those secrets hidden in plain sight, but an important teaching on how to grow your Aloha and be a happy person. People are people. They do 'whaht dey do', dah kine, all dah time. Someday they'll get there. We have to do a lot of forgiveness in this life . . . again and again. You jus' gotta love 'em!"

### A Ceremony for Hina, Goddess of the Moon

THE MOON, WHICH IS CALLED *MAHINA* in the Hawai'ian language, had been waxing over Kealakekua Bay. I had been watching it each evening growing bigger and bigger. Now it was finally a full moon. Energies were up and everything was feeling full, especially my brain. There was a kind of "spaced out" feeling that I sometimes feel with the full moon. Sometimes it made me drowsy and at other times energized.

I got a phone call from Aka inviting me down to the bay to have a ceremony for the Goddess Hina . . . Goddess of the Moon. I

was glad this time that I felt energized. We met at K Bay and then went and parked at nearby Manini Beach. We walked down the lava stone pathway out onto the rocks at the point, which embraced one side of K bay on its southern edge. Aka had about eight or nine women with her, and we were all sitting or standing waiting for the full moon to rise. The waves were breaking on the rocks with an undulating, rhythmic sound that was quite mesmerizing. Aka began to speak to us of the elements, and the moon, the sun and the stars. She said the old Hawai'ians used to talk to everything and make prayers for everything. She said, "In the old days, everything was honored. We knew we were part of nature, and we knew that without the sun, the moon, and the stars we wouldn't have a life. Without the water and the plants, we wouldn't have a life."

Aka has a beautifully expressive speaking voice. It was soft, lilting and melodious, almost as if she were singing. No wonder the Gods and Goddesses loved to listen to her, I thought. Her mother, Auntie Fern, had told me that she was one of the old ones, come back . . . not only to help her own people, but all people. Auntie Fern said Aka had a big mission, and Auntie was anxious for Aka to manifest it fully. "We are counting on her, but she has a mind of her own," Auntie had said.

Aka raised her *pu* and toned long and deep, and then began a beautiful prayer in the Hawai'ian language. We were encouraged to say our own prayer silently . . . especially, to give thanks for all the abundance in our lives. If anyone complained about their life, Aka was quick to list all the good things that person had to be grateful for. Then she would make a prayer for any obstacle to be removed quickly in order to bring a positive change. One of the women started to cry, and Aka went over to her and hugged her, and they spoke softly to each other. With the waves on the rocks, none of us could hear what they said. Then Aka broke out in prayer, looking up to the sky. "*Ke Akua*, please help my sistah here. Please protect her and her Ohana, and the ones that are near to her by heart or by blood. *Okie* (cut) the forces that would seek to diminish the light! Rebuke them, bind 'em, lock 'em up. *Ke Akua*, you do with them what you deem fit. Please remove these obstacles and blanket her with your unconditional love. Please open the way, for my sistah here. And we give thanks. *Mahalo lui noa, Ke Akua! Mahalo!*"

Aka was a strong force for the positive and held a dim view of negativity, as she said it was food for the dark spirits, who seek to diminish the light. "When we complain or get angry, jealous or fearful, we are providing food for the dark ones. We also hurt the flow and power of our own *mana*. We don't want to feed 'em. We want to commune with the divine forces, the creative forces that bring all the goodness, peace, and harmony into our lives."

This little talk was followed by a prayer and a Hawai'ian chant for Hina, Goddess of the moon. When we were finished, we filed down the path, which was now well lit by moonlight. Everyone was going to make their way back to their own *hales* (homes). I was going to spend the night with Barbara and enjoy breakfast with her in the morning. Aka was used to making the long drive back to Ocean View. The full moon would illuminate the landscape for her. Where vestiges of worry or negativity had lodged before, now our hearts were brimming with gratitude, love, and compassion for ourselves and each other. *Mahalo nui loa, Hina,* Goddess of the moon, for lighting our pathways in the night.

### Huki Lau and Fishing Spots

ONE DAY, AKA AND I WERE TALKING about the different methods of fishing here in Hawai'i. She mentioned the *Huki Lau,* which took me back to the time in Moorea when we participated in a *Huki Lau.* Our Tahitian friends in Moorea invited Christina and I to participate in a fishing expedition with a *huki lau* net. *Huki* means pull, and *lau* means leaves, or fern leaves. When walking the net out into a shallow part of the bay, one toe would secure the bottom of the net to the bottom, and the top of the net would be held up by the hand, neck high. It ended up in a horse-shoe shape. Sometimes small, transparent bait fish would be placed inside the area of the net to lure bigger fish, which eventually would be trapped inside. People on shore pulled up both ends of the net. With either style, fish would be caught. Our Tahitian friends laughed and laughed watching me walk the net out into the bay in an arc. Fish were plentiful, and fish on the plate was an *ono* (delicious) meal.

There are local fishing spots up and down the coast of the Big Island. I often went down to the shore at the end of Hawai'ian Paradise Park. Here there are cliffs and water that can be so rough that the crashing waves send up high plumes of white spray. I loved walking along the top of these cliffs listening to the music of the waves.

The locals fish there, and some are good rock jumpers who harvest the *Opihi* (a mollusk: limpet) that stick tightly to the rocks. They are quick with their knife and sack. They harvest the *Opihi* while the wave is out, and then quickly jump onto higher rocks to safety before the next big wave comes crashing in. However, this is dangerous and a lot of people have drowned harvesting, thus giving *opihi* the name: "the fish of death." *Opihi* served in a local feast is a delicacy and is usually a treat served at graduation time.

If you are a *haole* and you want to be *pono*, you won't try to go fishing with the locals. They have lost too much to colonization and tourism already, so best leave "feeshing" alone. "Jus buy duh feesh" at the market. My brother Scott and his wife Geri sent me money for Christmas to buy a fishing pole and reel so I could catch my own fish. They didn't realize that this would not have been *pono* for me, so I did something else with the money. That story will come later. It is a good Christmas story.

## *Local Color . . . Orchids Everywhere*

HAWAI'IAN PARADISE PARK, also known as HPP, was a great place to take walks. The central paved road slopes gently down towards the ocean. It is lined with fields of wild orchids . . . pink, purple, lavender and white. It was always a happy drive to come home, feeling the high vibration of orchids on both sides of the road. When I turned right, onto my street, the pavement ended and the street became a road of red dirt. Right after a rain, there were large mud puddles of water and the road became slick. The neighborhood children loved playing in the puddles. There were guava trees and lilikoi vines on a vacant lot across from the driveway.

One day while walking a new route, I passed an orchid farm. There were numerous greenhouses and screen cloths above tables full of orchids, at all stages of growth. I must have been peering through the fence, as an elderly Hawai'ian man waved me over to the entrance and invited me to come in to look around. He was rather short, brown-skinned, and had happy eyes. His short gray hair, rumpled trousers, and brown shirt told me a story of a man who worked hard. He carried a watering can in his hand and spoke with a wonderful, sing-song, pidgin English. "Orchids do not like to have "der" feet too wet," he said. "Have you evah been to one orchid fahrm?" he asked. I told him no, I hadn't, but that I loved orchids and found the many colors and varieties to be so beautiful!

I was then treated to a full tour of the greenhouses and screened areas. Orchids of all kinds, sizes and colors were everywhere. There were baby plants that had never flowered before, and there were large mature plants full of beautiful flowers. While talking with this man, who turned out to be the owner of the farm, I discovered that he raised orchids for export. He was friendly and loved talking story. He encouraged me to stop by, to "talk story," and to pick up a few orchids, each time I took a walk. Before I left, he showed me some of his prize specimens and told me about the fine art of growing orchids. The Hilo and Puna district, with frequent rains and warm sunshine, was the perfect environment for growing orchids.

Before you know it, I was taking orchids home each time I went for a walk and passed his nursery. He invited me in, when I walked by. He offered me a few more flowering orchids, for about three dollars each. I was developing an orchid collection in my little cottage. It was looking beautiful now with such a big assortment of orchids.

The orchids were lavender, pink, yellow, white and purple, beige and brown, and lime green ones. Some appeared to have faces. My little cottage was like the inside of a greenhouse. The orchids that he charged me for three dollars would cost twenty dollars or more in a California nursery. The addition of the orchids in my cottage raised the vibration and made it a happier place. *Mahalo nui loa, Ke Akua.*

### Lomilomi with Kumu Dane Silva

THE TIME HAD COME FOR THE *LOMILOMI* WORKSHOP. There were about eight Japanese ladies in the workshop. Dane's friend and business partner, Mariko, was helping to teach the class and acting as a translator. Yuki was there too, as an assistant and musician. The class was held in a large, open room in the downstairs of Desmon and Stacy Haumea's house. Desmon and his wife, Stacy, were also cooking for the class, and the meals were served at a long table on a big outdoor lanai.

There were at least four massage tables set up, and each one of us had *lava lavas* (sarongs) that we used for draping the body. Kumu Dane gave demonstrations of the *lomi* massage on different parts of the body. He would pick a person, and then demonstrate and talk as he did the demonstration. There was the back, then the shoulders, the neck, the hips, the legs, the arms, the hands and the feet. Everyone had a turn to be a "demonstration model." The workshop was also about prayer, the love for the body, and using various methods from the culture.

We learned to drape the person we massaged with a *lava lava* (sarong), giving modesty to the person being massaged. Then we moved it when we were ready to massage another part of the body. A Ti leaf was placed at the top of the table for protection, and we learned a prayer to say before starting the massage. Much of the class was practice. We paired off with each other and practiced the moves that we learned, with Kumu Dane, Mariko and Yuki watching us and correcting us when needed.

We learned to use our knuckles, fists, forearms, and elbows so we would not get arthritic fingers, like those of many massage therapists, from over-use of their fingers and thumbs. We learned to use our own body as a vehicle of *hula* and *lua*, so that we would not tire ourselves out. Our own body was used to stretch and dance, using hula moves that would channel healing energy to not only the person on the table, but to ourselves as well. The bent-kneed postures and long stretches felt good. It was true that it was not tiring doing *lomilomi* in this way. I could see that it was like a figure eight of energy flowing from the practitioner to the client and back again to the practitioner and so forth.

Kumu Dane gave a fascinating demonstration with Yuki of how the *hula, lomi lomi* massage, and the Hawai'ian martial art, *Lua*, were all interconnected and related in their grace and style of movements.

Desmon and Stacy served such delicious meals, and after lunch we had a cultural lesson of weaving *lauhala* (pandanus leaf) mats. This was a very important part of the Hawai'ian culture in the past. It was a meditative experience, and I kept thinking of all the mats that had to be woven to make the beds, floor coverings, and walls that were used in the *hales* (houses) of old.

We also made *"lomi* sticks" which we made out of guava wood. The bark is peeled and the branch needs to have a small crook branch coming off of the main branch. The wood is very flexible, and one can take the *lomi* stick and massage the part of your back that you can't reach with your hands.  The short crook branch coming off the main branch of the *lomi* stick is a wonderful probe for sore muscles of the shoulders and upper back. I had been a certified massage therapist for a long time, but now that I was learning *Lomilomi*, I felt it was a superior method to what I had been practicing before. A year later I taught my young grandchildren three percussion methods that I had learned. The way I taught my grandchildren was to call them, "choppers," "fists," and "cupping." This class was just an introduction to *Lomilomi*. I did not know if I would be able to take the more advanced classes. How generous Kumu Dane was to invite me to partake in his class.

### *Thanksgiving*

I WAS EXCITED WHEN I RECEIVED AN INVITATION by Desmon and Stacy and Dane to come to Desmon and Stacy's Ohana for Thanksgiving. It would have been sad to spend this holiday alone. At home I always cooked a big dinner with many entrees, and we often had guests in addition to family. I was told that the turkey was going to be boiled in oil. Well, this was humorous, as it worked just fine, and tasted great, but somehow much of the oil escaped onto the patio.

Everyone brought something to share and I decided to bring something very non-Hawai'ian – apple pies. Dane had spent the earlier part of the day making *sushi*. The feasting took place on long tables in the back yard, and the eating and drinking went on for many, many hours. Everyone was a little happily lit on beer and mixed drinks. The music started playing and various musicians showed up as the evening wore on. This was truly *kanikapila*, backyard jamming of slack key guitar, ukulele and Hawai'ian song.

### *Thanksgiving: Talk Story (Mo'olelo)*

THE STARS WERE OUT and Desmon started telling us about being a crew member on the Hokule'a, and how they had to study and learn the constellations while they trained for the voyage. As they were navigating primarily by the stars, which was called 'celestial navigation', they had to learn the constellations as well as understand how the stars rose, crossed the sky, and set. As he talked, we all looked upward at the bright stars above and imagined being on the voyaging canoe, hearing the splashing of the waves on the two hulls and the sound of the wind whipping against the sails.

The crew members took turns sleeping in the hulls of the canoe. But the navigator could only take catnaps and had to be aware and awake almost all the time. He had to watch for the changes in the wind, the waves, and the swells. And the stars were the guiding light. When there was cloud cover, navigating was more challenging.

Dane began talking about Clay Bertelmann and the Makali'i. Clay had been a captain of both the Hokule'a and the Makali'i. "You know," Dane said, "the Makali'i has been a floating classroom for hundreds of Big Island children who are learning about voyaging. With other Polynesian visitors who have come for training, maybe even thousands have been trained. In the old days an entire *Alapua'a* (Hawai'ian land division from the shore to the mountain top) would build a canoe together. But with the Makali'i, the Big Island community raised money for the canoe and built the canoe." Dane went on to quote Clay, "Our canoe is our island and our island is our canoe." He quoted the Hawai'ian, *"Wa'a he moku, he moku he wa'a.*

Think about this," Dane said. "A successful journey depends upon everybody getting along, as an *ohana*, as a village."

I remembered a story that my friend, Alapaki, had told me a few years before. He had a shop in Keauhou and was a friend of Herb Kane, the famous Hawai'ian artist. Herb Kane, after designing the voyaging canoe, had been the first captain of the Hokule'a when it made its first inter-island 'test' sails. Alapaki was a tanned skin, middle-aged man with glasses and a receding hairline of gray hair and a short beard. He had an open and kind face. I loved sharing stories with him, as he was always friendly. He inquired about my home in California and my family. Paul and our children had met him too, as we went to his shop each time we visited the Big Island. Alapaki's welcome and Aloha was not based on whether anyone bought anything in his shop either.

Alapaki's *aloha* was just a part of his friendly nature. I loved looking at all the Hawai'iana arts and crafts in his shop. We knew each other for many years by now, and we always ended up talking story. This day he was showing me some paintings and prints by Herb Kane that he had for sale. One of them, displayed on the wall, was of the voyaging canoe. He told me that Herb Kane had done research on the design of the voyaging canoes of old Hawai'i, both in the Bishop Museum and by studying old Hawai'ian petroglyphs. Alapaki went on to tell me that Herb was the first captain of the Hokule'a.

"On one of the voyages," Alapaki said, "the canoe got caught in the doldrums." He asked me if I knew what the doldrums were. I said, "Yes, when there is no wind or currents for sailing." He said, "Yes, the canoe was stuck in the doldrums and couldn't move. Remember that on these voyages they did not use motors or any type of instrument navigation. All the crew members prayed and sang for the winds and currents to return so they could sail again."

Alapaki's eyes got large as he said, "A big pod of dolphins showed up, out of nowhere. The dolphins actually created a current by swimming around and around the canoe again and again and faster and faster." His voice got more and more animated as he continued the story. "With the help of the dolphins, the canoe was able to move forward just enough to catch a current and then a good sailing wind." He said, "Dolphins are very intelligent beings and they help us, especially when we pray for help." I inwardly knew that and agreed with him. What a wonderful story, I thought. I shared Alapaki's story with the guests at the long table where I was sitting. Everyone had a story to pull out . . . and the stories kept rolling out as more and more drinks were poured.

By midnight a lot of good Hawai'ian musicians had come by. There were lots of drinks. Some people were drinking shots, but most people were drinking Corona with lime. People started to dance. I was getting a kick out of watching Uncle Benny dance by himself. He was having a ball, twirling and shaking and bouncing as he moved with the music, wearing a big grin on his face. Suddenly, with a fast fling of his arm, his wedding ring flew off his finger, rocketed through the air and landed somewhere on the lawn. Soon there was a crowd of people crawling around on the lawn, searching for his ring with matches and lighters. Finally, his ring was found, and he said, "Good thing too, cuz my wife isn't here tonight. She'd be givin' me one big stink eye, and worse, if I came home without my ring." But he wasn't the only one. One of my earrings flew off later, and got lost in the grass as well. It was found a few days later.

As the night went on, the air started to get a little chilly. Mariko, who was sitting across the table from me, was shivering in a sleeveless dress. I went into the house and got a blanket and wrapped it around her shoulders. I liked this pretty Japanese woman, who had such a sweet and delicate *mana*. But I could also feel her strength and determination. She told me about attending University classes in Hawai'ian culture. She may be Japanese, I thought, but she is also Hawai'ian at heart. She was a business partner of Kumu Dane. Being Japanese, she had many connections in Japan. She was able to arrange for Japanese students to come to Hawai'i and attend Kumu Dane's Long Life Lomilomi workshops and cultural teachings. She also helped to facilitate classes in Japan. This collaboration worked well.

Word-of-mouth in Japan earned Kumu Dane many Lomi students, who have a love of all things Hawai'ian. The more massage being done in this world, the happier and more relaxed everyone will be, I thought to myself. Getting regular massage is an indirect pathway to family harmony and world peace. If a body feels happy and relaxed, it is impossible to be grouchy or start a war.

A lot of people were here, and the group got larger as the evening went on. There were many conversations going on at the same time. They were becoming looser and more animated as the drinks continued to be poured. The eating continued too, late into the night. The turkey was delicious and the food table was never empty. My pies were gone.

As this Thanksgiving night wore on, a number of good musicians dropped by and started singing songs and playing slack key guitar. Everyone loved *kanikapila* or backyard jam sessions. And the singing and guitar music was just beautiful. One of the musicians said that, when a song comes to you, it is a lot like catching a wave. Many Hawai'ian musicians are also surfers. Music, Hula, Lua, Lomilomi, paddling, and surfing all have similarities . . . flowing grace, timing, sensitivity, inspiration, and flow. And of course, they all have *Mana, Aloha* and the blessing of the culture.

### Talks and Reflections about Kalapana and Uncle Robert

DANE SAID, "We should all go down to Kalapana some night with our sleeping bags and spend the night looking at the stars and feeling the *mana* of the ocean as the waves break against the shore."

Kalapana beach was new land. In the late 1980s and 1990, the Kilawea volcano was pouring streams of lava down to the towns of Kaimu and Kalapana. Uncle Robert Kel'iihoomalu had been born there and still lived in these village areas. His home was an outpost of the Sovereignty Movement, and a Hawai'ian flag blew proudly in the breeze near his "Awa Club."

Uncle Robert was an iconic, big-boned Hawai'ian man who made me think of King Kamehameha the Great. He and his family grew Awa and other traditional Hawai'ian foods and medicines. On Wednesday evenings and Saturday mornings, a farmers' market was held here. As always, Hawai'ian music filled the air, which came to be called Kalapana Slack Key. People talked about the lyrics of songs, and that sometimes there were two or three layers of meaning in the lyrics of a song or poem, and this was called *kauna*.

Many people saw Uncle Robert as a legendary Hawai'ian man, as he believed in keeping the old Hawai'ian traditions alive. His skin was brown. His hair and mustache were as white as snow, and his bright eyes were intelligent and full of passion and inspiration. Kapua once said, "Uncle Robert has huge hands, the size of baseball mitts." Kapua went on to say that the outside of his hands was rough, but the inside was soft. Uncle Robert was a religious man and was always said to have a heart of gold. He was willing to talk to all people who came by to visit his garden and Awa Club, and he accepted everyone, no matter what race, gender, or color they were.

It was always good to visit Uncle Robert. When living on the

UNCLE ROBERT

PAINTING BY KOKO MOMI KAWAUCHI JOHNSON

Hilo side, I sometimes went down to the end of the road. What had been the continuation of the road was now buried by the hardened lava flow of the late 1980s, which had "miraculously" separated and gone around Uncle Robert's property on both sides. One day he told the story of when the lava was heading to the villages of Kaimu and Kalapana. People had to escape quickly as their homes were burning up and cars were being buried in lava. This was just part of the reality of living close to a live volcano. The black sand beach was inundated and the Queen's Baths were devoured, disappearing under hot molten lava. They had been formed by collapsed lava tubes filling with fresh spring water. The bowing coconut trees, over the Queen's Baths, burned up. In the old days they had been pulled over with heavy twine, so they would be bowing to the Queen as she bathed.

The Chain of Craters road that led to the Wahaula Heiau was also closed, as it too was buried in lava. Eventually this *heiau*, dedicated to the God, Ku, was completely buried and could no longer be seen. Uncle Robert, his wife, and family refused to leave their homes and placed sacred Catholic scapulars, Ti leaves, and steel wool on the four corners of their property. They prayed that their home and land would be spared. I never remembered to ask him the importance of the steel wool, and I still wonder. The family felt it was a miracle when the lava flow, approaching their home, went around it, leaving it safe, amidst vast fields of fresh new lava. Uncle Robert used to fish on the shoreline very close to his house. But after all this new land had been created and hardened, he had to walk about a quarter of a mile to get to the water.

The Star of the Sea Painted Church had also been in imminent danger of being devoured and burned by the hot flowing lava. This pretty, Roman Catholic Church was built in 1927, in honor of St. Damian of the Lepers. The beautifully painted interior of this church was historic. In 1990 Uncle Robert, members of the congregation, and many local friends, in a monumental effort, moved the historic church to a new and safe location. Timothy Kern, who participated in the saving of some homes and the church,

STAR OF THE SEA PAINTED CHURCH

said that seventy-eight men in seventy-two hours had done this mighty feat. It is said that just as the big truck carrying the church was pulling out and driving to safety, the lava came and covered the area where the church had been. What timing and what a feat of devotion! Perhaps Mother Mary and Tutu Pele collaborated on the miracle of saving Uncle Robert's home and the Star of the Sea Painted Church.

## Other Stories, Thanksgiving Night

A LOT OF MO'OLELO "TALK STORY" was about the *kupuna*, the elders who preserved tradition, inspired the young, and kept the link to old Hawai'i alive. It felt good to hear these stories, under the stars, on Thanksgiving night. We were all feeling grateful for so much this evening: for the *kupuna*, friends and family, and this beautiful *aina*. I was certainly enjoying myself, but kept thinking of the Thanksgiving dinner at home that Paul had prepared for the family. Sometimes we celebrated Thanksgiving with my siblings, Lacey, Scott, and Debbie, and their families. I kept thinking of all of them and missed those family gatherings.

Desmon came out of the house where he and Stacy were cooking up another late night meal, and invited all of his guests to spend the night. I told them that I lived so close by that I was going to drive home. He probably thought I had too much to drink, but I didn't, as I nursed a couple of drinks all night long. I got high mainly on the *mana* and *aloha* all around me. Desmon continued to try to convince me to stay, by saying, "We always spend the night together after one of our parties, because the best part is breakfast and coffee in the morning."

I didn't want to reject his hospitality but I declined, knowing that I wouldn't get any sleep with a group of people sleeping on mats in a large room. As I drove home at two or three in the morning, I was grateful to have spent this Thanksgiving with warm-hearted Hawai'ian friends. I would park out by the road and wa

lk to my cottage, as I didn't want to awaken Debra. This was the first Thanksgiving that I had spent away from my family, and I missed them. It was the first time I had eaten both turkey and home-made *sushi* at Thanksgiving. The people, *aloha*, stories, music, and food that were shared will remain etched in my memory and heart forever.

I GOT MAIL FROM MA'ATEA, more commonly known as "Tea" (pronounced Tay- ah) from Moorea in Tahiti, saying she was coming to the Big Island. She wanted to stay with me. I had a blow-up mattress and fixed her a nice bed. I wanted to reciprocate hospitality to this wonderful Tahitian friend. She had offered our daughter, Christina, and I a three-month stay in her wonderful native houses on the Island of Moorea, right across the channel from Tahiti in 1993.

My cottage was festive with orchids and bowls of tropical fruit for her arrival. I picked Tea up at the Hilo airport and treated her to a *sushi* dinner in Hilo before we returned to the cottage. I told Debra that I was going to have a Tahitian lady friend visit me for a few days. I told her a little about our history, and she seemed pleased for me.

Tea carried herself with such grace. She had both humility and a dignified high-mindedness, even if these terms seem contradictory. She was in her sixties, but she was still a slim and exotic beauty which blended the best of her Tahitian and French features. Her short, black, wavy hair set off a classic face with slightly almond eyes. Almost all modern Tahitians carry some French blood as many French colonizers mixed with the native people. I thought to myself that the good looks of Tahitian men, women and children is "human art" at its best, as the people of the islands of French Polynesia were stunningly beautiful and handsome. In Moorea the people look like they just stepped out of a Gauguin painting.

Tea had descended from Tahitian royalty and her family members owned large tracts of land on the islands of Tahiti, Huahine, and Raiatea. Her brother and family own and live on their own personal island in the Gambiers Island chain. Tea's own place in Moorea was a gorgeous piece of land right on the lagoon, right next to an ancient *marae* and large coconut palm grove, which had once supplied Copra for export.

Tea grew up in outrigger canoes, paddling or motoring to nearby *motus* (small islands) to fish and picnic. There were many parties in Pape'ete with her mother and other leading citizens of Tahiti. When of debutante age, Tea was sent to school in France.

187

When we first arrived in Papeete, our daughter, Christina and I had lunch with Tea's mother, Madame Purea Raisin. Even as an elder, she was a queenly beauty. She had the presence and appearance of royalty, even though Tahiti had already become a French territory. After all, when writing a letter to Tahiti, the final part of the address must say: *Polynesie Francaise* . . . French Polynesia.

Madame Raisin had natural elegance. She wore a beautiful mauve silk blouse trimmed in mauve lace. Her long hair, woven and twisted neatly on the top of her head, was secured with old-fashioned tortoise shell combs. She wore a long necklace of the largest and most beautiful real black pearls that I had ever seen. The necklace was a family heirloom, and I wondered if it had once belonged to a Tahitian chiefess or queen.

As an American, you can go to Tahiti on a three-month visa, but you can't live there unless you marry a French or Tahitian citizen, or bring a business that would be beneficial to their economy. Of course, the business must be approved with careful scrutiny. It is not an easy long-term destination for American "ex-pats."

Our first night together, Tea and I stayed up late having some wine and fruit and talking away like school girls at a slumber party.

NANCY IN MOOREA

I had to catch up with her life. She had one daughter living in California. Another lived in Kauai, and Tea mentioned that she had raised her children in Waimea, here on the Big Island. She was fond of calling Waimea, "Kamuela," which is the other name for the town, and which means "Samuel."

Tea told me of an excursion she had made to the private island that her brother owns in the Gambiers. She then took a book on the South Sea Islands out of her suitcase and there, in the book, was a photo of Tea and her brother and family in a motor boat. His private island was in the background. She presented this coffee table book to me as a gift. The following day we planned to drive over to Puako on the other side of the island. A six-year-old grandson of one of her old friends was having a birthday party.

After we had lunch in Waimea (Kamuela), Tea wanted to drive me to the neighborhood where she had lived when her children had gone to the local high school. Her former husband lived on the Big Island, and that is how she migrated up from Tahiti. We drove into the neighborhood and I realized that we were close to Barrie Rose's house, where we have wonderful parties and dinners.

I kept following Tea's directions, and soon we were pulling into the cul-de-sac where Barrie lives. Then Tea pointed to the house and said, "There's the house I used to own." I couldn't believe what a coincidence this was! I had spent a lot of time in "her" house. I had even house-sat for Barrie Rose on two different weekends when she and Kapua went to visit his mother in Oahu.

We went up to the door, as I wanted to introduce them, and I thought it would be fun for Tea to see inside for old time's sake. But no one was home. Too bad, I thought. This made me think of karma, and how interconnected everything and everyone is, in this web of life. Was it just a coincidence or was it a synchronicity? The web of life and the interconnected nature of everything seemed to be boldly manifesting all the time here in Hawai'i.

### Hau'Oli La Hanau (Happy Birthday)

THE BIRTHDAY PARTY WAS FUN! In the host's yard was a large fish pond, constructed of lava stones and concrete for the cultivation of fish. Each child had a fishing pole and we watched as their excitement grew. Every child was pulling up at least one Tilopia, as that was the variety of fish that was stocked in this pond. Aquaculture was an ancient tradition in Hawai'i. All the islands had fish ponds close to the shoreline for cultivating fish. I loved seeing the kids having so much fun. Only in Hawai'i would kids go home with fresh fish as party favors. They were all so excited about eating their fish for dinner.

This fish pond made me recall hearing about the fish pond project on the Big Island, which was a joint effort between Hawai'ian *kupuna* (elders) and Hawai'ian youth and was funded by grants. The youth dug and created the fish ponds for the elders and then stocked them with edible fish. They also planted fruit trees and gardens for the elders. This was also a means of bringing the youth to the elders so that they could build relationships. The *kupuna* had a lot of wonderful old stories. Their stories were teaching stories, so the cultural teachings could be passed from one generation to the next.

What a wonderful project, I thought. I had spoken to some of the *kupuna* who had made close friends with some of the young people who came to help them. A young person can always use another grandma or grandpa in their life. And a grandma or grandpa can always use another grandchild.

As the sun began to set over the western ocean, Tea and I walked out on the beach and rocks at Puako. Once again I found myself telling Tea how appreciative Christina and I were to have had the gift of care-taking her place in Moorea for three months. She asked, "After Dave went back home to the ranch, I'll bet you and Christina were bothered by the local men." I told her that it was true. They were actually in our yard one night, creeping around and whistling. We felt it was not an idle threat, and everything inside of us told us to leave at once. We dressed quickly in the dark, grabbed our keys and purses, and made a sudden dash for the pick-up truck. We left in a hurry! We called Meme and Bob from the pay phone at the nearby Chinese store, and they told us to come to their place at once. From that time on Meme and Bob insisted we stay at their house at night. So after that, we were at Tea's during the daytime, near the village of Maatea, and at Meme and Bob Brocious's at night on the shore of Opunohu Bay.

It had been one of the most magical times in our lives. I told her how we had become a part of Meme's church on Moorea, and that the people had adopted us like family. Knowing local people opened up many wonderful experiences and friendships for us too. Going to church on an island is a quick way to make new friends. How many churches have mango trees that drop ripe mangos right outside the church window? And in how many churches do you get adorned with dozens of shell leis when you leave to go home?

Tea paused and said quietly that she never goes to church. I asked her if she followed old traditional Tahitian ways. She said, "No, all that has been lost in our family. We still have the land holdings from the family that we descend from, and the *marae*, but the old traditions are mostly lost. My parents sent me to France for my education. Oh, we still make *leis* and *monoe* oil from the Tiare flowers and fresh coconut oil. We still have feasts using underground ovens and take outrigger canoe trips to the *motu*, but we don't have any spiritual traditions that we follow. Some of my friends do the traditional drumming and dancing. I have a close friend who is the leading traditional drum maker."

Tea looked sad. She said, "I'm so '*fiu*' (bored and fed up) right now. I come back to see my old house in Kamuela today, and now your friend lives there. It is as if none of that old life of mine ever happened. It was so long ago and now there are only memories that tug on my heart. There are so many family memories here, and they were happy days. I had so many friends here too. Now I am with you, and you are telling me that my place in Moorea is the most magical place you have ever been. I guess I take that place for granted."

Tea had been divorced for a long time. She always felt a more suitable partner would come along, but up until now, this partner had not shown up in her life. And it wasn't for lack of suitors, as many men admired her. But none of them were quite right. She said, "I have so much, but after seeing my life through your eyes, I realize that I take some of the good things in my life for granted. But, you know, my kids are grown now and I am a grandmother. I love being a grandmother, but it would be so sweet to meet a nice man to share my life with."

Tea is so beautiful and has a natural grace and charm that made it so easy to be with her. I could feel a tinge of melancholy in her at times, but she could turn right around and dazzle you with her wit, soft laughter, and her bright smile, showing perfect, pearly-white teeth. She is not taxing or tiring to be with either. When driving around *holoholo* with Tea, it was like being surrounded by a soft, sun-kissed breeze. Tea was easy to love!

There is something about island people that is so unlike mainland people. Growing up in the natural elements and beauty of a temperate climate is one influence, but there is more. These people absolutely absorb the beauty, the salt air and breezes, the ocean waves, and the colorful flowers and birds into their very being. They seem to be infused with their environment, and in some ways they *become* the island. No matter where they live, later in life, it is always there, inside of them, emanating island energy and the blessings of their ancestors. Main-landers rarely have this flowing island *mana* the way island people do, no matter how much they love the islands.

## Kalapana with Douglas

DOUGLAS AND I MET AGAIN, BY SURPRISE, at the Pahoa health food store. I remembered that I first met him here, on the day that he took me to visit Green Lake. I told him about my visit from Tea and that I was going down to Kalapana today. He and I hadn't seen each other for a while, so he asked if he could come along. "Of course," I said. We drove down from Pahoa under the large arching trees and took the Red Road, which is the long way to Kalapana, but also the scenic route. We drove along the ocean and could see the white caps cresting on the waves of the ocean as they crashed upon the rocky shore. The road was narrow and rolled up and down, like a pre-school roller coaster. The rain forest on both sides of the road was beautiful with filtered sunlight bathing vines and trees and ferns. Banana trees were interspersed here and there, with their large leaves rustling in the breeze.

When we arrived in Kalapana, we parked close to where the locals were selling Hawai'ian crafts on their folding tables. I meant to return another day to look at their crafts for Christmas presents for my family at home. We went to look for Uncle Robert, but he wasn't home. We decided to walk on the path that goes out on top of the now hardened lava flow that had formed about one quarter of a mile of new land in the 1980s. We sat down at the ocean's edge and watched the waves for a while. A group of people approached the shoreline near by. We could hear them sobbing, with wails and cries of such deep despair.

Douglas gave me a hand and pulled me up to my feet, saying, "We'd better go over there and see if we can help these people." So we walked over to them, and Douglas asked them in such a soft and gentle voice, "Is there anything we can do to help?"

They began to talk to us, all at once, eager to tell us the story of their mother's death. There were two sons and two daughters whose mother had just died. They told us about her death and the funeral that they had just attended. They all broke out into sobs again. She sounded like a most wonderful mother, as they paid tribute to her, between sobs. They said they had come to the Kalapana shore because their mother loved this place, and she would have preferred to have her service here by the ocean.

Douglas suggested that we all hold hands and offer a prayer for her, right here on the new land that had been created by Kupuna Pele. He said, "This is really a specially blessed place." They were eager to do this. As we all held hands, Douglas offered a most beautiful prayer of gratitude for this wonderful mother, and it ended by his wishing her well on her journey into the heavens. All the cries and sobs had stopped now, and heads were bowed.

After the prayer, Douglas began singing "Amazing Grace" in a beautiful singing voice. I had never heard him sing before. I joined him, and immediately they all joined in. Here on the lava, strangers were united in love and compassion for one who was a newcomer in the heavens. A gesture of love for those who were bereaved brought us all together in our humanity. They all seemed to know the words of "Amazing Grace," as we formed a circle and became a beautiful, spontaneous choir.

When we finished singing, we continued to hold hands in silence. Then we all hugged each other, and off they went looking happy and telling us how much better they felt and how they could feel their mother's spirit, here by the ocean, in this little ceremony. As they walked back to the parking lot, their figures became smaller and smaller, until they disappeared.

I thought how very few people would have intervened in a situation like this. Douglas, with deep compassion and respect, had no fear of reaching out to people to share his love. This was one person, born on the mainland, who truly emanates island energy and true Aloha.

We continued to sit along the shoreline for a long time in silence. My mind was free of thoughts. It was never an awkward silence with Douglas . . . more like meditation. As the sun started getting low in the sky, clouds moved and streaked into a certain design around the sun. It looked as if a pyramid was drawn with light rays playing upon a few beautifully placed thin clouds. How beautiful, I thought. The pinks, roses, golds, mauves and silvers in the sky were breath-taking, colors ever-moving and changing. Clouds, and their ever-changing shapes and colors, brilliantly illustrate the age-old teaching of impermanence.

Douglas spoke after this long silence: "Our creator shows us special things if we take the time to be quiet and gaze upon the natural world. My father, being an Alaskan native, always taught me to get involved with people, to reach out, to give a helping hand, to give a meal to the hungry, water to the thirsty, and comfort to the suffering. Today, so many people live inside of their own isolated world, and are afraid to talk to strangers. To me, there are no strangers. I see myself in every other face. My heart is the same as their heart. Our joys and sufferings are the same."

I thought to myself, that Douglas was a most unusual man – this man who lived in a tree house, had no bank account, no car, no driver's license, no phone, no P.O. Box, no electricity or running water, and almost never handled money; this man who harvested and roasted wild coffee, over a camp fire, in a large black iron skillet, and served sunrise coffee to the people who lived in the bushes. And this man who made guitars, ukuleles, and wooden spoons from "found" wood to trade for food at the health food store. I had never met anyone like him before. It seemed to me that he, himself, was an endangered species, of the homo sapiens variety.


### Lovey's Sumotori Son-in-Law, "Everyone is Beautiful"!

AFTER A BUSY WORK WEEK CLEANING HOUSES, it was the monthly weekend to go to Honolulu for the next HACBED Training program. I had met Lovey at the last meeting and discovered that we lived close to each other in Hawai'ian Paradise Park. We agreed to go together and leave my car at the airport. Lovey had come from a Hawai'ian family of eighteen children, all born from the same mother.

As we drove to the airport, she told me stories of growing up and raising chickens and vegetables, as there were so many mouths to feed. There was always hunting wild pigs and fishing to supplement the natural fruits that grew on the island. With a garden of taro, blue sweet potatoes, and breadfruit trees, the grocery bill could be minimized. But they always had to buy their rice and Portuguese sausages. The tops of the Taro were delicious greens that tasted a little like spinach. Lovey told me what it was like to grow up in a household with this many kids. She was one of the oldest and was a grandmother now.

She shared with me that her daughter was married to one of Hawai'i's famous Sumotori (large Sumo wrestlers) and lived with him in an old plantation house in nearby Kea'au. These Sumo wrestlers could easily be up to five hundred pounds or more. The Hawai'ian Sumotoris could give the Japanese Sumotoris a "good pounding for their money."

On our way to the airport, we stopped briefly at her daughter and husband's house, and there he was, Lovey's son-in-law, larger than life, lounging his large Sumotori body, clad in only a loin cloth, on the upstairs *lanai*. This was a sight to see, this iconic athlete looking (as the Hawai'ians say) "SO DA KINE!"

Paul and I once met the brother of one of Hawai'i's top three *sumotoris*, Aki Bono. Aki Bono's brother and wife were selling homemade jewelry at the warm ponds on the Hilo side. We chatted with them for a while. Apparently Aki Bono was an exceptionally tall Sumo wrestler and one of the most famous of the Hawai'ian *sumotoris*. Brother IZ honors him in one of his songs.

Sumo wrestling started in Japan, but Hawai'i adopted it too. It was not hard to become so large in Hawai'i, as Polynesians have a culture of eating and more eating . . . and then more eating. Food is a celebration! Hawai'ians really enjoy their food or "grindz," as some of the locals call it. I remembered breakfast at Meme's house on the island of Moorea. There were the slim baguettes of French bread that were delivered to the mailbox very early in the morning. That was paired with *pate de fois gras*. Then there were fish pancakes: small, transparent fish from their bay sliced small and put into the pancake mix with chopped green scallions and topped with gravy made from mushroom soup. So delicious!!!

Hawai'ians enjoy cooking and pleasing their friends and family with *ono* (delicious) food. If you enter a Hawai'ian home, you will be offered food right away . . . or it will be placed in front of you with a gracious smile. Hospitality is one of the ways of showing Aloha. Bringing vegetables, fruit or fish to share when visiting is another Hawai'ian tradition, especially if the family you're visiting has many mouths to feed. Having taste buds and the enjoyment of eating is one of the great pleasures in life.

There is no real beauty stigma against becoming a large woman or man in the island cultures. Hawai'i, Samoa, Tonga and Tahiti not only have big-boned people, but they often become very large. There is no body shaming in these cultures. And with some of these Pacific Islanders, their large size is almost all muscle, especially if they are swimmers, surfers, and paddlers. In ancient times the Hawai'ian royalty tended to become extremely large. Some think that it was a sign of beauty and wealth. Very thin people were seen as sick, starving, or malnourished.

Polynesian women are made to feel that, if they are large, they are beautiful and honorable. There were always jokes about how each cell of the body emanates *mana* and *aloha,* but I don't think they were always joking. Large ladies and gentlemen are not discrim- inated against, and often they are dancers and musicians who are adored in their culture.

There was a famous *"gros monsieur"* (large man) in Tahiti who was a five-o'clock evening newscaster. He wore a huge Aloha shirt and danced at the end of his newscast, thrilling his almost all female audience. As he danced, his belly would ripple and wave, from side to side, under his shirt. Tahitian women would rush home to see him every day, as he was their super-star. Americans would not understand this Polynesian "everyone is beautiful" philosophy. I thought about poor American girls and women who develop anorexia and bulimia trying to be stick thin. "Too bad," I thought.

Brother IZ sings a beautiful rendition of "Somewhere Over the Rainbow" as one of his signature songs. He was the supreme example of a *gros monseiur* and may have been over six hundred pounds when he passed away from weight related complications. He sang like an angel, was deeply spiritual, and dearly loved.

However, he had a shorter life due to the strain his weight had on his heart. The medical profession chides some of the Pacific Islanders for a tendency to be overweight, reminding them that there is a detrimental relationship between excessive weight and diabetes, hypertension, heart disease, and a potentially shorter life.

Aka said one time, "If we have a shorter life because we are big, no problem. We know we are coming back. We would rather love our life . . . enjoy our grindz, dancing, singing, and spreading Aloha than worry about our size. Having a shorter life is not so bad." "Quality rather than quantity" was what she always said to me. Years later this proved to be a prophetic statement.

Nobody blinked much about someone weighing five hundred pounds. A few local friends thought I had a "fetish" because I was in the camp of "Everyone is beautiful," and wanted to introduce me to the most eligible large gentlemen of the island. However, I did remind them that I had a partner and family back in California, so in actuality, I wasn't interested in getting together with any man, large or small. However, the real truth is that these large people are usually extraordinarily sweet and DO seem to emanate a lot of Aloha.

Many large Pacific Islanders don't care to listen to medical advice or statistics. I appreciate good health practices, but I dislike discrimination for a person's looks, size, or physical disabilities. However, the medical profession is correct, and even traditional Hawai'ian health practitioners warn about the dangers of these conditions and other ailments due to excess weight.

Paul and I have a son who is legally blind. He has a condition called "aniridia." His eyes appear "all black," as the brown, blue or hazel iris never developed. I have heard sad stories from him about teasing and bullying he's received due to the appearance of his eyes. Many people seeing these "apparently" dilated eyes accused him of being high on drugs, even when he was very young. I loved the lesson I learned on the Island of Moorea that "everyone is beautiful" . . . short or tall, big or small, young or old. This is how it should be.

## The Turnstile Incident at a Kona Market

ONE OF THE SADDEST EXPERIENCES I had in Hawai'i this year was seeing a large, large gentleman get stuck in the turnstile that was (at that time) the only entrance to a particular grocery store. I happened to be shopping in the store and witnessed this event as I pushed my cart around shopping. The only way they got him out was to have a tow truck come with all the necessary tools to dismantle the turnstile. Finally, this poor, traumatized man was released, after shouting repeatedly, "I nevah gonna shop in dis store again." I felt so sad for him. On my next trip to the Big Island, I noticed that this same store no longer had turnstiles. On the visit after that, the store was *pau* (finished, gone).

## Aka's Sister, Kela, Weighs in on the Subject

ONE DAY I WAS SPENDING TIME with Aka's sister, Kela. We discussed the models in magazines that look like stick figures, looking almost

like they just escaped a concentration camp. They have been the standard of female beauty for years in the modeling business in the United States. Kela told me that too many young women get sick, sometimes becoming anorexic or bulimic, trying to look super thin like runway

KELA PULE, ANNI McCANN, AKA PULE

models. She said, "In Hawai'i, love handles can be seen as sexy." One time she said to Paul, laughing, "Come feel these love handles, Paul. I'm a triple Queen. I don't have a weight problem; I have a height problem." She could pull out her guitar and make you roll in laughter with her own racy renditions of old favorites. A big belly on a man or woman is "more of you to love." A big butt has more shake and wiggle for the dance, and is an asset when dancing to "If it's not jam, it must be jelly, 'cause jam don't shake like that."

### The One-Year-Old Birthday Party
*Hau'oli La Hanau* (Happy Birthday)

AFTER ANOTHER ONE OF OUR HACBED WEEKENDS, Lovey and I were on the inter-island flight from Honolulu back to the Big Island. My car was parked at the Hilo airport, and I was going to drive Lovey home. We had had a full weekend of training in grant writing and learning to find matching funds from foundations. It was intensive learning and very interesting. We all hoped to try our hand at grant writing to help the already existing non-profit organizations, as well as new ones that were springing up in this post 9/11 economic challenge.

One of the best parts of HACBED trainings was being able to meet so many interesting people from all the different islands. We would get reports about what kind of projects were happening on the other islands. The Big Island had a few representatives who were helping start more *Awa* (also known as Kava) cooperatives and farms. *Awa* was a cash crop. I never realized that there were so many varieties of *Awa.* It was used as traditional drink and sometimes a ceremonial drink. It was often served in half of a coconut shell and there were *awa* bars spread across the islands. When drinking it, your mouth could get a little numb, and along with it came an interesting kind of relaxation. As a medicinal it was used to reduce pain, relax muscles, and to help people get a good sleep. As a muscle relaxant, I had quick benefit from it when I had torticollis of the neck a few months earlier. However, dosage is very important, and it's good to consult a *la'au lapa'au*, herbal practitioner.

When we arrived at the Hilo airport from Honolulu, Lovey tried to call her husband from the phone booth. He didn't answer, so she said, "Ah, he's gone to the hall where the family's 'one-year-old birthday party' is already under way." With one family car she would not be able to get there, unless I dropped her off at the party. She asked me, rather apologetically, if I would mind going a bit out of my way to drop her off at the party of her one-year-old grandson.

"I would be happy to do that," I said, as I had nothing planned. So she began to direct me to the large hall on the outskirts of Hilo. Suddenly she said, "Have you ever attended a one-year-old birthday party in Hawai'i?" I told her that I hadn't, but that I knew it was one of the biggest celebrations in a person's life. I imagined that, in the old days, if a baby lived through the first year, it would show strength and good health which would be something important to celebrate.

She then said, "Why don't you come in as my guest. You will be able to meet my whole family . . . my *mo'opunas* (grandchildren), all my brothers and sisters and their kids and their kids, the aunties, the uncles and all the cuz's." I told her that I would love to come with her. As we opened the door to the huge hall, it was like entering a joyful realm, as it was richly decorated with flowers and streamers and happy Hawai'ian faces. A large buffet was at the far end of the room, with every kind of local food, and a bar for soda and juice. A band was playing Hawai'ian music, and people were sitting at long tables, eating and visiting. Some people were dancing on the open floor in front of the band. There must have been four hundred people in the room, people of all ages, all relatives of Lovey and the one-year-old child. Lovey scanned the crowd, lighting up as she spotted her husband and relatives. After she hugged her husband, she greeted and hugged the little grandchild who was being celebrated, and who was all dressed up for the occasion. There were tablecloths, bowls of fruit, and tropical flowers on every table, and many of the relatives were wearing home-made flower leis and flowers in their hair. Married women wear a flower behind their left ear, and single women wear a flower behind their right ear. Lovey introduced me to many in her large family. I think I met most of her eighteen brothers and sisters. I was thinking that this group would not be here today if it weren't for her mother and father having such a large family. This was the original eighteen and probably all of their descendants. What a family! They were all so gracious and friendly to me.

Ahh, I thought, this family has one very large gentleman amongst them, and he was heading our way. What a sweet face he had. If he were to hug anyone, they would disappear in the folds of his largeness. He gave Lovey a big bear hug and then she introduced him to me as her younger brother. I stuck out my hand to shake hands. But he took me by surprise, and gave me one big bear hug. Yes, he did have ESPECIALLY good vibes and BIG ALOHA, and for a brief moment I disappeared in the midst of his special *mana*. After meeting so many people I have to say I couldn't remember a single name, but I will always remember their kind and friendly faces. Lovey and her husband and I made our way to the buffet and filled our plates with *luau* pig, *lomilomi* salmon, poi, poki, macaroni-potato salad, rice, chicken long rice, *lau laus*, *haupia*, custard pie and coconut cream birthday cake. That was for starters, as there were many, many salads and side dishes.

Then the grand moment arrived and the one-year-old boy was taken up to the stage with the musicians, and talks and honors began. Gifts were placed all around on gift tables, and there was a birthday money box for the traditional donation gifts. This child was blessed and prayed for . . . to have a long, happy, healthy and beautiful life. Everyone conveyed their blessings on this one-year-old boy, and the atmosphere was filled with the *mana* of the *Aloha* spirit. What a beautiful tradition, I thought. I was so thankful to have been invited. It didn't matter to me or to any of the family that I was not part of this Ohana. If I was a friend of Lovey, I was welcome. I had eaten too much. Hawai'ian buffets were dangerous to the waistline and the hips. If I went to many parties like this, I would soon be calling myself, a "*Grosse Madame*."

### "*Iron Man*" Triathalon

"IRON MAN" IS ONE OF THE MOST FAMOUS Triathalons in the world. People from all over the world participate in it. Kailua-Kona is where the event begins and ends. This side of the island is served by the Kona International Airport and was once the capital of the Hawai'ian island chain. Later, the capital was moved to Lahaina, Maui, and eventually it was moved to Honolulu, Oahu.

I was never able to see this famous event. I did, however, see people training for it. I watched a few regulars swimming all the way to the monument and back in Kealakekua Bay. I saw people riding bikes up the Kohala coastline to Havi, and I saw a lot of people running. One thing I saw in these men and women, which they all had in common, was their muscular, athletic bodies. The event starts out with swimming in Kailua Bay. *Kailua* means "two seas," and the two currents can be challenging for swimmers. Then it becomes a bicycle race all the way through the Kohala desert to the town of Havi and back again. The third part is the running race. Since it is a world famous Triathalon, participants and spectators flood the Big Island for the event. It makes me think of King Kamehameha, who was able to lift the incredibly heavy Naha stone. He probably could beat all these contestants in all the categories. Except I don't think he ever had a bicycle in his day.

### The Bob Marley Kids

DOUGLAS CALLED ME ON THE PHONE from the health food store and said that a friend had given him two tickets to a concert with the Bob Marley kids in the Hilo auditorium. So he offered me a ticket if I would pick him up and take him there. We went, and it was a great concert. Once we got there, we went our own separate ways. He danced with many different people, and in groups of people, and I did too. It was a great vibe! About every other song was a Bob song and then the next song would be Bob's kids' songs, and so forth. It was easy to be right below the stage, if you danced. I could imagine the spirit of Bob Marley "over-lighting" the auditorium. Douglas was going to go out afterward with some friends, so I left alone when the concert ended. I wasn't used to being out at night. Seeing him laughing and having so much fun was a social side of Douglas that I had not seen before. It was fun to see, and it was a nice treat to have been given the free ticket, as I never get tired of Bob Marley's songs.

### "Bereft" – The Worst Day

IT WAS A WORK DAY AND MY JEEP broke down on the way to Betty's house. I had to have a tow truck take the car to a repair shop. At least I still had a valid AAA card. I caught a ride to Betty's house with someone I happened to know. It was a full moon on December 3rd, and it was one of those full moons that felt unsettled and chaotic, or at least it felt that way to me.

When Betty and I got into her car and started out, we heard a terrible grinding sound and HER car stopped running. Now her car was out of commission too! She knew someone who was driving to Waimea, so we moved all of our cleaning supplies out of her car and put them into her friend's vehicle. We must have looked comical with all our mops and brooms and dusters hanging out of the open-air jeep. But neither one of us was feeling comical. The full moon was magnifying our frustration. All day neither one of us was able to get into a very good mood. That negative energy set the tone for the rest of the day. Nothing seemed to go right, even with the house cleaning. Everything was like an hour glass that was turned upside down. Everyone has had a day like this once in a while, when everything starts out wrong. And then the irritable reaction and bad mood snowballs and gets worse. That was the kind of day we had. And as the Native American storyteller, Johnny Moses, says at the end of his stories, "And that is all!" . . . but that was not all.

At the end of the cleaning day, Betty was able to call one of her best friends who worked as a hearse driver for a funeral home in Hilo. After a long wait, he arrived in his big, black "traditional" hearse. He had time off from the job until someone died and needed to be picked up. I thought to myself, 'How appropriate that we would be riding in a hearse, like dead bodies, on this day from hell.'

Since neither Betty nor I had our cars, I asked her kind friend if he would mind taking me to the Hilo airport, where I was going to try to rent a car. This was not far off our route and he was happy to do this. But like the rest of the day, within five minutes I was denied a rental due to some glitch with my credit card. So I asked Betty's friend if he would mind the extra twenty minutes to drive me home to Hawai'ian Paradise Park. He was very willing to drive me home, but Betty said that she did not want him to go out of his way. I knew she was as frustrated as I was. So they dropped me off at the Hilo Walmart to let me figure out how I was going to get home. He looked at me rather apologetically, when I got out of the hearse. I thanked him. It was already dark, and the full moon was rising.

Outside, I found a pay phone and started calling everyone I knew. No one was home, or they weren't answering their phone. I even called my landlady, but she didn't pick up either. It was the Christmas shopping season and Wal-Mart was "decorated to the nines" with Christmas decorations. Local families were happily shopping with excited children in tow. They had a Santa in the store, too. Suddenly I felt that this misadventure, of coming here to Hawai'i, was a huge mistake. This had to be a fool's errand . . . and I was the fool.

I kept calling people, but with no luck. I was starting to feel homeless and bereft. The Christmas spirit was making me even more depressed. I should be home, I thought, with my own family, where I have a house of my own, a ten-acre farm, grown children, two tiny grandchildren, and a loving partner, who even agreed for me to take this "sabbatical." We both had felt that we each needed space to grow, and find out who we were "now," after the whirlwind and many years of raising five children. Somehow at this moment the idea of our 'finding ourselves as independent beings' felt stupid, foolish, and probably selfish too.

I was so down-hearted that I started entertaining dark fantasies. I even called home, and no one answered our home phone either. Even if despair and fears are fleeting, it can take us down many self-pitying dark alleys of thought. I was sinking into my shadow side, which was now rising up to meet the full moon. I sat down on a bench outside the store. I asked a few families if any of them were going to Hawai'ian Paradise Park or Pahoa. The answer was repeatedly, "No, so sorry," or "Good luck, sistah!" I called a taxi, but it never came.

The full moon was rising higher in the sky as time went by, and I actually had a good look at that full moon shining over Hilo, shining over Walmart's parking lot, which was spread out, filled with hundreds of cars, right in front of me. This was not a Hawai'ian bay filled with outrigger canoes and a shore lined with coconut palms. This was corporate America infiltrating this culture, with a fake Santa and canned Christmas music. I found it disgusting. Paranoia and negativity had sunk its teeth into me. I was not remembering Aka's teaching about negativity being food for bad spirits. I thought about all the honeymooners who come to the islands and stay in hotels on the water's edge. They gaze at the full moon, from their lanai, and feel the romance of Hawai'i. But when your energy is spinning in the wrong direction, in a negative vortex, you can feel as if you landed in the black underbelly of Hawai'i, with the beauty and magic nowhere to be found.

The full moon on this night did not feel friendly, or at least not to me. It was not my romantic full moon. It was simply a big body of matter, out in space, magnifying a bad day, breaking down our cars, and causing mishaps and dissension between Betty and I. And we had never had a whisper of dissension ever before. It had always been fun being with Betty each time we worked together. But tonight I saw the frustrated side of her which was a mirror reflection of my own. I was upset that she wanted me dropped off in the dark, when her friend was willing to drive me home. I had no easy way to get home.

In that moment I decided that I was done with this cleaning job and living on this side of the Island. The mold allergies were causing me trouble too. Was this decision impulsive or decisive, I wondered? Either way, I had just made up my mind. I need to get out of here, I thought. I already had mold allergies from all the rain and mildew, which often morphed into sinus infections. Kapua was helping me with Chinese herbs and acupuncture, but a mold allergy was still a problem. Kapua suggested that I move to Kawaihae, which is one of the driest places on the Big Island. He felt that I would feel much better. As a practitioner of traditional Chinese medicine, he said it was not healthy to have a constitutional damp condition and live in a damp place. It makes the underlying condition manifest damp illnesses, such as mold allergies and sinus infections.

As I thought of Kapua, I dialed his number in Waimea. He might have a solution or suggestion for me. I had already ordered a second taxi, but it didn't arrive either. Kapua didn't answer his phone, nor did Barrie Rose. Kapua, i.e. Edyson Ching (son of Eddy), had become my big brother, my so "da kine" Hawai'ian brother. Kapua's mother was native Hawai'ian and his father was Chinese. It was interesting how he had traits of both cultures. But this night he wasn't home. There were a few times when we rescued each other, during challenging times, or helped each other move, from place to place. I wished he would answer his phone. Even Rika, who rarely goes out at night, wasn't picking up her phone either.

I was making quick decisions in these dark moments. I had to acknowledge that this side of the island was not so good for my health anymore, even though I loved so many things about it. There had been many magical experiences here. Soon it would be time to leave. I would either go home or relocate to another part of the island. I made this decision to move right in this very moment, on this lonely bench outside of Walmart, as the Christmas music played on and on. Going back home to California, early, would feel like a defeat. I did not want to be a quitter. I still had not accomplished the experience, realization, or state of being that I had come here for. I thought to myself, "Tutu Pele is not done with me yet." My own dark underbelly was exposed to me. My "me-my" self glared at me. "I am half baked," I thought. I was not dough and I wasn't bread either. I started to cry. I hid my face and kept blowing my nose in a large cleaning rag that was in my backpack. No one going in and out of the store knew how much agony and despair was sitting, like a pitiful lump, on this bench outside. No one even noticed me, as the self-pity escalated.

I felt like a panhandler with no cup. But in the end this short episode gave me deeper empathy for the despair of lonely, homeless people. After about two hours and many trips to the phone booth, I finally was able to reach my landlady. Debra told me she had been taking a nap but would come to pick me up right away. I felt incredibly grateful to her. I knew I would offer her an extra massage or two for doing this big favor for me. I was so happy to see her car drive up in front of the store. I got in, and off we went to Hawai'ian Paradise Park, which was about thirty minutes away, depending on how fast one drives. She was my angel this night and her rescue was a big blessing. From that time until now I am thankful to Debra. I sighed a big sigh of relief and thought, "All's well that ends well."

When I got back into my cottage, I went to sit on my screened porch. The moon looked beautiful, shining on the big avocado tree and lawn right outside of my cottage. Gratefully, I thought, the full moon looks a lot better shining on this big tree than on the Walmart parking lot.

## "Whaht" Happened Yesterday?

THE NEXT MORNING, I WOKE UP FEELING "fabulous!" What happened to the self-pitying waif, the little match girl who cried on the Walmart bench in Hilo last night? She was gone, banished, transformed, and ready to make good on the decisions made with deep feelings, in dark moments. Yes, this crying person was going to move. Yes, she was going to quit the house cleaning job.

Leaving the close proximity of *Kupuna Pele* would be hard. Moving would not mean leaving good friends, for long. With a car, driving and visiting was not difficult. There was an influx of fresh, new energy surging through my body. The next adventure was about to begin and there was no more fear. Suspicions and dark thoughts had dried up with the morning sun.

What happened yesterday and last night, I wondered? This part of the purification that *Kupuna Pele* talked about in my dreams had not been understood yet. What created this cascade of negativity? And why did everything "go to hell in a hand basket" yesterday, one small obstacle after another, like a domino effect? They all seemed to loom larger and larger. The negativity escalated and, even symbolically, we took a ride in a hearse. Our vehicles were down, just as people's vehicles are down when they die, and then get transported in a hearse. So symbolically it all seemed like a kind of death.

Also the thought was coming to me that reacting, instead of responding, was another pitfall in yesterday's drama. We both got very upset that both of our cars broke down. What if we had responded differently and just chalked it up to a need for maintenance, with a timing that was awkward and inconvenient? If we had not both gotten so irritated and negative, the small mishaps at our cleaning jobs probably wouldn't have happened either, which only added fuel to our negative states. Aka always stressed that getting into a negative state and being angry, mean, or fearful is just "food for the negative entities" that are always floating around looking for their "fast food diet." I can remember a part of her prayer to clear obstacles: "*Ke Akua* (God), *Okie* (cut) and rebuke the forces that seek to diminish the light. Tie 'em up, bind 'em and lock 'em up. And *Ke Akua*, you do with them as you deem fit." The even-

207

mindedness that Tibetan Lamas, Hawai'ian spiritual teachers, and Native American medicine people teach and emulate was what we needed yesterday. But we also played off of each other getting more and more triggered and frustrated, until Betty became frustrated with me and I descended into victim-hood. Without negativity I'll bet I would have found a ride, right to my doorstep, from some nice local family. Or one of my friends would have picked up their phone and come for me, hours earlier.

But the negativity blocked everything from flowing. Positive manifestations could not come through this negative screen that I had created. Another thing I noticed about being in a negative state is that one reverts to self-centered narcissism. Everything becomes about "me" and "my" instead of "we" and "us." And what about the suspicions that came out under stress? This was not really the underbelly of Hawai'i, but my own underbelly: the dark, pain-filled side that usually hides in the unconscious mind, the sheath of pain that each and every one of us has . . . until it gets triggered, and we choose to locate and purify it. It is good at hiding, and it can sometimes leak out in various, more subtle forms: sarcasm, mean-spirited humor, cynical remarks, martyrdom, defeatist attitudes, complaining, or passive aggressive behavior. Aha, I thought. Now I am getting it! The next phase of this purification is locating the underbelly, having a much more acute awareness of how it leaks, and seeking to purify it. This was not about my cleaning partner, as she was just a "prop" or catalyst in this drama, as I was, for her. It was not my job to complain to her. We were mirrors of each other on that particular day.

I needn't focus on her or how I felt hurt in the moment. She had done many nice things for me, especially giving me a job when I really needed one. And we had had many good times and laughs together. We also shared stories of ancient civilizations and anthropology. It was time to be grateful that I was getting these clarities. And I knew these changes might take many more years to master. I wanted to talk this over with Aka and I was going to see her soon. I kept thinking about the lucid dreams of *Kupuna Pele* that had inspired me to come here in the first place. I had prayed for a chance to drink deeply of the essence of this culture. I prayed to her for guidance. In the dreams *Kupuna Pele* appeared dancing, in a fiery, volcanic orange cloud and invited me to come to live on the island. She told me I needed to come "for purification." I had no idea what that was going to entail. Now I was beginning to understand.

### Douglas at Makena Beach, "Slippahs" and Spoons

THE JEEP HAD BEEN REPAIRED IN THE SHOP and now I had a car again. Since it was such a beautiful day, I decided to go to Makena Beach. This was my friend Terry Walker's favorite place to swim with the dolphins, but the currents could sometimes be rough and often too tricky for tourists, unless they are really strong swimmers. Makena Beach is beautiful and sandy and was the place where Terry had most of her dolphin swims, as she lived on the Hilo side of the island. Terry had spent so much time bonding with the dolphins at this beach that she became quite an expert. She wrote several books about dolphins, and one contains the proper protocol for swimming with dolphins. She, being like a mermaid, introduced me to my very first dolphin swim in Kealakekua Bay in 1997. It was so special for me to have Terry by my side as guide and instructor that first time.

I looked, but Terry was not here today. There were locals sunbathing, stretched out on big beach towels. A few small children were making sand castles. Waves washing close to the castles filled their moats and threatened to wash the castles away. But the children didn't care. They were absorbed in play and imagination. I made my way down to the far end of the beach, and who did I run into but Douglas. We sat down on the sand and had a nice chat. He asked me if I loved the Marley family concert, and I told him that I DID love it. We went our separate ways at the concert, and I found myself dancing with groups of strangers throughout the concert. I was caught up in the mesmerizing music of these legendary Jamaicans. I thanked Douglas again for the free ticket that he had given me.

He went on to tell me that he often came to this beach and had a small *kuleana* (responsibility) here of helping visitors to know the proper protocols about the beach and the dangers of the currents. One, of course, was not dropping trash on the beach. Another was letting visitors know about the strong and somewhat unpredictable currents which were not far, offshore. He had a trash bag with him and had already picked up some trash from the beach. He said the local people appreciated him interfacing with the visitors, so "they" didn't have to do it. Douglas was always gracious and polite in the way he spoke to people, so I know any suggestions he made to people were done with Aloha.

His slippahs were lying next to him on the sand, and I noticed that they were badly worn out, and falling apart. I decided to surprise him. "Can you come to Hilo with me, Douglas?" He said, "Sure, what do have in mind?" It was a surprise! First I treated him to lunch and then took him to a store and bought him a new pair of "locals." To see his childlike excitement, you would think he got the best Christmas gift ever. "Well, it is not quite Christmas yet," I said, "but you are overdue for a new pair." He laughed and knew it was true.

When I took him home to his tree house, he invited me to climb up. On a bench opposite his work chair were his neatly laid out hand-tools. Some half-finished musical instruments were on a table. A few hooks on the wall sported his clothing. A nice big window looked out at the ocean, which was down the mountain, in the distance. There was a bamboo shade that could be pulled down in rainy weather. Douglas was a master of the tiny house and tidy housekeeping. A broom and dust pan stood in the far corner with a pile of wood chips and shavings. He showed me some new wooden spoons that he had just crafted. Each one was of a different kind of wood and each one was unique. "You know, I never cut trees down to make my spoons and instruments," he said. "I always use 'found wood' that I am guided to find." Then he said, "Merry Christmas," as he handed me three beautiful wooden spoons. "You will love using these when you go back home to California," he said. Well, I thought, he must know something that I don't know. What a treasure to have these hand-carved gifts from this pure-hearted friend.

### Rika and Storytelling

SINCE I WOULD PROBABLY BE LEAVING my cottage soon, I invited Rika over for one of our dinners and visits. After dinner, she settled herself into a comfortable wicker chair. My landlady had borrowed my CD player again, so we weren't going to listen to music or practice hula. Even though it had been a warm day, we were both sipping on cups of hot green tea. She asked me if I had ever taken anyone else to see the mural at Punalu'a Beach Park that Herb Kane had painted. She had introduced it to me the year she and I both managed Paleaku Gardens for a few weeks. I told her that I only took a few people whom I trusted to see it. I had taken my partner, Paul, our daughter Christina, her husband Rudy, and our grandbaby, Lilliana. Rika stood up and looked at the family photos that I had displayed on a table. The big green leaves of the banana tree outside the window cast a greenish hue on the photos. "Oh, your granddaughter and grandson are so cute. I wish I could meet them," she said.

She asked me how the family was doing, as she had already met Paul and our son Mike in the past. I told her that Paul was busy, as ever, running Blue Dolphin Publishing, and about all the umbrellas that I had sent to Lilliana. Then I told her what Rudy and I experienced when we took our family to see Herb Kane's mural in the old ruined hotel. I explained to Rika how Rudy and I both saw the miniature figures moving and speaking! The painted figures on the mural were speaking in the Hawai'ian language and moving around as if alive. When Paul, Christina, and baby Lil turned the corner to the mural alcove, the figures stopped speaking and froze back into position again, as painted figures on the mural. We both saw and heard this amazing transfiguration!

"Ahh, amazing!" she said, as she laughed. "The energy is so strong in that mural. I am not surprised you had this experience. I wish I could have been there with you. There's lots of magic here on the Big Island, and Herb Kane is a very special man. He's connected to the ancestors," she said.

Our grandson, Doc, had been born three weeks before I left for Hawai'i in 2001. I got a lot of pictures of him and his sister, Lil, on my computer through email. When I went to the computer and tried to get the pictures of Doc and Lil, with her umbrellas, to show Rika, somehow the computer froze. Both Rika and I tried to fix it, but neither one of us had any luck. Then Rika started asking me questions about our family's connection to the Western Shoshone native American tribe and our son-in-law's training for running the sweat lodge, and his Grandmother Eunice. Since the evening was young, I launched into telling her a story. Rika was always an avid listener and she asked a lot of questions. And that combination keeps a storyteller telling. I wanted to tell her the story of when Lilliana visited Hawai'i as a baby, the year before.

### *Flashback: Storytelling with Rika: Grandchildren (Mo'o'puna) and a Previous Trip to Hawai'i*

I OFTEN THOUGHT ABOUT MY FAMILY and my grandchildren. I have five children, three sons and two daughters, with my husband, Paul. All the children were grown up now and we were new grandparents. When I went to Hawai'i, everyone in the family said I would be paving the way, as the scout, and they would all move over, before long, to join me. Well, it never happened that way. We have a tendency to get tethered to our homes, jobs, and friends. Our granddaughter, Lil, was a little over two years old and our grandson, Doc, was just a few months old. I was missing their baby days, and I often packaged up gifts and mailed them off to both of them. Rudy and Christina were also raising Jeff and Johnny, Rudy's sister's boys. They were good big brothers to the little ones.

As a tiny girl, Lil was fascinated by umbrellas. At that young age she already had quite a collection of umbrellas, all with different colors and designs that I had given her. We have numerous photos of her smiling as she modeled different umbrellas, spin-ning them around above her head. She was beautiful, with long, curly black hair, tan skin and brown eyes. Her bright eyes were very intelligent and she had a strong but sweet nature. She seemed in every way to be "an old soul."

Our daughter Christina had married Rudy, who is a Native American from the Western Shoshone tribe. His family came from a colony (reservation) in Battle Mountain, Nevada. Lil looked Native American like her dad . . . but perhaps she looked a little like great grandma Eunice Silva, Rudy's grandmother who passed away three years earlier. There were signs that pointed to the possibility that Lil could be the re-birth of Grandma Eunice, but that's another story, and one that can never be proven.

### *Grandma Eunice, Western Shoshone Medicine Woman*

EUNICE SILVA LIVED TO BE ABOUT 111 years old, and she ran her last sweat lodge on our Nevada City property exactly a month before she passed away. She, and spiritual leader and medicine man Corbin Harney, had trained Eunice's grandson, Rudy, to run the sweat lodge, too. Eunice had been my spiritual and herbal teacher for the last five years of her life. She was also a recognized medicine woman who went to Washington D.C. as an elder-activist and representative of the Western Shoshone tribe. She had gone there in her full tribal strength, wearing braids and ribbon dress, and speaking out about the injustices of stolen Shoshone land, desecration of burial grounds, and the land rights of her people. Shoshone ranchers, activists, and sisters, Carrie and Mary Dann and their family, were good friends with Grandma Eunice Silva, her cousin, Grandma Florence Vega, and Corbin Harney. They and quite a few others were active in standing up for the rights of their people.

The Ruby Valley Treaty, which gave permission for white people to cross over Shoshone land, had never been officially broken, but it was not honored due to the white people settling on Shoshone land. These Shoshone elders insisted that the treaty be honored and that they be compensated for loss of land, mineral rights, and more. The United States has a shameful and habitual history of dishonoring the treaties they made with Native American tribes. These elders spoke up both locally and in Washington D.C. about lost grazing rights, nuclear contamination of their land by the Nevada Test Site outside of Las Vegas, Nevada, the seizing of sacred sites for mining on Shoshone land, and the desecration of sacred burial grounds.

Grandma Eunice was there to protest the disturbances and thefts of the burials of her own ancestors, her mama and her mama's mama, and farther back, who were buried at the ancestral ceremonial ground one hour outside of Battle Mountain, Nevada. It was called Rock Creek Canyon by the white people, but the Shoshone name was *"Bahzagohmbah,"* which means "otter waters." Her Shoshone name was *"Bahnzawoing,"* meaning "keeper of the otter water grounds." Even today otters swim in the creek there. Grandma Eunice truly was the keeper of the ceremonial grounds, along with her cousin, Florence Vega, who was also over one hundred years old. They had companioned each other through life and had some great stories to tell about when they were young in the late 1800s.

On Rudy's wall hangs a wonderful black and white photograph of Eunice and Florence, out in the desert, walking along with their botos. In the Shoshone language, a "boto" is a stick or cane. In their case the boto was used for both an aid in walking and also as

GRANDMAS EUNICE AND FLORENCE, PHOTO BY LINDA PUTNAM

a healing tool. The stick was made of a straight elderberry branch, which was gathered from a specific, very special elderberry tree on "Stevens" Mountain. The pith on the inside of the branch is soft, and dissipates with a little time, rendering it hollow. Grandma Eunice showed me how she uses her breath and blows through the boto onto different areas of the sick person's body reclining below her. I thought about the way the Tibetan masters use their breath for healing, blowing on a person, while praying. The Hawai'ians place great value on the breath also. I thought about the way Aka uses her Pu to blow on a person's chakra centers to balance their energy. Eunice was one to be reckoned with, as she didn't mince words. Her words had power. She could be wrathful without ever uttering a swear word. She was also a revered and renowned medicine woman and herbalist. All across the country, she was known for healing Native American people. She was especially famous for helping people recover from cancer, with her sweat lodge prayers and doctoring, and a bitter tea, made of several different plants.

Our grandson, Doc, looked a lot like Paul, with fair skin and brown hair. Rudy said, "I only have one son and he ends up looking like my father-in-law." However, Doc was named after Eunice's brother . . . Uncle Doc Blossom, who was also a medicine man, like his sister. Medicine ran in the blood of this family and, knowing the descendants, I can truthfully say that there are some very gifted people in this family.

### Lilliana's First Birthday in Hawai'i

WHEN LILLIANA WAS ABOUT TO HAVE her first birthday in 2000, Paul and I took our daughter, Christina, her then husband Rudy, and baby Lil to the Big Island for a vacation. Rudy had many "deja vu" experiences while he was on the island, and kept feeling he had lived here before.

### Auntie Fern Meets Baby Lil, at Kealakekua Bay

THE FIRST DAY, WE TOOK EVERYONE down to Kealakekua Bay to meet Auntie Fern at her shop. It was March and the whales were still in the waters offshore. The first thing she said to us, after "Aloha," was "Oh my goodness, she looks just like my daughter Aka, when she was a baby!" She oohhhed and aahhhed over the baby, and Lil gave her a big smile. Auntie Fern said again that she had never seen another child before that looked so much like her own child, Aka, at that age. We explained that Lilliana's looks came from her Native

215

American blood line.  She murmured to me that Lil was also connected to the Big Island and was a relative of their Ohana. This puzzled me, but she didn't say any more. I already knew better than to query Auntie Fern about details.

Auntie Fern picked Rudy out of our group and took him over to her van. She presented him with *The Book* of *Mormon*. "Be sure to read it!" she said. Rudy hugged and thanked her and said, "I will, Auntie."  As we drove away, Rudy said, "There is something about Auntie Fern that feels so familiar to me. I feel like I know her. This is really crazy. I am having *deja vu's* all over the place."

This particular day we were going to make a trip around the island, and Paul and I were going to play tour guide. Rudy recounted an experience and a dream that he had during the night: "Last night I was laying there, awake, and they came in the room and looked at me . . . just looked at me. It was really crazy." "Who was looking at you, Rudy?" Paul asked.

"Well, they were the spirits from here – you know, the old ones . . . the warriors," Rudy said. "They all came in and had a look at me. Boy, did I have goose bumps. I just laid there like this," he gestured with a stiff, stoic, reclining pose, arms held tightly to his sides. "They are really powerful and had those curved hats on!" he said. I asked, "Well, did they say what they wanted?" He said, "No, they just came to look at me. They wanted to know who I was. I think they recognized me from a long time ago." After Rudy told us about this night time visitation, he continued on, telling us about a dream he had later that night. "There is a man that we are going to meet today. He is waiting for us. We will meet him somewhere on our drive today. I will recognize him, from my dream, when I see him."

We drove south and went by the coffee fields of south Kona. Poincettas, bougainvillea and plumeria trees were blooming in people's yards along both sides of the two-lane highway. The flowers and coffee trees of south Kona gave way to the *ohia* forests, which then gave way to barren lava fields, as we approached the southern tip of the island.

### Soul Recognition and Reincarnation

WE STOPPED IN OCEAN VIEW, and then, as we approached South Point, Rudy said he had "chicken skin" again, and said he knew he had been here before, a long, long time ago. "I am sure I am getting this right," he said with excitement. "This is my old home, right down there at the very southern end of the island. I launched my canoe from there. It was a long, long time ago. And I had a twin sister too, that was waving good bye to me. Oh my God, I am getting so emotional. I can't handle it. I think I'm gonna cry," he said.

"Soul recognition, I thought to myself – the soul recognizes other souls and other places that we knew in previous lifetimes. It can be a powerful and emotional experience. I felt the same way in the islands, and also in Tibet, and in Italy, while visiting the home town of St Francis in Assisi. These were old homes that I knew and remembered. I had no doubt and I didn't doubt Rudy.

### Flashback: La Blanche in Tahiti . . . and Her "Deja Vu's"

OUR DAUGHTER, CHRISTINA, had a similar experience in Moorea and Tahiti, when she was sixteen years old. She told me that she was an island girl, so why did she have blue eyes, white skin, and blond hair, when she should have brown eyes, tan skin, and long wavy black hair? Christina was so pretty that the young men of Moorea gathered to catch a glimpse of her by the many small bridges that crossed fresh water streams on their way to the ocean. Christina's long, honey-colored hair had been bleached almost blond by the sun during the three months that we stayed on the island of Moorea. The young men were all playing their ukuleles for her when we passed by in our "*camionette*" (pick-up truck). She hung her head out of the window, smiled, and gave them eyebrow language. "La Blanche, La Blanche," they would shout, as we drove by to the sound of their quickly strumming ukuleles. They knew that we drove to the other side of the island each day. So all over the island the coconut wireless had proclaimed her, "Madamoiselle La Blanche." She had become a local celebrity without even trying.

I remembered that, when Christina was two years old, she practically busted out of her car seat with excitement every time she saw a palm tree when we drove through the Sacramento Valley. She waved her hands, tried to stand up and said, "My trees, my trees!" Now she was grown up and a mother, and she had brought her baby daughter to Hawai'i. As we continued our tour of the island, we passed the small town of Na'alehu. Rudy got very excited about this southern end of the island. "I could live here!" he said with excitement. We stopped here at a country store to buy a loaf of their famous zucchini bread, dotted with chocolate chips.

### Meeting Raymond at Punalu'u

WE CONTINUED ON TO PUNALU'U BEACH PARK, the Black Sand Beach, and the *heiaus* that were there. Christina and I pulled the picnic lunch out of the car. As we walked on the famous black sands of this beach, Lilliana pointed and cried out with excitement, as she spotted the big sea turtles basking in the sun. She pointed and laughed! She reminded me of her mother, when she saw palm trees as a baby. How fun to share this experience with my family and baby granddaughter.

As we walked towards a picnic table, a very large, bare-chested man started walking towards us. "There he is. There he is!" shouted Rudy. "That is the Hawai'ian man that was in my dream. He said he would be waiting for us. It's him, EXACTLY like he looked in the dream!"

The man came up to us, looking like he just stepped out of a Herb Kane painting of old Hawai'i, and said, "Aloha, welcome! I've been waiting for you." Rudy looked like he was going to pass out. No matter how any times spirit messages are confirmed, we always act surprised, as if it were the first time it ever happened. The man introduced himself as Raymond, and then we all introduced ourselves to him. After we talked for a while, he said, "This girl is very special, and I would like to have a ceremony for her today." He told us how important his culture was to him, and that we needed to go by the principles of nature and to let nature be our teacher. We needed to keep the old ways and traditions alive. Indigenous cultures could lead the way in this world in teaching conservation and caring for the land and oceans. He told us that he didn't travel much, as he needed to stay here, where he was born, where he had his energy nourished, and where he was protected by his *tutus*.

Rudy shared that he was Native American and had been taught to run the sweat lodge by his grandma Eunice, and by spiritual leader and "Indian doctor," Corbin Harney. Rudy told Raymond that nature was just as important to the Native Americans as it is to the Hawai'ians. And Rudy continued to say, "I am the prayer person, but my brother Santiago is an Indian doctor, just like Uncle Corbin, my Grandmother Eunice, and her brother, Uncle Doc Blossom. Rudy was tan with a strong, well-built body, and a curly pony tail that trailed down the back of his shaved head. He had deep, penetrating brown eyes, and stood tall and straight, like a Native American warrior of old. Raymond said to him, "Suck up the ocean, and we're all one people."

### Naming Ceremony for Lilliana Mahana

RAYMOND TOLD US THAT HE HAD LEARNED the Hawai'ian language and sacred chants from his *kupuna*. We spent more than an hour sharing back and forth with Raymond. Then he asked if we would permit him to do a blessing ceremony for Lilliana and a naming ceremony. We stood in a circle and held hands. The whole ceremony was in the Hawai'ian language. While Raymond chanted and prayed, a current of electrical energy circled through our hands. A feathery feeling touched the tops of our heads. Even the baby scratched the top of her head. A heavenly blessing, I thought. Raymond gave her the name *"Mahana,"* telling us that it was one of his Ohana's family names. He told us that the meaning of the name had to do with God's love and the warm rays of the sun.

Afterward, we shared our picnic with Raymond at a table near the *heiau*. After a while we heard a crack and the bench split in

half, tipping up like an up-ended teeter totter. Raymond rolled to the ground, in what looked like a slow motion martial arts fall. He got up, quickly rubbed his hands all over himself, gave a little shake, and said he was not hurt. When he got up, he smiled and said, "See how soft the Earth is?" Then he added, "My *tutus* said that, by cracking the bench in half, I was not to share too much more. Maybe I already said too much," he said, smiling a rather cryptic grin.

Well, much of what was said was in the beautiful, musical language of Hawai'i. We didn't understand the language, but we felt the blessing, and we were going to respect his *tutus*. He ended by telling us that *Mahana* had an ancient connection to this island, and that someday she would be back. She had a *kuleana* (spiritual responsibility or sharing) here, he said. Grandpa Paul picked up the newly named *Mahana*, and she smiled and laughed and reached for her grandpa's nose, the way babies do. Somehow, through divine guidance, she had received a very special version of the one-year-old "Baby Luau," which is a tradition celebrated for local babies on their first birthday. It was strange that Auntie Fern recognized her, and now Raymond had too. At a much later time I told Aka this story, and she brightened with a big grin and said, "Ohhh, you met my cousin Raymond. He lives in Pahala."

### *Puzzle Pieces Fit Together, Aka and Rudy's Ancient Memories*

AT A LATER DATE, WHEN AKA MET RUDY for the first time, she looked stunned. She told me that she recognized Rudy as her twin brother, from another life. "It was on the Big Island, which was, at that time, a part of the ancient continent of Lemuria," she said. And without any prompting from me, or anybody else, she told a story about waving goodbye to her twin brother, after she helped him launch his double-hulled canoe from South Point. "Chicken skin" was taking over my whole body, as it was the same story Rudy had told us a few years earlier. Later, when Aka met Lilliana *Mahana* for the first time, she said, "This girl looks like me. I am going to call her 'Little Aka'."

Aka did not know, at the time, that Lilliana *Mahana* had met Aka's mother, Auntie Fern, when she was one year's old. I told Aka that Auntie Fern had told us that Lilliana looked just like her when she was a baby. Aka laughed and said, "Wouldn't it just happen that my twin brother, from another life, would have a baby girl that looked just like me? Oh, we are all so interconnected in this web of life." So from that time on, Lilliana was not only called "*Mahana*," but "little Aka" too.

### The Mural by Herb Kane

NEXT, OUR FAMILY WAS GOING to pay our respects and honors to Tutu Pele by making flower offerings at the crater of the volcano. After that we would visit Hilo and the Hamakua Coast, before returning to Keauhou on the Kona side. But FIRST, I wanted to show them the

mural in the old ruined hotel complex next to the Black Sands Beach. This mural, painted by Herb Kane, depicted Hawai'ian people and

221

their daily village life before colonization. The mural, twenty-four feet wide, was perfectly intact and had survived the 1975 *tsunami* that

had destroyed the hotel. I always paid homage to these "real looking" old Hawai'ians every time I was in the area.

The mural depicts a double-hulled sailing canoe coming into the cove of Punalu'u, and on the shoreline there are chiefs and Ali'i

welcoming them. Warriors are standing behind them, and another man, carrying a *pahu* drum, is running to join them. In the distance is the Heiau. Behind the fish pond, which is directly behind the beach, are the *hales* (homes), constructed of bamboo, *lauhala* leaves, and pili grass. There is food and drink being prepared, and I am guessing that the men are preparing Awa drinks. Underneath an open shelter, people are eating or preparing something. A young man is fixing his outrigger canoe, and next to him is a white-haired *kupuna* with a cape of Ti leaves over his back, and he is sitting with a young boy.

We slipped into the building without anyone seeing us, as

there was a "No Trespassing" sign strung on a rope across the entrance. Rudy and I walked ahead of Paul and Christina, who was carrying Lilliana Mahana. We carefully picked our way over the broken pieces of concrete and wires that were lying all over the floors. As Rudy and I approached the little alcove where the mural was displayed, we heard voices . . . unmistakably . . . and they were speaking in Hawai'ian. Strange, who's in there? I wondered. We rounded the turn into the alcove and, to our shock, Rudy and I saw and heard the figures in the mural moving about and talking, like living people. We were tremendously shocked, but had each other to validate this very brief experience. It was a living, moving mural and brought to mind a book that I had read, as a child, called, *The Book of*

*Live Dolls.* Paul and Christina, who was carrying Lilliana in her arms, approached the alcove. Immediately, the Hawai'ian figures froze into position and were silent.

Paul, Christina, and baby Lilliana Mahana entered the alcove, but all was still. Rudy and I were in shock, but had each other to validate what we had witnessed for a brief time. We all studied and admired the perfection of the mural. Only after we got going again, in the car, did Rudy and I tell Paul and Christina what we had seen and heard. It was hard to believe, but it really did happen!

Our next stop was the volcano. We would have Lilliana Mahana throw a bouquet of flowers over the ledge of the volcano's crater, as an offering to Kupuna Pele.

My pretty Japanese friend, Rika, had been smiling and nodding during the telling of these stories. There were a few times when her eyes got big. Now she and I both began to yawn. Before she left for home, I gave her a bag of ripe star fruit. The tree outside of my cottage was loaded with this pretty fruit that looked like a gold star when it was sliced. I hated to see the fruit wasted, as so many of them were falling on the ground. "When you get your computer to 'unfreeze,' please show me the pictures of your grandchildren and family pleeeese," she said.

# MY STAY ON THE HILO SIDE NEARS AN END

## The Computer Rescue

I DROVE TO DOUGLAS'S TREE HOUSE early in the morning so that I could have fresh roasted coffee with him and his crew of friends. A few people were already sitting around drinking coffee and talking story. The sun was slowly rising in the east and casting little sparkles all over the ocean. There is nothing quite as lovely as sunshine on the water, and the little glints that dance around like jewels on the vast blue expanse. It was a long way to the east to touch California and my family. I had a lovely morning meditation just sitting and watching the sunrise with a mug of coffee, sweetened with Honaka'a natural honey. Life felt very sweet. It had become more simple being in nature so much of the time, and I found it created a feeling of clarity and peace.

I often stretched out on two plastic floaties, "noodles," at the Warm Pond and meditated in the soothing water. I put one noodle under my knees and another under my neck. Then I could just float and go into a blissful, empty space. It felt as if ions and lifetimes of stress was releasing from my body. If unpleasant images or feelings arose, I would breathe them out, with a long sustained breath. I also loved swimming in the ocean and always felt like a mermaid.

For years, Paul and I and our children had our vacations in Hawai'i, on the Kona side. Much to Paul's distress, I was known to swim far out in Kealakekua Bay or Honaunau Bay and stay for over two hours. Paul said to me one time, "You were just a little dot out there. And then I couldn't even see you anymore. You really worried me." I had to promise not to do it again. It was easy to get into the zone beyond time and space. This was especially true when the dolphins approached me to swim together. I had learned to float long ago as a teenager, in France, while living outside of Toulon, on the seashore at a place called Rue Fort Sainte Marguerite, Cap Brun. The secret of "not getting tired" was to swim and then float, with total relaxation. With just a few little movements of the hands, under the water, a person could stay afloat and rest on the surface of the ocean or the sea. If the water was not too choppy or icy cold, it was possible to rest this way for quite a long time. When there is no stormy sea, this is a good thing to know about, and it can be life-saving. I did not swim during storms or right after storms, as there could be a dangerous rip tide and undertow. I learned this at our sandy cove in France when I was thirteen. A strong man had to pull me out of the undertow on a sunny day right after a storm. However, when floating, there is a tendency to drift, up or down the coast, if one is not paying attention to landmarks on shore. And with currents I learned to swim cross-current, instead of directly into them. I remember that Aka had to tell visitors numerous times not to stand on a rock on the edge of the ocean. More than once a rogue wave came up to wash a visitor into the ocean. If the person got caught in an undertow or couldn't swim, they could drown.

How could I ever live without the ocean? I wondered. It seemed like I was totally bonded to the ocean and the dolphins and whales. When I was a small child, I had many dreams of swimming with dolphins and whales, our eyes gazing at each other as we swam along together. Auntie Fern and Aka were right about getting in the water and using the salt and water to clear the energy . . . and the Pu and the breath to clear the channels. I had not forgotten what they had shared with me, and I was being mindful of practicing and clearing. I remember how Aka forgave the man who killed her pet pig. She never held a grudge, or ruminated about what someone may have done to hurt her. "Let it go," she would say. Or she would say, "Ohhhh, poor ting!" about someone who was mean-spirited. A grudge would have been a storm cloud sitting on top of her shining sun, and she liked to keep the sun shining on everyone around her, as well as herself. She was a happiness generator!

Again the thought came, "Don't waste the wisdom of others, by not listening or following their wise advice." To have people like

Auntie Fern, Aka, and her sisters in my life was an incredible blessing. And all the other "cast of characters" were a blessing too. They enacted every imaginable archetype, even the difficult ones. Being in the water much of the time was helping me get into more sustained relaxed states. Even at the risk of getting wrinkly "prune" hands, I stayed in the water for long periods of time. It was a lovely place to muse or just go empty without thoughts. When a thought would arise, I might follow after it or maybe not, just resting in the natural state of the mind. It was easier to meditate in the water, than on land, for me. Having this time away from family was also a chance to discover how I manifested in the world, without the enmeshment with others influencing the outer manifestations of life.

When the group sitting around the morning campfire dispersed, I asked Douglas if he knew anything about computers. He laughed, and said they were not a part of his lifestyle any more, but that once upon a time he was good with technical things. Ahhh, I might be in luck. "Would you mind coming over to my place and having a look at my computer that 'froze'?" I asked. "No, I don't mind. Do you still have a surplus of starfruit?" he asked. "I would love for you to take some off my hands," I said. I had a huge bowl of them in the kitchen and a lot of them were frozen in the freezer, sliced as starfruit popsicles. And there were more that were dropping to the ground.

### The Deal Breaker

So, OFF WE WENT IN THE JEEP. Douglas had never been to my place before. We went into the cottage. It took him about three minutes to unfreeze my computer. I thanked him and slipped a bag of starfruit into his backpack. He asked me if I would give him a ride to Pahoa, as he wanted to meet a friend. We left right away. As we were walking towards the jeep, my landlady came out of her door, yelling and screaming at us at the top of her lungs. What a shock! She screamed that I needed to get this hippy off her property immediately! "Don't ever, ever, let him come over here again!!!" she shrieked, at the top of her lungs. She went on and on, having a full-fledged tantrum.

227

We hurried towards the jeep and drove away. I was mortified that she would insult my friend. Not only that, but he was clean and tidy and did not really look like a hippy at all. He had a pony tail, but lots of people had pony tails. We had been very quiet, and we stayed for no more than five minutes. She and I had no written rental agreement. As a tenant, I paid rent each month with a verbal arrangement which, up until now, had worked out quite well. She had never told me that I couldn't have guests over to visit. And a few friends had visited me here at the cottage before. My friends had been as quiet and respectful as I was, and she never complained. I felt totally bewildered.

An emotional assault is always worse, when a person is "wide open" and vulnerable, like after the morning's meditation. Once when I was giving a *lomilomi* massage to my landlady, I asked her if she had ever been to Green Lake. I told her that Douglas had taken me there, and I asked her if she had ever met him. She said she hadn't, and it was also unlikely that their paths would have crossed. What could be angering her so much? I wondered. I felt upset and sad at the same time.

Could I do it, could I do it, I wondered? Could I be like Aka and just "let it go," or say "Poor Ting," with sincere compassion? At this moment, I could not. The tantrum and hurtful words were too painful for me to stay here any longer. It would now be goodbye to this beautiful arboretum that surrounded the buildings, dozens of palms and tropical fruit trees, the white pineapple patch, the papaya trees, the stately old avocado tree, and the banana tree at my window that housed my little gecko friend who visited me every evening.

While driving to Pahoa, Douglas said to me, "I don't think you should live there anymore. This isn't a good environment for you. You have no freedom, with a person treating you like this." I apologized to him for the hurtful words she said about him. He said, "Water off a duck's back, for me. You're the one who was the target." I told him that I was thinking it was time for me to move over to the other side of the island. "Well, if that works best for you. But if you need to put a tent up on my land for a while, you're welcome." I thanked him for his generosity, but said I was pretty sure it was time to go over to the Kona side. If I wavered before on this decision to move, now I was sure.

I continued feeling stunned by my landlady's behavior. It was getting close to Christmas, and I knew that her husband would be coming home soon. After several months off-island on his job, he usually had a few months to be home. Maybe she wants the cottage back for him when he gets home, I thought. It definitely could be a nice "man cave." But, what a way to get me to leave! I had been a good tenant, keeping the cottage clean, being very quiet, paying my rent promptly, and fulfilling the trade agreements that we had arranged. How differently the day began, with my musings about relaxation and clarity and all the blessings of this journey. How fast the weather can change. I wondered if clear, pure, happy energy could act as a catalyst to provoke an angry person into a rage. It was like a lightning strike on a blue sky. Life had a weird way of crashing a rogue wave onto oneself, when one is vulnerable or in a happy, blissful state of mind.

I felt like I got caught in an undertow and was being swirled around and pulled out to sea and then washed back in again. Tumbling violently in the breaking wave, I would have to use all my strength to crawl out, against the tug of the current, to sprawl, exhausted, on the sand. I thought of the advice of Hawai'ians, "Never turn your back on the ocean." I had been vulnerable this particular morning. I had turned my back on "the ocean" and got knocked over by a rogue wave. I often forgot, in my prayers, to pray for divine protection.

Aka and Auntie Fern told me that "protection" was an important thing to include in our prayers. I prayed every night for my family and loved ones to be protected, but I often forgot to pray for myself. For me, prayers are positive thoughts, intentions, petitions, and visualizations for manifesting positive results. I believe they are heard, in the unseen worlds, by divine beings. I have a few friends and family members who are atheists or agnostics. However, by their kind actions I recognize them as spiritual. They may find that essence in nature. Usually we can agree that God or no God, afterlife or no afterlife, life and death are in the realm of "the great mystery."

By the law of resonance, the thought forms that are projected out by intentions, visuals, and prayers often bring back to us, or to others, the intended results for what we are praying for. There is the often unexplainable "dead reckoning" that a navigator of the ancient canoe culture uses to steer his canoe "into the box" or destination, without instruments. The mind, heart, prayer, and knowledge of the stars and the ocean are the instruments.

I thought of Aka's prayer which always asked, *"Ke Akua,* blanket my loved ones, near and far, those connected to me, by blood or by heart, with your divine love and protection. Clear any darkness, seen or unseen, conscious or unconscious, from my loved ones here. *Okie* (stop, end) the forces that would seek to diminish the light. Nurture in them, *Ke Akua,* all that is good and life giving. *Mahalo nui loa Ke Akua. Mahalo nui loa."* I knew that Auntie Fern Pule, her daughter Aka, as well as my family at home, all prayed for my safety and well-being while I was here on the Big Island.

### Finding the Tiare Flowers and Saying "A Hui Hou" to Kumu Dane

I WENT TO HILO TO DO SOME ERRANDS and, on this day, there was a light rain instead of one of Hilo's downpours. I walked past the old theater and remembered the play I had attended not long before. It was a play about a *Maori* grandmother and granddaughter. It was intriguing, as they spoke mainly in their native language, and the grandmother was transmitting stories and songs to the grand-daughter. At the end of the play there was a huge applause from the audience and the shouts of *"hana hou, hana hou,"* which roughly translates to "one more time" or "encore, encore."

I dashed around doing my errands in the quaint back streets of this old port town. Very few people were around. Then I realized it was Sunday. I noticed a hedge of Tahitian Tiare flowers around the grounds of the newspaper office. I got so excited seeing these deliciously fragrant, five-petaled, white flowers all over the trimmed hedges of the *tiare* bushes. They reminded me of our stay in Moorea. Knowing that the rain would brown them, I started picking them and put them carefully in a bag. Their fragrance was heavenly, much like a gardenia.

When I had a big bag full of these deliciously scented flowers, I went to my car and headed over to Desmon and Stacy Haumea's house. I knew that Kumu Dane was teaching a *Lomilomi* class there this weekend, and I thought the students may want to make leis of the flowers during their break-time. When I entered the classroom, the students were weaving *lauhala* mats, as Kumu Dane had invited a cultural specialist to demonstrate the technique. Kumu Dane came over to me and told me to join in and make a mat for myself. He was always the epitome of generosity and hospitality. I offered him all the *tiare* flowers. He poured them out and we put them in a shallow plate of water to keep them fresh. "Ahhhh, don't they smell so fragrant?" he said.

I told him that I was planning to move to the Kona side, and I wanted to thank him for sharing so much with me – the *Lomilomi*, the voyaging canoe, and so much of the culture with his old-time Aloha. These soul family connections are precious, I thought to myself. I quickly remembered how, a little less than two years ago, I had met Kumu Dane, Luther, and Desmon in Maui after they had sailed on the Makali'i into the harbor in Hana. I thought how one thing can lead to another, and then another. What blessings! This trouble with my landlady was just "small kine" as local people say in pidgin. The blessings were far greater than the troubles, or the *pilikia*. My heart felt full and happy thinking about that day in Hana

231

with our son, Mike, when the Makali'i anchored in the bay and we happened to meet Kumu Dane, Luther and Desmon. What an auspicious meeting, and what good brothers both Kumu Dane and Desmon had been to me.


## Flashback: Remembering Tandem Lomilomi Massages with Auntie Angeline in Kauai

I THOUGHT ABOUT WHAT KUMU DANE had said one time about how we would have a happier world if everyone was able to get massage. His Long Life *Lomilomi* teachings had reached many, many people from all around the world. There were lots of people who were now certified massage therapists who had taken his classes. That made me think of the rapid healing I had had from Kumu Dane when I had such a very stiff, painful neck. I too believe in the enjoyment and healing that massage gives to people.

One year when Paul and I were in Kauai, we decided to have a four-handed *Lomilomi* massage. We drove to Auntie Angeline's in Anahola, but we didn't know exactly where it was, as the directions were, "If you get to the Kilauwea lighthouse, you have gone too far. You may have to pass the town of Kapa'a . . . and then look for a papaya orchard on the right, and you have found it."

Auntie Angeline's name is Angeline Kaihalanaopuna Locey. She was a Hawai'ian *Kupuna* (elder), which literally means "wellspring," and *Kumu*, teacher of *Lomilomi*. She had studied and worked with Auntie Margaret Machado. In recent times Auntie Margaret was the most famous *Kumu* of *Lomilomi*. She had a school of massage and healing on the Big Island of Hawai'i in Kihei. Her motto was that *Lomilomi* was true "loving touch." Now that Auntie Margaret has passed away, the school in Kihei is being run by family members who were trained by her.

Auntie Angeline, an elder herself, was strong and healthy and wore a wide smile. Her demeanor was very sweet and humble. After arriving at her place, we were ushered into a hexagonal building where we undressed and laid on benches in a small screen-house which was being infused with steam. But unlike most steam baths, this steam was neither hot nor cold. It was the perfect neutral temperature and our bodies felt good, dripping from the mist. We reclined on the benches and listened to soft Hawai'ian music as it blended with the hiss of the steam.

After some time of drifting with few thoughts, we were called and shown to two unadorned massage tables with plastic covers, on the outside deck. Here we were vigorously massaged with a blend of red clay earth, oil, and red Hawai'ian sea salt. This was to cleanse and purify the pores and exfoliate dead skin. It felt wonderful, and this part of the treatment was slightly abrasive, brisk and stimulating. Then we were sent back to the steam room completely painted, to recline on the benches again and steam for at least another half hour or forty-five minutes. The next step of this delicious treat was being led to outdoor showers on the deck to rinse off all the salt and clay and return to the massage tables.

Each of us had two masseuses. I believe Auntie Angeline's daughters joined her, and she spent time with both of us . . . with an additional *lomilomi* massage person in order to make up "four hands" each. Then the great bliss began, with four hands sweeping long, deep strokes up and down the body, covering every square inch, modestly and gracefully avoiding private areas. Generous amounts of oil were applied, creating easy access into tight spots and a smooth glide up and down the body. The two people were so in sync with each other that it sometimes felt like one person with many arms and hands. Forearms, elbows, fists and knuckles were used on the tight areas. Percussion was used: rhythmic hand-cupping, lightly pounding fists, and chopping with the sides of the hands. Sweeping open hands opened rivers of *mana* inside the energy channels. There was no difference in style, pressure, or vibration between the two practitioners. It all just flowed like ocean waves, or perhaps more like the hula, graceful and languorous . . . pleasurable, soothing, yet at the same time, awakening.

Now there was surely something more than massage going on here, as deep, radiant warm heat started percolating up from the core of our bodies along with the deepest feeling of peace and relaxation. The heart chakra unfolded like an opening flower bud, and loving feelings, with no inhibition, started flowing outward in all directions. "Ah . . . we ARE all one. Love IS everywhere, really! I do love everyone," I kept thinking.

This part of the massage was given with generous pourings of oils with tropical fragrances, so that the four hands could slip and glide and make long, deep strokes up and down the body from the toes to the shoulders and neck . . . then long strokes down the arms, to the hands, and ocean waves on the belly. From time to time a slight breeze came up and the fragrance of nearby *plumeria* flowers teased my nose with their lovely aroma. When we were positioned face down, there were long, deep strokes up and down the back. My back became eager for more. It was the unrelenting desire of "massage greed." "More, don't stop," the back seemed to say, as if it were an entity separate from myself. The oil soaked deep into the layers of the skin, moisturizing every surface.

A spontaneous long, deep sigh took me into the center of relaxation. Now this is how a human being is meant to feel, I thought. Finally, this bliss came to an end, and the four women, wearing oily *mu'u mu'us*, led us back to the showers for a rinse off and then off to the dressing room. Oh, how wobbly I felt, and I could see that Paul, too, was pleasurably "out of body," saying Mahalo to his two *wahine's Lomilomi*. When we were dressed, we said a grateful goodbye to Auntie Angeline and her helping massage angels. I expressed that I would love to learn to do *Lomilomi* and how much I would love to learn from her.

She said, "You just did, by having this massage. Remember, everyone is beautiful, and you love every cell of their body. You infuse them with Aloha." Then she said I would learn from her some day. (Jumping ahead . . . years later, she came to our home in California with one of her advanced practitioners, Ann Lemieux, and taught a four-handed *Lomilomi* class in our converted barn in Nevada City, California. The request was answered.)

Standing in the parking lot after this transcendental experience, we were trying to decide who was grounded enough to drive the car back to Kapa'a. Neither of us felt able, but we walked around a little until I felt I could drive safely. Paul was "smooshed" and in such a state of relaxation that it lasted a long time afterward. He had trouble tying his shoelaces. Hawai'ians usually wear slippahs (flip flops). For Paul, driving was not an option.

# An Io Hawk

I WAS ON MY WAY TO VISIT KAPUA, Barrie Rose, and Jeannette up in Waimea. They had found a short-term job for me. It would be living-in and care-taking an elderly man in Kawaihae for a month or so. If I wanted the job, I would go to meet him and his house-cleaning ladies, who were interviewing prospective caregivers. After this I planned to go to visit Aka, and her mother, Auntie Fern, at Kealakekua Bay, and Barbara DeFranco at Paleaku Peace Gardens. As I was driving up the windy road of the Hamakua Coast, I noticed an Io Hawk flying a few feet from my car window, right alongside of me on the driver's side. It was rare enough to see an Io Hawk, but to have it flying next to my car was really astonishing. I kept expecting it to disappear any second, but it kept pace with me, as if we were flying together in formation.

Aka had shown me the Io Hawk in the past and told me that it was very special, and that it was rather rare to see an Io. In addition, her own name was Haleaka Iolani, "Iolani" meaning "heavenly hawk." So the Io hawk was an *Aumakua* for her.

It had already been several miles and the Io was still flying beside me, keeping perfect pace with whatever speed I went. How strange, I thought. I had heard stories that powerful *kahuna* can send their astral body into a bird, especially an Io hawk, and embody it for some purpose . . . like looking or watching something from a distance or protecting someone. Or it could be a messenger, or a blessing from an *Aumakua*. Native Americans I had met told me about a similar belief, as did Tibetan Lamas.

I had no idea what it meant, as it was so unusual. If it was a messenger, I was not getting the message. I knew that it was a special blessing though, and I said, "*Mahalo,* brother or sister Io. You are so beautiful. *Mahalo,* for your blessing." My prayer was inspired by Aka's many daily prayers of appreciation. Finally, the Io flew off in another direction, leaving me completely in awe and wonder.

## A Care-Giving Job in Kawaihae

AFTER VISITING KAPUA, BARRIE ROSE AND JEANNETTE in Waimea, Kapua told me he would come along in his car to be there when I met the older man named Ray. His house was on a hill overlooking a small cove near Kawaihae, which was noted for hosting whales that sounded during the night. It was also close to Spencer Beach, which was one of my favorite swimming beaches.

Ray was in his nineties, and he looked a lot like my father. He was over six feet tall and had very thick, bushy eyebrows that perched like two bird nests on top of his glasses. He used a walker and had a scowl on his face, as he had stage-three cancer and was in pain. He was still able to get to the bathroom and was able to shower and dress himself.

He would need meals prepared for him, and someone to be around during the night and most of the day, except when he was napping in the afternoon. He would need someone to run his errands, shop, and drive him to his doctor appointments. His home was very nice, and there was a swimming pool in the back yard. His wife had died a few years earlier. He had a large, friendly dog that wanted to jump up on me and lick my face. If I decided to take this job, I would have a nice private bedroom and bathroom. And I would be paid too. This could be the perfect place to recover for a while from the mold allergies that inflamed my sinus. I decided to take the job.

## HOLOHOLO KONA SIDE


### *Kealakekua Bay: Seeing Aka and her Sister, Kalehua*

THIS WEEKEND I DID NOT FIND AKA at the shop, but was told that she was at Honaunau Bay, over by Pu'uhonua o Honaunau, the City of Refuge. Aka's older sister, Kalehua, was at the shop this time with her mother, Auntie Fern. Aka's sister showed me the jewelry and *lava lavas* that the family made, and we talked for a while. She was sometimes called "Miss Aloha," as she was so full of Aloha, smiles, and humor. She was also named "Fern," the same as her mother.

Kalehua had a delightful musical laugh, and her eyes were lit with love. Why does everyone in this family feel so familiar to me? I wondered. I teased her, asking her if she was "Fern" today, or "Kalehua"? The full name was Kalehuamakanoe and it was a very powerful name. It was the same name as her mother's. She told me that it translated to Fern in English. But Kalehua was the shortened version of the name. At times I called her "Fern" and at other times I called her "Kalehua." Sometimes I felt that her "Miss Aloha" persona was "Fern," and her powerful *Ikaika wahini* (strong woman) persona was "Kalehua." Aka's daughter Suzy had been gifted with the same name as well. Fern always took to teasing very well, and she teased me back. But if she needed to "stand and deliver," she would instantly become Kalehua. And I came to know the difference. She, too, was "a receiver" like her mother and her sister, Aka. But each of them had their own style. Over time I came to realize that each member of this family was gifted, each in their own unique way.

There was a lot of laughter and fun with this family, but there was also a very serious side. The oldest sister, Wanda, and her husband Jerry Iokia and their family lived on Oahu in the old family home. Three other sisters, Lisa, Lehua, and Kela lived on the Big Island with their families. One of Aka's brothers lived in Oahu and one lived on the Big Island. It was a big family and a very close and spiritual one.

JERRY, NANCY, WANDA, AKA

## Hawai'ian Names

IN INDIGENOUS SOCIETIES, especially the Hawai'ian and Native American, names have powers and carry *kuleanas* or spiritual duties or responsibilities. There are times when names need to be changed, if a given name is too powerful and creates illness or obstacles.

There are stories of a serious illness disappearing when a name that is too powerful or not appropriate is changed. The famous hula dancer, Auntie Iolani Luahine, Aka's great aunt, had to have her original name changed. While she was a child, she had a serious eye disorder which cleared up almost immediately when her name was changed. The hawk has wonderful eyesight, so being given the new name of Iolani (heavenly hawk) empowered her eyesight to be healed.

Haleaka Iolani's (Aka's) name never needed to be changed. She was recognized by Auntie Iolani Luahine, her parents, and other gifted seers as a *Kapu* child, a sacred child, one who would bless the people, one to be protected and prayed for so that no negative forces could interfere with her destiny.

In another story that I heard, a baby was given a very powerful name. The baby had repeated convulsions and was in threat of dying. A seer in the family divined that the child needed to have her name changed. As soon as the new name was given, the convulsions stopped immediately. *Pupuka* means "ugly or unsightly," and sometimes babies and puppies are called *pupuka*, even though they are really seen as sweet and cute. Babies may be spoken to sweetly while they are being called "*Pupuka*." Oral traditions from the past believed that, if you called a baby "*pupuka*" (ugly or homely), bad spirits would not be attracted to them and bewitch them. Aka's very beloved dog and sidekick was named "Pupuka." I didn't understand why, until I learned about this tradition which was a carry-over from the old days. I have talked to Hawai'ians who strongly believe in the power and appropriateness of names that are given to Hawai'ian children. It is all very mysterious to Caucasian people. One local friend of mine said that she was aware of quite a few infant and toddler deaths which she felt could have been avoided if their names had been changed. This might seem like superstition by the dominant mainland culture but many Hawai'ians believe in the power of names.

### *A Chat About Family History with the Two Ferns*

"AKA WAS NOT REQUIRED TO DO HOUSEHOLD CHORES," said Aka's older sister, Fern. The oldest sister, Wanda, was in charge of the house, the kids, and the chore list, when their mother, Auntie Fern, was at work. She was only a child herself, but took on adult responsibility. Their mother, Auntie Fern, was a police matron in Honolulu. Wanda took good care of little Aka and all the other children, and was a great enforcer of the chore detail. There were lots of kids, and Wanda was in charge of making sure everyone got their work done "before Ma got home." In this house, if one person didn't do their chores, the whole gang would be in big trouble. Aka's sister, Fern, who was eight years older than Aka, once told me about a time when someone was supposed to wash the dishes. That day the dirty dishes were piled into the cabinet under the sink. "When Ma got home and found what had been done, oooooooh, we all had to line up, and we were all in trouble," she said.

When Auntie Fern was pregnant with Aka, she had dreams of her daughter before she was born. She knew she was carrying a *Kapu* (sacred) child. This child was never to wear hand-me-down clothes. All of her clothes needed to be sewn for her, even her bathing suits and underwear. Aka was exempt from chores, as she was not required to be a part of the work crew. As soon as Aka could read, she devoured one book after another, as she was intrigued with learning everything! She was interested in everything and was so *akamai* (smart). All of Aka's brothers and sisters knew that Aka was special and gifted. Perhaps she would have the God-given power to bring the heavens down to touch this earthly realm someday. She was destined to have many different kinds of gifts which would manifest as time went by and as she matured.

### Another Visit with Auntie Fern

IT WAS NOW ANOTHER DAY and I had a craving for *lau laus* from

Ka'aloa's Super J's restaurant. I brought two plate lunches from Auntie Janice, one of the owners of Super J's, to Auntie Fern down at Kealakekua Bay. We sat and ate our lunch and watched the bay from the chairs outside Auntie Fern's shop. "You know," she said, "I taught Janice

some tricks about making *lau laus*. And now she does a good business with them." I had never known that before and was a little surprised. Auntie Fern said, "We had a *lau lau* business over on Oahu and all the kids helped."

Today was unusual as Auntie Fern didn't ask me to jump in the water and wash the "buggahs" off. Besides, I didn't have my bathing suit on this day. She said, "It's a shame you never got to meet my mother. She was a very wise woman and she knew so much about our culture. When Aka was very young, we sent her to live with Tutu. That, of course, was my mother, Matilda Makekau. Grandmothers are called *tutu,* or *kupuna wahine* in our language. She was also called Tutu Pua. Wanda spent several years with my mother. She took our *kapu* child under her wing and taught Aka a lot about the old culture and spiritual things.

"Her house was right here in Napo'opo'o. This house was just a short walk from the shop here. Auntie Io (Iolani Luahine) lived there too and some other aunties. Through some misfortunes we lost the land. That's a long story and we won't go into that. The house isn't there anymore. It was torn down and there is another house there now." Fern looked a little downcast when she told me about losing the land and the house.

Aka had once made a rather cryptic reference to their family home and land that was lost. This was obviously something very sad for the family. Aka always had thoughts of trying to get the land back, but she said that it would have been too entangled legally. Something had happened, but it was never made clear to me. And I didn't want to be *niele* (nosy). But little by little I was hearing about Aka's childhood from different family members. At this point a group of tourists came up to look at Auntie Fern's wares, and she got up to greet them. I thanked Auntie Fern for sharing these stories, and said good bye, "*A Hui Hou,* Auntie!" Her little dog, Pule, tried to follow me to the jeep, but Auntie called him back. Then she turned her attention to the tourists, who were fingering her colorful, hand-sewn clothes hanging on racks in front of the shop.

I DROVE SOUTH, DOWN THE RATHER RAGGED ONE-LANE ROAD to Honaunau Bay and Pu'uhonua o Honaunau, also known as "The City of Refuge." This narrow road was close to the ocean, but heavy brush obscured the view. It had dips and ruts, and I had to be careful to pull way over when an oncoming car approached. There were about four miles between Kealakekua and Honaunau Bays. The *mauka* hillside rising on my left was bare except for brush and had been the topic of discussion by the *kupunas*.

I thought of Auntie Moana Kahele (Mona Kahele), who knew every square inch of this South Kona landscape like the back of her hand. She knew the old place names of beaches, bays, villages, and old trails. Trails were used *mauka to makai* (upcountry to seaside) during the old days. But travel by water in canoes was the most common way for the local people to get from one part of the island to another. Thank goodness, Auntie Mona has shared her vast knowledge of the history of this South Kona region, or it might be lost today. So many place names have been changed just in her lifetime.

I found Aka at Two-Step. She had just gotten out of the water after a swim. She shook her wet hair and wrapped her red lava lava around her wet black shorts and sports bra. Then she walked across the lava to give me a big wet Aloha hug. "You wanted to cool off, didn't you, sistah?" she said with a laugh.

"Now I don't need a swim to cool off," I said. "I just had lunch with your Ma," I said. "Did you spoil her, bringing her a *lau lau* lunch again?" Aka asked. "Yep," I said, "and she really told me a lot about your childhood today. She told me how you went to live with your *tutu* right here in Napo'opo'o." "Oh," Aka smiled and said, "Did she tell you why they sent me to live with my tutu?" I said, "Yes, because you were a *Kapu* child, and you needed to be trained in the old ways, and there was some issue with electricity."

"Well, that's a big part of it," Aka said, "but as a little child I was blowing up the electricity in the house. My *mana* (spiritual energy) was too strong for the lightbulbs. I think I blew up the toaster and some other things around the house too. This started, they told me, when I was in my crib. Well, there's something else I should tell you. Don't let me use your computer, as I have a bad track record with them too," she said, with a long, loud laugh. "My own computer is okay, because I talk to it 'real sweet', and then we get along just fine."


### *Learning from Tutu Pua (Grandmother)*


"MY GRANDMOTHER TAUGHT ME SO MANY THINGS about the old ways," Aka said. "She was a Makekau and a sister of the famous Hula dancer, Iolani Luahine. We called her Tutu Pua, but her English name was Matilda." Aka looked nostalgic and was quiet for a minute, before saying, "I really miss her, but she visits me from the spirit world, and perches on my head when she wants to talk. You see, there are times when my ancestors talk to me or through me." Aka then told me that her grandmother had passed away when she was a teenager. She continued the story by telling me that "Tutu took me to the forest, up *mauka* (up country) to gather plants. Some of the plants were used for medicine and healing. We gathered flowers, ferns, and greenery for *leis* and head adornments. We collected grey green strands of a moss-like plant which is called 'Pele's Hair'." Aka always had a lot of it hanging in long strands from a clothes line around the outside of her house.

Most Hawai'ian homes are bordered with the sacred *Ti* plant. Some were green and others burgundy red. Aka and her grandmother also gathered the protective Ti leaves in order to weave and braid them into *leis*, and wrist and ankle bracelets. Aka said, "The Ti plant is a protector, and that is why my 'grandmudder and dem' taught me how to use these plants for their special protective

medicine. Almost every Hawai'ian home has a Ti plant hedge growing around it, and this tradition continues today. Having Ti plants around the house was common for both the *Ali'i* and the *Kanaka* in the old days. *Kanaka* is the true name for Hawai'ians. It is what they called themselves before colonization. Later we were called Sandwich Islanders and then finally, Hawai'ians.

"Auntie Iolani Luahine, better known as Auntie Io in our *ohana*, as well as Auntie Helen and Auntie Rosalie were there, too, some of the time," Aka said. "Auntie Io was gifted in a special way, as the ancient Goddesses danced through her. She was a trance dancer, 'a receiver', or 'mystic' as we say. Her body was a vehicle of ancient Hawai'ian sacred dance for the Gods and Goddesses. She was particularly close to the goddess of dance, Laka, and the volcano goddess, Kupuna Pele. She danced *Kahiko* (old style of *hula*), clicking stones between her fingers and sometimes using two sticks to create her rhythm. Then there were *hulas* that required the *Ipu Heke* drummer. The drummer sat on the ground, with a drum made of two *Ipu* gourds, cut and precisely glued together. The *Ipu Heke* drummer counted out the rhythm. The first drum beat was hit on the floor and then the next two were made with the hand on the drum. 'Ummm pah pah, Umm pah pah. . . .'

"Tutu and I worked with the gourds that were used as *Ipu Heke* drums and calabashes. *Pu's* were made from large bamboo, and *Pueos* were made from small crafted coconuts. Earth drums and nose flutes were made from both large and small bamboo. Big gourds were used for cooking and storing water and food in the old days. The *kanaka* would put hot rocks and water into the gourd and food was cooked in this boiling water. The people had gardens and fields that grew in the middle lands above the ocean and below the forest. This was the farming region. They grew pumpkins, squash, sweet potatoes, taro, breadfruit, gourds, and other vegetables. Many of the farming families grew a small patch of sugar cane too, long before C&H and other sugar companies were on the islands."

### *Two Favorite "Canoe Foods"*

"THERE WERE MANY, MANY *ULU* TREES (breadfruit trees) in this middle region too," Aka said. "This area was the breadfruit belt. This region was a half mile wide and eighteen miles long and there were thousands of breadfruit trees. Breadfruit is so delicious and nutritious, and can be fixed in so many ways. It's a real survival food, just like *taro. Kalo*, or *Taro*, the root that produces *poi*, was grown in the region too. They said that thousands of pounds of both taro and *ulu* were produced there. Breadfruit and t*aro* are two of the canoe foods brought here from the early Polynesians around 1200 A.D. They also brought the pig, chicken, and dog. Breadfruit was a main source of nutrition just like *taro*. We still eat both of these foods today. They're both 'onolicious' and 'ononutritious'! Remember when I brought you fried *ulu*, and *poi*?" I did remember and I loved both of them.

I told Aka that I loved breadfruit and liked it best roasted in hot coals. Christina and I had eaten it when we were on the island of Moorea. I mentioned the old breadfruit tree that I had admired on the grounds of the iconic Painted Church on Painted Church Rd. "Tutu said that the breadfruit forests helped bring in the rain to this agri-cultural region of Kona. Now most of these trees have been cut down, and there is less rain because of it. It's really a shame. Isn't it interesting that trees can have such a big effect on the weather? Everything is so interconnected in this web of life. Because of inadequate rain, many families here on the Kona side have large, round catchment tanks on their property to gather rain water. In the old days, rain was collected in large gourds and sometimes stored in large bamboo.

"Relatives in the Waipio Valley grew our *taro* (a.k.a. *kalo)* and they got their *poi* by pounding *taro*. You've probably seen the stone *poi* pounders, right?" Aka asked. "Yes," I said. Aka looked at me with a mischieveous look and asked, "Got *poi*?" I said, "Absolutely! It's always in my fridge." I noticed that a lot of local people asked each other, "Got *poi*?" with big smiles on their faces. It was definitely part of the local diet. I guess I was a rare *haole*, because most *haoles* don't like *poi* unless they add a lot of sugar. But I liked this smooth fermented pudding.

### *The Dolphin Crowd*

THE DOLPHINS WERE USUALLY IN EITHER Kealakekua Bay or Honaunau Bay. Both bays were known to those who swim with the dolphins, as the dolphins like to be in either of these places during the day. They like to be in shallow bays during the day, which is their rest time. People would ask, "Where are the dolphins this morning? Where's the pod?" Sometimes the dolphins would swim a little farther south and be in the waters off of Ho'o'kena Beach. But they could show up anywhere along the Kona coast.

There were people who had web sites who scoped out where the dolphins were each morning, and then posted the information on their site. Many of the dolphin swimmers, with their snorkels, masks, and flipper fins would then make a bee-line to the location. Cars would fire up their engines and caravan down to the current dolphin location. But the dolphins don't live with appointments or schedules, so they could be gone by the time the crowd arrived.

Sometimes some of the dolphin swimmers reminded me of the 49er miners in the gold fields of California, frenzied to find gold. I had mixed feelings about swimming with dolphins. Of course I loved swimming with them too, and I understood their enthusiasm. However, it felt as if the dolphins were being exploited and harassed all too often. Aka and her mother felt the same way. Some people were very respectful, but some others were not. It was great fun for people, but there were some downsides for the dolphins.

Kealakekua Bay was also a birthing ground, or nursery, for these *nai'a* spinner dolphins. It is their bedroom, as dolphins sleep in the daytime after hunting at night. That's why they usually return to relatively shallow bays early in the morning. They sleep one hemisphere of the brain at a time. Often they would swim in a circle in pods of about thirty, coming up for air every few minutes, and sometimes to leap and spin. But most of their sleep takes place in the daytime. To observers they don't look like they're sleeping, as they keep swimming and breathing as they sleep. At night they go out into the open ocean to fish, where they feed on mackerel, bait fish, and squid.

Aka told me that, due to the harassment by some tourists and kayakers in the bay, and "dolphin swimmers" who try to chase or grab them, the population of the dolphins had seriously diminished. When a dolphin does not have the peace to sleep, they can be tired when fishing out in the ocean at night. A tired dolphin is more vulnerable to shark attacks. She also told me that, when she was a child, there were hundreds and hundreds of dolphins in the Bay, and there was still a sandy beach next to the Heiau.

Hawai'ian people do not generally seek out swimming with the dolphins. If a dolphin approaches them, while they are swimming or out fishing, then that is considered a natural encounter. But swimming out to follow dolphins or swim amongst them, grabbing for a fin, or trying to touch them, was something they would never do. Auntie Fern scolded people from time to time and gave them stern advice about letting these beautiful creatures have their peace, to rest. "Kealakekua Bay is a *nai'a* (dolphin) sanctuary and nursery, and they use this bay to rest and birth their young!"

### The Night Marchers and Fireballs

I HAVE HEARD STORIES of the *Huaka'i po,* or "night marchers," who are sometimes called "night walkers." The night marchers are a troop of ghost warriors walking across the land, at night, in certain places, and on certain historic trails on the island. It seems there are certain places to stay away from at night, as one does not want to encounter these spirit warriors, from what I've been told. These stories are not concocted to scare tourists or mainland residents, as many local people have seen them over the years.

Fireballs are also mysterious manifestations. Different things are said about them, but what I have been told is that a practitioner of *ana ana* (praying someone to inflict harm or death) can send a fireball to target someone they wish to harm or kill. Locals told me that in the old days, if you cursed, long and loud at them, they would dissolve. There are stories about people feuding in the same village sending fireballs back and forth to each other's homes. And the cursing would blow up the fireball before it hit the house or family. If this is true, it must have been some kind of dark sport, like black-arts dodge ball. However, these rare stories are exceptions to the rule, as *Aloha* and shared cooperative living was what characterized the *kanaka maoli*.

Most local friends have said that these dark arts are no longer practiced in modern times. I would guess that things like this rarely happen. During this year I did actually see a fireball. I was visiting a family in the up-country coffee fields. We all saw one flash by on the road in front of their house and continue down the road. It was round, the color of fire, and was larger than a beach ball. Some stories tell of *Kupuna Pele* moving from one Volcano to another in the form of a fireball. It is said that there is often a volcanic eruption of the volcano that the fireball moved to, either immediately or within a few days.

I do not pretend to know the truth about fireballs, but they are phenomena that quite a few people on the island have seen. Actually there is probably nothing to be feared if one is "*pono*" (good), has a good heart, and travels on this island with respect for both the seen and unseen worlds. Just to be sure though, bring out your loudest and worse curse words if one is heading your way. There are so many stories of fireballs that one can't totally dismiss them. Ancient peoples of all cultures had people who knew the esoteric arts, both good and bad.

On the Big Island things get quiet early in the evening. Except for Kailua Kona, most people turn in early and don't tend to go out much at night. I always had a feeling that Hawai'ian nights belong to the spirits and that people belong inside at night. I felt more respectful than scared, but I did value my intuition that led me to avoid nighttime excursions. When I did go out driving at night, I always had the feeling that the air and land was thick with spirits, a feeling I don't have back home.

## Aka Reports About Visiting Japan, and The Timing of the Earthquake

I DID FIND AKA AT HONAUNAU BAY. She was sitting in the shade and got up and gave me a big Aloha hug as I approached her picnic table. As usual she was working on a craft project, a small coconut shell which she had carved into a *Pu'eo* nose flute. In the Hawai'ian language, *Pu'eo* means "owl," and the sound of this small, traditional flute is like the hooting of an owl. She put the flute up to her nostril, and with her breath, she made the soft, hooting sound.

"Well, sistah Nancy, where have you been? When are you moving back to this side?" she asked. I gave her an update and told her my plans. She was happy to hear that I would be moving closer. I told her about the Io hawk that had flown along the side of my car, for a number of miles, on my way over here. "No matter if I sped up or slowed down, that Io kept right beside me on my left and would make eye contact with me. It really was so unusual, and the hawk kept pace with me for a number of miles," I said.

"An Io is always a blessing, sistah, and I have it on the highest authority that our *Aumakua* are protecting you," she said. And no more was said about it.

Aka was wearing her sports bra with a *lava lava* (sarong) tied across her chest. I asked her about her recent trip to Japan. "Remember how we all got in the water and prayed about it before I left?" she asked. I remembered very well. I was upset about the construction project also. It was slated to be condos and a golf course. She launched into the story, first telling me of seeing Japanese friends, teaching workshops on *Ho'o'ponopono*, and making many good connections. "So many Japanese people love the Hawai'ian culture," she said.

She told me that a Japanese corporation was indirectly invested in this large building project, which was slated to be built just *makai* (downhill) of a nearby town. The developers seemed to ignore the fact that there was a large burial ground on this hillside and below. The *Ivi* Committee (bone or burial) had met a number of times, outraged that corporate power was infringing on the cultural and spiritual rights of Hawai'ian people. Auntie Mona Kahele had spoken to me, passionately, about this, and so had Auntie Fern.

Aka went on to tell me that, when she was in Japan, she addressed the board of directors of the corporation. She paraphrased the talk that she had given to them. I believe she began her public address with a chant and a prayer, which was her custom. She then gave a history of the proposed construction project and how it was desecrating a large burial ground and some sites that were sacred to the Hawai'ian people.

The bulldozing had already begun and bones had been unearthed. Aka asked them how they would like it if someone from another country started to dig up their grandparents' graves in order to build a luxury condo development and golf course? That question seemed to bring the issue home to them.

She continued her talk with her usual eloquence. I had noticed that when her *tutus* were "perching," her speech became unusually eloquent. There was never any pidgin in it. It also helped that she had attended law school in Arizona. She could keep up with the best of the lawyers with her quick wit and sharp intelligence, as well as her sensitivity to culture and tradition. She knew a lot about Japanese traditions, so she appealed to the board members with analogies that related to their own culture.

As she came down the elevator of the tall building in Japan, she noticed a lot of security guards standing around in the lobby when she got out on the ground floor. She had no idea why they had been called in. She was not trying to incite a riot by speaking to these board members. But maybe they thought that she was seeking

251

publicity about the issue. I wondered if there had been an article in the Japanese newspaper about Aka's visit.

Just as Aka and a few friends left the lobby and stepped outside the building, a strong earthquake shook the building she had just left. She and her friends steadied themselves and held on to each other . . . as the ground shook and the building swayed.

The many security guards looked at her with wide eyes, as if Tutu Pele herself had just given the building a good shake as a big exclamation point to her talk! After all, this Hawai'ian woman had wild hair, wore a red *lava lava*, and was a formidable woman who could blaze fire out of her eyes . . . when it was needed. Her size, compared to most petite Japanese women, was also impressive. Aka's unforgettable image, reminiscent of Kupuna Pele, had just emerged from the shaking building when the earthquake began. The timing of it made the security guards look at her with trepidation and awe.

After she told me this story, she said that she thought the corporation was going to pull their investment out of this project. She had a good feeling about it. "At least it has gotten the ball rolling, even if it takes a few years to stop the project."

### *Birds as Vehicles for Spirit Visitation*

LATER, I LEARNED FROM AKA, her daughter Suzy, and her sisters, Wanda and Kalehua, that the cardinal bird is often the vehicle for the visiting spirit of one of their *tutus*. She said it was always a happy thing to see a cardinal and she called it "Tutu." Whenever Aka saw one, she would say, "Oh, Aloha, Tutu. You are so beautiful! Look at you! Mahalo for visiting today! And of course seeing an Io Hawk is a great blessing too," she said, giving me a knowing glance. In her melodious voice she thanked the birds, the flowers, the trees, the ocean . . . everything . . . for being so beautiful, for being so "life giving." I was starting to realize that her life was a walking prayer. Later she shared that loving and being a part of all of nature's beauties was part of the teaching of *Ho'omana*.

Aka's walk was a walking hula, graceful and gracious, and at one with nature. Yet, as a large, full-breasted woman she was tall and strong as a warrior. She had a posture that was straight and tall, which spoke of confidence and determination. Later when she came to the mainland and needed to buy shoes, she found out that she wore a size thirteen shoe. At home she was either barefoot or wore "slippahs." She asked me, "How can you pick up the grounding energy of the *aina* wearing shoes? The feet are for absorbing the grounding earth energy." I laugh now, remembering how we would both compare the bottoms of our feet with each other. Both of us had thick "shoe leather" callouses on the bottom of our feet from going barefoot as much as we could. "We dance barefoot," Aka said. "We are connecting with our sacred *aina* with our feet. I often think of Auntie Io and the gracefulness of her *hula*. I can imagine that watching her was like seeing the Gods and Goddesses come to life."

Aka would tilt her head and smile a big smile with laughing eyes, and her hands would swirl and twirl, as if dancing *hula* with her Auntie Io. Sometimes she would dance the *hula* so gracefully, with or without music. She truly was Iolani . . . the heavenly hawk, descended from *Kahuna nui* and royalty, and in the ancestral line of her Auntie Iolani, the magical Hula dancer.

### *Auntie Io . . . Iolani Luahine*

IOLANI LUAHINE (HARRIET LANIHAU MAKEKAU) WAS BORN on January 31, 1915, in Honaunau, Napo'opo'o, the Big Island of Hawai'i. She was sometimes called, "The high priestess of Ancient Hula," or the "last handmaiden to the Hawai'ian Gods." She was the youngest of five girls but was *hanai'ed* to her great aunt. She first studied with this great aunt, Keahi Luahine, who was her grandmother's

sister. This great aunt was a well-known *Kumu Hula* (*hula* teacher) and dancer in Honolulu, who followed the ancient Kauai school of Hula. She was a descendant of many generations of court dancers on the island of Kaua'i, who performed at sacred ceremonies for royalty and chiefs. She was also invited to be a royal dancer for King Kalakaua and the future Queen, Lili'uokalan'i and their court. It is said that even King Kalakaua danced *hula*.

During Iolani Luahine's university days she studied *hula* with Mary Kawena Pukui, who was also a student of her great aunt, Keahi Luahine. Iolani Luahine taught *hula* and performed in many places. George Na'ope (1928-2009), a famous Kumu *hula* and traditional chanter, was one of her students in the art of pantomimic *hula* dance. He later founded the Merrie Monarch Hula festival that honors the last King of Hawai'i. This festival takes place in Hilo every year. Later in life Iolani Luahine was a historian and a docent for the different royal palaces, both on the Big Island and on Oahu. She was a curator of the Hulihe'e Palace in both the 1950s and the 1970s. She was a dancer, chanter, and teacher of *Kahiko*, which is the ancient form of *hula*. In 1972, she was named a "Hawai'ian Living Treasure," before leaving this world on December 10, 1978.

I knew that Aka's graceful walk, and the way she led *hula* lines with visitors, were inspired by learning *hula* from her famous Auntie Io. As some people break into song, Aka often broke into lovely dance and melodious prayers. Her sparkling eyes, big smile, and hugs could fill anyone with healing *mana*. There was nothing self-conscious about her. She was vibrant, happy, and natural. Her laugh could be deep and raucous, echoing good fun, a good joke, or just "plain enjoyment." When I would ask her, "How are you today, Aka?" she would always say with great gusto, "Fab...ulous!" And she was. And then she would say, "And sistah, how are YOUuuuuuu . . . the real you? How are youuuuuu?"


### *Swimming with Aka in Honaunau Bay*


"LET'S GO GET IN THE WATER and wash dos buggahs off," she said, laughing and mimicking the words that her mother always said to me. She could move back and forth effortlessly between the

254

eloquence of the King's English and local *pidgin*, and sometimes a mixture of the two. I was wearing my swimsuit under my clothes, so I quickly took the clothes off and packed them into my beach bag. She took off her lava lava and was ready to swim, with her black shorts and black sports bra, a quick and ready-made swimsuit. We walked over the lava to "Two-Step," scooted down, one lava step at a time, and jumped in the water, making a huge splash, just as a big wave washed out.

The water was chilly at first but very refreshing, as we splashed around like two breaching whales. But then we glided and dove down . . . to the underwater world of kaleidoscopic beauty. The light beams on the water created different shafts of reflecting light, and everything moved and shimmered. Incoming waves re-arranged the water, shifting our vision of the underwater landscape. The diverse and beautiful reef fish and clusters of coral broke up into prismatic shapes and colors, for brief moments, and then cleared. We found the large sea turtles, on the south side of Honaunau Bay, swimming together in a group of five. We drifted amongst them, without bothering them in the least, and they were not afraid of us.

### *Visiting the Honu (Sea Turtles) with Aka*

WHILE WE WERE SWIMMING, we found the large sea turtles close to the canoe launch. They were feeding on algae a little farther out, in water that was over our heads. This is where we usually find these large and old *honu*. Aka was looking for something and examining the shells of each of the turtles, without touching them. They swam beside us, their flippers moving slowly and gracefully, and with their ancient eyes looking directly into ours. Again the proper protocol is important to know. "Do not touch the sea turtles. Do not harass them by chasing them, and do not disturb or move them when they are sunning themselves on a beach."

Aka was only looking, and not touching. It felt like we were in a totally different realm among these beautiful, large *honu.* Aka's long, salt and pepper hair streamed out behind her as she swam like a mermaid amongst "the old ones."

After swimming for a while, enjoying the beautiful colors and shapes of the reef fish swimming below us, we swam over to Two-Step and got up and out of the water. The help of a gentle, oncoming wave helped to wash us up onto the first step. Before that wave pulled us back out again, we quickly climbed up to the second step and onto the shore. When it came to waves, timing was everything. After our swim, we walked over the swirled *pahoehoe* lava – once molten, but now cooled into hard, rope-like ripples – to the picnic table. The table was shaded by a tree. Dogs, without obvious owners, wandered around this area, looking for a hand-out or discarded

snacks. A Hawai'ian flag, anchored to the *lanai* of a house on the north end of the bay, flapped in the breeze. The soft, sweet Kona breezes felt like being kissed and cleansed at the same time. Bells and chimes tinkled softly in the distance from someone's breezy lanai.

Aka let out a deep, hearty laugh when she saw me bringing star fruit out of my beach bag. "Sistah, what are you doing to those star fruit trees, over there, to make them produce so much fruit?" She laughed as she said everyone would think of me as the star fruit lady, if I didn't "change it up."

So I pulled out one of my giant avocados and we quickly devoured its delicious green fruit. "Ah, so *ono!*" she said. She had a bag of dried fish and squid and some rice and *poi* in her bag. She liked that I learned to eat with my fingers when I was in Tahiti.

"Fingers and hands are for eating. Who brought forks to the *Kanaka* (people), anyway?" she asked, arching her eyebrow as she laughed.

We both continued to eat our lunch with our hands and fingers. Aka's hands were wide and long and were the hands of a healer and wise woman. They were the hands of a Hawai'ian *Ali'i*, an old one come back. These hands had been busy all her life, farming, fishing, healing, dancing, cooking, sewing, gathering, crafting instruments and *leis*, holding her beybeys, caressing these beloved children, and petting her many dogs.

And how could I forget the big *Aloha* hugs these hands and arms gave, and the love that emanated from her wide open heart. And these hands could shake out a good "*shaka*" too. We shared and ate all the food that we had, with our hands and fingers, without leaving a morsel. Between us, we never had "leftovers." I wondered, whoever dreamed up forks and spoons, anyway?

### Aka's Honu Rescue

WE BEGAN TALKING ABOUT THE SEA TURTLES, and Aka reminded me of the legend of her people arriving on the Big Island on the back of a flying *Honu* (sea turtle). I asked her if it represented a star ship and she nodded. "Yes, we come from the stars. Actually, we are very connected to the Pleaides," she said, raising her eyebrows three times in rapid succession. "The flying Honu arrived on the island, which at the time was Mu (Mo'o), or as we may have heard it called, the legendary continent of Lemuria. During my life I have seen plenty of these star ships around Kealakekua Bay. Some say that there are star beings buried up on the top of Mauna Kea. I have seen ships many times, in various parts of the island," she said. I said, "Well, how could we assume that we are alone in the Universe?" "Right," she said, "we're not." She got a faraway look in her eyes and was quiet for a while. "Someday I will return to the stars, when my *kuleana* (spiritual responsibility) is complete."

I told her that I noticed her looking carefully at the shells of the *Honu*, while we were swimming in the bay. Again she nodded. "I was looking for the *Honu* that I rescued some years back," she said. She began to tell me her story. She found a *Honu* with its shell badly cracked. Somehow she was able to take it home and set it up in a kiddy swimming pool. She went to the ocean every day to harvest 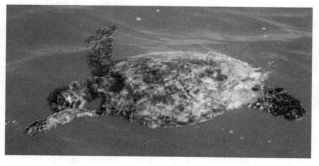 algae for it to eat, and she worked on healing the *Honu* over quite a period of time. People told her that the shell would never be able to heal, and that with a broken shell the turtle couldn't live for long. She wouldn't believe them, as she believed in healing and miracles. Finally, the shell of this *Honu* did knit back together again . . . and when it was healed, she took the *Honu* down to the ocean and set it free, to find its *ohana*. Sometimes she would see it, swimming with the other *Honus*. "It was bitter sweet to let it go, as I had become attached to it, but it belonged with its own *ohana*."

### *Aka and I Dream up a South Kona Ice Cream Factory*

"TOO BAD IT'S NOT MANGO SEASON," Aka said. I know you love mangos, sistah!" I said, "It always seems that I miss mango season every year that we visit." "How's that?" she asked. I replied, "That's because we usually visit in February and March." Then we got talking, discussing one of our favorite ideas, which was starting a Kona Ice Cream factory, featuring tropical fruits, nuts, and coffee. It would make use of the local fruit and nuts, and the many unused "falls" – fruits that hit the ground or are wasted. Aka and I thought it would be great if it were run by local youth that needed work after high school.

Aka began to talk about how we shouldn't waste food, and then followed it by a conversation that we would often have in the future – the idea of an ice cream factory, run by the local youth, and making use of surplus tropical fruits. We sat there thinking up single flavors and flavor blends, and pretty soon we had made ourselves hungry for ice cream. It was such a warm day that it sounded SO good. "How 'bout chocolate, coconut, macadamia nut ice cream?" she said, pursing her lips together in a kiss and smooching the air. "Or some of this white pineapple sherbet? So many mangos, passion fruit, bananas and mac nuts go to waste."

You could sometimes see wild pigs in the Mac orchards eating up the nuts on the ground. They also hung out under the large, old avocado trees eating avocados. She said, "My kids, Ola, Lilinoe and Suzy, can run the factory and be in charge. They're so *akamai* (smart). *Mo'o'poona* (grandkids) can take it over from them, 'laytah.' I'll be there to sample the ice cream." It could help support their *ohanas* (families) in the future, and even help fund the "Mission Aloha" land.

We mused and salivated, creating flavors with our imaginations: Chocolate-Macadamia Nut, Coconut, Coconut-lime, Banana-Macadamia nut. Banana-Chocolate, Banana-Chocolate, Mango-Lilikoi, Lemon-Lime ice, Starfruit-Papaya, Mango-Lilikoi, Coconut-Mango, Kona Coffee-Chocolate, Vanilla-Macadamia nut, Chocolate swirl with Chocolate, Kona Coffee-Chocolate and Coconut. "Oh," she said suddenly, "How 'bout Nancy's Starfruit Gelato?" "Mmmmmmmmm," we both said, tasting the wonderful flavors, virtually, with our imaginations. It was a fantasy, of course, but a fun fantasy.

### *Paleaku Peace Gardens*

THAT EVENING I ARRIVED AT PALEAKU PEACE GARDENS just in time to make dinner with Barbara. I loved this kitchen because, instead of glass windows, it was a framed-in screen room with a roof. Tropical foliage and a small *koi* pond were right outside the kitchen door. The breezes always felt cooling while cooking. There was a long table in the kitchen, covered with gaily decorated oil cloth. The refrigerators and food storage "cubbys" were behind the kitchen in a large pantry.

I really liked and respected the way Barbara organized her center. People on retreats and residents had to wash, dry, and put away their own dishes and clean the sink traps. In my house, at home, family rarely remembered to clean the sink traps. It is an annoying task when left to only one person. This was a brilliant protocol and it worked seamlessly. Barbara was not harsh but she commanded respect, and her guests followed her rules.

This beautiful evening, we joined a yoga class on the open, covered platform after dinner. The spectacular Kona sunset cast golden light on everything in the garden, as we did our stretches and postures. The class ended with a guided meditation, just as the golden hour gilded everything a crimson gold, which slowly morphed into soft shades of pink and gray.

This spot of magical beauty was a teaching and learning place, with Tibetan Lamas, Hawai'ian cultural experts, and with other visiting teachers. The big covered platform was also where Barbara, Cindy, Rika and I had taken Hula classes with Kumu Hula Peccelo Day.

There was also a shrine room with a Tibetan Buddhist altar and thangka paintings hanging on the wall, which depicted deities sacred to the Buddhist tradition. Some very prestigious Tibetan Lamas had visited and taught at Paleaku Peace Garden. Namkai Norbu Rinpoche taught the sacred dance of the Vajra here. Lama Tharchin Rinpoche and Lama Thinley Norbu Rinpoche had collaborated on sculpting a life-size statue of Padmasambhava.

GURU RINPOCHE, PADMASAMBHAVA, IN NEVADA CITY

Padmasambhava, also known as Guru Rinpoche, was the miracle working, lotus-born saint who was the first to bring Buddhism to Tibet from India. He was also renowned for ridding Tibet of trouble-making demons. He converted them into wrathful guardians of the Buddhist faith. We have a similar, life-sized statue of Padmasambhava on our land in California (above), which was sculpted and empowered by the Nyingma lama Chagdud Tulku Rinpoche in 1984.

Barbara and I shared a love and appreciation of cross-cultural spirituality. We always thought it was an interesting coincidence that we both – Barbara, and Paul and I – had sponsored statues of Guru Rinpoche on our land, hers in Hawai'i and ours in California. Hers was looking west towards Tibet and ours was facing east towards Tibet. But, as the world is round, I guess either direction would lead to Tibet. The whole intention of these empowered statues is to broadcast universal peace, compassion, and blessings to all beings everywhere on this earth, and beyond, into unlimited space.

Paleaku Peace Gardens had an art studio too. Two artists were in residence at this time. One of them was our mutual friend, Kaaren Soby. Kaaren was from Canada and, on this journey, her husband stayed home to tend the homestead. Kaaren and I called ourselves the "toilet dakinis" as we laughed and joked while we were doing our work trades at Paleaku Gardens. Part of our work was cleaning the public areas.

Kaaren is a fabulous artist and did gigantic flower paintings on large canvases. She was another friend that I could talk privately with. We discussed the stage of life that we were in, as we were almost the same age, in our later fifties. We discussed marriage, children, freedom, and spirituality. We triggered each other's sense of humor, and we laughed a lot. Kaaren had a deep, loud and boisterous laugh that could make anyone laugh with her.

Paleaku Peace Gardens also had a sand *mandala*, covered with a glass case, which had also been created by Tibetan monks. Usually the sand *mandalas* are destroyed after a ceremony, reminding us of the impermanence of all things. But in this case an exception had been made, and the *mandala* had been left intact for people to see as they toured the shrine gardens. There was also a *mandala* painted on the floor as a guide for dancing the "Dance of the Vajra," as taught by Namkai Norbu Rinpoche.

Our friend, Carol, a gifted poet, joined several other friends, from time to time, to perform this complex but beautiful dance on top of the painted *mandala*. All over the land there were shrines to all the world's religions and beautiful plantings of shrubs, trees, and tropical flowers. A double row of palm trees, forming a sloping pathway, led to the tall, white Buddhist *stupa*. From this vantage point one could look down the hillside, far below, to view both

Kealakekua and Honaunau Bays and the ocean that stretched out endlessly, until it disappeared by rounding the curve in the earth. From Paleaku it was about a ten or fifteen-minute drive, winding downhill, to get to either one of these ocean bays.

Paleaku's gardens also had a labyrinth, a Native American medicine wheel, and a Tibetan Green Tara statue and shrine. A little distance away was an Islamic shrine, a Mother Mary Christian shrine, a Jewish shrine, and a miniature *heiau* to honor the Hawai'ian culture.

I enjoyed sleeping in the loft of Barbara's kitchen house. This was a favorite sleeping nest for me, as the energy here was so clear

and sweet. I loved the way the breezes and fragrances wafted over me all night long. Sometimes, as I was falling asleep here, I entertained a fantasy that all the shrines and their guardians and religious leaders gathered together here at Paleaku Peace Gardens for an interfaith dialogue during the night. During the dialogue they realized a universal spirituality. It transcended the differences and points of conflict found in the world's religions and spiritual traditions. I wondered if the human race would ever be able to evolve beyond greed, war, and domination, to embrace peace and cooperation. I knew that individuals could do it, but it seemed countries still could not. One of the greatest teachings of the dolphins is that of the "Unity Community," as dolphins get along and cooperate as a pod.

In the morning Barbara and I had coffee, and she invited me to join the Paleaku Ohana for Christmas. I happily accepted the invitation. Christmas was coming soon and this would be my first

Christmas away from my family. It wouldn't be the season for jackets, hats, and gloves, but the perpetual season of bathing suits, shorts, and flip-flops. Now it was time to head back to the Hilo side, as I would soon be packing up and moving to Kawaihae. Barbara generously offered for me to return to Paleaku Gardens after I had finished the care-giving job with the elderly man named Ray. I really appreciated her generosity, as I knew that Ray was very sick and may not have much time left.

All over the gardens of South Kona, large garden patches of poinsettias were blooming. This was a reminder of Christmas at home, but poinsettias would never grow in our cold, icy yard at that time. There were red ones, white ones, and pink ones. Flowers bloomed all year long, and these islands are a paradise for flower lovers. Fruit stands appeared here and there along the belt road in South Kona too. People with small farms or acreages either sold their fruit at their stand, or left it unmanned for people to donate on the honor system. Papayas, bunches of little finger bananas, and avocados were in abundance. Wild pigs could often be found under avocado and macadamia nut trees, fattening themselves on these delicious island foods.

# HOLOHOLO ON THE HILO SIDE

## Back to Hawai'ian Paradise Park and Mauna Kea

SUNDAY MORNING, I STARTED BACK to the Hilo side. The drive was always enjoyable. Beauty was everywhere in Hawai'i, and the scenery changed often, as the Big Island had at least twelve different ecosystems. On the high road to Waimea there were spectacular views of Mauna Kea, the highest mountain of the island, and mountainsides that rolled down to the ocean, which looked small and far away. It had been good to see Aka and her sister Kalehua again. And it was also good to touch in with Barbara and Paleaku Peace Gardens again.

## The Io Hawk

AKA AND KUMU DANE

As I RETURNED HOME and came through the door of the cottage, the phone was ringing. It was Kumu Dane and I was surprised, as he rarely called me. He just had a few words which made me "scratch my head" and

264

wonder. He said, "Did you have a good time over on the Kona side this weekend?" I said, "Yes, were you over there too?" I asked, wondering how he would know I went over there. "No, I was here in Pahoa . . . How did you like that Io Hawk?" he asked. I had previously thought that the Io hawk was somehow connected to Aka and her *ohana*. She had the hawk as part of her name . . . *Iolani*, heavenly hawk. But who knows? Some things are just plain mysterious. I wouldn't ask any more questions. Auntie Fern had taught me not to be so *niele* (nosy). Some things are just better left a mystery.

### Niele means "Nosy," Another Teaching from Auntie Fern and Aka

AUNTIE FERN HAD SCHOOLED ME to stop asking so many questions and not to be *niele* (nosy). She told me it was important to listen, to pay close attention to everything around us, and to learn to listen to our *tutus* or elders for guidance. "It is important to get our answers by developing greater inner awareness and discernment," Aka said. Auntie Fern always told me that the spacious mind is peaceful and happy, and is not cluttered with worries or other people's business. Her eyes would light up, and then she would look at me and make a gesture with her fist, screwing the air, in front of her nose, as she said, "Don't want to be too *niele* (nosy)."

Aka had also schooled me in the "*niele*" teaching. She too would make the gesture of her fist screwing the air in front of her nose. Then she would say with a chuckle, "Nose for nosy." I would always laugh at the face Aka and Auntie Fern made with this gesture. I knew all too well that they meant nosing into other people's business was not a good thing to do, generally speaking. Aka said, "Having other people's business in your head is like having mainland rush-hour traffic going through your brains. Same if you listen to the news too much. That will spin your energy down instead of up. Being informed can be good, but dwelling on the world's pain isn't. Sometimes you do have to get involved with people, as your *na'au* may guide you to help someone. But other times, just pray for them when they have problems. Your guidance will tell you what to do. Let your *na'au* (gut level instinct and heart) guide you. When you are clear, you will always do the right thing."

## Merging with Nature

WHEN WE WERE SITTING TOGETHER, either in the mountains or at the ocean, Aka would breathe deeply and tell me that we could merge with the sky, the clouds, the ocean, the flowers and the mountainsides. She always talked to the trees and the sky and everything around her, and thanked it, telling it how beautiful it was. One time she told me that this was actually a part of the teaching of *Ho'o'mana*, which is the old Hawai'ian religion based on nature.

"Merge with the ocean. Merge with the tree. Deeply love all of nature's beauty. All of nature is *Ke Akua's* gift. And we are a part of that too," Aka said. *Kahunas* and masters from many different traditions often speak or teach in hints, rather than state the obvious. Aka's words reminded me so much of the teachings of the Tibetan Lamas, who teach us to let the mind become as vast as space and to merge with the sky, and let thoughts just drift through the mind like clouds, until they disappear, finally . . . without effort.

## Overlays and Ancestral Healing

ARE WE BURDENED BY SUBTLE OVERLAYS, or do we fly free? I asked myself. I was wondering about this, this morning. And do we sometimes overlay our friends and family members with our judgments and silent criticisms? I got to thinking today about how Auntie Fern talked a lot about not being too *niele* (nosy). We think a lot about our family and friends and the dramas that they are going through, both good and bad. Is this just simple caring, or is it being *niele*? I wondered. Does it take us off center and uproot our grounding? A big realization came to me today. The more time I spend meditating here on the Big Island, the more I realize why Auntie Fern always tells me to get in the water and wash those buggahs off. It was not just spirit interference or "feeding" that was clinging to me, but layers of my own thought forms that get stuck to my auric energy field.

What about people like Aka who sing throughout their day and pray multiple times of day, praising *Ke Akua* and all of nature around her? She speaks to the trees, the flowers, the birds, and the ocean, and tells them how beautiful they are, and how grateful she is for their lives. And she does the same with people, pouring real Aloha and positive energy into them. This type of projection and overlay is extremely uplifting and positive for the person receiving it. What if all of us could do this and sustain these loving states? I wondered. It would be a happier world.

I thought of getting in the water and washing the buggahs off. Sometimes "the buggahs" could be negative projections sticking to our auras in the form of judgments or criticism from others. The salt water surely did release these "barnacles," and I always felt clear and bright when I got out of the water. To find our own unique clearing methods is so essential to our well being. Part of the lesson for me is to let others be free to be themselves, to do their own life, without our inner gossip about them, and sometimes, our unrequested advice.

I thought of judgments I had from others about this hiatus I was experiencing here in Hawai'i. When I had tears in front of a friend one day, they thought I was having a nervous breakdown. Others thought that, because I was separated from my husband, we didn't love each other any more. Another person thought I was having a terrible time here in Hawai'i, just because I had faced challenges. None of these judgments were true, and were not helpful. I, too, needed to be free of *niele* judgments, so I too, could fly free. "*Noa Noa*" means "free, free."

### Ancestral Healing

I THOUGHT OF AKA AND ALL HER TEACHINGS about how we carry the blood of our ancestors, which holds their talents, strengths, fears, trauma, and good and bad deeds. Today's science calls this "epigenetics." She had shared with me ways of clearing the ancestral line. Part of the ceremonial prayer for our ancestral line entailed

267

praying for forgiveness of them and for them, wherever they happen to be, at this very moment, in time and space. This phrase was interesting to me, as it covered them whether they still resided in the heavens or whether they had been re-born. When the ancestral line is cleared, we are more directly connected to the purity, divine love, and power of our creator. Aka often referred to all of us as butterflies who had to go through the worm and chrysalis stages before emerging as a beautiful butterfly . . . that could fly free.

## *Two Surprises at the Pahoa Post Office*

### *Stacy's Gift*

IT WAS GETTING TO BE just a couple of weeks before Christmas. I went to the Pahoa post office to check my mailbox on Monday morning. There was a small package for me from my oldest daughter, Stacy, and a letter from my brother, Scott and his wife, Geri. Stacy is only eleven months younger than my oldest son, James. Stacy is smart as a whip and some people call her a "brainiac." But she has both beauty and brains and by her own description, she is "in the business of saving lives," as she is a nurse in the Intensive Care Unit, and an Emergency Room R.N. Growing up and continuing into the present, Stacy consumes at least one new book a day. And her reading includes every topic imaginable. If I ever want to know something, I ask Stacy. She has a delightful and sometimes naughty sense of humor. When I think of her, I hear her infectious laugh. In her carefully wrapped small package was a beautiful gold and garnet ring. I put it on immediately and it fit me perfectly. I came to tears at her thoughtfulness and how much this meant to me right now. I missed her. And I missed everyone in the family, especially because I would not be with any of them for Christmas this year. Next I eagerly opened the letter from my brother Scott and his wife, Geri.

MY BROTHER, SCOTT VASAK, besides being a solar contractor, is a fisherman, in the tradition of our father, Otto Vasak and his father, Ottokar Vasak, who was born in Bohemia and educated at Charles University, in Prague. These men are not primarily fly or ocean fishermen, but lake and trout stream fishermen. This is a particular breed of individual who loves rambling through the woods and up and down the banks of remote streams and lakes. Our oldest son, James, had been initiated into the fishing clan by my father. He never forgot some of the main rules. You never wore white shirts as the fish could see you, and you had to be quiet, very quiet, as the fish could hear you. We had many fresh trout dinners growing up. My father did, however, sometimes get a good catch as a fly fisherman as well.

Rainbow and German brown trout were the prizes brought home for dinner, breaded in flour and cornmeal, and fried in garlic butter over a campfire. This tradition has passed down through the family, with my oldest son, James, being tutored by my father as to what Panther Martin lures to use, and how to creep along the streams stealthily so as not to spook the fish. It was always quite competitive between my father and my son, James, as to who could bring home the larger catch. It must hark back to survival issues and who would be the best provider for the village. Who is the best hunter or fisherman? My grandfather once caught a super-sized Muskie up at a lake in Hayward, Wisconsin. He was interviewed on the radio like a celebrity. Like many Bohemians, who immigrated from the old country, he was also a *"houby"* hunter, who knew his mushrooms. He hunted rabbits and collected berries. My grandmother, being an excellent Bohemian cook, made braised rabbit with mushroom and sour cream/dill gravy. Mushrooms dried on screens in the basement, and the basement shelves were filled with berry jams and other jars of fruit that Grandma Zdenka had canned in the summertime.

Ottokar Vasak was my grandfather, and he was the one who introduced me to the greatest cathedral of all – he loved the woods, lakes, rivers and streams! The woods and all of nature was his cathedral. Besides being a man of nature, he was an incurable romantic. He left little love notes in the kitchen cupboards and dresser drawers for my grandmother to find. He also gathered wild

269

violets and brought beautiful little bouquets to her from his tramps in the woods. And this romance went on into their elder years and for the rest of his life.

Scott and Geri's letter included a check, a Christmas gift from both of them, for one hundred and fifty dollars. It was earmarked for fishing equipment. They thought that, if I fished here in Hawai'i, I would be able to stretch my finances. How kind and generous of them, I thought. Again I was moved by the love and generosity of my family.

But, I had come to realize that the local people really did not appreciate having *haoles* invade their fishing spots. I often watched the fishermen fishing with their rods along the rocky shoreline at the end of Hawai'ian Paradise Park. Having listened to the conversations of many locals, I knew colonialism had already robbed the Hawai'ian people of too much. The last thing they needed was one *haole* woman joining them at their fishing spots. No, no, I thought. I mustn't fish here. Scott and Geri's idea was great, but due to the cultural considerations I opted to "not" buy the fishing equipment.

### Christmas Shopping at Kalapana

I WAS PACKING AND GETTING READY to move to Kawaihae. My landlady had not discussed her outburst of temper, and I did not bring it up either. We would just "let it go." I had already given her notice, and I was busy cleaning the cottage thoroughly so as to leave no traces of myself. My father had always taught us to leave a place as clean or cleaner than we found it, and this applied to the "outdoors" as well. He made sure we knew how to completely extinguish a campfire and leave no traces of ourselves at our campsites, or on the trails.

While I was cleaning, I got a sudden impulse to drive down to Kalapana, and later I was glad I did. My Christmas shopping was solved in one fell swoop. Kalapana means "hole in the sky." I am not sure why this beautiful place has that name. I drove up and saw Uncle Robert's flag moving in the breeze.

There were some nice local ladies who had their craft tables set up. I was drawn to one of the tables, as the lady had such a nice, open smile and a very magnetic energy. Her table was spread with an array of beautiful hand-made crafts. Some things were made of coconut shells and others were woven of *lauhala* . . . bracelets of various designs, mats, hats and purses. Seeing her wares made me think of Auntie Mona Kalele, who had made her living, early in life, by weaving hats and mats from *lauhala*. There was jewelry too, made of bone, beads, shells, and *kukui* nuts. There were essential oils of tropical flowers and lotions and salves. So I shopped and shopped, finding something special for each family member back home. I had been financially pinched since I quit the house-cleaning job. The check from my brother enabled me to treat everyone to really nice Christmas gifts. As this lovely local lady carefully wrapped each gift in newspaper, her friend tallied up the purchases for her. Small children were playing around the table.

Everything was bagged up, in two big bags, and I had paid her the exact amount, which came to exactly one hundred and fifty dollars to the penny. She then seemed to slip into a bit of an altered state, that was reminiscent of Auntie Fern and Aka. She said to me, "You have a granddaughter, who is still a very small girl. She has a very strong connection to this island and some day she will come here. When she comes, I would like to offer to teach her Hawai'ian herbology. I am a practitioner of *La'au Lapa'au*. I am serious Auntie, as I can see and sense her as a very gifted person. It would be an honor and a joy to teach her."

She then asked for my phone number and I asked for hers. "If Lilliana Mahana visits Hawai'i in the future, I will bring her to meet you, Auntie." I said. She then reached under her table and pulled out a very precious, hand-made piece of *Tapa* cloth, that she had made herself. I knew that the process of hand-made tapa cloth took hours and hours of work and care. "I want you to bring this to your *mo'opoona* (granddaughter) when you go back home. Have her put it up on the wall. It will be a blessing for her." I thanked her profusely, as I knew that the process of pounding this cloth from the bark of the Mulberry tree was difficult and time-consuming. She said that the designs were designs from her *Ohana*. Once again I was stunned, as I had not mentioned having any grandchildren while I was buying the gifts. This piece of *Tapa* cloth was very precious.

Then I remembered that I had brought some expensive children's jackets and clothing, which were donated "for Hawai'ian kids" by friends at home. I had them in the back of my jeep, and I brought the bags over to the table and offered them to this woman, as the children who were playing around the tables seemed to be hers. When she saw the bags of children's clothing, she suddenly burst into tears. At first I didn't know what had triggered her tears. She continued to weep softly and tried to speak between tears. Finally, she was able to tell me that their house had burned down recently, and that they had lost almost everything. The *keiki* (children) didn't have many clothes, and the family was sleeping in tents on their land. "There are some very old traditional elders in the family too," she said. They too were sleeping in tents.

She continued saying that, up until today, she didn't think they would be able to have their traditional Christmas dinner because they couldn't afford it. The 9/11 2001 Twin Towers tragedy in New York had caused family members here on the Big Island to lose jobs. The visitor industry had employed many local people, but the visitor industry was almost non-existent right now. It had been about three months since the event, but the Big Island was still in an economic crisis and few tourists were traveling. She told me that with my Christmas shopping, she now had the money to shop for a big Christmas dinner on their land. Her emotion was contagious, and I too was moved to tears. Oh, my goodness, I thought, this is the best Christmas ever, to be able to help this family have a Christmas dinner together after their house fire.

"*Mahalo nui loa Ke Akua!*" she said. *Ke Akua* guides people to help others and sometimes uses those who listen to their *tutus* to be the ones who *kokua* (help) and carry out errands for *Ke Akua*. Immediately I thought of Auntie Fern and how she counseled me to constantly listen for guidance from the *tutus*. If I had been part of the footwork of helping this family have a Christmas miracle, then it was also a miracle for me and the best Christmas gift ever.

I remembered that early this morning I did get a nudge to go down to Kalapana. Subtle nudges may seem unimportant, but nudges from *Ke Akua* and a host of angels and ancestors are often subtle. And my brother and his wife would be blessed, too, for their part in this Christmas miracle.

## A Mysterious Phone Call

A FEW DAYS LATER, JUST BEFORE I discontinued my phone service at the cottage, I got a mysterious phone call. It was a *kupuna* (elder) and he was speaking to me in Hawai'ian. His voice was sweet, but the voice of a very elderly man. Of course I didn't understand, and I thought he had gotten the wrong number at first. Then he began to speak in English and said, "Thank you, Auntie, for giving us a Christmas dinner. *Mahalo nui loa*! *Ke Akua* blesses all of us." Then it dawned on me that it was the *kupuna* (elder) of the family which had had the house fire, and that he was the traditional elder who was a native speaker.

I told him that I was grateful too, and wished them all a Happy Christmas and continued blessings for recovering from their fire. His voice had such *mana* (spiritual energy) and *aloha* that I cried for a few minutes after we hung up. I sat in the wicker chair and realized that I had been truly blessed through the connection with this family. I remembered a phrase from the Bible about how it is greater to give than to receive. "How true," I thought. If we can run errands here on Earth for divine angels and *Ke Akua*, then we are blessed to have this *kuleana* (spiritual duty or responsibility).

## Mike Tomson Visits Hawai'i

MIKE TOMSON IS A FAMILY FRIEND from Grass Valley, California. He is a contractor, story teller, and a teacher of "non-violent communication." Mike had a unique upbringing, spending his early childhood years on the island of Palau in the Micronesian Islands. Later he lived on the island of Saipan and Guam. He was a kind of wild child who totally embraced this island culture, feeling right at home in it. His parents had been hired as school teachers for these islands. Mike's young spirit loved this native culture, and he soon walked like the native people, barefoot and grounded. He has a big smile with twinkling, mischievous green eyes. He liked to pat his belly, testimony to his love of good eating, or as they say in Hawai'i, "grinds." Mike has never lost that walk, his big smile, and his long, warm-hearted hugs. Even though he is white, he is often seen as a Pacific Islander. Islanders recognize each other by what I call "island energy," and he definitely has that island vibe.

Not long after arriving in Pilau he spent very little time at home, roaming the island. His parents knew that the local people would look out for him, and they trusted him to make wise decisions.

 He learned the native language and attached himself to the "navigator of the island." A navigator is one who navigates a canoe without instruments, as was done in ancient times. Navigators navigate with stars, swells and waves, birds and intuition, which is sometimes called "dead reckoning." Mike had many adventures in the water and received training in voyaging and navigating. He has told me many fascinating stories about his life on Palau, and later in Guam, with wistful nostalgia in his eyes.

Having met Clay Bertelmann, his family and group of Hawai'ian voyagers, I thought Mike should visit Hawai'i and meet all of them too. It would be a bit like soul retrieval into a part of his past that was so wonderful and adventurous.

Kumu Dane Silva had recently taken me to the Bertelmann home in Waimea and introduced me, so I felt certain that I could help facilitate Mike meeting these voyagers. I called Mike back home in Grass Valley and asked him if he couldn't break away from work and come over for a visit. Soon he booked a flight to the Big Island. He was intrigued, ready for some island time, and he made it happen. Shortly after Mike arrived, we drove around the island together and I showed him some of my favorite places along the way. At one place near South Point we stopped to watch the whales breaching. Then we stopped at the Black Sand Beach at Punalu'u to see the sunbathing turtles. When we arrived in the Hilo area in the evening, Mike stayed in a kind of hostel/hotel, and I went to stay with a lady friend nearby.

The next day we discovered that the Tahiti Fete was happening in the big Hilo auditorium, so we spent an entire day there watching one group after another perform Hula. The performances were stunning, with participants from many island communities besides Hawai'i, Tahiti and other Pacific Islands. Dozens of Hula *halaus* (schools) performed with their traditional costumes and drummers. *A halau* is a school – *ha* means "breath" and *lau* means "many," so it means the dancers breathe as one. Some groups from Japan performed, and many Tahitian groups had traveled to Hawai'i for these performances too. It was a spectacular show, and we sat in the bleachers with families and Mike walked around from time to time taking numerous photographs of the beautiful dancers.

It was fun circling the island, and Mike enjoyed the local food as much as I did. *Poke*, a raw fish dish, was a favorite, and later I would take him to Super J's on the belt road above Kealakekua Bay to enjoy Janice's *lau laus*.

### Another Visit to the Bertelmann's with Mike

MIKE AND I HAD GONE TO KAWAIHAE on two different days to the place where the Makali'i is usually docked. It was not there. We found out later that the canoe was up on blocks in dry dock in a nearby industrial area. Not wanting to give up, we tried a third time by heading north on the highway, up towards Kawaihae. Close by was the Native Cultural School where Clay's wife, Deedee Bertelmann, was teaching. We drove down a gravel road along a rather barren stretch of coastline, to the location of the school. We met Deedee and her daughter, Pomai. As Deedee's daughter was just about to go home, Deedee told us to follow her, "if we could keep up with her fast driving" up the hill to Waimea. After a fast ride up the hill, we arrived at the Bertelmann's house. Clay, some of the voyager crew, and a few Maori visitors were putting a new roof on the house.

Mike, who is a contractor, had brought a laser-level from home. And that tool was just about to come in handy. When we drove up to the house, we saw Clay, Shorty and Luther, and several other men up on the roof. Mike quickly introduced himself and offered a large, perfectly cooked Taro root to Clay Bertelmann as a traditional offering. He immediately asked if his help was needed. Before long Mike was up on the roof helping them engineer the challenge of bridging two sections of the new roof together. Mike's laser-level helped to solve this problem. Mike laughed with me later, saying, "I had no idea why I decided to bring this laser-level along to Hawai'i. Later Mike gave the level to Luther as a gift.

I joined the women who were in the house planning a dinner for the large group. Before long the men would be coming down off the roof and they would be tired and hungry. So off I went to the Waimea KTA to get some food as my offering to the group effort. The banging of hammers, heavy footsteps, and heavy thumps were heard up on the roof. Suddenly one of the Maori men fell through the roof. He was holding on to the rafters with his hands and dangling. Mike went over and held on to him and gently coached him to be calm, so he could pull him back up on the roof without falling.

As Mike began to get acquainted with the crew, he was able to share that he had met Mau Piailug, the famous navigator from Micronesia, in 1970. Mau had come to Hawai'i to teach the Hawai'ians traditional navigating. Mau sailed with the Hawai'ian crew in 1976 on the long voyage to Tahiti. The voyage was about 1,500 miles and took thirty-one days. We women were cooking down below in the kitchen, and I thought to myself, "Mission accomplished!" I knew, from that point on, Mike's friendly and helpful personality would carry him into the water on the voyaging canoe with the Makali'i crew. It never took long for Mike to make friends, and doing a roof project was a perfect way for Mike to meet the voyagers. As we all ate dinner together after Clay offered a *pule* (prayer), I realized that we were eating with some of the original crew members of the Hokule'a. They had followed the ancient sea road, Kealaikahiki, from Hawai'i to Tahiti. These brave, pioneering souls and their voyaging canoe were the first to follow the ancient sea road and complete this voyage in modern times. The Hokule'a and its crew had not only made history but changed history in proving that ancient peoples could cross oceans in voyaging, sailing canoes.

Mike, perhaps without realizing it at the time, passed several important tests. He made a traditional offering to the captain of the Makali'i. He humbly helped in a group project of voyagers, and he helped pull one of the crew to safety. When sailing on the ocean in the voyaging canoe, the crew needs to know that each one of their crew members can be trusted and can remain calm in emergencies. Helping each other and trusting each other is essential out on a rough and stormy ocean. It can mean life or death. "Our canoe is an island."

### Love Blossoms for Two Couples

BEFORE LONG I TOOK MIKE UP TO Barrie Rose's house in Waimea, as I wanted to share my friends with him. There he met Kapua, Barrie Rose, and Jeannette. Kapua and his girlfriend in Hilo had recently broken up, and I had helped him move up to Waimea, where he was teaching at the Acupuncture College. He introduced me to Angela Longo, who was the head of the school. Barrie Rose was a beautiful woman who owned a lovely home in Waimea. She was divorced, but had children who were still living at home. Jeannette was in the midst of a divorce. One day I helped her move out of the house that she had shared with her husband. A looming divorce is traumatic, especially when there are children involved. She cried, and I was able to hug and comfort her. Little did I know that soon she would be smiling again and renewing her dreams.

Jeannette is a tall, lovely woman who had lived in Australia. She felt confused about what was next in her life. She had a job as an administrative assistant to a movie producer who lived part-time on the Big Island. We women all supported each other in the transitions that we were going through. It was wonderful to have Hawai'ian friends, but it was also wonderful to have these two *haole* lady friends. We talked about our spiritual paths, men, children and relationships, and our hopes, dreams, and disappointments. We discussed how we all had missed recognizing "red flags" in our lives. As we got older, we got a little wiser. One night we had a dinner party and I invited both Kapua and Mike. I thought that Mike and Kapua would get along, and I was sure that Kapua would introduce Mike to many other Hawai'ian brothers, as well as some other voyagers.

Kapua was trying to form a Big Island's men's group. I told Kapua that a funny movie could be made on this theme, following the lives of some of the Hawai'ian brothers, who often called to each other, "Hey, Brah." I went on telling Kapua that the movie could open with the title *"The Big Island Men's Group"* spelled out in black lava stones, or white coral chunks in the lava fields north of Kailua Kona. As an example, there was an array of messages written this way, like the names of lovers written in white coral on black lava or black lava stones, and which spelled out messages, often surrounded by a heart, outlined with stones. The title of the movie spelled out in rocks could be filmed from a helicopter. And there could be some great Hawai'ian music for the sound track.

Mike ran healing groups in "Non Violent Communication" in California, and I thought that he would like to join Kapua's men's group. Our Hawai'ian friend, Soli, was a famous activist for indigenous Hawai'ian rights. He overheard Kapua discussing this men's group and, arching his eyebrow skeptically, asked, "Whaht kinnah mens?" We all laughed and the subject was dropped. I smiled to myself thinking of Aka's expression, "Drop it like it's hot." Kapua told me later, "Hawai'ian guys don't really go for this idea. Their idea of male bonding is surfing, fishing, hunting pigs, barbeque, and drinking beer." And that would be Coronas with lime.

Before long, everyone had met, and there were two new couples falling for each other. Kapua got together with Barrie Rose, and before long he moved into her house. Mike took a fancy to Jeannette, and another relationship began. Now Barrie's house became the scene of some wonderful times, as we often had dinner party get-togethers or excursions. Other friends joined us, and we had a group that became very bonded. Everyone was a good cook too, and that made for *"ONO"* (delicious) dinners. I'll never forget how Soli taught me the proper way to julienne carrots for a stir fry. It seemed that all these Hawai'ian "brahs" were master chefs.

# A Red Cedar Circle for Christmas

KAPUA TOLD ME ABOUT A NATIVE AMERICAN MAN named Johnny Moses (Whis.stem.men.knee, Walking Medicine Robe). Kapua explained that he had spent a number of years as Johnny's student up in the Northwest, above Seattle. Johnny was a descendant of Chief Seattle and a number of prominent healers and medicine people. Kapua explained that a Red Cedar Circle was a ceremony that had originated with the Northwest tribal people. The cedar leaves from the Red Cedar trees were used as a smudge. Different medicine songs had particular purposes and were sung in rounds. Between the songs, prayers were made by the people attending the circle. Since Kapua had spent years with Johnny, he had learned the songs and the drumming. People who attended would either bring a drum, a rattle, or a bell. Since these tribes were associated with the Shaker Church, the prayer rounds were a blend of Shaker and their own Native traditions. Candles, bell ringing, and all night healing ceremonies had derived from the Shaker Church. An offering blanket in the middle of the floor had a candle on each of the four corners, and there was a bowl of offering water in the center of the blanket. Story telling was another part of this ceremony. The stories almost always included animals. Some of them were a little off color, but very funny.

This particular night Kapua was conducting a *Peshelt*, which was a traditional "Give Away." He had gathered and purchased gifts which would be paraded around in a circle by the group while a song was being sung. When the song concluded, someone sitting in the circle would be given the gift. Jeannette and I were far from home and would be missing our family Christmas, so being gifted by Kapua's generosity was much appreciated at this time of year. I had tears of gratitude when Kapua wrapped a beautiful blanket around me. I was sitting beside Soli on a couch, and the next round of songs and dance stopped right in front of Soli. A beautiful blanket was also wrapped around Soli. I then realized that Soli and I were the eldest in the group, both being in our late fifties. Prayers were again said after the Native American songs, the drumming, and the tinkling of bells. At the end of the ceremony everyone had a pile of gifts in front of them, and a candle-lit meal was being set out on the dining room table. This had been a beautiful prayer ceremony. Each one of us had made prayers for many people. We felt the blessing of both Christmas and the Red Cedar Circle, and the medicine people of the Northwest tribes. I was hoping the family back home was able to feel the love and prayers that I was sending to them across the ocean.

*Mele Kalikimaka* – Merry Christmas

## Christmas is Coming . . . The Mongoose is Getting Fat

CHRISTMAS CAME AND WENT QUICKLY. I drove to Paleaku Peace Gardens, and all the residents, as well as some locals, gathered around a beautiful Christmas tree set up in the large screened-in dining area. We had each brought a gift and exchanged the gifts around the tree. Then we had a wonderful Christmas dinner together. It was a sweet occasion. I was so grateful to Barbara for inviting me to this wonderful Christmas day, as I was really missing my family. The family and I had several phone calls back and forth during the day. I have to say that I felt guilty for not being home. But Paul gave me such a wonderful gift. He told me that he would be coming over to visit me in a few months. Now this was something wonderful to look forward to. I wondered where I would be living when he came. The family had received the Kalapana gifts in time for Christmas and loved these mementos from Hawai'i. It was strange to experience Christmas in the tropics and to see the poincettas blooming in the gardens and on local hillsides. Being warm, wearing shorts and sundresses, and going for a swim on Christmas was something new.

## Kupuna Moana (Mona) Kehele

KUPUNA MONA KEHELE VISITED THIS DAY, as she and Barbara were good friends. Again we spoke about *Ho'o'ponopono* and the way she was raised. Her style of *Ho'o'ponopono* was Christian-oriented. When she was a child, she had to arise early in the morning as she was being taught *Lau' lapa' au* (herbal gathering and medicine). She and her *tutu* went out, with their buckets in hand, to gather medicinal plants as it was getting light. Some of the gathering locations were at quite a distance or far up in the mountains. I always loved listening to Auntie Mona. She was one of Hawai'i's living cultural treasures. Her real name was Moana, but Mona was written on her birth certificate. She had such sweet energy, and both love and wisdom emanated from her. She liked having me drive her home. We would pass Choice Mart (a local grocery store) and drive up the hill to her home. She often told me of her married days living in Miloli'i with her husband who was a fisherman. She cleaned and dried a lot of fish in her day. It was mostly *opelo*, which is mackerel scad. But there are others that want to eat the mackerel besides fishermen: tuna, *ono*, *mahi mahi*, marlin, and dolphins love the *opelo* too.

Once she told me about stone monuments, called *ku'ula*, on the shore of fishing villages, that were supposed to bring a plentiful catch. She had grown up in South Kona and was a renowned expert about the history of this area, the sacred sites, ancient trails, and old place names. I felt honored to spend some time with Auntie Mona. She carried in her memory so many of the old, traditional ways, and she was a fluent, native speaker.

Barbara had a gift for me that I have 'til this day: a little silver and enameled box with a gold coin inside. How precious I thought. I hugged her and thanked her deeply. She said it was to remind me of the flowing gold of our higher consciousness. I looked into Barbara's large, beautiful brown eyes, and I saw a sister and was deeply touched. We had so much in common. I envied her ability to manifest and to inspire people to help and contribute to Paleaku Gardens. It was something fantastic that she had created here, one step at a time . . . one shrine at a time. So many people have lived here, gardened here, attended events here, helped here, and benefited from the healing energy of the place. It was and still is a sacred space for community and visitors.

## THE MOVE TO KAWAIHAE

### Considerations About Moving from the Hilo Side to Kawaihae

As a practitioner of Chinese medicine, Kapua had tested my pulses and looked at my tongue and questioned me about my symptoms. All this, and the excess mucus that I described, told him that I had a damp constitutional condition. Living in the damp, rainy climate on the Hilo side would just perpetuate the mold allergies that I had developed. I needed a drier climate and Kawaihae, which was much hotter and drier, was the antidote.

I was going to miss all the rainbows, the rain forests, being close to Kupuna Pele's volcanic crater, and the friends that I had made: Lomilomi class, Kumu Dane, Desmon and Stacy, Rika and others. I would miss the monthly Shamanic drumming group, water aerobics, and "Intenders for the Highest Good." I would miss the occasional spontaneous outings with Douglas too, and the ladies at Kalapana who had become friends. And then there was Lovey and her family. There was sadness in this move but, on the other hand, excitement arose in me thinking that I would be much closer to Auntie Fern and Aka, Barbara, Carol and Kaaren. Living on the Hilo side, I had missed my Kona friends. But I could always drive back here to this lush, tropical side of the island for a visit. It was only a few hours away.

I knew that the job taking care of Ray would only last for a short time. Barbara had invited me to come back to Paleaku Gardens when this caregiving job was over. This *holoholo* tour of different island locations entailed a lot of moving, but I had a relatively light load. It wouldn't be so bad. My massage table was the biggest thing I had to move. A computer, a small boom box, some boxes, bedding and clothes were the rest of it.

It was interesting living in different parts of the island. I felt like a gypsy, keeping my belongings small, and ready to move at any time. My friend, Stan Padilla, back home in the Sierra foothills, always says, "If you're a gypsy, be sure to fly your colors." He himself has gone through life in a colorful way. As a Native American from the Yaqui tribe in Northern Mexico, he has painted the most cosmic paintings and public murals, and made beautiful jewelry. He knows how to live life as art, and he sees art in nature and every act of life.

Moving around was both exciting and a bit stressful at the same time. There were about twelve or thirteen micro-climates on the Big Island. I had not actually lived in Waimea, in the green upcountry of ranches and cowboys, but I had done house-sitting there a few times for Kapua and Barrie Rose. By spending a few weekends up in Waimea, I got a taste of how it feels to live there in the midst of rainbows, mist, sun and clouds at the foot of the sacred mountain, Mauna Kea. There are two micro-climates in the town of Waimea. The west side is drier and the east side gets much more rain. The people were friendly here, and on the weekends I was here, I attended Billy Mitchell's church.

### Inner Compass

ONE TIME, AKA SAID TO ME with a big wink of her eye, "Do you ever check in with your inner compass?" She went on to say, "I grew up with *Aloha* and *Mahalo* to the ones who give all life. This is how you check your inner compass. Ask yourself: Is your mouth kind, or mean? How aligned are you with the greatest will that there is? How aware are you of loving each other and tending to each other's hearts and needs? How aware are you of living the dream and manifesting the dream?"

These were some very deep questions, and when she would wink at me in the future, and ask how my compass was working, I knew exactly what she wanted me to do: to check in with myself on this list. Check, and double-check!

## *Moving to Kawaihae*

MY 'ADOPTED' BROTHER, KAPUA, CAME TO THE RESCUE when it came time to move from the cottage in Hawai'ian Paradise Park to Kawaihae. I said my goodbye to Debra and expressed my gratitude for being able to stay in her cottage and beautiful land, which was a true arboretum. As we said goodbye, I felt a spark of love in my heart. I thought of her essential nature of sweetness that I felt in her every time I gave her a massage. I was glad that we were on good terms. What had upset me earlier seemed small and far away by this time. This cottage had been a beautiful place to land, and I was very grateful. We never really know what someone else is going through, so we forgive people when they splash out at us. She was happy that the cottage was so clean and ready for her husband's arrival home.

Through my friends Barrie Rose and Jeannette, I had heard of a short-term "live in" job taking care of an elderly man named Ray, who had cancer. Kapua and I packed both of our cars with my belongings, and we drove over to Kawaihae. We drove up the Haumakua coastline, then up the hills to Waimea, and then down the long, steep, winding road to the western coastal town of Kawaihae. This is the location Kapua suggested I live. The Makali'i was moored there. It was also one of two harbors for the big shipping company, Matson Lines. Spencer's Beach Park was close by and was a nice beach for gentle swimming. Then there was the best fish taco place on the island, as well as a homemade ice cream/shave-ice shop. The kids and youth have a canoe club there too, and I enjoyed watching them practice their paddling while standing on an old lava stone wall which had been built in the 1800s. Long ago this wall had been used as a holding pen for cattle, and from here they were shipped to Honolulu.

# A Brief History of Kawaihae

KAWAIHAE, WHICH I HEARD MEANS "WATERS OF WRATH," was a relatively barren and dry place in the 1800s. Located about thirty-five miles north of Kailua-Kona, it had been a favorite surfing spot for the earliest surfers. European and American ships arrived there and trading had taken place. The sandlewood trees on the hillsides and upcountry of Kohala were harvested for shipment abroad. China wanted this wood for incense and fine furniture. Native Hawai'ians harvested the trees, but they were poorly paid. Because this wood was so coveted by the foreigners, deforestation took place quickly. In addition to this quick deforestation, young sandlewood trees were being eaten by the relatively newly introduced cattle. So the forests of sandlewood trees that were so beautiful and precious began to disappear.

Kawaihae also had an ancient salt production area where hollowed out lava pans were filled with sea water. After the water evaporated, the salt remained. This salt was originally used as table salt and for preserving fish. It was also bartered and shared with other parts of the island. Later the salt was used for curing and preserving meat. After visitors started arriving on the island, the salt was sold and traded to the whaling and merchant ships.

Captain Vancouver had gifted King Kamehameha I with cattle which later came to be called Vancouvers. They had been turned loose on the Island and were *kapu* (forbidden) to hunt during Kamehameha I's lifetime. Before long they had multiplied into large wandering herds. They became a nuisance, eating crops, and sometimes attacking people. *Paniolos* (cowboys) were brought in from Peru, Mexico, and Portugal to rid the island of the wily and dangerous wild cattle. The bulls were targeted and often either castrated or killed for meat, hides, and tallow. Beef jerky was made from the local salt and the meat of the Vancouvers.

A cattle business was beginning to thrive up on the Waimea plateau, and before long there were cattle drives from Waimea down the mountain trails to the coastline harbor at Kawaihae where the cattle were shipped to Oahu for slaughter. Then the Parker Ranch started importing cattle and grew their own herds, no longer choosing the tougher meat of the wild cattle.

Whaling and other ships seeking supplies came to Kawaihae as well, to buy or trade local food. They especially coveted the preserved salted beef and potatoes that were grown on the hillsides. Whaling was so widespread that the whale population in the Pacific began to be seriously diminished.

The next big impact on the culture was the influx of Christian missionaries around 1820, who taught the Native Hawai'ians that their own religion was evil and that they could only be saved by Christianity. At this time the old religion was banned, and *tikis* and other ceremonial objects of the *heiaus* were destroyed. This was the end of the traditional Hawai'ian culture and *kapu* system.

Missions and churches were built of the local stone and cemented with a kind of lime made of melted coral from the reefs. Damage to the coral was immense. Coral is not inert but a living organism. Hawai'ians had always taken care of the coral reefs and had made their stone temples, foundations and walls with a dry stacking technique. They knew it was not good to disturb the living coral reefs. In addition, with the influx of the whaling and trade ships, visitors brought the horrors of smallpox and other diseases. Almost half of the native population of Kawaihae died. Colonization brought tragic consequences to the Hawai'ian people.

In 1882 Captain Matson, who was a Swedish-American, sailed his three-masted schooner to Hawai'i carrying food and other supplies for the new plantations. His sailing vessel returned to San Francisco filled with sugar. Claus Speckels, sugar tycoon, financed many new ships for Matson that would both import and export to Hawai'i and other Pacific destinations. This became the Matson Navigation Company. Later, passenger steam ships were built by Matson to bring tourists to Hawai'i, but this fleet of ships was retired in the 1970s, as air travel became the favorite way to visit Hawai'i. Matson supply ships are still coming and going daily. What would the islands do without them, I wondered?

## A Temporary Home in Kawaihae

KAPUA AND I ARRIVED AT RAY'S with our two cars and unloaded my things. Then we talked to Ray for a while before Kapua left. When I said goodbye to Kapua, he was shaking his head and said, "This is one 'kine' tough character. You got your work cut out for you."

Ray was in pain and ornery from it, which was understandable. I told him that I would bake him an apple pie the next day. He liked the idea. I thought that would cheer him up. Walking was a little hard for him, so I toured the house by myself. It was a nice modern home with a swimming pool in the back yard. After having tea, we went to bed, as it was dark by now. Ray's house was up on a hill above a cove known to be a favorite abode for humpback whales. During the night I could hear their sounding . . . the deep, primordial scales that echoed off the ocean and the steep cove walls. Some of the *kupuna* at the beach told me later that Ray's neighborhood had been on an old trail for the Night Marchers, or Night Walkers, as some people called them. However, I was glad that I never experienced them.

I had to say goodbye to my gecko friend in the cottage in Hawai'ian Paradise Park. Now I had whale friends just a short distance away. It was a comforting  sound and a little bit other-worldly. I remembered all the vivid dreams I had as a child and teenager in which I was swimming for miles and miles, right alongside whales and dolphins. The ocean had been in my consciousness for a long, long time. In my dreams a whale would often be swimming beside me. His eye looked into mine and penetrated me, to my depths, with an unspeakably wise transmission. The reverberations of their songs and tones echoed in my mind, as I drifted off to sleep . . . in a new bed, in a new house, in a new little town.

Waking up to a sunny morning, I jumped out of bed knowing that I was on duty and must get dressed and ready to help Ray with his morning routine. We had two doctor appointments up in Waimea, and while there we did some other errands, including getting ingredients for the pie. Even though my family in California loved my apple pies, Ray did not. I had to remind myself that people with cancer have a hard time with appetite and taste. Nothing really tastes good.

Ray needed help getting into the doctor's office. A strong arm was enough, as he was good at getting around with his walker. One doctor's office was up a steep flight of stairs. That was hard for both of us. So for several weeks I shopped and cooked for him and took him to frequent appointments. Ray's golden lab dog and I walked to the road to pick up his paper every morning, and again to the mailbox in the afternoon. I did tasks and errands for him, but other than laundry, cooking and dishes, I was not required to do any of the cleaning. Local cleaning ladies came in every week. It felt good to be off-duty from cleaning. Most of the time Ray just wanted to sit in silence, but sometimes he wanted to talk. He had been reviewing a lot of personal history. Over the several weeks that I was there, he recounted his life story to me. It was all very interesting. He had had a long, full life. I was a good listener, and by talking to me he had a chance to look back on his long life of ninety-some years.

In the mid-afternoon Ray took a long nap, and this was my time off. I drove just a few miles to Spencer's beach, where I could take a daily swim. Almost every day some *kupunas* would be at a picnic table, under a tree, playing guitar, ukulele, and singing. Often they invited me to sit with them. One of them had his young grandchildren with him, who were not quite old enough to go to school. A trip to the beach had a happy sound track! This melodious, lilting Hawai'ian music and the swim was the highlight of my day. The sandy beach was wide and sprawling, and the ocean waves were usually quite gentle here. As the shoreline curved out of sight, there was a large stand of palm trees in the distance. I never noticed an undertow while swimming here. But the ocean is changeable and as Aka always told me, "Never turn your back on the ocean. When jumping breaking waves, stand sideways. You can keep your eye on her that way."

Another piece of local advice is to avoid swimming at dawn, at dusk, or on cloudy days. These are the feeding times for sharks. There were facilities for camping at Spencer Beach with well-kept and clean showers and bathrooms. One time the park was filled with teenage campers from a Big Island church. The day they were there I was sunbathing on the beach and lazing in the water while listening to them singing hymns in the Hawai'ian language. 'Such a beautiful language,' I thought, as gentle as the soft breezes that blew here.

Above the beach on the hillside is the famous Pu'ukohola Heiau, which means Temple of the Whale. This massive Heiau was built by Kamehameha I and emits a powerful aura all around the area. Sometimes I indulged in an ice cream or shave ice on the way home. The *lilikoe* (passion fruit) shave ice with vanilla ice cream was my favorite. Children loved a drink called P.O.G. It was a combination of passion fruit, orange, and guava juice. My grandchildren would love P.O.G. as well as this tropical ice cream shop and all its many delightful flavors, I thought, as I headed home to Ray.

I tried my best to give Ray good healing energy, as I knew he felt so poorly. He was in pain, but not yet to the point where he needed a nurse to administer morphine. His condition was heading in that direction though, and I could see that he would not be able to live in his own home for very much longer. The end of life scenario, with cancer, is usually very sad and very painful. I tried to give him quality time and company and his favorite meals. But his appetite was blunted and nothing tasted good to him anymore. His complaint was that food tasted either like cardboard or ashes. It was hard watching someone suffer this way. I felt so much compassion for him that I did not take his grumpiness personally. I knew that he might be afraid of his next stage, but he didn't want to talk about that. He was of the old school stoicism of the "stiff upper lip."


### A Tour of the Hospital in Waimea


ONE SUNDAY AFTER BILLY MITCHELL'S church service, I was invited to have a tour of the Waimea hospital (North Hawai'i Community Hospital) by one of the ladies at church, who was an employee of the hospital. Waimea is also known by the name Kamuella, which means Samuel. In the front entrance hallway there was a large, colorful painted mural depicting a doctor and nurse on one side, and a *Kahuna* healer and his team of healers on the other. This hospital honored evidence-based Western medicine as well as Eastern and Indigenous healing modalities. If a patient requested it, *Kahuna* healing medicine and prayer were allowed in this hospital. I had also heard that acupuncture and therapeutic touch (the laying on of hands) was sometimes used before and after surgeries, if a patient requested it. Dr. Earl Bakken had been deeply involved with this hospital. He was instrumental in inventing the digital pacemaker. As I walked through the hospital, I found it to be quite unique in design. It didn't smell like a hospital either, and the rooms seemed to all have doors that went out into patios filled with beautiful flowers and plants. The lady giving me the tour told me that not only was the food local and delicious, but that the kitchen staff was known to pray over the food as it was being prepared. She also told me that many doctors from the mainland and from other countries come to see and learn from this hospital. Another Hawai'ian lady who I met at church told me that the hospital site had been chosen by following ley lines that came down from the sacred mountain. Looking up to the heights of Mauna Kea, I saw a ring of clouds around the summit. Some local people say it is the *lei* of the mountain Goddess.

### *"Got Poi? The KAPA Dinner Radio Show with Kahikina*

ONE OF MY FAVORITE RADIO SHOWS was the dinner show on KAPA radio. It was hosted by a hilarious man, Kahikina, who entertained his radio audience with pure Hawai'ian humor and warm *aloha*, laced with plenty of *da kine* pidgin English. *Poi* is a staple of the traditional Hawai'ian diet. It is steamed and pounded Taro root, which is like the texture of a pudding. It is kind of a pinkish gray. Many mainlanders don't like *poi*, but I did. The locals always asked, "Got *Poi*?" Riches in traditional foods were often better than money, especially *poi*, *lau laus*, *luau* pig, freshly caught fish, chicken long rice, *lomilomi* salmon, and *haupia* (a jelled coconut dessert).

Kahikina ran contests, made commentaries about local news and various characters and local sports teams, but his dinner show was my favorite. As Kapua and I were driving to the house in Kawai'ihae, Kahikina came on the air with the usual opening to his dinner show: "Bruddahs, and sistahs, Aunties and Uncles, *keikis*, Muddahs and Faddahs, cuz's, *kupuna kane* (grandfathers) and *kupuna wahine* (grandmothers), all over dah island, from Hilo to Kona, from Havi to Na'alehu, from Puako to Honaka'a, from Waimea to Pahoa, all over dah island people arh asking dah question . . . yes, people arh asking dah question . . . long pause . . . and then with a loud and dramatic announcement, "Wats fo dinnah?"

Maybe I got some of the towns wrong, but this is the jist of the opening to his dinner show. Kahikina, whose full name is Tommy Kahikina Ching, would go on to give the recipe for tonight's "dinnah" and suggested that all the *kane* (men) coming home from work, in their pick-up trucks, and *wahine* (women) out in town, should stop at the grocery store to get the list of ingredients for his evening recipe. And then in a most humorous way, he  would describe how to prepare the recipe. He once described the wrong way to chop up an onion and it had me laughing for the longest time.

Another very humorous show he did was all about how to eat at a buffet. He said to go for what you don't get at home: the prime rib, the prawns, the crab legs, etc. "Skip the jello! Don't fill up on what you have at home." Kahikina is still an iconic figure on the Big Island today. He is back on the air on KAPA radio now in 2022, and continues to do a lot of charitable work for the "Food Basket," which collects food and donations for families with food insecurity. He is still in the "dinnah" business. "One dollar and one can." You may see him raising money for the Food Basket in the parking lot of grocery stores, outdoor markets, and maybe even on a golf course.


## *Imagining the Past at Lapakahi*


ONE AFTERNOON, INSTEAD OF GOING FOR A SWIM, I decided to take my two-hour break, while Ray napped, to visit Lapakahi State Park. It is about twelve miles north of Kawaihae up Highway 270, which is also the Akoni Pule Highway. Lapakahi is a partially restored ancient fishing village, farm and settlement that is estimated to be about six hundred years old. There are many lava stone foundations of houses and storerooms. A few houses that have been restored by the State Park resemble the original *hales*. The bamboo structures were covered with pili grass or pandanus for leak-proof roofs. There was a trellis structure in the village still growing Ipu gourds. Some of the gourds were large and looked as if they were ready to pick. Who had planted and tended the Ipu gourds, I wondered? Was it the Kupuna that I had met at Spencer beach, who was making an *Ipu heke* drum? In the times before colonization the gourds would be used for calabashes, baskets, drums and many other useful things.

I took the self-guided tour and learned that this village had some stone ruins that surrounded fields which once supported an elaborate watering system. Stone pathways wound through the village remains and then led right down to the pebble-filled beach, which was once a launch for fishing canoes.

The old village site was empty now. I saw the last visitors leave and get into their car. I continued to walk around, trying to visualize the entire village as it once was. I imagined the people busy with their daily activities in the fields, children playing, and fishing canoes being launched. I sat down on a large rock and closed my eyes. Soon I was focusing on my breath, deep inhalations and longer exhalations, which led me deep into inner space. In this quiet and peaceful place, I listened to the little waves that were breaking on the beach. There were the occasional calls of sea birds. I could imagine the laughter of children and the beautifully soft and poetic Hawai'ian language being spoken by their parents. There was still *mana* here, left behind from the people that lived here and prayed here over many years. What would these ancient people think if they could come to see the remains of their village today?

## *Beaches and Puako Petroglyph Archeological District*

BY NO MEANS DID I GET TO ALL THE PLACES I would have liked to visit. Instead of visiting all the popular beaches, I tended to go to beaches that were close to where I lived. There were a lot of beautiful beaches north of Kailua-Kona. I did visit Hapuna Beach which is at mile marker 70 on Highway 19. It was voted Hawai's best beach one year. It is a white sand beach which is long and beautiful. I also liked Anaeho'omalu Beach, popularly known as "A" Beach. It's only eight and a half miles from Hapuna Beach. Kua Beach is especially beautiful and only a few miles north of Kailua-Kona.The turn off is to the left opposite the Veterans' cemetery. There are also beautiful beaches, open to the public, at many of the hotels along the coast north of Kailua-Kona and south of Kawaiehaie.

There were two places I really wanted to visit but didn't, which were the Green Sand Beach (Papakolea beach) near South Point and the Puako Petroglyph fields. The Green Sand Beach at South Point is not easy to reach. Most people walk in as it is illegal for vehicles to drive there. People who had viewed the petroglyphs, dating back to ancient Hawai'i, told me that I needed to start the walk on the Malama trail by going to the east side of Holoholokai Beach Park. The road to the park is found on Hwy 19, north of Kailua Kona between the 73- and 74-mile marker. This area has at least three thousand different petroglyphs.

I never swam with the manta rays either. Some people go to the Sheraton Hotel, in Keauhou to book an after-sunset "Manta Swim." There are manta swim venues in other hotels north of Kailua-Kona too. I have been told that swimming with these graceful and harmless sea angels is every bit as awesome as a dolphin swim.

## A Little Secret Beach

THE HOUSE CLEANERS WERE WITH RAY this evening, so they told me I could have the evening off. Kapua, Barrie Rose, and Jeannette picked me up, as Kapua wanted to show us a beach that was known almost exclusively by locals. We drove to a remote parking lot, then walked on a narrow path through a little grove of trees and bushes for about ten minutes. Finally, we were stunned to come upon a little cove of calm water and a white sandy beach. Not a soul was on the beach, so we had the place all to ourselves. What a lovely discovery and what a great swim we all had as sunset approached. While lying on the beach, we got to talking about the ambivalence many people have about dolphin swims and dolphin healing. As the sun was setting and we all watched for the green flash, I began to tell my friends about the incredible relationship that my friend Joanne had with the dolphins.

### Flashback: Joanne's Dolphin Healing and an Exception to the Rule

YEARS BEFORE I MET AKA, Paul and I were in Mau'i and met Joanne, an old friend who was living in Kula, Maui at the time. She had survived, and was completely healed, from a case of leukemia, and was eager to tell us her story about the healing abilities of the dolphins. When Joanne lived on the mainland, her feelings of sickness and weakness led to a diagnosis of leukemia. Over a period of time she underwent a number of unsuccessful treatments. Finally, her doctor gave up, and suggested that she "get her affairs in order."

Joanne decided to move to the Big Island of Hawai'i to enjoy her last months in a place she really loved. She is a person that never gives up! She was living close to Kealakekua Bay and she knew that others were going out in the morning to swim with the dolphins. She longed to do it, but she was just too weak to swim. Some friends decided to make this dream come true for her. During this time, she met and became friends with Joan Ocean, who has led many people on dolphin and whale swims over the years. Joan helped her get into the water . . . with a board to hold and with a friend on each side of her. In this way they guided her through the waves. The salt water felt refreshing and it buoyed her up in the water. This went on for a few weeks until she had the strength to swim with her board all alone.

One day a dolphin approached her in a relatively shallow part of the bay. It sonared her and seemed to want to play. The dolphin presented her with a leaf. The dolphins love to play the leaf game. They drop a leaf in front of you for you to pick up, and then you swim away with it and drop it somewhere for them to pick up. When you have been with dolphins for a while, you soon come to recognize individuals. Like people, they have personalities, sizes, shapes, scars, and markings on their bodies. I have seen cookie cutter scars on dolphins that come from shark bites. Soon Joanne realized that the same dolphin was coming to her every time she went to the bay. The dolphin seemed excited to see her, and it would jump, leap, and spin as if celebrating their human/dolphin connection. As time went on, they would swim together.

Joanne stopped thinking about being sick, as she was feeling better and stronger! She thought that, if this was her death journey, then it was quite wonderful. All the elements in Hawai'i soothed her body. The Aloha spirit in the atmosphere warmed her heart, and her new dolphin friend was pure joy! Joanne's dolphin played the bubble game with her, too. It would blow large bubbles underwater and telepathically invite her to go into the middle of the bubble. She would enter and feel a delicious, high-frequency energy. Slowly the bubble would rise to the surface and it would pop. Joanne loved the feeling as she ascended with the rising bubble. As time went on, she felt like a mermaid. The board had long ago been discarded. More than six months had gone by, and she had not died, as her doctor had suggested she might.

Joanne's dolphin would sonar her body regularly, but one time the dolphin really alarmed her, as it rammed its nose into her solar plexus with a lot of force. She wondered if for some reason he was becoming aggressive. However, she later felt that "this ram" was the turning point in her health condition. There was a warm, effervescent feeling after she got out of the water that day. She felt as if she had champagne, bubble-like energy sparking vital energies in every cell of her body. After this ramming, the tides turned for Joanne's health. She started feeling really well.

*{Now, a new Regulation that protects dolphins was passed September 28, 2021. This regulation is authorized under the Marine Mammal Protection Act and N.O.A.A. (National Oceanic and Atmospheric Administration) fisheries. It prohibits swimming with, approaching or remaining within fifty yards of Hawai'ian spinner dolphins. It applies to all persons, kayaks, canoes, boats, paddle boards and drones. Snorkelers and others breaking this law have been and will be prosecuted. The exception to this regulation is if a person is snorkeling in the water and happens to be joined by a pod of dolphins.*

*Dolphins rest in the day time and hunt in the ocean at night. Tired dolphins are prone to shark attacks, and human nasal mucous in the water can cause dangerous and sometimes deadly upper respiratory diseases in dolphins. Human interference has been detrimental to the rest cycles and feeding patterns of the dolphins, especially with increasingly large numbers of visitors who want to swim with the dolphins. It is best to cultivate "armchair surfing" or "shoreline gazing" to connect with the dolphins.}*

### Joanne's Leukemia Is Healed

MY FRIENDS HAD BEEN LISTENING TO THE STORY and were worried that tourists might start trying to grab the fins of dolphins. But, I told

them that this story is not an invitation for either well or ill people to grab the fins of dolphins. This is really NOT *pono* (correct) and is not allowed in Hawai'i. It would be considered harassment.

I am only telling this unusual story because it is very rare and it is a story of true healing. For a long time, Joanne didn't go to the doctor for check-ups or tests. She was just enjoying her last days on earth, and she didn't care any-more if she was going to die. She surely did not feel like a dying person! She felt great and had lots of energy. After two years she went back to the doctor for tests for her leukemia. To her great joy there was no trace of the sickness, and she knew who had helped her heal. *Mahalo lui loa* to *Ke Akua* and the dolphins, as *Ke Akua*, it is you who gave the dolphins this healing gift. This healing adventure took place on the Big Island of Hawai'i. The last time we visited her, Joanne was living on Maui. She continued to be not only well, but had radiant good health. She was forever infused with the *mana* of the dolphins and is a dolphin sister, who has been gifted with the energetics of the dolphins.

### *A Four-Wheel Drive Challenge to Beautiful Makalawena Beach*

ONE BEAUTIFUL DAY KAPUA CALLED ME and said his friend Margaret from Seattle was visiting him and maybe we could show her around and take her on a little adventure. Little did I know then what he had planned for us. I picked them both up in Waimea, and we made our way down to Kawaihae and then south on the main highway. On the way down the hill Kumu Dane called and wanted to know what all of us were doing. Kapua put it on speaker and we all shared an Aloha. Dane said, "Whaht, you're going to drive in?" We came to a certain area where we saw a lot of parked cars along the side of the road. "This is it," said Kapua. "We don't need to walk in because your Jeep is four-wheel drive."

Kapua wanted to drive my jeep, as he said we were going to a beach that required four-wheel drive and he was experienced with "off road." The other option was walking a few miles over lava rock to the pristine white sand beach. It took me a while to get over being angry about this torturous ride. We entered the black lava and the car went "Bump, Bump, Bump, BANG" . . . over huge lava blocks for a time that seemed endless. 'The poor jeep,' I thought. 'It will be ruined.' Margaret did not like this bumpy ride at all either. She kept saying, "Well if it was my car, I wouldn't let Kapua ruin it like this.

The shocks will be shot after this. The car will be too!" This ride made the chuck holes in the sandy dirt roads of the Nevada desert seem like nothing. We were creeping along about two miles per hour, as the non-existent road was so bad. It was not lava gravel or rocks, but big blocks of uneven lava that sometimes seemed like huge steps that we were climbing up and down and driving over.

When we finally got to the beautiful, white sand beach, both Margaret and I were in a bad mood from the terrible bumpy ride, and my fear for the jeep. In my book, Kapua's name was "MUD," as my mother used to say . . . at least it was this day. It was hard to relax and appreciate the beauty of this beach after this stressful ride. I couldn't help but think that we had to go out the same way we had come in. The beach was lined with beautiful coconut palm trees and little pools a few yards from the ocean's edge. People were bathing and lounging about. Since there were almost no cars, I figured that these smart people had walked in.

The sky was so, so blue on this day, and the gentle trade winds were making the palm fronds sway to and fro. The beach was beautiful, and the sand was so very white. People were enjoying swimming and floating in the ocean. It seemed that the ocean floor descended very, very gradually here, and the waves were very gentle. There are so many beautiful beaches in Hawai'i, and the water feels delicious on the skin . . . at just the right temperature. But after admiring the scenery we were brought back to the reality that we had to re-trace our steps to get back to the main road. Kapua took the wheel again and navigated us out as gently as possible. It was impossible to avoid "Boom, Boom, Bang!" He tried some rodeo jokes about riding a bucking bronco, but Margaret and I were not sharing his humor this time. After surviving this ride, I refused to drive to any of Kapua's four-wheel drive adventures again. It was *PAU*, as they say in Hawai'i, and *PAU* means FINISHED.

{P.S. As of this writing, Kapua tells me that the road is smoothed out now, and we should try it again. "Whaht-evah"!!! I don't think so.}

# The Ipu Heke

ONE OF THE *KUPUNAS* AT SPENCER'S BEACH had just finished making an *Ipu Heke* drum. His two grandchildren were spellbound as he explained and demonstrated each step of the process to them. Today in Hawai'i there are so many layers and gradations of culture. Tourists, hotels, and modern stores are only an outer skin. Traditional people kept the old culture alive and passed cultural practices on to the younger generation. I was so happy to know that this culture was actually experiencing a renaissance! It would not die out, in spite of colonization.

I watched the *kupuna* completing his drum over a number of days while I was at the beach. The two gourds were glued together: the larger gourd on the bottom and the smaller on the top. This elder had grown the gourds in his own garden. He watched the small delicate gourds ripen to a large and perfect size, as they climbed a hand-made trellis made of strong sticks and twine. He had to cut the gourds and hollow them out first. I came in on the process when he was smoothing them on the outside with sand from the beach. "Who needs one kine sandpapah, when you got sand at da beach?" he asked me, with a little laugh and happy  eyes. There was a time in the history of Hawai'i when Ipu gourds were grown in abundance. They were used as callabashes for water, food, and medicine. Netting made of twine, called a *"koko,"* was made to go around them, in order to carry them or hang them up high in the *hale*, where rats couldn't get into stored food.

But the *Ipu Heke* was a drum, used as a rhythmic accompaniment to the Hula. "Umm, pah pah, Umm, pah pah" was the rhythm that this happy *kupuna* was drumming out with his fingers. His *Ipu Heke* was finished. The first beat would be hit on the ground or floor, and then he would beat out the second two beats with his weathered brown hand. His wizened face and sparkling eyes smiled as he listened carefully to the acoustics of his new drum. The *kupuna* had carefully tended this *Ipu* plant in his garden, from planting the seed, the emergence of the very first sprout, to the mature gourd, and then to his finished drum. His *ho'opuna* (grandchildren) had watched every step. Now hula dancers would dance to its beat. He had made it with so much *aloha*, in the old way, and was planning to gift it to a friend who was a *Kumu Hula*.

Hawai'ian Proverb
*I le'a ka hula i ka ho'opa'a"*
"The hula is pleasing because of the drummer."

## The Whales

WHALE SEASON IN HAWAI'I BEGINS in November and continues until May each year. January and February are the peak months. These *Kohola* (humpback whales) make a yearly migration from Alaskan waters and come to the warmer waters off the Hawai'ian islands to birth their young. At times the humpback whales come into Kealakekua Bay. When snorkeling in the bay, if a whale enters the bay, one can hear a symphony of whale songs which often accompany the high-pitched whistles and songs of the dolphins. These ocean mammals, sometimes having forty-ton bodies, can breach out of the water high into the air, creating explosions of bubbles and white spray. Anyone out on a whale watching boat, who has witnessed a whale breaching close to the boat, knows what a thunderous sound the splash makes. White spray and bubbles remain on the surface of the water.

When the whales slap their tails, they can make a huge spray as the tail can weigh up to seven hundred pounds. When you're out in a boat and a whale breaches near you, you feel the raw power of this ocean mammal. Sometimes a whale will "spy-glass," rising out of the water with only their head and large eyes. Having a whale's eye looking at you is a powerful feeling. Sometimes they appear to wave their flukes (fins). Hearing their duets, and their calls and responses while snorkeling in the bay, are one of the loveliest sounds I've ever experienced. I always imagined that they were singing us back to remember who we are, to remember many things that we once knew, which reside behind the veils of our conscious mind. Some people feel that they help us to remember life before this life, or life in the stars. I've even heard some people say the Akashic records are sung in their songs, and that the whales are the keepers of the Earth's archives.

### Whales, Rain and Loneliness

LAST NIGHT I LAY IN BED LISTENING to the rhythmic beat of the rain on the roof. Ray was sleeping soundly, graciously out of pain for the duration of his sleep. I could hear his breathing in the next room. We kept our doors cracked, so I could help him if he needed me. I was hoping that Paul would come over to visit me soon, but it would be hard for him to leave a very busy printing and publishing company. The business had rather rooted us in Nevada City, in the California gold country. We still had some adult children living on our land, and he was looking after them too. He didn't know for sure if he could get away. I was missing him, and the loneliness that I felt became even stronger while I lived with Ray and all his suffering pain. I wished that Paul could be with me to hear the whales sounding in the cove below. He would surely love listening to them as much as I do. I imagined him being there with me, under the crisp white sheets and the Hawai'ian patchwork quilt with the *ulu* (breadfruit) design.

But we were both still discovering ourselves as separate independent beings and no longer as enmeshed individuals who had lived together for many years. We were both tired out from both physical and mental hard work. We had almost forgotten who we were as individuals. I had to remind myself sometimes that I had chosen to come to the Big Island. Paul had agreed and given his blessings, thinking it would be good for both of us. It was a type of soul retrieval, in this new stage of life, after raising five children. The children were young adults now, and our grandbabies were still babies. I sometimes described this hiatus, of what would be almost a year in Hawai'i, as my sabbatical between being a mother and a grandmother. This was certainly unconventional, and I am not advising this for others either. It shocks some people. But it seems that the people who understood it the most are women. It seemed to trigger insecurity and criticism in some men. Others thought it was a good idea. I was glad that Paul was not insecure.

I secretly wished that Paul would sell the business or move the business over here to the Big Island. But as I said, we were quite rooted on our ten acres, living in our old farm house that sat on top of the 1800's Davies Gold Mine and stamp mill. In my heart I knew Paul wouldn't be able to move the business to this island that we both loved. But sometimes loneliness crept in, like a dark coverlet, especially while listening to the rain in the dark of night.

Mingled with the sound of the rain was the ancient sounding of the whales in the cove below Ray's house. Their soundings climbed up and down the scales in major and minor chords and rhythms. They had their own unique symphony. It is said that every year the humpback whales have a new song. Whether they are the whales that migrate from Alaska to Hawai'i, or the whales that migrate from Alaska to Mexico, they all sing the same song each year.

The whale operas felt like a call to remember, to go deeper, beyond our present incarnation into the ancient past. They were sounds that spun the mind out into the stars and the galaxies. Ordinary time and space stopped, and the mind emptied itself of trivial things, memories, wishes, and concerns. But the loneliness remained. In my mind I could still hear the rhythm of the brand new Ipu Heke drum being played by the *kupuna* at Spencer Beach. The vivid memory of it resounded in my mind and blended with the whale songs. The beach was dark now and empty of picnickers, sunbathers and swimmers. It could purify and renew itself during the solitude of a dark and rainy night. Tomorrow the sun would shine again, gleaming and reflecting on the water, and the kupunas would be playing their ukuleles and singing the beach awake, once again.

## Rhythm and Prayers

RHYTHM IS AROUND US ALL THE TIME. When we begin to notice, we become attuned to it. There are layers of rhythm too, from the subtle sounds of our own heartbeat to a deeper layer where we can attune to the heartbeat of the Mother Earth. There are so many rhythms . . . from birds, animals, frogs, crickets, wind in the grass or trees, raindrops, the sounds of whales and dolphins, and the myriad sounds of water: dripping water, rain, babbling brooks, waves, and waterfalls. I thought of winter back home with the silent rhythm of snow falling. The first rhythm we know, in this life, is the heartbeat of our mother, while we are still in the womb. And all around the world, people have made drums and sat in circles, drumming and making rhythms with sticks, rocks, and shakers that echo even more subtle rhythms under the surface of the Earth, in the millions of years of Earth history.

As I was drifting off to sleep, I prayed for my family and friends back home, and I prayed for my friends here on this island. I especially prayed for Ray, that he might have comfort and peace. I liked a phrase from Aka's prayer: "*Ke Akua* (Creator), blanket all those who are connected to me, by blood or by heart, with your divine love, protection, and healing." Her mother, Auntie Fern's words echoed in my mind as well, "Pray and pray and pray. Make your life a living prayer." I had not forgotten. I was not going to waste the wisdom of the elders.

### Flashback to Moorea: The Training of a Drummer

WHEN READING A BOOK, I always feel that books are missing a sound track: the ambient sounds that might accompany a certain scene: the calls and responses of birds, crickets, waves, the sound within a conch shell, of frogs, or the wind in the trees. Movies often provide a musical sound track to accompany the scene, but with a book, our imagination must help fill in the sounds and images that we might be hearing or seeing if we were "inside" the story. Sometimes there are sounds that are unfamiliar to us. If one has never heard palm fronds blowing in a tropical breeze, or soft waves lapping on a shore of sand and shells, one would not be able to imagine it, or hear it in one's own mind.

Our daughter, Christina, and I stayed on the island of Moorea for three months in 1993 when she was sixteen years old. From our beach we could look out across the water to see the island of Tahiti in the distance, only twenty-eight miles away. Christina was enrolled in home study as a junior in high school. The next year she returned and stayed for another three months with a Tahitian family with whom we had become close friends. While in Moorea, we met a Tahitian man who was reputed to be the best traditional drummer on the island. He had students of his own, who had to go through the same rigorous training that he had when he was young. At night, we could hear the Tahitian drums from our little bamboo-framed home with the thatched pandanus leaf roof.

One day the wife of the Tahitian drum teacher described her husband's drum training to us. First, his master gave him an assignment which would last a number of months. He was to study and absorb the rhythms of nature before he would be given lessons directly on the drum. The sounds of the waves on the shoreline, the raindrops, waterfalls, the different rhythms of wind and breezes, the sound within a conch shell, bird calls and songs, crickets, the scurrying sounds of the land crabs as they make a mass alarm exodus into their holes, frogs, the rolls of thunder and the cracking of lightning, the sounds of the dolphins and whales and the myriad sounds of ocean waves in different kinds of weather. He was to listen for rhythm in everything around him and after these months of listening and absorbing, his drum master would finally bring him face to face with the drum.

Our bedroom house was perched right on a lava rock foundation on the edge of the lagoon. Waves lapped up on the rock walls and lulled us to sleep at night. In the distance we could hear giant waves crashing up against the barrier reef that surrounded the island. A big white mosquito net cascaded down around the sides of our bed from a ring attached to a large bamboo "rafter" on the ceiling. We often commented that it was like sleeping in a protective cocoon.

On a distant beach, farther down the shoreline, we could see a bonfire and hear singing and the beat of Tahitian drums. Sounds carried beautifully across the water, and it seemed as if the many coconut palms, all around us, acted as loud speakers, bringing the primal drumbeat and voices right to us on the wind. Next to this land there was a grove of tall coconut palm trees which had been planted for the export of Copra (coconut meat) years ago. Now the industry had stopped, but the palms dropped abundant coconuts which littered the floor of the coconut grove.

Most locals fished. The lagoon was dotted with canoes and a few motor boats that would stay still while the people were fishing. The women would often fish bare-breasted, looking much like the women in Gauguin's paintings. There were sand sharks in the lagoon, but the locals said they were harmless. The fishermen and fisherwomen caught a variety of fish which had an array of delicious flavors. I still remember one fish that tasted exactly like crab, and another very close to the texture and flavor of lobster. From our bedroom house we could make out the canoes gliding along at night, fishing with torchlight. It was like a dream-scape, especially during the full moon, and we had to "pinch ourselves" sometimes to realize that we were living this particular dream in real time. It was so much like I imagined old Hawai'i to be.

### Ray, Holding You in a Sacred Way

TODAY, MY ELDER BROTHER RAY, I see tears in your eyes, as you sit on the lanai, overlooking the ocean, with the bougainvillea vines dancing all around you in the breeze. They are vibrant with colors of magenta and white. Just as birth is an entry into this world, death is an entry into the heavenly world from which you came. These transitions are sacred, and there are so many ways to die. As Aka and I said to each other, one time, "There are so many ways to get your 'ticket' to the next world." Whether we have a long or short life, or "how" we die, is really a great mystery, too.

Aka and I know that there is an afterlife. As receivers, we had both received unmistakable messages from friends and relatives "on the other side." Being who she is, gave her abilities way beyond mine. She literally lives in more than one world at once, slipping between the veils of the worlds, with grace and ease, like a *hula*

305

dancer. She was in communion with her *tutus* all the time. And she acknowledged them many times a day in her prayers. Aka did not know Ray, but she was making distant prayers for him, as we had talked on the phone about Ray's condition.

I spoke silently to Ray. "Ray, the doctors have now given you the word that you need to be in a care home, where you can receive morphine for the pain that is becoming more intense for you every day. What are your tears telling me? Are you in pain? I imagine that you don't want to leave your home and move a step closer to your inevitable death. Or is it the existential feeling of eternity looming in front of you, as the great mystery of not knowing what will become of you. Or do you wonder if you will be able to bear the pain, as it gets worse? For those of you, without faith, like yourself, you have no idea if it's suddenly and finally all over, or if there is some form of life afterward. When I tried to speak to you of my belief in after-life, your lip curled with disapproval and skepticism, and you said something about weak people needing religion as a crutch. You are snapping at me more often now. I know the pain must be unbearable. You are losing weight and you are weak, slumping in your chair during fitful naps and moaning in your sleep. Your shirts are hanging loosely on your broad shoulders that once stood so straight and strong. You don't want to lie down now as you don't want to give up. You have always been a tall, proud, successful man, and this weakness and pain is not 'what you signed up for.' Becoming helpless in a sea of pain is even worse than the things that happened to you during the Second World War. I reach over to take your hand, and in an unusual show of strength you yank your hand away from mine. A few moments later I reach over for your hand again. This time you accept me holding your hand and tears start to roll down your cheeks. We just sit in silence. If I could just pray and make your pain go away, I would. Ray, in my heart, I hold you in a sacred way.

## MOVING TO KONA

### *A Return to Paleaku Peace Gardens*

I WAS BACK AT PALEAKU GARDENS AGAIN, as Ray had been moved to a nursing care home and was now receiving the proper type of pain medication. He was much more comfortable now, but slipping in and out of consciousness. I would not forget Ray, and I wondered why we had met on the Big Island at the end of his life.

Once again Kapua had helped me move, filling the moving day with dozens of jokes. He sometimes told the jokes more than once, but we always laughed, as the way he told them, in animated pidgin English and his own robust belly laugh, was hilarious. One of them was, "Do you know what a Gozunda is? My grandma had one." I would say, "No, what is a gozunda?" Then he would say, "It is an old fashioned chamber pot. You know, it gozunda da bed." And then he would roar with laughter. His laughter was infectious and I would always join him. I thought of a friend who always said that "laughter clears your jets." His next one was: "Do you know anyone with cranial-rectal syndrome?" And I said, "No, what is it?" He laughed for a while and then between laughs, squeaked out, "Someone with their head up their ass." Then he told of a class he took in the college of Traditional Chinese Medicine. His Chinese herbal instructor was a Chinese woman with a thick accent. She was giving them instructions on laxative herbs. She then said, "You got to lube da tube to float the boat." There is only one Kapua, and somehow he gets away with it, as his delight in his own jokes is just as funny as the joke itself.

I was back in my sleeping loft above the kitchen in Barbara's house on the grounds of Paleaku Peace Gardens. I always felt this was the very sweetest place in the world to sleep. Barbara and I were back to having breakfast together. We sat together and went over the day's plans before she went to answer phone calls and do paper work in her office. There was also a workshop scheduled soon, with Faisel, a Middle Eastern spiritual teacher, who teaches about the different states of consciousness in a very colorful way. I was looking forward to helping with and attending this event. Now that I was so close, I was able to snorkel again in Honaunau Bay, commonly known as "Two Step," and I would be able to see a lot of my Kona-side friends. The mold allergies had completely cleared up while I was living with Ray in Kawaihae, and I felt very healthy. It was good to be back in Kona, at Paleaku Gardens, and close to the dolphins and other friends.

### Corals are Living Beings

I MET CINDI HANOHANO PUNAHAOLE at Paleaku Peace Garden while I was staying there for visits in 1999 and 2000. She and Barbara are really good friends and the three of us participated together in a Hula class with Kumu Hula Peccelo Day. We also enjoyed visiting together in the kitchen after Hula class. One time Cindi invited me up to her home above the Kailua Kona airport, which had been her parent's home. I have rarely seen such a beautiful garden with so many varieties of beautiful plants and flowers.

Cindi is a Hawai'ian woman who was educated in a one-room school house on the Big Island in the nineteen fifties. Later she attended college on the mainland. She grew up learning how to survive on the land. Her father taught the children how to grow gardens, fish, hunt and dress the animals, and prepare them as food. All this was done with great respect. Her jobs on this island have always been about marine conservation and taking care of the land, the coastal areas, and ancestral sites. In the past she helped to preserve ancient fish ponds. Today she is the Project Director for Kahalu'u Bay's Education Center.

As a favorite snorkeling bay, there are up to 400,000 visitors a year. She and the volunteers who help her are deeply involved with educating visitors about the bay, the reefs, the marine life, and the coral. Visitors almost always want to cooperate with helping protect the bays and corals after learning about their fragility. Cindi's style with people is gentle and filled with *aloha*. Corals are living beings that have most often been damaged by sunscreen pollution and people standing on them. There are some "relatively" reef-safe sunscreens on the market today that are less harmful to the coral. Through education, locals and visitors alike are learning how to protect the corals. They are fragile living beings that are also the homes of so many reef fish and sea life.

### One of My Funniest Friends . . . Kaaren Soby

KAAREN AND I MET EACH OTHER while we were both staying at and doing "work/trades" at Paleaku Gardens. She was from B.C. Canada and about the same age as I was. She had short, blond, wavy hair, was tall and graceful, and had a youthful figure. Most of all what I recall is her pretty face that was almost always wearing a big smile with dancing, impish eyes. Her daughter was the same age as one of my daughters. One of the things that we had in common was that our husbands were both at home and we had come to Hawai'i on a "so-called" sabbatical or long retreat.

We both felt a need to explore ourselves, as ourselves, alone, finally, after many years of marriage and child rearing, land and house work, and jobs. Kaaren felt the same way. Kaaren's husband, Larry, was also as freedom-giving to his wife as Paul was to me. How very lucky we were. Kaaren is an accomplished artist and painted a beautiful mural at Paleaku Gardens. When she cared for some land, *mauka* of the highway, she had a large lanai with a beautiful distant view of the ocean stretching out far below. Here, she painted numerous sunset paintings, which were very beautiful.

Both Kaaren and I practiced Tibetan Buddhist meditation, so while cleaning at Paleaku Gardens, we called ourselves the "toilet *dakinis*." We scurried around doing our chores in the morning so that we could spend the afternoons swimming and snorkeling. What a life! Kaaren's home was in the back woods of British Columbia with only snow mobile access in the cold and snowy winters. I lived in another winter cold spot in the Sierra foothills of California. Here we were in Hawai'i, in the winter, with temperatures in the high seventies and low eighties (F), and weather that was delightful for swimming and sunbathing. In spite of a loneliness that we sometimes felt, we were having a good time.

Kaaren was able to do the graceful "Dance of the Vajra," which was inspired and taught by Namkai Norbu Rinpoche. She danced with a few others on the specially painted mandala, which was set up by Rinpoche on a platform floor at Paleaku Gardens.

Kaaren and I, coincidentally, had come to the island with the same intention, to have an opportunity to experience ourselves, alone, away from family, in this culture that we both love. I kept a diary, but Kaaren's diary was far more creative, filled with hilarious cartoons of her adventures and misadventures. While we were at Paleaku Gardens, living and doing work trades, Kaaren painted a beautiful large flower mural that was uniquely her own style, but in some ways reminded me of the work of Georgia O Keefe.

There was a cartoon on the cover of Kaaren's diary that showed a car, half covered with lava, and a very funny caption that went with it. I laughed and laughed as I flipped through Kaaren's cartoons. So much of what she cartooned and wrote about were identical to adventures and misadventures that I, too, had had.

Back home, Kaaren and Larry had a large piece of land in the remote north woods of British Columbia, complete with dense forested areas and a small lake. This was the perfect retreat space! Larry, like Paul, was very liberal in giving his blessing to his wife to go for a long adventure on an island in the middle of the ocean. I feel that both of these wonderful men had to be a little bewildered at times about these wives of theirs, who didn't yet know each other when their call to the island came. Kaaren, like me, was led by dreams and spiritual guidance. However, besides the high times swimming in the ocean and sharing funny stories, when we weren't working, we both were severely tested. Both of us had moments of homesickness and tears, and sometimes wondered if coming here was a big mistake. But soon these moments passed, and synchronicities, magic, and wonderful people helped the tears to evaporate.

We both laughed and pondered seriously about the purification that Kupuna Pele exacts from newcomers who try to stay on the island for longer than a short vacation. Locals like to tell stories about *haoles* who come over and some of the crazy things that happen to them. They would say, "So and so just got blown off the island." There were more than enough stories about visitors who broke their ankles on lava rocks, got centipede bites on their lip, or had sicknesses or other mishaps. Kaaren said to me one time, "You just don't come over here to mess around ... eh?" Oh yes, the ever-present Canadian "eh" was part of Kaaren's lovely voice and speech. And she had one of the loudest laughs in perhaps the whole world, except perhaps for a Tibetan Lama we know who could rival her laugh. When Kaaren laughs, you can hear it a long way away! It is such a raucous and jubilant laugh that, no matter how you might be feeling, you start laughing with her. It's infectious! When she was with Aka and they both laughed . . . now there was a joyful sound!

Back home in Canada Kaaren was an activist and showed her artwork in local galleries. Her high energy fueled her talents and her laugh. I loved to watch her swim out into the bay with such a trim and strong body that was right at home in the ocean. We shared the love of the tide pools, reef fish, turtles, and the dolphins and whales. Soon Larry would be coming for a visit, right around the same time that Paul was coming to visit me. We planned for the four of us to have a few dinners together. How different it would be to be with partners again after being alone for so long.

### Some Thoughts on the Hawai'ian Language

IN HAWAI'I, VERY FEW PEOPLE ARE STILL FLUENT in the Hawai'ian language. Auntie Mona Kehele grew up speaking Hawai'ian in her home and was a fluent speaker. At one time it was illegal for the people to speak their own language. This was one of the tactics of the American government in their attempt to assimilate the people and eliminate their culture. This was much like the inhumane practices and genocidal, mass slaughters imposed on Native Americans. But now with the recent renaissance of the Hawaiian culture, which started in the nineteen seventies, the Hawai'ian language is again being taught in schools, and children's books are being published in Hawai'ian, so there is a current resurgence of the language. Most Hawai'ians speak English but often salt-and-pepper their sentences with a large array of Hawai'ian words and phrases. They remember these words, as they were used at home by grandma and grandpa, and mom and dad. Today, the language is being taught again by remaining native speakers. Immersion schools in the 1970s required parents to speak Hawai'ian at home to the student.

Many of the songs of Hawai'i are in the Native Hawai'ian language. It is a soft sweet language, consisting of twelve letters, the vowels and a few consonants: A E H I K L M N O P U W. (W's are pronounced like V's.) When it is spoken or sung, the sounds seem to reflect the swaying of palm trees, the waves touching the shoreline of sand or rocks, and the swirling rippling receding of the waters. The language is as sweet as the tiare, the tuberose, the pikake, and the plumeria flowers. The tones touch and open the heart. Island people, living close to nature, spoke a poetic language that reflected the islands and the waters that their canoes traversed.

*Kauna* refers to several layers of meaning in a chant or song, much like the embedding of outer, inner, and secret meanings. Even though it is a poetic, gentle language, it can also be fierce, coming from the mouths of warriors or *lua* (Hawai'ian martial arts) masters. It was the intention of the communication that dictated the tone of voice, either the softness or the fierceness.

I learned to chant a beautiful chant from Kumu Hula Peccelo Day. We would chant it as each of us entered the *Hula halau*, when Barbara, Cindi, Rika and I and others were taking Hula lessons at Paleaku Gardens. I'm not sure I can remember all of it now. Aka taught me two different chants in the Hawai'ian language. Many a time we stood together on the shore of the ocean and chanted together. Her *mana*-filled chanting voice is embedded in my memory forever.

### A Chance to Paddle

I LOVED WATCHING THE PADDLERS going out to the ocean from Honaunau Bay. They would launch their six-person canoes from the boat ramp and go out to the ocean through the bay. One day I was standing by the boat launch and a group of local women paddlers found themselves short one person. They looked around and asked me if I could fill in. I shocked myself by saying "Yes." So off we went! This was certainly an exercise in group mind and perfect timing.

The moment of dipping the paddle into the water and coming out of the water had to be precisely synchronized with the rest of the paddlers. For me it took great concentration, as I didn't want to be the "one *haole*" who threw off this precise rhythm. It didn't take too

long before I got the hang of it. I dipped my oar in and pulled it through the water at the same time as the other oars. Someone called out "*Huki*" (pull) every time we needed to change sides. Before long we were paddling out of Honaunau Bay and into the ocean.

We paddled up the shoreline for about forty minutes before turning around and coming back into Honaunau Bay. Paddling was more strenuous once we were in the ocean, as the water was a little choppy and had more current. To increase our speed, we had to use more upper body strength. I wondered if my strength would hold out, as this was the first and only time I had ever done this. Fortunately, all the swimming I had done had built up pretty good strength in my arms and shoulders. I noticed that the other women had very muscular arms. They were training for a future race. By the time we paddled back through Honaunau Bay, I was feeling comfortable with the paddling and was less nervous. It was fun and a fulfillment of a semi-conscious wish.

As we paddled into the bay, the City of Refuge, Pu'uhonua o Honaunau, was on the right hand side of us. We passed the large *heiau*, the coconut palm trees, and the little sandy beach that had once only been used by the *Ali'i o*r chief class. In the past this place was truly a haven and refuge for people who had broken *kapu* (laws). If *kapu* breakers were able to get to this place, they would be spared possible death. They could become a part of this society and be safe. It was a village of refuge and rehabilitation before the arrival of visitors and colonization.

As we approached the shallow water and the boat ramp, we got out and lifted the canoe out of the water. Not much was said, but everyone had a look of contentment on their faces as we all had had a good paddle and felt refreshed. I thought to myself that my arms would surely ache the next day, but they didn't. I thanked the women for inviting me and then walked away. One of the women smiled a friendly smile and shook out a *shaka* for me, which I returned.

### Helen's Birthday with Aka and the Whales

MY DEAR FRIEND HELEN WAS COMING to the Big Island for a vacation and was bringing her son Jay and his daughters. They had accommodations in a nice hotel in Kailua-Kona. Helen wanted to do something "special and Hawai'ian" for her 75th birthday. In the evening she planned to have a dinner with her family in an open-air restaurant along the edge of the ocean. So I hatched a plan: a birthday surprise! I called Aka, and we discussed the idea of a ceremony for Helen. Aka knew just the place, the picnic grounds at the City of Refuge, Pu'uhonua o Honaunau, right on the edge of the ocean. I volunteered to bring the picnic, and Aka planned to arrive on the 18th of March, at high noon. I decided to invite Rika along, as she wanted to meet Helen. Rika and Aka were already friends.

We picked Helen up at the hotel. Her son and grand-daughters were going snorkeling somewhere else and wouldn't be coming with us. We had already bought the picnic makings at the KTA, as they had the famous, delicious butter rolls that Aka loved so much, and . . . they had *malasadas* (Portuguese donuts). Some were filled with taro and others were filled with jam. They also had a wonderful deli. So my cooler was filled with drinks and deli treats, and *huli huli* chicken from the *huli huli* man, and of course, Aka's favorites, the buttah rolls, and of course, the birthday pie, a blue sweet potato and cream cheese pie with whipped cream on top. So *ono*!

Helen and Rika and I arrived first, parked the car, and claimed a nice picnic table. As we got set up, Helen was in such a bubbly, happy mood. She "ooohhed and aaahhed" over the beautiful setting: the ocean, the waves hitting the rocky shoreline, and the swaying palm trees. Oh, how nice the weather was here in March! At home in Nevada City, it was still winter and very cold.

Aka drove up to our picnic table driving a green forest service truck. Beside her was her ever present little dog, Puka, who had the presence of a king in a dog's body. Also in the truck were her daughter, Lilinoe, and her granddaughter, Shai Shai, and Shai's father. We all gathered around the table. Aka had a wide and expansive smile on her face and gave Helen and I a hug that completely enveloped us in her big Aloha and big love. Here was a woman who was not afraid to love. She loved and hugged everyone. Even the stiffest, most uptight people melted down, softened, and smiled after an Aka hug. Pupuka, Aka's dog, jumped up on the bench of the picnic table with his nose twitching in all directions, smelling the *Huli huli* chicken (spit-roasted) and buttah rolls. He just knew he was a human being in a dog's body, and he wanted to be treated as such.

Aka decided that we would have the ceremony first and the picnic later. She had hand-crafted a beautiful *haku po'o lei* for Helen's head, and she placed it upon her head saying, "Happy Birthday, sistah Helen." Then there was a *maile leaf lei* that she placed around Helen's neck. Aka said, "I was lying in bed this morning, having my morning prayers and meditation, and I was talking to my brothers and sisters, the whales. I have it on the highest authority that they will be here today to attend this birthday celebration, Helen."

I wondered how she could be so sure of this. She said it with the confidence of utter knowing. Aka led Helen out to a spot which she knew all her life. It was a little hole in the lava rock that Aka called a *puka*. She asked Helen to stand above the *puka*, with her legs on both sides of it, as it was a power spot, a spot of blessing and energy. Her toes loved the feeling of the water in the *puka*. Helen immediately began to wave her two arms, like flapping chicken wings, as she felt the energy go up her legs and spine to the top of her head. "Ohhh, ohhhh, ohhh," she uttered, as she was feeling the energy all through her body. Aka started chanting for Helen, said a prayer over her, and poured a little water from a shell onto her head, almost as if she was baptizing her.

NANCY, HELEN AND RIKA

I was thinking to myself, in a certain way, to have a ceremony with Aka, you do become a Hawai'ian at heart, as brother IZ says. And you do get baptized by *Ke Akua* and his angels, as Aka's heart is pure and her motivation is always to bless. As unconventional as it is, it is sacred. After this part of the ceremony, Aka walked over to the place where the lava rock met the ocean waves. She had her *pu* in hand, raised it to her lips, and toned three, long deep tones to the direction of the south, then to the west, and then to the north. We were assembled in the east on the shoreline.

Suddenly, whales were coming to us from the three directions that she had called to. They were like dogs coming quickly to a dinner whistle, and how they entertained us . . . breaching, spy-glassing, and playing in the deep water so close to our picnic table. The water gets very deep, very quickly, right off this particular shore line. At one point in the ceremony Aka had Helen throw her *maile leaf lei* into the water, and then there was a closing prayer and chant. "Now sistah, let's go grind (eat). It's your birthday and you will go first." Lilinoe had all the paper plates, cups and napkins set out. There were deli-cartons and other delicious food for lunch. Everything was ready for the birthday picnic.

The whales continued to jump and play and entertain us the whole time we enjoyed the food. Aka's little grandaughter, Shai, was delighted with the whales. Later I asked Aka, "How did you do that?" She smiled and said, "I was born with certain gifts, sistah. I am closely related to the whale brothers and sisters, and like I told you before, I have the gift of 'calling'." She just said this in a matter of fact way, but with no ego and no pride.

So what we had witnessed was Aka "calling the whales" with her *pu*. Again, for her the extraordinary is ordinary. In a family like Aka's, where each and every one is gifted, nothing like this would be a surprise. I leaned over and whispered to Aka, "Aka, do you believe in love at first sight?" She laughed so loud that her belly shook and she said, "Sistah, I fall in love at first sight with each and every person I meet. I love 'em all . . . and I am here to give my Aloha, and to share the teaching of Aloha. Real Aloha IS falling in love at first sight, with each and every braddah and sistah."

Aka talked with Helen for a while and we all visited with each other and fussed over Shai, Aka's little Hawai'ian grand-daughter whose smile was full of sunshine. Rika loved meeting Helen and felt like adopting her as an Auntie. Aka surely had the Aloha spirit and so did her daughter, Lilinoe. Puka finally had his chicken and buttah roll, and was under the table chowing down, or as Aka often said, "Getting a grind on." And if the food was really delicious, many local people said it "broke dah mouth."

At the close of our time together Aka walked over to the ocean's edge once again. We were all behind her. There was a closing chant and a prayer . . . "*Mahalo nui loa Ke Akua* (our creator) for all the blessings that you so generously bestow upon us, each and every day, and on our sistah Helen, on her birthday . . . and *mahalo nui loa* Helen, for coming all this way to celebrate your birthday on our beautiful *aina*. We give thanks . . . *Mahalo nui loa, Ke Akua* (Thank you, creator)."

Then Aka took her *pu* out to the ocean's edge and started speaking to the whales and told them that they could go now . . . and thanked them for coming to join us today. She blew her *pu* in the same three directions and off the whales went, swimming away to the north, south and the west. Blessed creatures of God, I thought. How I loved the whales and dolphins, and I couldn't be happier that I had been able to arrange a birthday like this for one of my dearest friends. I felt so very grateful to Aka, as wherever she goes and whatever she does, she creates beauty, welcome, and the feelings of kindness and love. And this is ALOHA.

## No Kine Pilikea (Trouble) in Hawai'i

AKA WAS STILL LIVING DOWN IN OCEAN VIEW, but her daughter Suzy was going to school up in Kona. Sometimes when Suzy wanted to stay overnight with a friend in Kona, Aka would call me from Ocean View and ask me to pick up Suzy at her friend's house and drive her to school. Suzy would talk me into getting *malasadas* on the way. I always enjoyed seeing Suzy, who was twelve at the time. She was full of life and full of fun! She carried a similar *mana* (spiritual energy) as her mother and grandmother Fern. She had the same name as her grandmother/auntie Fern, "Kalehuamakanoe." I could see that some day Suzy would grow into being a spiritual guide and have this *kuleana*, just like her mother, grandmother, and great grandmother. To this day I love Suzy, and she now has four beautiful children. Her daughter, who is her oldest, is also named Kalehuamakanoe.

One morning Aka asked me to meet her down at the bay around 11 in the morning. She often drove up from Ocean View to K. Bay to run the shop with her mom. But this day was different. She wanted me to sit in with her on an unusual type of *Ho'o'ponopono* session. A woman who we both knew would be coming to see us in the park next to the bay and the *heiau*. She was a stunning young woman from California. Aka told me that it would be confidential, like all *ho'o'ponopono* sessions, as she was going to have to talk to this woman about some *pilikia* behavior . . . and *pilikia* means trouble.

It seems that Aka had "plenee *pilikia* complaints" from some of her Hawai'ian women friends. Apparently a particular woman had been going after, and cheating, with some of their husbands. Of course some of the cheating husbands had "snowed" this woman with complaints about their wives. Other persuasive remarks complimented this woman on her beauty. "She was so irresistible that they had to 'have her' and it would be an experience they would always treasure." Oh boy, how young, beautiful women can be naïve, I thought. She believed these old standard lines, hook, line and sinker. Aka had been taught high moral standards and would not tolerate this behavior, as it was hurtful to her women friends. She would be a warrior in battle for her friends and family. Since we both knew this woman, we were the ones who were going to talk to her about it. It would be just the three of us.

The woman arrived at the bay and walked cautiously, picking her way over the rocks, to the picnic table where we were sitting. She smiled, but when seeing our expressions, her face turned serious. Aka said, "Sit down, sistah. What we are going to say today is going to be said out of caring for you and also for the community . . . my other sistahs and bruddahs and their *Ohanas.*" Aka began with a prayer: "*Ke Akua,* we ask that you be with us today as we talk together and seek understanding. Help us to be right with you and with each other. We ask for your guidance and blessing today as we seek peace, love, and harmony between ourselves and our larger *ohana. Mahalo nui loa* for all you give us each day and the blessings that you so abundantly shower upon us."

Without mentioning any names, Aka launched into some of the stories that she had heard from her women friends. She asked the young woman if these things were true. At first the woman said it was none of our business and why should she reveal private things to us. Aka went on to say that she was concerned not just for her friends but the community at large, and that this problem had been "delivered onto her plate." "I respond to whahtevah comes on my plate," Aka said to the woman. "There are sisters who are really hurting because they have told me that their husbands have been sleeping with you." Some are thinking about a divorce and divorce can hurt the children, as well. The woman then launched into all the reasons the men had given her, listing their complaints about their wives.

"You seem to believe in spiritual energy and things like individual and collective energy. Isn't that right?" Aka asked. The woman nodded. "When there is a disturbance in the community, it becomes a disturbed energy in the collective. This is an island surrounded by miles and miles of watah. Everything is more intense here, energetically. We are living on top of a live volcano. No joke, that they call this island the 'dirty laundry island'. Tings that are not *pono* about us – and that means all of us – rise up to be washed and cleaned. And then we have Kupuna Pele in the Volcano, and she knows when a *wahine* (woman) is not *pono* (righteous or good). She knows about jealousy! And my correction is gentle compared to what she might do. One woman in pain can be felt, on some level, by all the women. Maybe we're not able to identify the disturbance, but there will be a *puka* (hole) in the energy. Several of my *titas* (women) are hurting. They tell me that their husbands are cheating on them, with you."

The woman hung her head and seemed to look down at her tan bare feet under the table. Then she said, "I don't have anyone. Okay, these men have needs and their wives aren't taking care of them, so what harm does it do?" Aka laughed a rather stiff laugh, lit a cigarette, blew the smoke out slowly and thoughtfully, and said, "That line is as old as the hills, sistah. Are you falling for dat, hook, line and sinkah? These *kanes* (men) see a young and naïve woman like you, and you know, it is kinda hard for them to resist you, looking so all 'da kine'." Aka went in and out of pidgin, like so many Hawai'ians. She was eloquent in the King's English, but could slide right into the thickest of pidgin at times. Sometimes, like now, it was a blend of both.

"I am not saying that these *kanes* (men) are right in hitting on you, either. They're not. But you already have a reputation here, and you are not a local. You are a visitor. You need to treat this culture with respect, if you are going to visit here from the mainland, and be *pono* with the locals an' 'our cultchah'." Aka went on, "Here is what you need to think about sistah: Either you are a friend to other women and are a sistah . . . or you are not a sistah. If you hurt other women by cheating with their companions or husbands, then you are not a sistah. When you are a sistah, all the other sistahs will be your friends, often for life. They will have your back. They will be there for you through thick and thin. But if you decide NOT to be a sistah, then you may find yourself alone, later in life, without friends. When your beauty fades and times are tough, the men won't be there for you either. And it will be too late, unless you decide to change now. If you make an offering, purify yourself five times in the watah, with *tapu wai*, have remorse, put these ways behind you, and then re-dedicate yourself to being 'a sistah', then *Ke Akua* may even bless you with a wonderful man of your own some day."

I said a few words to her too and told her she probably didn't know the pain a wife feels when her husband cheats on her. She admitted that she had never been married or in a serious long-term relationship. "It really hurts!" I said. "You are really young. You just think you are a free spirit having fun, but you probably never realized that the coconut telegraph carries gossip all around the island. The men may brag to their friends about you, and then the word goes out. The men will hit on you, and the women won't trust you. When you go to the grocery store, you may get 'stink eye' from the women."

The woman said defiantly, "Why are you judging me? It's not good to judge . . . and you're both judging me." "This is not about judgment, sistah," Aka said tenderly as she reached across the table to hold her hand. "This is about correction, for your own good, and your own happiness. Earlier in my life, I, too, needed some corrections. I have not been perfect. I was not judged, but I WAS corrected. A correction is said with love and a person's best interest in mind and heart. When there is no correction, everything just gets worse." "We all have our blind spots," I added. "I needed some corrections too, when I was younger."

Aka's elders had called upon her to help patch the web. Aka often talked of the web of life that connects all of us and how each of our actions affects this web. "We want the web of life, which connects all of us and all of nature, to be sparkling with goodness and love," she said. "Everyone knows everyone's 'biznis' here, and whaht everyone is doing, all the time, especially on 'dis island'," Aka said. "The coconut telegraph prevails!!! There is no hiding. We all need to be *pono* (good) here and *akamai* (smart). The island is like a canoe. We have to work together and look out for each other, for our very survival, as island people. One person that goes crazy or causes disharmony can tip over the canoe. It is important to remember too, that we are all guests of Kupuna Pele, and when she needs to, she can be a tough mistress."

Aka snuffed out her cigarette in an empty tin can that she carried with her. She now spoke softly to the woman with a voice that was like velvet. "The choice is easy, sistah. You either are a sistah or you're not." Now the floodgates opened, and the tears began to pour down the woman's face. She put her face down on the table, on top of her folded arms, and sobbed quietly for a while. Finally, she looked up at Aka and said in a wee, small voice, "I want to be a sister."

*{P.S. In recent years, I saw this woman here in California. She gave me permission to share this story, without her name, of course. She said this day was a turning point in her life. It was the beginning of the beautiful, happy life that she has today, which includes a wonderful husband and children.}*

## Hawai'ian Laughter

ONE OF THE THINGS I LOVE SO MUCH about the Hawai'ian culture is the perpetual laughter inside and outside of Hawai'ian homes. Hawai'ians love to laugh, and their humor pervades the culture. They poke fun at each other, but they poke fun at themselves the most, and see the humor in small, everyday things. They make each other laugh, as they know it lightens the load of everyday problems and stress. Science says it creates endorphins, which are the happiness hormones. Humor lightens our view of life and helps everyone have the resilience to get through hard times. The "Big Aloha" love and laughter keep the people strong and united . . . with giggles or belly laughs.

With a good joke or poking fun at oneself, a disagreement can evaporate. I wish I could remember all the good laughs I had while living on the Big Island in Hawai'ian homes and gatherings, but I will share a few that I do remember, as I remember laughing so much of the time. Not taking oneself too seriously is a good way to avoid having a big ego. Being able to say, "I'm sorry," when having hurt someone's feelings or making a mistake, is also a sign of humility and grace. "Oh, *Kala Mai* . . . I'm sorry or excuse me" is a phrase one hears a lot. I heard Aka make a prayer one time that went like this: "*Oh Kala Mai, Ke Akua* for anything harmful I have ever done, either consciously or unconsciously, intentionally or unintentionally." No one wants to hurt or be offensive to others.

When Hawai'ian people start to kid you, then you know you have been accepted. They watch to see if you can laugh at yourself. If you can, you will be kidded more and more and then, more than likely, be accepted as a friend. My friend, Kapua, like many Hawai'ians and Native Americans, loved fart jokes and bathroom humor. When getting prepped at the hospital, with a group of surgery candidates for a hip replacement operation, he mentioned that he was going to choose the anesthetic option of the macadamia nut-coconut-chocolate-covered morphine suppository. One lady, who was also a surgery candidate, said to him, with a complete poker face, "Oh, I didn't know that they offered that option."

Speaking of his Native American teacher, Johnny Moses, Kapua said that Johnny always said, "Some people think that their sh#t don't stink, but their farts give them away." Another joke from Kapua is: "You want to make God laugh? Just tell him your plans." One of Kapua's favorites is to say, "All my life I thought my name 'Edyson' was because my mother named me after Thomas Edison. One day, when I was grown up, I asked my mother why she named me after Thomas Edison." She laughed and said, "No, I named you after your father, Eddie. Edyson means 'son of Eddie'." He said back to her, "Well Ma, I'm glad you didn't name me after you, or I would be Bettyson." Someone else told me that you never wear shoes or slippahs (flip flops) inside a Hawai'ian home. It is polite to leave them outside on the steps and lanai. But occasionally you may not get your own slippahs back, as someone with old torn up slippahs may take a better pair on their way out. Local people joke about this. "Oh *kala mai*, didn't mean to, brah!" If you're the last one to leave, there may be slim pickings.

### Singing with Aka and Redemption

I ALWAYS CALLED AKA THE *"KARAOKE* QUEEN." She had a *karaoke* machine, loaded with hundreds of songs. She often sang an hour a day, with the microphone to her mouth and her graceful body moving and swaying to the music. Aka's mother and father were entertainers, and sang and played in the hotels for weddings and big events, so Aka and her sisters and brothers grew up in a musical house.

Aka's mother gave music lessons in their home, and the whole family sang and played instruments. They are all talented too, as I have had the pleasure of hearing them sing. Aka imitated for me the way her ma, Auntie Fern, would twirl and slap her big stand-up bass fiddle. I never got tired of listening to Aka sing. Famous for getting shy singers to sing, she pulled me into her chorus a number of times. "C'mon sistah, hit it! Belt it out! Give it your heart and soul! There's nobody that can't sing. Give up on this shower and car singing and bring it out! Just do it. The more you relax, the more your throat will open up! You'll be surprised. Nevah, nevah think back to school or church chorus when someone told you that you are 'tone deaf,' 'can't carry a tune,' or are 'off key.' When people are nervous, their throat closes up and that's what happens. Let it rip! Just relax." And this talk was ended with the biggest of belly laughs.

We were off and running with our favorite, "Redemption Song" by Bob Marley. We must have sung that at least a hundred times together. "Emancipate yourself from mental slavery. None but ourselves can free our minds. See sistah . . . just look at you . . . just listen . . . moh bettah all dah time. You're on it like a bonnet."

One day she commented on "Redemption Song" saying, "Everyone needs redemption! We all do things that we regret. Our ancestors need redemption too, and that's why we do *Ho'o'ponopono* for them as well. Imagine seeking and receiving forgiveness for everything ever done by your ancestors that might have hurt, harmed, or destroyed any life force in the past, all the way back to when your line was first created . . . or seeking and receiving forgiveness for those that have done harm against them . . . releasing them fully from the ties that have bound them, even in the spirit world. Now imagine freedom for all of them . . . thousands and thousands, if not more. All this helps to clear the blocks for us and all of our descendants. And by doing this, genetic ailments can be healed, and the way is opened for us to access ancient wisdom. When our inner channels are cleared, we become so much more intuitive, and receiving messages of divine guidance becomes a normal way of life. Best of all, we become clear enough to be of service to others, and to the divine."

I was trying to take this all in and thought of numerous ways I needed to more deeply forgive certain things I had done, and things that were done to me. Aka looked at me pensively, intuiting my thoughts. She continued with this talk: "We may feel ashamed and guilty about some things we have done. We all have that little secret closet inside of us that holds our guilt, shame, or regrets. That closet can also hold resentments, hurt feelings, and grudges towards other people. You know *da kine* – can be large or small. Sometimes that closet door opens up at night if we can't sleep, an' we re-run the movies. How many rocks can we put in our boat before we sink it? To keep our boat afloat, we need to breathe, pray, forgive, and let it go. Sometimes we need to do a ceremony to help us unload all of these rocks."

Suddenly she broke out in another song by Bob Marley, "Oh, please, don't you rock my boat." I had to laugh, as my daughter Christina and I listened to this song almost every day during our stay on the island of Moorea. Bob was literally our soundtrack for those magical three months.

Aka resumed speaking after I stopped laughing. "We are new people, every new day, and we can redeem ourselves by changing our habits and our behavior that isn't so *pono* (good). Sometimes we need to realize our own part in creating *pilikea* (trouble) with someone we resent. Pride and ego can get in the way of being honest with ourselves. We are free when we are sorry and make a sincere promise to change in a good way. Guilt and anger has a way of blocking our energy and our creative forces. Our *mana* becomes stifled, and then we are no longer able to create positive manifestations. But when we forgive ourselves and make changes and also forgive others, well . . . that is redemption! This goes for ALL of us and this is one of the reasons I love this song so much."

Aka could speak the King's English more eloquently than most, and when she was bringing through her *tutus* from the other side, her English was flawless. But from time to time, she would slip

325

into pidgin, when she was having fun or being casual. Pidgin flows with the jungle-like growth outside, the birds singing, and the blue, blue ocean with white caps on the shoreline. Pidgin is a lilting song that rolls off the lava and sand and then, glides like a bird flying *mauka* (uphill) into the cloud banks, which sometimes shroud the mountain tops.

When we were done singing, Aka would put her arm around me, emit a big belly laugh, and praise the improvement in my voice. At a later time, Anni McCann stayed at Aka's house too. She is a professional singer, song writer and recording artist, with a most beautiful and versatile voice. She could sing opera, Leonard Cohen, her own songs, and everything in between. Aka loved Anni, as Anni in her chorus up-leveled both duos and group sings.

We laughed a lot with these karaoke songs, and sometimes we stamped our feet and even threw in some back up singer "sha la la's" and "shoobie do wahs." Sometimes we would *hula* around the house and if there were a lot of us, we would make a traveling, dancing *hula* line through all the rooms of the house. There was plenty of laughter, joy, and love flowing. Aka got a lot of shy people to sing with her, and it gave them confidence and joy. I miss those days on the Big Island singing with Aka. Sometimes before a group meal she would lead us all in a song called "Love at Home." She cheered me on, and gave me the confidence that was ripped away from me in Sunday school when I was told not to sing anymore. A true healer heals in many ways, in the places where we are hurt or broken.

## "Ice"

WHETHER IT BE HAWAI'IANS, NATIVE AMERICANS, ABORIGINES or any other indigenous people, there is a resulting vulnerability caused by colonialism. It has suppressed their cultures, outlawed their languages and spiritual traditions, stolen their land, and desecrated their sacred sites. Injustices, greed for land and resources, as well as enforcing new rules for the people, led some of the people to escape the resulting emotional pain, with drugs, alcohol, and suicide. Stripped of using their own languages in public, or conducting their ceremonial cycles and being forced into "reservations" or small allotments of land, has caused anger, depression, and hopelessness in many of the people. The colonizers, feeling superior, rationalized these things with their belief in "manifest destiny." Based on "this world view," colonizers felt entitled to steal from and control native populations. With the belief that they had "God on their side," they were the very ones to introduce alcohol to native people who weren't able to tolerate it.

In recent years in Hawai'i, there has been an ICE epidemic. This is methamphetamine usually made at home in "ice kitchens," which makes this dangerous drug easily available and affordable. A quick jolt of energy from the drug often addicts those in the building trades and other jobs, making them think that they could work harder and faster and be more productive and energetic. But along with this false "energy" from this highly addictive drug, comes erratic driving and other "behaviors," marital strife, fights, and domestic violence. After the "high" there is an inevitable crash. Natural energy patterns are completely disrupted. Addicted people are not themselves anymore. To go to work the next day requires more ICE for energy, and the pattern goes on. People's personalities change. Brain damage occurs with long-term use, and families split apart.

It is not only in Hawai'i that this epidemic is taking place, but also on the mainland and many other places in the world. We also have this problem in our hometown of Nevada City, California. The term "tweeker" came about to describe Ice addicts, as they would fidget with this unnatural, speedy energy, tweek everything around them, and often steal from friends, family, or strangers to satisfy the addiction for the next high. Ethics and moral principles taught in church or family could be easily erased from memory by this drug use. Car accidents, incidents of domestic and other violence increased in this beautiful paradise. *Kahunas*, healers, and living cultural treasures do what they can to help curb this epidemic, as they are the keepers of the traditions, the culture and ceremonial cycles. Rehabilitation centers are filled with people getting well. This problem began to be called "the underbelly" of Hawai'i. And it is in the population, across the board, in all races and nationalities that live on the Big Island. But it is not only a problem here, it is a big problem on the mainland, and crosses all races and cultures. Some people call it the devil's drug. Returning to traditional ways, ceremonial cycles, rehabilitation centers, and access to inspiring leaders often provide healing and solutions for this plague.

*A Short Poem I wrote about Addiction to ICE (or Meth)*

"They entertain dark spirits …
Even yet, the butterfly sails over the garden gate.
'Metamorphosis,' the butterfly whispers in their ears,
as it alights upon their breasts, as if on a flower."

## Feng-Shui with Fatima

FATIMA HAD COME TO LIVE on the Big Island from Brazil. She was a most beautiful and graceful woman. While staying on the island during this post 9/11 time, one had to take any kind of job that was available to make ends meet. Fatima was cleaning houses on the Kona side. On several occasions I filled in for her usual cleaning partner.

It was a pure pleasure to work with Fatima. She was a joyful being, like a nature sprite that had an eye for beauty. Her black hair framed a beautiful face with dark, soulfully kind eyes. I didn't really know anything about her at the beginning, but we had two days in a row of cleaning and re-arranging a house while the owner was away. "The owner gave me permission to re-arrange furniture and art work any way I want to, while we work on her house. You and I can make these decisions together," she said in her soft and lilting Portuguese accent. So she put on some wonderful Brazilian music, and we danced as we mopped, scoured, dusted, and vacuumed the house. While we worked, we consulted each other on how the furniture and artwork could be re-arranged to be more *Feng-Shui* and pleasing.

As we had permission, we put some things away in labelled boxes that made the house look too cluttered. We moved and re-arranged furniture. Fatima was strong, even with her slim, petite frame. We matched in strength when moving things around, and it was like play with her. There was music and dance in all that we did.

To my amazement, our artistic senses matched on all of our decisions, which I found to be most unusual. I remember that at the end of the first day she asked me to ponder whether we would make one particular bedroom lavender, or green? She asked me to think about it overnight. On the morning of the second day we arrived with our Kona coffee. We had pondered color schemes and both of us came up with exactly the same ideas. 'Amazing,' I thought. We would continue our process of transformation. We both agreed that the bedroom would be purple and lavender and the paintings would be the ones of lagoons and palm trees. So we switched out color themes finding all the right things to finish the rooms. We had an array of curtains, duvet covers, sheets, and accent cushions to choose from. And then there was a large beautiful collection of art to select from. We had a hammer and picture hangers and did our picture hanging very carefully, both eyeballing and measuring.

In the kitchen Fatima placed a large bucket of beautiful white and purple orchids that she had bought at the outdoor market early that morning. Each room became more and more beautiful with the re-arrangements of furniture and art. Bouquets of orchids were placed in every room. "Orchids raise the vibrational energy," she said to me. It surely seemed to be true, as the house was humming with a beautiful, shimmery energy. And I remembered how good my little Hilo side cottage felt with my large orchid collection. After the bouquets were placed, she sprayed the house with an aromatherapy spritzer that filled the rooms with a delicious subtle fragrance that smelled like pikake, tuberose, tiare and gardenia flowers. Then we played bells and chimes in each room. With each additional gesture, the vibration of the house seemed to be happier and higher in frequency.

With all the new color schemes, art, and furniture rearrange-ments, the house did not look like the same house. It was transformed! It was beautiful! Everything was sparkling clean. The sinks were scoured clean, wiped out dry, and the faucets were polished. The floors gleamed and the rugs were spotless, without a trace of lint. The stove sparkled and begged never to be cooked on again. But the shiny clean spotless beauty was only temporary. It is the nature of this world that dust falls upon everything, and oil and grease dirty stoves, kitchen counters, and walls. But for this day everything was perfect. The homeowner would be coming home this afternoon and would find her house a place of uplifting beauty and happiness. Fatima was unique. In two short days I had learned so much about transformation and energy from her. A clean and beautiful house truly uplifts the spirit.

Now that we were finished, we decided to sit on the patio and have some iced tea. I did not know much about Fatima before these two days, but during our cleaning job she had mentioned having had domestic problems in Brazil with her former husband. As a result, she had not been able to see her beloved son for many years. It was a complex story full of medieval mystery and intrigue. Somehow it seemed that her son had disappeared. She had no way of discovering his whereabouts. She missed him, and her eyes filled with tears when she spoke of him. He would be a young adult by now, I thought.

As we drank our tea, she gave me the next installment of this mystery story. She recounted taking a walk along the northern-most ridge above Kealakekua Bay. This was the trail that went from the trailhead near the top of Na'po'opo'o Road that goes all the way down to the Captain Cook monument and the bay. She continued by telling me that she felt it was a most mystical place and a kind of portal between worlds. As she walked, looking out at the bay and the ocean stretching out below her to the horizon, she saw a young man walking up the trail, coming towards her. She thrilled with recognition and the certainty that this was her long lost son. He looked just as he would look, being years older than the last time she saw him. He smiled at her with a broad smile of recognition and love. As she was about to embrace him, he passed by her and, when she turned around, he was gone! She was in shock and despair. There was no place he could have escaped to, in just an instant. Where could he be? She thought her hopes and prayers had been answered. He did recognize her. She felt the love in his eyes and heart as he approached her, but her heart sank as she made her way home in tears. She stopped at the post office to pick up her mail, and in the mail was a letter to her from a relative in Brazil saying that her son had recently died in an accident.

As she got to this part of the story, both of us had tears streaming down our faces. "Oh, how can you bear it?" I asked her. "Oh," she said with a soft sad smile, "You just bear it. And you take that love you have for your son and give it away to everyone else around you. You broadcast love. You put love into people's houses when you clean. You listen to people and comfort them when they are sad. My son came to me on that trail. Without a doubt, I know that it was him. He was happy! He showed his love for me and then just disappeared into thin air."

## *Musing as Dawn Breaks, Paleaku Peace Gardens, Painted Church Road, Kona*

ARISING FROM DREAMS, IN BETWEEN WORLDS, A CORRIDOR of light appears as my dream slinks around the corner, out of sight and lost to memory in the files which hold other dream-scapes, dream adventures, and dream people. Crowing roosters and the clucking of chickens blends with peace doves cooing out a pretty mantra, spreading light from coffee plant to coffee plant, to jewel ornamented papaya trees and medicinal Noni fruit, looking like cream-colored grenades hanging from the branches of glossy-leafed bushes.

Pick-up trucks, with drivers on their way to work, cruise down the curvy Painted Church Road. The drivers smile at anyone walking along the road, and raise a hand to shake out a *"shaka"* – either a lively one . . . or a slow, lazy one. A beam of light touches my heart, and I feel fresh with the new morning. Kupuna Pele, her *aina* (land) and people, have helped to extract from me that which no longer serves my new direction, as well as those things which had closed inner heart doors, locking in the radiance and hiding the gems.

Opening like a flower bud, in sacred moments surrounded by spirit guides, ancestors, angels, and good friends, the heart slowly unfolds and flows like molten gold. Older brothers and sisters in the spirit world, hold out a helping hand and whisper words of love and encouragement. How amazing to be graced, in rare moments, by these beings who knew the suffering and joys of this life . . . but conquered duality, learned to remain equal . . . one sound, one taste . . . one heart.

I deeply relax and surrender to the Aloha and the *mana* flowing from flower to tree to bird, to ocean from whale to dolphin to human, to be cleansed by soft breezes or in salt water. Puddles of old tears dry on salty ocean rocks to join a marvelous and beautiful ocean habitat, filled with blossoms of light rays in indigo water that mesmerize the mind as it wings its way to a higher frequency.

The sonar and clicks of dolphins, cruising in formation below the surface of the bay, give notice that they will soon surface. They circle on the surface for a while, undulating, before leaping and spinning with their silver bodies gleaming in the sun. Then suddenly they dive in unison, in a beautiful synchronized water ballet. Instinctively they glide and turn, dive and ascend, at the same time, as a pod, without a leader. When they surface, fine mist appears above their blow holes as they exhale. Collective consciousness is easily apparent in a pod of dolphins. I join them in my imagination.

Soon they surface alongside me as I float in the water above them, to breathe and blow, to swim, undulating, and eventually, to spin in joy, as if celebrating their abundant life force. Endless effervescent bubbles circulate through my body, awakening and enlivening my whole being, just watching them and being near. I embrace life and renewal! It is good to follow a life of compassion and truth. Together, as we walk this path of life, we are all in school on this Earth as one human, ripening our hearts and our wisdom, doing our best to get it right this time.

And as I recall resting upon Pele's swirling lava hair on the shoreline near the cresting water, my heart leaps with excitement and joy as I watch the *keiki* (youth) glide across the bay in their outrigger canoes, paddling in unison.

The young ones are paddling out the old rhythms of ancient water people with the canoe and the paddle. Others sail the replica voyaging canoes. They look to the stars, the waves, the swells, and the birds for guidance. They use no compass and no instruments as they re-enact ancient trans-oceanic voyages. They are bringing back the old voyaging ways that brought happiness and balance to the people. Canoe racing was a big sport for both the youth and adults alike. Paddling was everyday enjoyment and preparation for the races. In the old days paddling was more than that; it was a major way of traveling from place to place and to other shoreline villages.

The Hula, the chants, and the drum blend in a dancing prayer of graceful movements, voice, and rhythm. Joined, they emanate *mana*, circulating life force back into the circle of life.

My heart is touched and happy. Partaking of these rich elements opens up a whole new life. I thank *Kupuna* Pele with a big "*Mahalo nui loa*" (thank you), as she has invited me, in dreams, to come here, for a while . . . for purification, to appreciate the abundant beauty all around, and to honor and respect it. My inner voice said, "Listen and remember."

I thank the dolphins, the *Nai'a*, for helping to transform my state of mind so quickly. Whether in the water with the dolphins or armchair surfing with them, at home or on the shoreline, they are so generous with their willingness to clear and uplift our energy. Their gifts are given freely and provide evidence of our interspecies relationships.

### A Public Letter from Aka

A LETTER THAT AKA SENT TO ME, and also shared with others, later in time on March 2, 2011, regarding our relationships with the dolphins, and after reading my book, *A Guide to the Dolphin Divination Cards*.

From Haleaka Iolani Pule:

### KA NAI'AU IOKEKAIMALINOA'OKON
### I LOVE DOLPHINS

*"As a native Hawai'ian who has spent more than 44 generations –*
*with all of them being powerful Kahuna Nui, High*
*Priest/Priestesses, helping, initiating, and activating healing on*

*many levels and for many beings – my Ancestors and I must share this with you:*

*"In my lifetime I have watched and experienced nai'a / dolphins in many different ways. I have watched them in the Ke Ala o Kahiki channel (between Moloka'i and O'ahu) as they used their sonar to stun a huge school of fish. In turn it made the fish go crazy and try to get out of the water, creating a boil, which in turn attracted the birds that would dive and grab fish to feed their young and themselves. Our fishermen would watch for the birds and follow them to the dolphins (na'ia), and then drop their long lines to catch ahi, mahi mahi, and ono . . . which in turn would feed us. The dolphins and the ahi, mahimahi, and ono all swim together in the deep, and the dolphins provide food for all of them . . . they are the greatest of providers.*

*"In Kealakekua Bay I have had the first-hand opportunity to watch the loving demise of these precious, precious ones that have*

*given, shared, provided so, so much, asking for nothing in return. I have, as a child body, surfed onto our shores with them on the same waves, and have watched them fill our bay at sunrise by the hundreds, many times over a thousand of them . . . so precise in timing that we could set our watches to their arrival. They would come in to sleep in our shallow, sandy bottom bay . . . as they don't sleep like humans do . . . they shut off their sonar and use the sand to help them see with their regular vision and rest up throughout the day, so that they can go out and hunt at night. They would leave our bay at sunset every day, seven days a week, 30 out of 32 days a month.*

"'Herds' is what these powerful numbers of dolphins together were called. Now we are lucky to see them in sub-pods (30-50) or pods (50-80), and they rarely come in, maybe 7-10 times a month if we are lucky. According to Jacques Cousteau, when a herd of dolphins break up in the ways they have now been doing for about 20-25 years, it is about survival. You see, when we love something, the knowledge is in our reach to educate ourselves enough about them to understand fully what we should do to not hurt them in any way, shape, or form. The dolphins' number one cause of death is not sharks. It is upper respiratory infections.

"When humans swim in the ocean, the first thing our bodies do is start releasing the mucous in our bodies through our sinuses and our throats and out the snorkel, leaving threads of sticky stuff behind. If you are swimming with the dolphins, it sweeps through the pod – the young and the old get sick, they slow down and they get eaten. So for those that are conscious about the effect that we have on everything around us, and are not so selfish about taking what they can, may the Creator's healing flow through each and every one of them. This is the same prayer that I say for the dolphins, as they are the innocents, sharing the medicine of living in flow with the universe, and in such a way that all realms can be accessed. And you can all purchase Nancy Clemens's dolphin divination cards and guide book to do the "real loving thing," which she calls "armchair surfing" – swimming with the dolphins, and having great sleeps at night, knowing that your "loving actions" are not leading to the demise of our brothers and sisters of the sea...."

*Mahalo from Kealakekua Bay, South Kona, Hawaii*
*Haleaka Iolani (Auntie Aka)*

P.S. Aka and her mother, Auntie Fern, would be happy that today, as of September 2021, it is illegal in Hawai'i to swim with dolphins or to follow them in boats.

ANDRE RIPA WAS BORN IN PARIS and loves dolphins as much as I do. We met on the Kona side of the island. Speaking in his charming French accent, Andre told me a little about his life and how he came to live in Hawai'i, on and off. Although Andre was fifteen years younger than I, we had a lot in common and became friends. We both laughed and said that souls don't have an age.

I had lived in France as a teen-ager, and loved the French culture. Andre's French accent and mannerisms brought me back to happy days living in France. Andre had also lived in Montreal, Canada. He is a healer who practices Reiki and facilitates healing groups. I had done the same thing in California.

At one time in Andre's career he worked with autistic children and took them to see dolphins in a large pool. The children seemed to improve and became more social and talkative after being around the the dolphins. The connection seemed to lessen the symptoms of autism while the children were in the water with them, and afterward too. They enjoyed the dolphins and expressed enthusiasm. Andre told me some impressive stories of healing from his days of doing this work with dolphins.

Sometimes we swam with other dolphin friends in K Bay who happened to come from many other countries as well as the mainland. It was fun having international friends who were dolphin spirited. Sometimes we went for coffee and drives to a number of beautiful spots on the Kona side of the island. Andre's energy was smooth and flawless, and it was easy to be with him, whether we talked or not. With admiration for this handsome young man, I thought to myself, 'He is an old fashioned gentleman.' Sometimes we just communed with the beautiful scenery and vistas of the ocean from the heights at the foot of Mauna Kea. Andre knew Aka too, and the three of us and others sometimes spent time together at K Bay or Two-Step.

One day Andre received the sad news that one of his dearest friends had passed away. He was so very sad that I suggested we go to the City of Refuge to make prayers for his friend. We were there about sunset, and just as our prayer reached a part about freedom of the soul, we witnessed a humpback whale breach into the air and land with a huge splash in the middle of Honaunau Bay. The timing of it was just so perfect. We both had the feeling that the soul of his friend was joyful and free.

I remember another day when we drove to Waimea and the soft mist in the air created a beautiful rainbow. As we gazed at this wondrous beauty that spread across the sky, I told Andre of my love of St. Francis of Assisi and my belief that he is the patron saint of not only animals, in general, but dolphins as well. He was familiar with this saint who lived in Assisi, Italy in the 1200s. I told him of my vision of Francis and how I believed that Saint Francis was the one who inspired me to write the book (*The Guide to the Dolphin Divination Cards*) that accompanied the *Dolphin Divination Cards*.

Learning that day that Andre's birthday was on the 4th of October, I told him that he must have a very special connection with St Francis, as October 4th is the feast day of St. Francis. Then I told him that I have two sons that flank this feast day . . . Michael on October 3rd and Sean (Tada) on the 5th. I offered to adopt him, as his American mother, and then I would have three sons all in a line on the week of St Francis. But I could never replace his real mother, who lived in Paris. He laughed and said *"Peut etre."*


### The Dolphin Dome


AS TIME WENT ON, IT BECAME OBVIOUS that some people who swam in the Bay were not respecting the *na'ia* (dolphins). Aka and I had spoken of this often, and now Andre and I were expressing concerns too. I shared a vision that I had had with Andre. It was an idea of having a "traveling dolphin dome" which would be a virtual reality way of swimming with the dolphins – using film images, sound, and holograms of life-sized swimming dolphins.

When I told Andre of this idea, he seemed amazed and then shared with me that he had an almost identical idea and inspiration. These ideas had come to us before we even met each other. This way, the dolphins would not be negatively impacted in their own environment, and people everywhere could experience the joy of swimming with dolphins . . . but of course, with simulated moving visuals: with waves, water sounds and dolphin whistles. We speculated about how a dolphin dome like this might bring stress relief and healing to people. Aka and her mother, Fern, loved this idea too. I never manifested this idea. However, Andre expanded the idea to include Native People chanting and dancing with the dolphins, Aka chanting, scenes in ancient Egypt, Tibetan monks chanting, and some of his own exquisite piano compositions, as background music.

In later years he developed whole dramatic shows, which were spin-offs of our original idea of a virtual reality dolphin dome. Today, at the time of this writing, Andre has a beautiful and gifted wife named Gianna who participates with him in these productions. She has a lovely singing and toning voice. After deeply connecting with St Francis, or Francesco, as Andre likes to call him, Andre and Gianna have made many pilgrimages to Assisi and chose that sacred spot for their marriage. I am happy to say that today Andre is fully conscious of his deep connection with and guidance from St. Francis.

## A Deep Phone Conversation with Aka, Messages from Heaven

ONE DAY, AKA CALLED ME SUGGESTING that we go to the Volcano soon, to make offerings and to chant to Kupuna Pele. Her vehicle was having mechanical trouble at the time, so she asked if we could take my jeep. I said, "Yes, of course." I knew that she wasn't going to drive over an *a'a'* (rough, sharp, lava blocks) lava field, like Kapua. When we went somewhere together, she liked to do the driving. She always said that because she lived here all her life, driving was easy for her and that I could just relax and enjoy the scenery. She also said that when Paul came over to visit me that she would take us to the Waipio Valley for a picnic and a tour of the valley, all the way up to the *"po"* (the head) of the valley. She also said we would all go to do ceremony at both the Waipio Valley and the Volcano.

We had a lot of time in the car together on our excursions and shared many long, deep talks. I remember so much of what she shared, but sometimes I forgot to write things down in my diary, and some things that she told me may be lost to my memory but has been absorbed somehow into my bloodstream. Aka was in a philosophical mood while we were on the phone, and she told me that she was communing with her ancestors on this day. She said that she felt a light, tingly, loving feeling when her ancestors perched on her head.

She said to me, "My *tutus* are perching." What she meant by this was that her ancestors in the spirit world were perching on her head. She had explained this to me in the past that this was the way ancestors communicated with her telepathically, from the spirit world or "the heavens," as Aka called it. Aka's mother, Auntie Fern, had also explained this to me. Then Aka asked me if I had paper and pen, and I quickly went to get some. "Please write everything down," she said, "as I can tell that my *tutus* are going to come through with something important to talk to us about, and you know I might not remember very much later."

She was reminding me of Ivan St. John, an excellent trance medium who I met in San Francisco when I was twenty-five years old. He brought through my late husband who had been killed in an accident just a few months earlier. The communication was so convincing and authentic that my knees were knocking together. I was so shocked and in awe finding out that Jim could talk to me from the spirit world through Ivan. And that was the beginning of my spiritual quest.

Aka and her family usually called their gifted people "receivers" instead of "mediums" or "seers." After breathing deeply several times, she began to speak. "You know, sistah, when love blossoms in our heart, we feel so very close to heaven. We are just souls experiencing this human life. But this is not the only life or the only place that we can experience life. It is hard to live in the density of this realm, as when we are free of it, we release ourselves like butterflies. We are no longer in a cocoon. But we are here until we fulfill our *kuleanas* (responsibilities)."

I thought, what if we were able to lift the veils while we are here on earth? What would we see? All the density and solid things would be seen as illusory, vibrating particles of energy and light. And then they can re-arrange themselves, always shimmering. I thought of Arthur Young and other physicists who talk about these things in scientific terms. I remembered my experience with a Tibetan lama, His Holiness Kusum Lingpa, who held my hand on our couch and inducted me into a state in which I could see everything as vibrating atoms, and nothing as solid.

"If we could lift the veils, we would be so surprised to see the spirits and ancestors that live in a different dimension. They can visit us here in our realm, but very few of us can see them. They vibrate on a different frequency. Sometimes we will be surprised to see them show up on photographs."

She was quiet for a few seconds, and I could hear her breathing getting deeper. Aka resumed talking: "There is an exuberance and lightness of our being in the heavens. Physical suffering drops away, and we float or fly through so many colors, lights, and landscapes . . . without blemish, without the tarnish of every day human life, filled with dramas and troubles, big or small. All the flowers and trees bloom together at the same time, and nothing ever wilts or dies. There is no dust! Everything is ever-living and always pristinely beautiful. There is celestial music and so many different realms. We go to where our soul resonates. When we 'go on,' our soul is set free from the density of this earth, which by comparison is like a ball and chain. And one ascends into realms of unspeakable divine love . . . and grace and clarity. The 'man in white', the Elohim, masters and angels are near, giving their blessings of healing and divine love.

"Many things that are obscured in our earthly life become revealed as both large and small epiphanies. Understanding and forgiveness for ourselves and others becomes easier too. In the atmosphere of divine love, one can see how greed, anger, jealousy and cunning in earthly life can affect us. Unquenched desires lead nowhere, as we cannot grasp money, things, or people for very long.

"Life is fleeting. It is like a dream, from the perspective of the heavens. Earth life can sometimes be heavenly, but it can also be hellishly painful. With either the hellish or heavenly perspective, we need to realize that this world is a world of duality, of light and dark, and good and bad. It is up to us what we choose to focus on, and it's up to us what we choose to feed.

"And what are we here to do? We are here to purify ourselves, to divest ourselves of pain, hurt, resentment, anger, and judgment. We are here to grow our humility, generosity, compassion and Aloha. We are here to forgive ourselves and others. We are here to share the Aloha that grows, opens, and gives from our heart. We can also develop the ability to recognize, open, draw upon, carry, and direct the flow of *mana* (true spiritual power). We are here to walk a path that honors the power of the Creator that flows through us. This is the secret that opens up to the magic that is always swirling around us, and we can learn to direct its flow. It helps us to manifest and to be more successful in all the good things that we aspire to do."

It seemed now that the message had come to an end. This voice was Aka's, but the words didn't sound like Aka's usual language. She was quiet for a bit, and said she was going to hang up now, as she felt like resting. Before she hung up, she asked me, "Sistah, did you write everything down? It's important, and I won't be able to remember all of it later. I have the jist of it, but it will fade away. Make sure you re-copy it into your *holoholo* diary, if you wrote it in your shorthand." Then she said, with a gentle laugh, "I am back now and I have things to do . . . the dogs need to eat. Pupuka is looking at me with that pleading look . . . he's ready to grind."

### *A Walk with Carol, Offerings at the Women's Temple*

I HAD KNOWN CAROL FOR A LONG TIME. She lived in Marin County, California and, after retiring as a University professor, Carol moved to Hawai'i. Her home was *mauka* (uphill) from Pu'uhonua o Honaunau (the City of Refuge), and she had a most fabulous tropical garden in her back yard. Everything thrived in luxurious abundance and beauty. Spending time in her garden was sensual and beautiful, as there was such an array of plants, flowers, and fruit trees, all planted in such an artistic way.

I remember that she planted Hopi corn every year, as she was taught by a Hopi woman who had loved and nurtured her. This was a kind of "spiritual adoption," very much like the Hawai'ians when they *"hanai"* (informally adopt) a person into their family. She also had chocolate plants with beautiful, hanging cacao beans. This garden, full of tropical plants and fruit trees, was a magical setting on the hillside overlooking the City of Refuge and the horizonless ocean.

As a gifted poet and photographer, Carol has a uniquely poetic way of viewing the world. One day I remember sitting in her garden as she read her poetry to me. I was an eager listener, as her poetry is beautiful and soul stirring. In recent years Carol has become a renowned poet, with over seven published poetry and photograph books, and many poems published in a variety of publications. One day, Carol suggested that we go for a walk along the coast, starting at the City of Refuge, which was directly below her home down a long, gently winding road with a sweeping view of the ocean.

We made *ho'o'kupus* (offerings), little bundles filled with fruit, wrapped up in a sacred Ti leaf. It is then tied with a strand of Ti leaf and adorned with flowers. Carol took me to the women's temple within the City of Refuge, and we made offerings and prayers there before starting our walk. This temple was not as large and imposing as some of the large *heiaus* here. It was a stone temple, but was smaller and shorter than the others, and most people might walk right by it without noticing, except for the offerings laid on the top of the stone platform. On the piled black lava stones of the temple were other offerings, some fresh and some desiccated, made by

unknown women. There were shell *leis*, little dried bundles of *ho'okupu*, and dried flower *leis*, which had been fresh and fragrant when they were placed there. Fresh flower *leis*, shells and stones, and various other things had also been offered.

I wondered what kind of prayers had been offered here, and for how many centuries? I imagined ancient Hawai'ian women coming here to pray. Were their prayers so different from ours, a prayer for a baby, or a male companion, a lost person or pet, for the healing of a sick or injured person, for forgiveness and pardon, or comfort for heartbreak and grief? Or perhaps a prayer would be a big *"Mahalo nui loa, Ke Akua"* (Thank you, Creator) for an answered prayer. Within some offerings were secrets, and maybe others had no secrets at all. Perhaps the offering was just an offering to the "Goddesses" or spiritual beings, who live in another dimension but are still aligned with this place. Carol had brought me here a number of times. The wind blew the palm trees this day. The fronds were bending and bowing with the ever-changing direction of the winds. The salt air was delicious in my nostrils. I remembered how many times I longed to be by the ocean, when I was at home in the Sierra foothills of California. White clouds scudded across the sunlit sky, but up *mauka*, dark grey clouds were gathering and clustering around the coffee fields that stretched up the Kona mountainside.

### A Walk on an Ancient Path

IN TIMES BEFORE COLONIZATION there was a yearly ceremony that lasted for several winter months, called the *"Mahahiki."* It was a time to relax, dance, sing, feast, and enjoy ceremonies and sports. There were competitions of all kinds: boxing, wrestling, tug of war, swimming races, surf riding, *holua* slide races, and many games. It was a time to leave daily work behind. The King and Queen and their retinues would walk ceremoniously around the island. Remnants of the pathway still exist today as large smooth stones on different parts of the island.

The Holua slide provided the *kanaka* with thrills, as this sport was fairly dangerous. One slide is located a little bit north in Keauhou. It is well known because it is still quite well preserved. The slide went from high on the mountain and ended near the shoreline of Keauhou Bay, on Ali'i Drive. This daring sport, only practiced by the chief class, was both dangerous and exciting. There were slides like this in other parts of the island but they are not as well preserved as this slide. The slide track is a mile long and has sharp curves, which were navigated by the rider shifting his body weight. Often the riders went up to sixty miles an hour, much like the modern-day sport of snowboarding. The rider had a small wooden and twine sled, called a *papa holua*. He would either lie down on the *papa holua* face first, or stand on it sideways. The track was constructed of lava rocks and smaller stones, then covered with dirt. Before a race, pili grass was put on the track and sprinkled with *kukui* nut oil to make it slippery. This was one of the many sports practiced during the *Mahahiki* season when big work projects were stopped for these

months. The *Mahahiki* season was dedicated to Lono, the God of peace, music and agriculture. After the advent of missionary influence, this sport ceased to be practiced. Missionaries had done much to turn the Hawai'ian people against their own cultural practices and religion. It took many years to reverse these laws, and thankfully, in recent years, starting in the 1970s, there has been a cultural renaissance.

Carol and I walked through the picnic ground of the City of Refuge and passed the foundation stones of an old village and animal pens. This had been a village where people once lived, but now only the stacked lava stone foundations were left, in square and rectangular shapes, with an over-growth of foliage growing inside and all around them. This village was just a few yards from the shoreline, so I imagined it had once been a fishing village. We continued on this walk and finally climbed up a hill to a spot that seemed to be above a sea cave. We continued on for a while, but decided to turn back, as we knew the trail would eventually take us to Ho'okena Beach.

As I walked, I remembered talking to Auntie Mona Kahele, who was an elder of eighty years old. She had grown up in South Kona. She was born in 1921 and was a historian from an early age. She wrote down the stories of the *kupuna* (elders) that she heard when she was a child. She was raised by her father's mother, Lokalia, and spent much of her time with other family elders. She loved the old stories and legends which were passed down through the generations. Even though she was young, she felt it was important to write them down. Her first language was Hawai'ian, as English was forbidden in her home. So at first the stories were written in Hawai'ian. Later, she translated them into English.

Perhaps Auntie Mona is best known for sharing old place names of towns, villages, bays, beaches, trails, and other locations of South Kona. She strongly felt that these original names should still be used today. Modern names had replaced many of the old names. She had multiple careers in her life: farming and assisting her fisherman husband by cleaning and drying fish. Later in life she was a teacher and did counseling and healing with herbs and the reconciliation practice of *Ho'o'ponopono*. In addition, she and her husband, Abel, raised many, many children, most of which were not their own.

One day, she told me a story as I was driving her to her home above Choice Mart grocery store. She told me that, when she was a child, she had to get up very early and prepare her bucket for going up into the high country to gather healing herbs with a family member who was a *Lau' lapa' au* (herbal healer). Auntie Mona was an elder now and could no longer walk the trails, but she had written books documenting old place names, and historical and sacred locations in South Kona. I enjoyed reading her book a few years after my return home, called *Cloud of Memories* by Mona Kahele, published in 2006 by Kamehameha Schools. When Auntie Mona visited Paleaku Gardens and talked about *Ho'o'ponopono*, as she practiced it, I realized that, as a Christian, she had taken the teachings of *Ho'o'ponopono* and adapted them to Christianity. The famous Auntie Morrnah Simeona had done something similar and shared these teachings on the mainland and even overseas to Europe. She actually passed away in Poland. Aka told me that Auntie Morrnah was her grand aunt, two generations back, on her mother's side.

However, the underlying principles of listening attentively, understanding, humility, forgiveness, healing, and love were the same as the pre-Christian version. It would have been wonderful to have been able to listen to Auntie Morrnah Simeona, but I was grateful to be able to know Auntie Mona Kahele. Often I drove Auntie Mona home after her visits to Paleaku Gardens. She was a treasure trove of stories and history. I wish I had spent more time learning from her. She emanated kindness and wisdom, and I always loved being with her. I told Carol that if Auntie Mona was able to be with us today, on this walk, she could tell us so many stories about this very place.

Several times we stopped to look at the ocean. The waves were throwing up huge plumes of white spray as we stood at a high point on the trail. How beautiful this place was! The winding trail went up and down, with trees and brush growing along the sides. Certain places were close to the ocean, and I wondered if there were little secret beaches below us. South Kona had changed from the days of Mona Kahele's childhood. But it was still beautiful and still carried the mystic voices of the past, which seemed to be carried on the wind. Carol and I made our way back to the City of Refuge, noting different plants, bushes and trees that were growing along the edges of the trail. Carol was very familiar with many of the tropical plants growing here, and she had many of them in her own garden. The ever-present Noni bushes dotted the area near the City of Refuge. Their green grenade-like fruit peeked out from under shiny green leaves that became cream colored when they were ripe enough to fall to the ground.

### A Brief History of the Overthrow of Hawai'i

IN THE 1800S, THE MISSIONARIES IN HAWAI'I had abolished surfing, *hula,* and speaking the Hawai'ian language. King David Kalakaua tried his best to restore the traditions that pre-dated the influx of missionaries.

On November 17th, 1886, King David Kalakaua (1836-1891) celebrated his fiftieth birthday with a festive Silver Jubilee ball and *luau*. Just a year later, in 1887 King Kalakaua was forced at gunpoint to sign a new constitution which was drafted by rich white businessmen. Most of them, like the big five of the sugar industry, were getting rich from their sugar and pineapple plantations. This new constitution removed almost all the power of the Hawai'ian monarchy.

King David Kalakaua was called the Merrie Monarch, as he revived the *hula, oli* (chanting), Hawai'ian music, and other cultural arts that had been repressed by the influx of missionaries. He often had large festive parties which included *hula*, chanting, and Hawai'ian musical performances. He, himself, was known to dance the *hula* as well. The following quote is attributed to him: "Hula is the language of the heart, therefore the heartbeat of the Hawai'an people." He tried valiantly to keep the culture alive. His parting words, as he died were: "Tell the Hawai'ian people that I tried." Since 1963 there has been a yearly, week-long Hula festival in Hilo in the Edith Kanakaole Stadium. It is called the Merrie Monarch Festival in honor of David Kalakaua, the last King of Hawai'i.

After King Kalakaua died, his sister, Queen Lili'uokalani succeeded him to the throne. She drafted up a new constitution restoring power back to the monarchy. Traveling around all the islands on horseback, she gained the approval and support of the Hawai'ian people for her new constitution. However, a thirteen member "Committee of Safety" was formed, consisting of rich, white businessmen. In secret they called themselves "the annexation group." They were determined to access more land for themselves by annexing Hawai'i to the United States. Eventually, they orchestrated a coup and proclaimed a provisional government. In order to accomplish their goal, they called in the United States military to help them take over the Iolani Palace in Honolulu. The Queen was deposed and put under house arrest. All power was taken from her. It was a very sad day for Hawai'i and the Hawai'ian people. The history of this "take over" is long and complex. Sovereignty activists have legal documents showing that the annexation, as a territory of the United States, was illegal. This annexation eventually led to statehood and in 1959 Hawai'i became the fiftieth state of the United States.

Many Hawai'ians are still angry about colonization, and there is still a viable Sovereignty Movement in Hawai'i. Passionate activists would like to oust the American government from the Islands. Aka's Uncle Abel Simeona is one of these activists. And so is Soli, whose full name is Soli Welokiheiakea'eloa Niheu Jr. Soli was a leading fighter and one of the early pioneer activists for the indigenous rights of Hawai'ian people. He and others got arrested when they supported the local farmers in the Kalama Valley, on the island of Oahu, who were being evicted from their land to make room for modern housing developments. The Hawaiian "renaissance" began in the 1970s. Soli was also one of the leaders and early supporters of ethnic studies in Hawai'i's colleges and universities. I told Aka that I had been blessed to have gotten to know Soli at the gatherings at Barrie Rose's house in Waimea. He and Kapua had been long-time friends and went "way back" to the activist days in the 1970s. My memory of him was his quiet modesty, his sharp intelligence, and his passion for the rights of Hawai'ian people . . . and, a great chef!

With American financial interests entrenched in the islands in the 1800s, and the influx of Americans and other foreigners, the whole sovereignty issue has become very complex. The missionaries were the first to be involved in this process and wanted to create a Christian society in Hawai'i. Early on, the Hawai'ians were stripped of the right to speak their language, dance the *hula*, or practice their original religion and cultural traditions. Even some of the sports and games of the *Mahahiki* season were discouraged or banned by the missionaries and their growing number of churches. Today Hawai'ian religious practices are protected by the American Indian Religious Freedom Act that was passed by the United States Congress in 1978.

### *"Drop It Like It's Hot"*

ONE MORNING I WENT DOWN TO THE BAY to swim and encountered Aka at the shop. Her mother, Auntie Fern, was there too, talking to some of the locals. Aka and I went over to Manini Beach, which was not far away on the south side of Kealakekua Bay. We took a brief but refreshing swim, entering the little sandy entrance with the waves swirling around us and tossing little pieces of white coral and black lava stones around in the surf, as waves broke gently onto the beach. Straight ahead of us was the north side of Kealakekua Bay and the *Pali*, a steep cliff-side that was the home of ancient burial caves and small herds of wild goats.

Aka's swim costume was a sports bra and a pair of shorts. For her, being "dressed" was wrapping a colorful *lava lava* (sarong) over her shorts and top, and tying it in front over her heart. It was almost always warm here in Kona. How wonderful to not need many clothes. As the day was still young, Manini Beach had not become crowded yet. It was a favorite place for parents to bring small children, as the entrance to the water was gently sloping and shallow. On the open grass were lots of empty picnic tables under large palm trees. We found one and sat down. Our conversation started off like it usually did, with chit chat about what we were doing, our families and local news. I told Aka that Paul was planning to come to visit me soon. She became excited thinking of all the things that we could do to make his visit a real adventure as well as a sacred pilgrimage. She had been waiting for this day for a long time. Many times she had talked about a plan for us to visit the Waipio Valley.

Aka told me how she planned to drive our jeep down the very steep incline into the Waipio Valley, as a four-wheel drive vehicle was necessary. Without four-wheel drive, people either walked down or rode a horse. We would bring a picnic and she would treat us with a trip to the *Po* (head) of the Valley. Having relatives everywhere, she had a key to the gate that guarded the back part of the valley which is not open to visitors. We would go there for a ceremony. She also talked to me about her plan for Paul and I to go with her for a ceremony at the volcano.

Our conversation deepened as we began to talk about the problems of racism and reverse racism on our planet. We talked about genocides of peoples throughout the world, and throughout time, and how racism and separation of races and cultures help to create these genocides and wars. The desire to take land and resources away from other people, and to kill them, was as old as the hills. This history saddened both of us. We have Native American friends who carry a deep heartache, and sometimes intense anger, over the colonization and mass killings of their people and their way of life. Broken treaties, lies, the slaughter of the buffalo, liquid genocide (introduction to alcohol), re-locations to reservations, outlawing their language and ceremonies, and the attempt to eradicate a culture and people had left deep ancestral wounds.

"Racism and reverse racism keep people separated," Aka said. "Migrations, wars, slaughter, rape, and hostile takeovers have been happening for thousands of years on this earth." "We live on a warring planet," I said. "The spiritual design and plan is for awakened people to help transform our Earth from a warring planet to a peaceful planet. This peace has to begin with each one of us. Oh, such unrealistic idealism I have. When I was young, I thought I would see world peace in my lifetime. Paul thought the same thing. Of course, it is not the Earth that is the problem. It is the people who live on this Earth."

Aka chuckled at my words and said, in pidgin, "True dat!" Then she went on to say, "It is a huge challenge, as it seems as if many people have conquest in their genes. The ancient Hawai'ians had methods for purifying this impulse in their genes. My *kupunas* taught me these things. When there is purification that goes all the way back through the ancestral line, eventually reaching *Ke Akua* (God), then true *Aloha* and Heavenly Father's power can be sincerely felt and lived, in spite of injustices and genocides. Direct power coming from our Heavenly Father can infuse the spirit of the one who has purified their ancestral lineage."

I went on to say, "The question is: What is it in people that would rather kill, make war or steal from others, or just not care? How do we purify that selfish impulse and desire to take from another, rather than the kind impulse to care about everyone?"

Aka replied, "There have always been conquerors and those who have been conquered. All peoples have done it, at one time or another. And many have had it done to them. This is world history on this planet, which, sadly, is like you said, still a warring planet. Perhaps it's still in its infancy of developing true Aloha. Our design is to transform in consciousness, to become one with God and "the man in white," and the consciousness and reigning spirit of this

350

planet, Mother Earth. We can become vehicles of the God energy coming all the way down our ancestral line to us.

"We need to take care of our Mother Earth. She has been so abused. There are people who have purified themselves and developed compassion and caring, and who no longer have any desire left in them to steal or fight or violate other people . . . or nature." Then she smiled and said, "I aspire to that unless someone is trying to hurt my behbehs and then you will meet 'Mother Bear'. We Mothers are protectors of our children. That is a sacred instinct too." And I replied, "And yet there have been moments when we have had compassionate leaders and societies, but before long greed and arrogance seems to creep in and take over. We have to get beyond that, and deal with the present. They always say that we need to learn from the past and that history repeats itself."

Aka replied, "But we need to be present now. Anger and resentment and hate of those who have conquered the people will only block one's own good energy. We call it *mana*, our spiritual energy and power. We learn from our *kupunas* (elders) that we hurt our own *mana* and diminish it, if we cultivate resentment, anger, and revenge. We harm our *mana* if we are unable to forgive. Somehow we seem to be destined and challenged to learn to live together in peace and cooperation. This comes from forgiveness and understanding and finding our own peace inside of ourselves. It's not so easy, sistah, but that's why we learn *Ho'o'ponopono*."

We paused in this discussion to gaze out on the bay to see a bevy of kayaks circling a certain area of the bay. Soon we saw the tell-tale fins of the dolphins swimming in a large circle, surrounded by the kayaks. "Our poor *nai'a* (dolphins)," Aka said . . . "poor tings, never get a rest from deez tourists. Most dem such nice people too. They just want a dolphin swim so bad.

"We Hawai'ians, even those of us who have been blessed with the teaching of Aloha, have our moments, when we mutter, under our breath, 'Those darn haoles.' Then maybe later, we might catch ourselves and think, 'Ahh, reverse racism is creeping in, right here inside of me. Oh, *Kala mai, Ke Akua!*' It is so pervasive, so easy to fall into. It is especially hard when it comes to parts of our island being desecrated by developers, invading our burial grounds, and decisions about land use made by people who are not Hawai'ian. I always say to myself, when a thought or words like this about *haoles* come to mind, we need to go color blind and return to true Aloha, an' just 'Drop it like it's hot'!!!"

I was going to go home and write in my diary about our conversation. I called it my "holoholo diary." Aka had nicknames for me, the *holoholo wahine* (holoholo woman), when she wasn't calling me the "Starfruit Woman." Later she called me "Nan-sea." This conversation seemed important to record.


### Aka's Kitchen


AKA WAS GOING HOME TO COOK something up for her family's dinner. Her furry side kick, Pupuka, hopped into the passenger seat beside Aka, looking like the regal dog that he was. Her children, Ola, Lilinoe and Suzy, would be home for 'dinnah', as Aka would say. She sometimes used an outdoor kitchen and had a super-sized wok with tripod legs. She told me she would boil up blue sweet potatoes, fry up some fish, and make a big salad, with papaya seed dressing. She liked to tell me her dinner menus as she knew I missed cooking for my family back home. Her cuz's had gone fishing and she had some good fresh fish to fry. I would joke with her and ask her to take me home in her pocket.

I had visited her kitchen. She had big tubs of honey and coconut oil in her kitchen. There were buckets of fresh fruits and vegetables for both juicing and cooking. These were all natural foods, and there was a bee farm on the road down to Napo'opo'o village, where her grandmother, Tutu Pua (Matilda Prim), used to live. Aka would often bring me a jar of this delicious organic honey. Her grandmother had told her that the coconut, its meat and water, could cure almost everything. Honey was a great healer too, especially the organic honey that came from the local bee farm.


### Akoni Pule, Mud Puddles, and the Mo'okini Heiau


ONE DAY ANDRE AND I DROVE UP TO WAIMEA and picked up Mike Tomson and Jeannette. Mike came from Nevada City for a visit upon my urging, but his visit had turned into a stay of several months. He had fallen in love with Jeannette and, as he had grown up on Pilau, an island in Micronesia, he felt right at home here. We decided that it was a good day to go *holoholo*. As the day unfolded, we decided to go up to the north part of the island and visit the town of Havi. I had heard that Havi was a very windy place and that it was a location where there was never, or almost never, any vog. As we drove into Havi, we saw a quaint little town comprised of old buildings that had been turned into gift shops, restaurants, coffee shops, and a few real estate buildings.

As we entered the town, there was a plaque on the left of the highway. We got out and looked at the picture of Akoni Pule and a description of how and why the highway from Kawaihae to Havi was named after him. I already knew that he was Aka's paternal grand-father. He had been in the Hawai'i state legislature and had done much to secure the funding to build this new highway. It was far safer than the mountainous, windy road that went from the up-country town of Waimea to Havi. Aka's sister, Kalehua, took Paul and I there, on another occasion, to see the house where Akoni and his wife Sarah had lived. There

KALEHUA POINTING TO HER GRAND-
FATHER, AKONI PULE

was a fresh water stream that came downhill from the mountains right beside the house, and there was abundant tropical foliage in the yard and behind the house. The house was no longer owned by the family. "We used to love to visit our grandparents and to play in that stream," Kalehua said. Aka and Kalehua's family had many happy visits to their grandparent's house when they were children. These were the North Kohala relatives, from their dad's side of the family. Later, Aka's sister Kela told me, with a giggle, that all of the kids loved bathing in the very private stream in their underwear. Many of their other relatives, from their mom's side of the family, lived in South Kona or on the Island of Oahu.

When Kalehua took us to this area, she pointed out some other Pule relatives' homes as well. She took us to a rocky ocean beach park where the whole family had celebrated birthdays and other big family occasions, under an open-air pavillion. "I can remember all the cooking that we did for those picnics and grindz . . . so ono . . . so onoz they broke dah mouth," she said. When the food is so delicious that it broke the mouth, then that's some really good food. There were a few times that day that I saw sweet, misty nostalgia in Fern's eyes. Mike and Andre were having a debate as how to get to the Mo'okini Heiau. We knew that we had to find the four-wheel drive dirt road that went to the Heiau and that it was close to the town of Havi in the North Kohala region of the Big Island. These two disagreed, one with a French accent and the other with a rising voice, but it was all in friendship and fun.

We finally figured it out and realized that we needed to look for the Upolo airport sign. We went down the airport road and were on our way, turning left after the small airport. It had rained earlier in the day, and the road was slick, muddy, and full of mud puddles. Even with my four-wheel drive Jeep, the car was sliding all over the road. Again, I was nervous about my car getting mired in the mud. Mike chided me saying that the car was built for these conditions. Was I a nervous Nellie, I wondered, or was my nervousness justified? We had also heard that this was a wonderful spot for whale watching. The whales were often seen breaching and diving in this channel, which was right across from the island of Maui. We looked out and saw white caps on the waves, and the wind was blowing hard, but we didn't see the whales.

We got out of the car and began to walk. Andre looked at his shoes and frowned. "Ahh, la boue!" – 'mud', he said in French. There was no way to avoid the mud and the mud puddles. We resigned ourselves to having muddy shoes. We walked by the birthplace of Kamehameha the First, which was marked with a plaque and some perimeter stone walls. Some say he was born in a canoe just offshore of this spot. After walking further, down the muddy road, we came upon the Mo'okini Heiau, which is said to be one of the oldest *heiaus* on the island and considered an archeological site. The Mo'okini Heiau is close to Havi, but located on an isolated grassy plain near the shoreline which is swept by the powerful winds of the north shore. It is one of the oldest *heiaus* on the Big Island and is said to have been built in 480 A.D. It is dedicated to the war God, Ku, and history tells us that there were thousands of human sacrifices made here. Heiaus, where human sacrifice was practiced, are called *Luakini heiaus*. For this reason, there are people who visit the Heiau that claim to see, hear, or feel ghosts. Many visitors feel an eerie feeling at this place. I felt it too and thought how it felt like a place "out of time."

The rock that was used as a sacrificial slab is still at the *heiau*. Those sacrificed had their bones crushed, which were used to make various implements, like fish hooks, for example. I have to say I had a creepy feeling when we arrived at the *heiau*. I was wondering if it had been a good idea to come here at all. I didn't want any sad spirits coming home with us. Suddenly I remembered how Aka always belted out, "No riders" when we passed a cemetery. I learned that Leimomi o Kamehae Kuamo'o Mo'okini Lum is the female *Kahuna nui* and caretaker of the *heiau*. Her father was the previous *Kahuna nui*. He selected her and trained her for many years, to take over the spiritual rituals and duties of the *heiau*. She took over these duties in 1977 after he passed away. The *heiau* is on her family's ancestral lands. She and her ancestors have been the *Kahuna nui* of this ancient *heiau* for many centuries.

Leimomi was born in 1926, and has been enjoying a long and full life. As a young woman, she was a police officer in Oahu. When she took over the duties of the *heiau*, she wanted to change the energy of the *heiau*, due to its history of human sacrifice. She did prayers and ceremonies to re-dedicate the *heiau* to the children of the world. She greets groups of school children who visit the *heiau* and speaks to them about the history of Kamehameha I and the history of the *heiau*. She has trained and appointed her daughter to take over as the next *Kahuna nui* after she passes away.

I was wishing that she was here this day so we might be able to hear her ancient chants. Jeannette and I walked side by side for a while catching up on girl talk, which centered mainly on our children and her new relationship with Mike. Jeannette was enjoying Mike's companionship. She said she had never met anyone like him. He was so open, so honest, and so adventurous, and a man who liked to talk about feelings. Neither one of them ever expected to find a romance in Hawai'i, but to their surprise they had. It made their adventure all the more magical. Soon Jeannette caught up with Mike and walked beside him.

Andre reminded me of the adventurous Tin Tin in the *Tin Tin* book series by Belgian cartoonist, Herge. He had an energetic, jaunty walk. I loved these books when I was a young teen-ager living in France. All that was missing was Tin Tin's little white dog, Milou. I laughed to myself naming an imaginary new Tin Tin book, "Tin Tin and the Mystery of the Mo'okini Heiau." I kept wondering why human sacrifice was done in the first place. One version of history tells us that it was introduced by a Tahitian chief who arrived on the island by double-hulled sailing canoe. I don't think historians are sure of the date.

The poor jeep was covered with mud when we left the area and got back on the road again. It was so interesting to share this experience with these friends. There were always laughs and warm feelings with this group. Now being chilly, we were off again to get a hot drink, up in Havi. As we left, I held up my hand and said, "No Riders."

### *The Great Kamehameha I*

KING KAMEHAMEHA THE GREAT
b. 1758 reign 1795 d. 1819

THE BIRTH OF KAMEHAMEHA I, also known as Kamehameha the Great, was about 1758 (his date of birth is not certain). He was born less than a mile from the Mo'okini Heiau. The infant was taken there for birth rituals before being taken to a remote location and hidden from chief Alapai and others who felt threatened by his potential future power, and might have wanted him killed. About the time that Kamehameha was born, a *kahuna* (priest) of prophecy said that a great leader was to be born that would conquer and unite all the islands.

356

Another prophecy about his birth was that when a light appeared in the sky, with bird-like feathers, a great chief would be born. The birth of Kamehameha I coincided with the appearance of Haley's comet, as it passed over the Big Island of Hawai'i. Today there are four statues of Kamehameha I. His name means "the lonely one" or "one that is set apart from others." As a boy he lived in the sacred Valley of the Kings, also known as the Waipio Valley. Each year on June 11th his statue at Kapaau, near his birthplace, is celebrated and covered with long, beautiful leis of golden flowers. There is a parade, songs, and a local Hawai'ian picnic lunch to honor his memory.

As Kamehameha grew older, he went on to study the arts of fighting and warfare. The fighting arts for strong Hawai'ian men were very vigorous. They trained and trained in the various Lua arts of strengthening their body until it became a virtual weapon. They also learned to fight with spears and clubs. At this time in history everything was made of stone and wood. Their favorite war club was a *leiomano*, a wooden club lined with the sharp teeth of a tiger shark. There were very high standards, discipline, and strict protocols about being a warrior. As Kamehameaha the Great grew up, there were visitors that sailed to the island in schooners. He was about twenty-one years old and actually present on the beach when Captain Cook first sailed into Kealakekua Bay on the Big Island. For many years one of his homes was behind the pond in the village of Kealakekua Bay. Foreigners introduced him to weapons and other objects made of metal, and trading began. Kamehameha made a point to learn the methods of warfare from these visitors. Later he was able to trade with these visitors for cannons and guns, which he used in his battles to win and unite all the Hawai'ian islands.

Another prophesy that was fulfilled was that the person who would be able to conquer and unite all the islands would be able to lift the long rectangular stone called the "Naha" stone. It weighed about five thousand pounds and no one had ever been able to lift it. But Kamehameha shocked everyone with his almost supernatural strength, and lifted the Naha stone. It is said in some old Hawai'ian writings that every time he was discouraged in battle or apprehensive before a battle, that he would encourage himself by thinking of how he had done that almost impossible feat. Today the

Naha stone can be seen in front of the Hilo public library on the Big Island of Hawai'i.

Kamehameha I began the campaign of wars to conquer all the islands and unite them under his rule. He now had cannons and guns that he obtained from English and American friends. Thus he and his warriors now had an advantage over the chiefs of the other islands, who didn't have these weapons. Through battles he conquered all of the big island of Hawai'i, and then Maui, Oahu, and Lenai. Before a war with Kauai could be waged, the head chief of Kauai surrendered Kauai to Kamehameha I. Now the islands had been conquered and were united under Kamehameha's rule. The prophecies had been fulfilled.

Eventually Kamehameha I settled in Kailua Kona, in the area of the present King Kamehameha Hotel, *heiau*, beach and boat launch. As it was the custom at that time for high chiefs to have more than one wife, King Kamehameha had many wives and descendants. He died of asthma in May of 1819 at the age of 82 or 83 at his home, Kamakahonu, in Kailua Kona. A Hawai'ian belief is that the *ivi* (bones) hold *mana* (spiritual power) and the bones of Kings and high *Ali'i nui* (chiefs) need to be hidden in remote areas. It is important that they are hidden where no one can find them and make use of their *mana*. "*Hunakele*"

in the Hawai'ian language means to hide the bones in secret. Even today no one knows where the bones of Kamehameha the Great are hidden.

## Every Day Aloha, A Whale Birth

ONE EARLY MORNING I DECIDED TO GET UP and drive down to K bay about seven in the morning. The dolphin swimmers were already arriving and pulling their fins and snorkel gear out of their cars. The previous day I was swimming out in K Bay and had encountered a pod of dolphins. I drifted on the water above the pod watching them swim below me in large circles. At regular intervals they all ascended in unison to breathe. They would dip and dive on the surface for a while and then dive again, as in a synchronized water ballet, to circle below the surface. I was enjoying their sonar sounds and whistles.

But then I became aware of the sounding of a whale joining the orchestration. How beautiful and ancient it sounded to me, as the sounds traveled through the water. I was swimming with my snorkel and mask on when I heard these whale songs, and wondering how far away the whale was, as sometimes they do enter the bay. It sounded close, but I couldn't see it. Now it was the next day and I had returned to the bay, not thinking about the whale sounds of yesterday. I had just had the impulse to go to the bay earlier than usual. Aka was sitting on the sea wall across from her mother's shop, playing her nose flute and facing the water. I was surprised to see her, as she, too, was here much earlier than usual. I went over and sat down on the stone wall next to her. I didn't speak, as I didn't want to interrupt her flute song. When she lowered the flute from her nose, she looked at me and smiled and said, "Aloha, sistah, do you know what's going on out there?" I said, "No, I don't." She said, ". . . a mother whale is about to give birth. I was playing a flute song to her to help her birth go well and welcome the baby."

The dolphin swimmers were still getting ready to go out into the bay. Suddenly Aka got up and left and started running up and down the beach, balancing carefully on the large rocks, calling out with authority, "No one in the water today. Stay out of the water. A mother whale is about to give birth. Show her some respect! Give her space! No one in the water today!" Even though the swimmers were unhappy, they minded Aka, knowing her and knowing that she and her mother, Auntie Fern, and her family were key "spiritual keepers and protectors" of both the *heiau*, the bay, and the dolphins and whales.

Aka came back to the wall and sat down beside me again and seemed to be tracking what was going on under the surface of the water. "Okay now, sistah, she is birthing that baby right now! Watch, you will see the baby come up for its first breath of air." I watched the water at the spot she pointed to. The baby whale popped up for its first breath of air. It was so exciting to witness this! As with all births I got tears in my eyes, feeling overcome with emotion. There was motion in the water and mama whale blew a big spout!

Aka began to play her nose flute again to welcome the baby whale. People on the shoreline of the rocky beach had been watching too. Some were cheering. Nobody was going into the water today. Aka had said so, and she was not someone to be ignored. After a while she whispered into my ear, "Sistah, do you know how big a whale placenta is?" I said back to her, "It must be huge." She replied,

"And do you know what is going to come into the bay to eat that placenta?" I nodded, finally understanding why she was so adamant about not wanting anyone out in the water. And she was careful not to scare anyone either. Again, I recognized her as a protector, a protector of the whales, of the dolphins, of the *heiau*, of the bay, and of the people.

360

*Fishing in Hawai'i and Tahiti*

ONE DAY, AKA AND I TALKED ABOUT FISHING and all the old fishing villages that used to exist on the Big Island. "Most of these fishing villages are no longer fishing villages," Aka said. "Milo'li'i is still a fishing village, and back in the day it was really busy, bringing in a lot of the fish that went to the Hilo markets. Dried *opela* was shipped to Oahu. The men would drive pick-up trucks at night, full of fish on ice, to get those fish to the Hilo market by morning. When I was young, I learned to fish from the shore and from a canoe. I could throw a small cast-net from the shoreline or from the beach in shallow water. The cast-net is circular and has tiny weights all around the edges. When you know how to fish and grow a garden, you will not go hungry on the Big Island."

I told Aka about my fishing experiences on the Island of Moorea. "Meme took me out in an outrigger canoe on Opunoho Bay at night, and we stayed out fishing all night long. Their home and land was right next to this bay, and had belonged to Meme's late mother who was an herbalist. The canoe had a small motor, but we hardly used it. A thick rope was dragged behind the outrigger canoe with hooks at various levels of the rope and baited with smaller fish. We had gotten the bait fish earlier in the day in a method called *huki lau*. The net was walked out into the bay in a hoop shape, which would be lined with Ti leaves. The fish were herded into the center. Then friends and family on shore pulled both ends of the net in, which contained the fish. Everyone who helped would share in the catch. The tiny bait fish were put in buckets for the night fishing."

Aka smiled and chuckled hearing about the way Meme and her family had chosen me to be the one to walk the net out into the shallow part of the bay. I told her the water was up to my neck, the whole time. She said, "They were sure having fun with you . . . kinda' testing you, eh? But you were a good sport. We have the *huki lau* tradition here too, just like the Tahitians. My father was an awesome fisherman, too. He was also a free diver and could hold his breath for a long, long time. One time he brought me black coral from a dive, while he was working and diving on a marine research vessel. I used that black coral to make some beautiful jewelry."

### Suzy, Slack Key, and Lunch

NOW THAT I WAS SO CLOSE TO K BAY, I saw a lot of Aka. I would drive down to the bay, take a swim, and often encountered Aka either at the shop or close by, at Manini Beach. Sometimes I would hang out with Aka's daughter, Suzy, who was twelve at the time. She and I were swimming one day and diving for stones. When we would come up from our dive, Suzy said we were to interpret what the stone looked like . . . sometimes a kind of animal or some familiar object. It was fun. We just kept diving and coming up with interesting stones, with unusual shapes. Suzy was full of life and fun! On another day Suzy, with her winning smile and ways, persuaded me into letting her drive my jeep.

Neither Aka nor Grandma Fern was around to ask. I was persuaded. My condition was that I sit next to her and that she drive very slowly around the little roads around K Bay and Manini Beach. She turned out to be a good driver, so I didn't feel nervous. "But Suzy," I said, "I am not going to let you drive to the Waipio Valley." We both laughed at that. Little did I know then, that I would continue to know Suzy and her partner and children years into the future.

One day after swimming with Aka, she said, "Let's take a walk and go visit my cuz." We walked just a short distance and came up the stairs to the front door of a house in Napo'opo'o village. This house was close to where her grandmother and Auntie Iolani Luahine once had a house, and where Aka and her sisters spent part of their childhood. Aka cracked the door and sang in, "Alohaaaa brah." Soon a tall, tan, bare-chested man with black hair came to the door and greeted her with a big smile, warm bear hug and *honi* (nose to nose greeting, sharing breath). He had tattoos (*kakau*) on his arms and an ivory-colored carved fish hook on a cord around his neck. The tattoos, which had a lot of geometrical shapes, reminded me of the tattoos of so many Tahitian men. Aka later explained that the fish-hook necklace had been carved from bone. It was very traditional in Hawai'i for good luck in fishing, boating and swimming.

Then Aka introduced me to her cousin and he welcomed me as well. Before you know it, he had sat down with his guitar and began to sing a beautiful Hawai'ian song. Aka seemed to know the words of the song and began to sing with him. Several beautiful songs later he excused himself and went into the kitchen. He called out that we shouldn't leave as he was bringing out some grinds (lunch) for all of us. Aka said, "No need brah, but you go ahead." Soon he came out with plates of lunch. He served us with a big smile and the Aloha was palpable. He asked me how I happened to come to the island and where I was staying.

After lunch there were a few more songs. I was mesmerized by the beautiful slack key guitar and the lyrical music. I relaxed back in a rattan chair and closed my eyes. I could visualize hula dancers dancing to this gentle music. I thought to myself that only in Hawai'i could you drop in, unannounced, at a friend's house, and be serenaded and fed lunch. It seemed so effortless and gracious. The slack key guitar and the graceful story telling of the *hula* are Hawai'i to me. Good live music enlivens the endorphins, creating a pleasure body, just as the dolphins do.

### Lomilomi Massage for the Kupuna

ONE DAY BARBARA DEFRANCO LET ME KNOW that there was a volunteer opportunity to share *lomilomi* massage with local *kupuna* (elders). The location was a South Kona senior center that had a regular weekly program for seniors. Each session included a speaker on nutrition, fall prevention, and other topics helpful to senior citizens. Several of us who had studied Lomilomi massage with Auntie Margaret Machado or Kumu Dane Silva took our tables to the Senior Center and happily offered our volunteer services. We set up our tables and waited for the lecture to be over. We understood that, due to the modesty of elderly Hawai'ian and Japanese people, we would *lomi* them with their clothes on. This was no problem as we were taught how to do this when we learned *lomilomi*. However, they did take off their socks and shoes. We gave each person a twenty-minute massage. One particular day I remember a lecture about nutrition, which was followed by a healthy snack. All the seniors, both men and women, were either Hawai'ian or Japanese. I kept thinking how cute they were. Some of them were shy and had not experienced massage before. When we greeted "our person," we asked them if they had any particular aches and pains, or injuries that we should be aware of, or areas of their body that needed massage the most.

This opening question gave them the chance to tell us a little bit about themselves and the condition of their body. We had a stool and helped them get up on the table. As we had learned in class, we began with a short prayer. I felt that many of these people had not had human touch for a long time. Most of them were widows and widowers. They especially liked having their bare feet massaged with flower-infused oil. I remember one lady who became tearful, saying it felt so good to be touched. She said no one had touched her for a long time, except for having her hair washed at the hair dresser. Another lady that I gave a *lomi* treatment to said that she still lived in her own home. She told me that a young teen-ager had become her friend and came to do yard work for her. She made him meals and "talked story" to him. He was so grateful to have an adopted grandmother that he planted a vegetable garden for her. Later he and his friends built a lava rock fish pond for her in her back yard. He was grateful to hear the stories of the old days and receive her Aloha. It was a wonderful example of the mutually positive connection that can happen between youth and elders.


### *Ho'o'ponopono: Aka Shares with a Few Friends*


AKA INVITED ME TO JOIN HER and a few of her guests from Japan. I was free and looked forward to meeting these Japanese ladies. We met in the park at Manini Beach. The weather was perfect. Aka told me that these friends wanted to hear about *Ho'o'ponopono*, and introduced me to each of these young women. They immediately addressed me as Nancy-san . . . the 'san' on the end of the name is a sign of respect. Their English was quite good too.

After some small talk, Aka seated herself at a picnic table and we all sat at the table around her. She had placed a Ti leaf in the middle of the table. She began with a chant and a prayer which was followed by asking the ladies how they deal with a family or work-related conflict. One at a time they told some stories of conflicts that they either had or still have in their life. One of the women told a story about being ostracized from her family because she refused to marry a wealthy Japanese business man that her parents had chosen for her. Modern Japanese women were pulling away from many old customs, especially arranged marriages. And if the marriages weren't officially arranged, daughters could be pressured to marry a man her parents had chosen for her. Others told stories of conflicts at work, or with boyfriends or husbands.

Aka began by telling us that *Ho'o'ponopono* was very different from mediation because it is a process that is over-lit by prayer and spirituality. It means making things right and bringing things back to love, peace, and harmony. The practitioner is traditionally a spiritual person who has had training in this healing art. Often it is an elder in the family who teaches a child or grandchild. The person being taught is taken along to *Ho'o'ponopono* sessions. Everything that takes place in the sessions is kept totally confidential. "My grandmother taught me and guided me by taking me to sessions that she conducted.

"*Ho'o'ponopono* means making things right with ourselves, others, our world, and the divine. Listening with empathy and openness is encouraged in order to understand another's point of view. Sometimes the sessions go on for many hours, or even days, in order to come to peace, harmony, and understanding. During a session of *Ho'o'ponopono*, the participants are all drawn together in prayer with the goal of reconciliation, and each person coming to understand the other's point of view. It is important to listen carefully to each person when they are talking, without interrupting."

Aka shifted into talking about a deeper level of *Ho'o'ponopono*. I had heard the previous explanation before from Aka, but I felt she was about to share something that I had never heard before. I was taking notes and I was glad that I could write so fast, as I didn't want to miss any of this. I knew it was very, very important. Everyone was listening attentively.

"We believe that we carry spiritual and collective karma within us. We feel that it is our responsibility, in this time of ascension, to clear, purify, and raise the vibration of our entire lineage: of both our ancestors and our descendants. We need to imagine seeking and receiving forgiveness for everything that was ever done by our ancestors and ourselves that might have hurt, harmed, or destroyed any lives in the past, all the way back to when our lineage was first created. We must also seek and receive forgiveness for those who have done harm against our ancestors, our selves, and our descendants, releasing them fully from the ties that have bound them, both here and in the spirit world. Now imagine freedom for all of them, thousands upon thousands, if not more. Imagine the clearing of all blockages for yourself and for your descendants. By doing this, you are healing genetic ailments and sicknesses that have been passed from generation to generation. You also open gateways that may have been blocked before, so that you can access ancient wisdom and knowledge. And when you are able to clear all of your channels, by very seriously practicing all of this, you will become much more intuitive. You will be able to receive messages from your guides and helpers in the spirit world and from the stars. When we are cleared like this and become so much more aware and intuitive, we can be of greater service to our friends here on Earth and to the divine."

# A Visit to Kumu Lanakila Brandt in the Kona Community Hospital

ONE DAY BARBARA GATHERED A GROUP OF FRIENDS and asked us if we would go with her to the Kona Hospital to pray for Uncle Lanakila Brandt, who was in the hospital. I remembered Uncle Lanakila, as he had conducted the ceremony at Paleaku Gardens a few days after I had met Aka the previous year. He was well known as a Kahuna of the God Lono and a Kahuna of the temple complex of *heiaus* at Pu'uhonua o Honaunau. He also was a Kumu Hula (teacher of *hula*) and a teacher of ancient Hawai'ian spirituality, language, prayers, and songs. I don't remember what he was suffering from at that time, but he smiled and greeted us warmly when we came into his room and formed a circle around his bed. We prayed together for his healing and well being, each of us offering a spontaneous prayer for him. Later when I learned more about him and his extensive knowledge of prayers and chants in the Hawai'ian language, I thought how ironic it was to have a group of women come to pray for him in English. However, he seemed very happy to have us visit. Even if we didn't know the healing chants that he has taught his students for many years, it was the sincerity of our prayers that seemed to make him smile.

## Mayumi of Ginger Hill Farms

MAYUMI ODA IS A WORLD RENOWNED ARTIST, often referred to as the "Matisse of Japan." She lived in California for a number of years and then moved to the Big Island of Hawai'i. In my opinion she is every bit as much a goddess as the painted goddesses which have given her world-wide artistic fame. Mayumi's graceful flowing motions and her pretty, delicate appearance, reminds me of a princess in a fairy tale. She is slender with dark salt-and-pepper hair and has wise and sparkling eyes. She often wears gauzy white pants and loose flowing white shirts. Her movements remind me of the story telling of the *hula*, artfully graceful, carrying a message and aura of peace and tranquility.

The first time I met Mayumi it was Aka who brought me to her house. Aka always told me how much she loved Mayumi-san. And now Aka wanted to share her friend with me. "Now you are in for a treat, sistah," she said to me, as we drove down the hill past her daughter Suzy's school. At the bottom of the road, she turned left into the parking area of Ginger Hill Farm. We parked on the mowed grass which was lined with banana trees.

Aka was aware that each of us had a close relationship with Corbin Harney, a Native American spiritual leader and anti-nuclear activist. "Mayumi has worked with Corbin too and has spoken against nuclear proliferation at The Hague, and at the United Nations World Court of Justice in the Netherlands," she said.

We went to the door. Aka cracked it open and sang in a long sweet, "Alohaaaaaa, Mayumi." Mayumi came to the door and welcomed us with a smile and hugged each of us. Then Aka began to tell Mayumi about me and my deck of *Dolphin Divination Cards* and the *Guidebook*. Aka said, "Nancy, here, has woven into her dolphin readings both spiritual and environmental messages." I was a little embarrassed about all the praise Aka was giving me. I promised Mayumi to bring her a deck of my little round dolphin cards and *Guidebook* sometime soon.

For many years Mayumi has conducted retreats at her home for Japanese students and visitors from all over the world. She leads them in Zen Buddhist meditation and yoga, and she teaches organic, sustainable gardening and cooking. It is all "hands on" and everyone participates in the gardening and cooking. Finally, she shares her great expertise in art and leads the students in either finding their artistic muse or enhancing a talent they may already have.

Her beautiful home has touches of Japanese architecture but is merged with a local Hawai'ian style. It is surrounded by the lush tropical foliage of South Kona. There is a koi pond with a curved bridge as one approaches the front door. Above the door are

Japanese-style posts and lintels. There is abundant ginger and *olena* (turmeric) growing on Mayumi's farm. As one approaches the kitchen door, one often sees baskets of ginger, turmeric, hard squashes, and other produce freshly harvested from the garden. Bunches of bananas are hung there too, to finish ripening. From the house there is a hill that slopes down towards the ocean. A winding path leads to gardens, cottages, and campsites.

I found Mayumi's art studio to be a magical place. There are high ceilings and large windows on two sides displaying nature's art outside the windows

. . . tropical trees, plants, and vines. As Mayumi and Aka took me to the studio for the first time, they watched my face, as I am sure it had a look of awe and wonder as I took in all the visuals. On the walls are large paintings (*thangkas*) of Goddesses and female deities. These paintings are larger than life, in bright, bold colors. They are tributes to the many aspects of the divine feminine. Some were Goddesses on boats with waves all around. A rainbow appeared in one of them. Goddesses would also be painted in gardens full of flowers and foliage with scudding clouds overhead. Some of the Goddesses were female Tibetan deities, such as Tara and Saraswati. These paintings are often as large as eight by ten feet and sometimes larger. A Green Tara *thangka*, of 11 by 14 feet, was painted for the Wood Valley Retreat and Dharma Center in the south of the Big Island. Mayumi has said that the different Goddesses and feminine

369

deities reflect qualities of what she is feeling or aspiring to at the time that she starts a painting.

I was just spell-bound . . . and couldn't stop moving my gaze from one painting to another. The Goddesses feel as if they could step right off the walls and mingle among us. I glanced over at Aka and Mayumi, and they both had serenely blissful looks upon their faces as they watched my reactions. At the moment they were not the animated teachers and activists that they both manifest so uniquely, but serene and blissful Goddesses themselves. Most of Mayumi's work is painted, silk-screened, or carved onto wood blocks. She also incorporates calligraphy. She told us that she does her painting and silk screening kneeling on the floor. I was just amazed by this. As my eyes surveyed the studio, I saw paints and brushes and other art supplies on the shelves of the studio.

Having tea and home-grown bananas and nuts in Mayumi's studio is a pleasure for the palate, as the eyes continue to scan from one large, beautiful and colorful Goddess to another. I was reminded of the Tarot card, "the three of cups," as the three of us savored the tea that Mayumi poured into three small Japanese teacups. It did feel as if the three of us were kindred spirits who were once again re-united.

Mayumi wanted to share some *olena* (turmeric root) and ginger with us, so we moved towards the kitchen, passing through the living room first. This large, comfortable room has often been the site of gatherings and meditation retreats. Yoga mats can easily unroll on the wooden floor. Some of her son G's beautiful and dramatic artwork is on the wall. This room opens up onto a large covered lanai, which overlooks a sloping yard and the ocean far below. Here so many delicious meals have been served. There is a very long table that accommodates large groups with a smaller side table at the end for the buffet.

I have had the pleasure of eating here with her group of students and local friends a number of times after this initial meeting with Aka. Koko Momi Kawauchi Johnson, another gifted artist, who is also a close friend of Mayumi's and Aka's, has spent a lot of time here with Mayumi at Gingerhill farms. Like Mayumi, Koko is a talented cook. The food is prepared in the kitchen, and almost all of it is grown in Mayumi's garden. Students are often chopping, peeling, and prepping the food. They may look up with a smile, as working with fresh organic vegetables makes this kitchen a happy place. *Mana* (spiritual energy) and delightful aromas pervade the house, moving from room to room, like the smoke of temple incense. The golden soup of pureed and seasoned kabocha squash with *olena* is surely the most savory and delicious soup I have ever eaten.

The Christmas season of 2001 Mayumi hosted a festive holiday party. Her two sons were there and many local friends. Festive outdoor lights lit up the lanai. There was fish, crab, other sea food, and vegetable dishes. Japanese side dishes were on the food table and as always the most delicious small, sweet bananas, grown on the farm. Vegetables, soup, rice, dates, figs, and nuts were offered along with homemade *mochi*.

Aka reminded us that we had a mutual friend: Corbin Harney. Mayumi shared that she had worked as an anti-nuclear activist in Japan and that she knew Corbin Harney, who was a Western Shoshone spiritual leader and healer. Paul and I had published Corbin's book, *The Way It Is: One Air, One Water, One Mother Earth* (1995). It is a book about the way Native Americans view nature and the way they protect and relate to the natural world. There is also a section about Corbin's anti-nuclear acti-vism. Corbin talked the book to Paul and I over many early morning breakfasts. Corbin most often would be up making breakfast for the family before dawn. He said, if we slept in, we would miss his stories as well as a hot breakfast. Paul took copious

notes around the breakfast table over a number of months. Then, using Corbin's "voice," he assembled the notes into a book, with organized chapters and photographs. This wonderful traditional Native American man was family to us and was like a grandpa to our children. It is impossible to estimate how much our present views have been influenced and changed by the early morning teaching stories, early morning prayer circles around a warming fire, the healing sweats in our lower garden, and our many travels into the Nevada desert with this spiritual leader. Mayumi and Paul and I share many things in common, as well as sharing two very close and dear friends: both Aka and Corbin.

{*This account of Mayumi and Aka took place in 2001 and 2002. In more recent years Mayumi gifted us with a treasured painting of Aka, which appears on the cover of this book. Mayumi has also produced several beautiful color books of her artwork, started creating textile art, and published a deck of beautiful oracle Goddess cards, containing a divination message paired with her art work in both Japanese and English.*}

### A Profound Talk with Aka

IT WAS THE GOLDEN HOUR BEFORE SUNSET, and Aka and I were walking around the labyrinthine pathways of the City of Refuge, Pu'uhonua o Honaunau. Shafts of golden light spread through the palm trees, casting long shadows on the large stone *heiaus*. These ancient platform temples were the places of ceremony during

centuries past, when this place was a safe refuge for people who had broken laws or *kapus*. Now Kahu Sam Lono and Kahu Lanakila Brandt were two of the Kahunas who still performed the ancient ceremonies of the old religion here. Uncle Lanakila was a Kahu of this place, like his grandfather before him, where he too had performed the rites of the God.

The sun was hanging low in the sky, like an orange lantern suspended above the ocean. Aka would usually be home at this hour fixing dinner for her family. Tonight she was staying in Honaunau, as each of her family members had their own plans. We sat down on some large lava rocks and pondered the shiny glints of tangerine light that were sparkling on the ocean, and the waves that were breaking on the shore, sending plumes of white spray up into the air. Soon she began to speak, gazing at the ocean the entire time. There was something deep and prophetic in her tones this evening.

"You will be going home soon," she said, in a matter of fact way. It's time for you and Paul to be together again." I agreed with her, but I did not feel finished with this time of inner growth and realization, and I did not feel that it was quite time to leave. I knew that Paul was planning to visit me soon. We would spend time exploring favorite places on the island, and we would talk and find warmth and comfort being with each other, as people do, who have had a long relationship. We would share what we had discovered about ourselves, living away from each other for all these months.

Aka began to speak again, "You and I have talked many times about the future, and we both know that the day is coming when I will be called upon. You and I have both spoken about and seen, ahead of time, trips to Europe, Russia, Japan, and other places where I will share Aloha and the teachings of my *tutus*. This is what I was born to do. Ma has been so frustrated with me at times, thinking I wasn't going to fulfill my *kuleana*.

{*Years later, I met a few of her wonderful European and Japanese organizers: Toshi Koamaikai, Saraspea Yuka, Gerda Fuchs, Heidi Oberli, Christa Bauer, and many others.*}

"On some level this will be an opportunity to share the teaching of Aloha as my grandmother and aunties taught me, but I also see a metaphorical suitcase of gold and silver, an abundance of finances that I am not used to having. This can swing both ways, as a blessing or a curse. I have always lived by the skills my *tutus* and *ohana* taught me, as well as faith and trust, and the gifts that spirit brings to me and my *ohana*. There are always gifts, filling our daily needs from our daily work, and from those who have gone on before me. There is such a feeling of trust and abundance that I never worry. The *aina* and the sea and the forest are so generous.

"So many people worry about money, or even obsess about not having enough, and wanting more than what they have. So many people think that money will bring them happiness and solve their problems. But when it arrives, it just runs through their fingers like water in a sieve, and before you know it, it's gone. And then all that fear and anxiety of lack is back again. Our modern lifestyle destroys our peace."

I thought of Douglas on the Hilo side of this island, living a life without money and being happy in a tree house. He had a similar philosophy of trust and appreciation of the little everyday miracles that occur, that rich people rarely notice or get to experience.

"You know," Aka said, turning to look at me smiling, "people may want to feast on me." She laughed and looked at me and asked

me if I was taking that literally? I said, "No," and didn't say any more, as she was slipping back into her altered state, staring out at the ocean. "They will be hungry, but it will not actually be me that they are hungry for. It is the *aloha*, the love, the teachings and *mana* (spiritual power) of my *tutus* and ancestors, that they will be hungry for. It will be inner peace that they are hungry for. And I will be happy to provide the feast for them. That is part of my *kuleana* (spiritual duty)."

She had a soft smile on her face and now the sun was lower in the sky. It cast a golden glow on her face, as she gazed into the sunset with a faraway look. She had only looked at me twice during this talk and she was not using pidgin English. She was a very well read person with great depth and intelligence. This particular evening, she was deeply philosophical. Even her style of speech was different. I knew that I had better pay attention and write these words in my diary when I got home.

"I always love the golden hour," she said, suddenly looking at me with a smile. You know, speaking of 'golden', gold and silver and jewels can create some really intense medieval dramas. When you think about it, all these things come from under the earth. Have you ever thought of that?" she asked me. I said, "Yes, our friend, Corbin Harney, the Western Shoshone medicine man, always says that we are emptying out the Earth's pockets with mining and drilling which is destabilizing our Mother Earth." Aka nodded at that and said, "Well, that's a good way to describe what we are doing."

Aka got up off the lava stone and stretched and held out her arms towards the setting sun and said a prayer of thanks to the sun for its life-giving gifts. Then she sat back down and continued her musings. "Think about it, gold and silver and jewels can cause a lot of problems. It was how money came into being. After being mined and brought up to the surface, they have caused people to betray each other, steal from each other, and fight with each other for centuries and centuries. It is kind of like the bad things that happen to greedy people who dig up the *ivis* (bones) of our ancestors to build condos and resorts on burial grounds. Greed can cause people to lie, exaggerate, and to create scapegoats for their negative projections and fears. Think about it. All these things are robbed from the *aina*, our Mother Earth.

"Somewhere in the genes, greed and fear seem to arise over money. Families often break apart and hold lifetime grudges against each other over inheritances and land disputes. And it's never, ever, worth it, to disturb our minds like this. I have seen these things happen right here. My grandmother and I have done *Ho'o'ponopono* with families that are set against each other. And sometimes people never come back from these betrayals. You gotta love 'em though, but, just maybe, it will never be quite the same again. You may have to love 'em from a distance."

Aka went on to tell me about some *Ho'o'ponopono* sessions she had with large families, at odds with each other, about disagreements over inheritances or land. She never disclosed names or details that would identify anyone, as she kept strict confidentiality in this work. I suddenly thought of my own metaphor of pulling up the "drawbridge of my moat" back home, when I felt overwhelmed. It was rare, but on a few occasions I had felt this way. I thought of the Gold Rush in my home town of Nevada City in the foothills of California and the robberies and murders that took place back in the mid-1800s. "Gold got a lot of people robbed or killed back in Nevada City during the Gold Rush. A lot of Native Americans and Chinese were killed. Bounties were offered, and there was an epidemic of hateful racism. There was a tragic genocide against both the Native Americans and the Chinese," I said.

Aka sort of chuckled ironically and said, "It's a shameful history alright. Yes, they got their golden ticket, alright, right into the next life." Aka went on, "You may be shocked to find that a lifelong friend or a friend of your children will slander you or your children. I'm a mother bear, and anyone that messes with my children will see that mother bear coming into their camp, ferocious and growling. NO ONE messes with my 'behbehs.'" I saw fierceness in her eyes as she spoke of the mother bear. I wondered what brought this subject to mind. Somehow I wondered if she was looking into the future, not only for herself, but for me as well.

"People can even get into your suitcase and rob it when you are sleeping." I wondered why she was referring to suitcases. "You know," she said, "if I ever gather a suitcase full of gold and silver and jewels, I would bring it home to my beybeys . . . just like a mother animal bringing food back to its young. It would be given to them, or a family member who is sick, or who needs food and medicine, or a house or an education.

"When the robber finds that the money is spent, or the jewels are all sold, what do they have left? They have empty pockets and they have lost friends. And what is left for the person robbed, but an empty suitcase and the realization that they have been betrayed by a friend? It is disappointing and it hurts for a while, but you gotta love 'em. Remember how Jesus said, ''Father, forgive them, for they know not what they do?'

"Forgiveness is important, as our own bitterness, anger, and hurt ends up hurting us. That is only one very important reason for forgiveness. There are others: bitterness and anger can tear up our insides and make us sick. Our *na'au* will be twisted and will not be able to work properly. And we won't be able to get those gut level hits and hunches that give us guidance and safety. And our heart won't be able to pour out *aloha*. It will be just a trickle. It would be a drought for the heart.

"Aloha and forgiveness puts love and peace out into the universe rather than anger and bitterness. Remember how I have always told you that negative emotions, like anger and jealousy and fear, create food for the bad spirits? They will come around to feed on it and cause harmful problems. But even with forgiveness, a previous friendship may never be quite the same again. It may be so tarnished that it may have to be distanced . . . or let go. But still, you gotta love 'em. Oh, *kala mai, Ke Akua* (forgive me, Creator) for any occasion in time and space that I have done harmful things, intentionally or unintentionally, consciously or unconsciously to others."

She had made this short but spontaneous prayer quite suddenly and it reminded me of the many times a day she prayed out loud. Aka went on to say, "We always need to look to ourselves first, to see our part, or to track what we have done to bring these things about. It may be tracked to a time long ago, or we may track it to something we had a part in more recently. And then forgiveness has to go all the way around the circle to include ourselves."

I thought of Eunice, the Western Shoshone medicine woman, from a Native American colony in Battle Mountain, Nevada, who lived to be 111. She had gone through these things too, over her long lifetime. Her father had been viciously attacked and killed by some gold miners. Some of her own people were jealous of her and even tried coming against her with bad medicine. She would say to me, "They can't hurt me. They ain't got nothin'!" She taught me that no matter what anyone has done to you, "Just smile and wave." And Aka's version would be to "smile and shake out a *shaka*."

The rosy, purple and gold-edged clouds that appeared after the sun sunk into the horizon were fading into pale pinks and grays. Soon darkness would draw a dark curtain over the clouds and shroud the nearby *heiaus*. Aka held up her hand and said, "*Mahalo nui loa, tutus* for being with us this beautiful evening. Please light our way. Give us your loving protection as we make our ways home." As she said this prayer, a wave of chicken skin ran through my body, head to toe. We walked back on the path that went between two stone *heiaus*, past an ancient fish pond and a thatched canoe house, and out of the historical park. I thought to myself, "Here in this place of refuge, where ancient peoples of Hawai'i were given refuge and forgiveness for breaking *kapus* and misdeeds, Aka had just shared deep insights with me about wrong-doings, forgiveness, and Aloha. Do ancient thought forms hang in the atmosphere, ready to be plucked like ripe fruit? I wondered. It was easy to imagine the group of people who lived here hundreds of years ago. As it got dark, they may have lit their path with a torch of *kukui* nut oil. They would be entering their thatched *hales* (homes) for the night. They would go to sleep, on stacks of *lauhala* woven mats, listening to the surf breaking on the rocks. Design-decorated *tapa* cloths, made of mulberry bark, may be hanging on the wall. Layers of history were embedded here. It was easy to imagine spirits from the past wandering the land, visiting their old haven of refuge which had saved their lives from execution.

We had reached our cars. Aka gave me a big hug, we said good night, each of us got into our vehicles. I waved goodbye, and Aka shook out a shaka. We had never had a talk like this before. It left me wondering. It was a strange conversation. This evening Aka didn't ask me to write our talk down in my diary, but I knew I should. Even though I was terrible at advanced math in school, I did have an uncanny memory and could often remember conversations word for word. I would be sure to write about this in my diary tonight, as it had strange and prophetic tones. I had no idea then that this diary would someday be expanded to become a book, and a tribute to Aka, her mother, Auntie Fern, their *ohana*, and the culture of Hawai'i.

## *"Paka" and Fishing*

KAPUA LIKES TO REMINISCE ABOUT "the old days" in Kona. In the 1970's and 80's he was young, and he and his wife were raising a young daughter. He told me about clever ways that local people grew *pakalolo* (*paka*), which is the local word for marijuana. It was a time when a lot of people were smoking it, and like the most excellent Kona coffee beans, it grew well here. Besides doing various jobs and farming, locals love fishing. There are many places along the coast that give up a good catch for local families. However, they are often places that are hiked into, in the dark, before dawn, over rough lava. These places are called "seeks" (secret spots). Speaking of themselves, they would often say, "The braddahs are on the shore!" and when they caught a fish they yelled out, "Feesh on" or "Shoots, I lost em." And don't ask me how I know. "Seeks!" I did eat some excellent fish dinners, from the outdoor grill, but it was the "braddahs" that caught 'em.

## *The Keoua Honaunau Canoe Club*

THE KEOUA HONAUNAU CANOE CLUB and Hawai'ian Immersion School was another innovation founded for the youth of the Honaunau area during the nineteen seventies era. This was the peak of the Hawai'ian cultural renaissance, and old traditions were being revived. It was called "Ho'ohanohano Na Kupuna o Keoua." Dixon Enos was the first person who told me about the school. He and his beautiful wife, Barbara, were raising a family up mauka from Honaunau Bay on a lovely little farm. One evening they invited me to their garden to sit and talk story around an outdoor fire pit. They had gathered a bundle of Ti leaves in a vase, to bless us, while we enjoyed the fire. Stories were brought out and one that I remember is about the Keoua Honaunau Canoe Club. The original *hale* was built right across the road from Honaunau Bay. It was a prototype of later schools that focused on Hawai'ian traditions and culture. This original canoe *halau* and school of traditional Hawai'ian culture catered to "youth at risk" and other young people who were more interested in Hawai'ian traditions than mainland style schools. They had fun paddling canoes, practicing for races, and learning about their traditional culture. Uncle Moses and Lilly Abraham, Tutu Clara Manase, Boots Matthews, Herb Kane, Clarence Medeiros, Diana Aki, Dixon Enos, Kapua Ching, and many others were involved.

The Keoua Canoe Club was closed in 1984 and the traditional *hale* gradually fell into disrepair. Around 2014-2016, the Keoua Honaunau Canoe Club received a grant to re-build the *hale*. Walter

Wong, master builder of traditional *hales*, directed his crew of apprentices and volunteers in the reconstruction project. The *hale* was dedicated to educational and ceremonial purposes. Carol Tredway documented the re-building of the *hale* in her beautiful drawing. Across the top of the artwork are: Calvin Kelekolio, Herb Kane, Haleaka Iolani Pule, Tutu Clara Manase and Uncle Joe (A.K.A. Sir Renwick Ili'ilipuna Tassill).

That same night, sitting around the fire pit with Dixon and Barbara, Dixon shared a story about his involvement in the

Kaho'olawe island Ohana. In recent history this island had been used exclusively as a U.S. government military base, with weapons and firing range. For traditional Hawai'ians this was a desecration of sacred land. After a number of protests, the activists, led by Georges Helms and others, finally succeeded in having policies changed so that Native Hawai'ians could have access to this island. Dixon prepared *awa* for a ceremony which was conducted there by Kahuna Sam Lono, which was attended by many Hawai'ian activists. This ceremony blessed this weapon-torn island and a *heiau* dedicated to Ku and other ancient sacred sites.


### A Phone Call with Paul


PAUL AND I HAD BEEN SPEAKING ON THE PHONE almost once a week throughout these months of separation. He always updated me on work at the publishing business and about the kids, our friends, the land, and the gardens. Since I had been living like a gypsy on the Big Island, people that I met had no idea that I had a home and ten acres of forest, gardens, and orchards back in Nevada City, California. I usually didn't mention the details about our land unless I was asked. If someone inquired, I was happy to tell them all about home. I wanted to live in the present moment by trust and faith.

Our adult children were grown up now. James was 42, Stacy 41, Sean 30, Christina 25 and Mike 22. They kept in close touch with both Paul and I. Mike, who was born with aniridia (no iris in his eyes) and was legally blind at birth, lived at home with us. Christina would call me and have me talk to the grandchildren over the phone. Lilliana was two and three and Doc was a year old. Lilliana was going through a phase of loving umbrellas, so I sent her several umbrellas by mail. The one she really liked was from the Hilo Zoo, and was covered with pictures of zoo animals. Christina had married Grandma Eunice's grandson, Rudy, so the children carried the Western Shoshone bloodline of medicine people. I missed these adorable children and Rudy's two nephews, Jeff 12, and Johnny 10, who also lived with them. It wouldn't be too long and I would be home and I could see them on a regular basis. On this phone call we were deciding on the best two weeks for Paul to pull away from work to come to visit me on the Big Island. Both of us were excited to see each other. So much had happened for both of us. Finally, a date was chosen and a ticket bought. I would be picking him up at the Kailua Kona airport and placing a beautiful flower lei around his neck.

## PAUL'S VISIT

### Arrangements for Paul's Visit at Paleaku Gardens

BARBARA AND CREW HAD some wooden platforms for tents on the part of the Paleaku land that was under some huge trees, often filled with birds. I had arranged with Barbara for Paul and I to sleep in one of these spacious tents. I did my work trade with Barbara ahead of time, so that the days with Paul we would be free to be on vacation.

### Paul's Arrival and an Assessment of our Inner Growth

THE DAY OF PAUL'S ARRIVAL HAD FINALLY COME, and I drove to the airport with great excitement. After buying a flower *lei*, I stood at the gate waiting for him to appear. His plane had landed, but it took a while for him to debark and come through the gate. It seemed like forever that I was waiting, *lei* in hand. Finally, his smiling face appeared. We wrapped our arms around each other and kissed, and then I placed the fragrant *lei* of *plumeria* flowers around his neck. He was really here!!! It seemed surreal to both of us as it was so many months since we had seen each other. I'm sure our smiles were tattooed on our faces. We went up to Sam Choy's in Keauhou for a glass of wine and an appetizer dinner. We could sit on the large lanai and watch the sun sinking into the ocean. As we relaxed, I saw the setting sun reflected in Paul's eyes. What a handsome man, I thought. His warm brown eyes smiled at me across the table. Having a slender, tall and strong body, I told him he was forever young. He

383

squeezed my hand in the old familiar way of people who love to hold hands.

We talked about how each of us dealt with being without the other during these months apart. We shared how we had both become more independent and the internal growth that had come from this hiatus. I no longer felt like the same person who arrived on the island in September 2001. The culture, both old and new, had slowly and subtly infiltrated my being and shifted my views. The *mana* and *aloha* shared with me had helped heal some old wounds and expanded my heart and my capacity to love. And I was so much better at being able to cut slack for the inevitable imperfections in myself and others

I talked to Paul about the ways that Aka, her mother, her family, and other local people had helped me to grow in so many new ways. They had given me uniquely Hawai'ian insights into issues that troubled me, too. I had always felt other people's energy, as my own. It was wonderful when I was around happy, relaxed people. However, my solar plexus would become tight and I wouldn't feel well when I was around very stressed or angry people. Here on this island I had learned so many ways to clear my energy. Swimming, walking in nature, praying, meditating, singing, and having some "alone" time each day were key for me. The relaxed island energy helped me to realize the difference between island energy and the more intense mainland energy. Aka and her family taught me that as an ultra-sensitive and receiver that I needed to create my own insulated world within this world. I can remember Aka saying "Worlds within worlds!" as a reminder. This was not a way of isolating or shutting things out, but of creating a protective buffer of light around me while interacting with "the world."

Paul had his own experience of being without me. He wasn't quite ready to voice it yet. He did say proudly that he had cooked and hosted our traditional Thanksgiving dinner, all by himself. He had bought Christmas and birthday gifts, decorated the tree and hosted Christmas for our adult children and baby grandchildren. And he had done an excellent job of it. Paul is a very sensitive person but does not have my issue of being a sponge.

Here we were together again on the Big Island. The old layers of true Aloha are always bubbling up like a spring from the sediments of ancient history until now . . . right out of the *aina* (land), the mountains, the rocks, right out of the clouds and the sand of the beaches. The Aloha is always emanating from the flowers too, which fill the breezes with fragrances all year long.

Aka's true compassion for difficult people was always a heart-felt, "Poor Ting." Her teachings on "tracking" helped me to trace the roots of family problems, tendencies and insecurities that come from family and through generations of ancestors. If the chain of pain is broken in the present generation, it helps both our descendants and our ancestors, "wherever they may exist in time and space, at this very moment." Aka's mantra, "You gotta love 'em!" had been embedded in me too. My pride and heart were not hurt when Paul shared that he did quite well without me, because he kept very busy. But he said he loved and missed me. He, too, needed this time to just be himself, without the enmeshment and petty grievances that naturally occur in long-term relationships. We loved each other without a doubt. It was a treat to be together again and to reunite, with each of us having gained a greater capacity to be independent, yet still love and understand each other.

What else had the culture taught me, Paul asked? Another Aka directive was just to "Chillax," have faith in *Ke Akua* (God) and the "man in white" (the Lord), and to pray many times a day! Hawai'ians are generally so much better at this than most mainlanders. And a sweet sense of humility and humor lightens everything. Part of the meaning of Aloha is to be humble, gentle, forgiving, loving and kind with ourselves and others. And let me not forget Aka's suggestion to sing for an hour a day. Aka's frequent prayers and gratitude throughout the day gave me an insight into her inner joy. She was not unlike us in some ways. She had a family too. She had problems at times. But she was so skillful in navigating her problems. She didn't hang onto problems, let alone nurse them tediously. And somehow they flew out the window and did not diminish her loving heart, joy, and relaxation. Somehow, just as some local people can "turn a typhoon," Aka could turn a problem into a blessing. At the end of this reunion day with Paul I finally realized that it was nearing the time to return home. I also had to reconcile myself to the fact that my family was not going to follow me over here to settle in Hawai'i, as they once thought. I missed Paul, the children, dear friends, and the budding lives of our grandchildren.

### A Vacation with Paul

WE WOULD PACK A LOT IN during this two-week vacation, as there were so many places I wanted to share with Paul. Aka had plans for us too. We started out having coffee and breakfast with Barbara in the Paleaku Peace Gardens kitchen. After that we went down to Kealakekua Bay to pay our respects to Auntie Fern, the Heiau, and the bay which is the birthing grounds and sanctuary for the spinner dolphins. We had a great chat with Auntie Fern, and in her candid way she asked Paul, "When are you taking this woman home?" I joked with Auntie and asked her if I was such a big nuisance. She wiped her brow and rolled her eyes, and Paul had a big chuckle over that.

Then she surprised me by telling Paul that she couldn't figure out how I had met so many of the important Hawai'ian people, all over this island, in less than a year. She went on to say most local people never meet even a few of these people in their whole lives. "How does she do that?" she asked Paul. Paul said, "Nancy basically loves people and, of course, follows her guidance."

We all watched the dolphins out in the center of the bay circling, diving, and spinning. The kayakers were making a beeline for their area, ready to jump overboard for a dolphin swim. Swimmers at the shoreline were quickly putting on their fins, snorkels and masks to head out into the middle of the bay to join the dolphins.

Fern frowned and said, "I just wish they would leave the poor 'tings' alone. This is supposed to be a dolphin sanctuary! The poor tings can never get any rest with all these people harassing them. They're supposed to be resting in the daytime." I recalled that they rested one side of their brain at a time. Auntie Fern continued, "This is where they birth their young. It's a nursery for their beybeys. They get so tired that when they head out into the ocean at night to hunt, they often get nipped by sharks. They also die from infections they get from human nasal mucous. I tell these tourists that we, local people, don't go out to swim with the dolphins. Some of these people try to grab them by the fins or touch them. This is not *pono* (good). We respect their life and we can enjoy them from the shore. I do every day."

Auntie Fern offered Paul a soda and then began to show him her wares, which were on racks outside of her rustic craft shop beside the Heiau. I was watching the dolphin paparazzi as they clustered around the pod, both swimmers and kayakers. I knew that I had enjoyed swimming with the dolphins too. The influx of dolphin-swimming tourists had increased year by year, and it had really become a circus. I was starting to adopt Auntie Fern's view too.

"How is that little grandbaybay of yours?" Auntie Fern asked Paul. They had met the year before. "She looks so much the way my daughter Aka looked, when she was a beybey." Paul went on to tell Auntie all about the children and the grandchildren.

Before long we were off . . . after hugging Auntie Fern, *A Hui Hou* (see you later), to drive the four-mile road to walk through the

City of Refuge and to check if there were any parking places left at Two-Step, Honaunau Bay. The bay had already become busy with sunbathers and swimmers so we decided to come back for a swim another day. We walked through the City of Refuge on its winding paths. We saw the little lava rock tables that were set up for the *pohaku* (stone) game that was played long ago. Little white and black stones were set up on a type of checker board. We wondered how this game was played. For a while we watched the canoe maker carve an ancient replica canoe. Then we looked at the replica thatched houses, the tikis, the *heiaus* and the tide pools close to the shore. I had done this so many times alone. I had been here with Rika and Andre and Aka, but most times I came here alone. It was a wonderful place to contemplate and 'feel through' the layers of history that abided here. Now, it was nice to take this peaceful walk with Paul, hand in hand.

### Dipping into History

ONE MORNING PAUL AND I WENT to Pu'ukohola Heiau National Historic Site, which was very close to Spencer Beach and Ray's

PU'UKOHOLA HEIAU, PHOTO OF MURAL BY HERB KANE

house, where I had lived in Kawaihae. It was also called the Hill of the Whale. The Heiau was dedicated to the War God Ku (Kuka'ilimoku). I had driven past it numerous times on my way to Spencer Beach. This Molokini Heiau was terraced in massive stone work, and it is thought that long lines of strong men passed the building stones, one man to another man, from the Pololu Valley about twenty miles away. This would have been a very long line, similar to a fire brigade, passing buckets of water. Thousands of men were involved in this huge project. It was started in 1790 and finished in just one year, in 1791. A prophecy was made by Kahuna Priest, Kapouhahi. He predicted that King Kamehameha I would be successful in conquering and uniting all of the Hawai'ian islands if he built the Heiau on the Hill of the Whale. We walked up and down the hill surrounding the area of the Heiau. No one is to go up onto the Heiau, as it is still an active Heiau. Hawai'ian descendants of *Ali'i* still conduct ceremonies there.

We were trying to imagine the building of this huge Heiau complex with the strong bodied men carrying and passing stones to those who were placing them. There was no mortar used, as Hawai'ians are experts at "dry stacking" stones. Kamehameha I's brother, Keli imaika'i, was in charge of the building project. I could imagine the extremely tall King Kamehameha I, standing atop the Heiau in his full regalia, feathered cape, and head helmet, gazing out to the ocean. Soon he would wage battle on the other chiefs of the Big Island, as well as those of the other islands. The King's warriors were in peak physical fitness. They practiced for hours the martial art called *olahe Lua.* They had many strenuous exercises for building maximum strength and developing fighting skills.

The *heiau* overlooks an older *heiau*, and below in the bay there is a third underwater *heiau*, dedicated to the shark God. It is said that the *manu* (sharks) still swim around this underwater *heiau*. At one time, food offerings were made to the shark God.

One of the first European visitors to the islands was amazed to see both Hawai'ian men and women, from all classes, wave surfing. In his journal he called them "amphibious human beings." They were seen as great athletes on both land and water. Kamehameha's own cousin, Keoua Kuahu'ula, had control of the east side of the Big Island of Hawai'i. He, who was a rival, was lured to the new Heiau, by being told there would be a peace treaty made between him and his cousin. When they arrived in their canoe, Kamehameha I ordered his cousin and companions killed and placed on the new Heiau as sacrificial offerings. A local person added on to this historical story. He told me that, when Keoua Kuahu'ula arrived in his canoe and realized that he was going to be killed, he cut off his

ARRIVAL OF KEOUA KUAHU'ULA, MURAL BY HERB KANE

own male organ so that he would be an imperfect sacrifice. I have no idea if this last bit is true or not.

True to the prophesy, Kamehameha I would conquer all of the islands. The chiefs of Kauai Island surrendered instead of fighting, once they saw that all the other islands had lost their battles. King Kamehameha I had the advantage in battle as his English and American friends had traded him guns and cannons and helped him mount cannons on his double-hulled war canoes. The other chiefs did not have these "modern" weapons.

ONE DAY PAUL AND I WENT *HOLOHOLO* with Aka's sister Kalehua, who was also called "Miss Aloha" or Fern. We had a nice swim at Spencer Beach and fish tacos in Kawaihae. Afterward, we drove up north on the Kohala coast to see the home of Sarah and Akoni Pule, her Kohala grandparents. The house was set back from the road a ways and surrounded by a jungle growth of tropical trees. We stood at the edge of the highway bridge and looked at a small year-round creek that came down the hill next to the house. The creek was shaded with palms and dense foliage. The house was no longer owned by the family, but Aka and her sisters had told me stories of memorable visits to their grandparents and playing in the stream. I knew that this place held many happy childhood memories for all the siblings in the family. I had heard the stories, but now Paul and I had finally seen this special place ourselves.

After reminiscing, we drove to some north coastal areas which had views of the island of Maui on the other side of the thirty-mile channel. The channel is named *Alenuihaha* which means "great billows smashing." It is considered the most dangerous channel in the Hawai'ian islands, having strong winds and rough currents. In olden times double-hulled canoes sailed across this rough channel from Kawaihae to Hana on the island of Maui. We parked for a while to see if we could see the whales spouting and breaching, as it was a favorite whale viewing spot, but none were in view. We drove back south, down the Akoni Pule highway, named after Kalehua's Grandfather Pule. His son, William Mahoe Pule Sr., was born on January 17, 1936 and passed away on May 18, 1978. I believe Aka was about thirteen or fourteen when her father died and Kalehua was a few years older.

We talked in the car about being disappointed not to see the whales today. And then, while we were driving, suddenly there came a loud whale song that seemed to be coming from inside of the car. It was loud, powerful, and undeniable. At this point we were several miles east of the ocean, too far away to hear the whales sounding. And it was not the car radio either. I said, "Oh Kalehua, you made this happen. You're a magical woman." She just laughed and shook her head, "No." Then Paul said, "We're driving on Akoni

Pule's highway. Maybe he brought the whales to us." At this thought, we all laughed. All three of us were amazed and realized that the whales, like the dolphins, are not bound by time and space.

I remembered Aka's words about the whales. "The whales use their songs to harmonize and keep the planet together. The ancient ones channeled what the whale songs and their knowledge meant. There is a chant called the *Pala Hoa* and that is a *kahola* (whale) chant." Aka wasn't with us on this memorable day, but her sister Kalehua was. The whales had shown up for us after all, in a most unusual way. As we kept talking about our "wonder" at this experience, an *anuenue* (rainbow) appeared in the blue and cloudless sky. We pulled the car over to a turnout, and I got out and took a picture of it. To this day I call that picture our "whale rainbow."

### A Call from Juni

ONE DAY WE GOT A PHONE CALL from our *Paniolo* friend, Juni Medeiros. He had been visiting Ho'okena with our mutual friend, Lenda Hand. Juni needed a ride back up to his ranch on the east side of Waimea. He also had been asked a favor by his friend, Parker Ranch veterinarian, Dr. Billy Bergen. Juni thought we might want to meet Billy, as he is a famous man in the Hawai'ian ranching community. For over twenty-five years Billy had been the veterinarian for all the animals of the large Parker Ranch in the up-country of Waimea. He has also written three books detailing the fascinating history of the Parker Ranch: the flora and fauna, the records and detailed observations of the cattle and horses, and his case histories. He is and has always been a good friend to the *paniolos* who live and work on the ranch.

One of King Kamehamea I's granddaughters, Chieftess Kipilane, married John Palmer Parker, who was the first Parker to settle on the island of Hawai'i. As a result, a very large tract of land, 500,000 acres, was granted to Parker and his wife by the royal family. At one time there was more than 50,000 head of cattle on the Parker Ranch, which has been sustained for over one hundred and sixty years. This was how the Parker Ranch began. But there is so much more history that Billy Bergen has detailed in his books. He is a great

Hawai'ian historian. My understanding is that Billy's son has taken over his father's veterinarian practice. However, it is clear to us that Billy would never completely retire.

On the day that we met him, Billy was about to oversee the collecting of sperm from a very high-end stallion on the ranch. In order to have this particular stallion mount the artificial horse, he needed to have a teaser horse in a corral nearby. According to Billy, not just any mare excited a stallion into the urge to mate. Since artificial insemination was done with very expensive breeding horses, Billy needed to have his favorite "teaser mare" brought from a distant Waimea pasture over to the Parker Ranch. And that is why Juni was asked to help.

My brother Scott Vasak and his wife Geri Orchard were visiting us in Hawai'i this week. So they came on this excursion too. We drove up to Waimea with Juni and went to a large pasture of grazing horses. Juni went through the gate into the pasture. He was going to bring the pretty little teaser horse over to the waiting truck and trailer. We watched Juni walk across the pasture with a lead rope in his hand. He looked so natural out there. The horses started to whinny and one particular horse got agitated when he saw Juni approaching the mare. She was clearly his mare too. Geri, being a horse woman, was giving us insights into what was going on within the herd. Juni seemed totally comfortable with the hoof pawing and whinnying of the other horse and walked among them confidently. Soon he had the lead around the mare's neck and was leading her back across the pasture where we were watching and waiting. The trailer door was opened and she loaded with no problem. We followed Juni and Billy Bergen and the horse trailer back to the Parker Ranch, where this pretty little quarter horse was put in a corral near the stallion.

### Taking Juni Back to His Ranch

AFTER A MOST INTERESTING VISIT with the vet, Billy Bergen, we drove to Juni's ranch, which was on the wet side of Waimea. We had always visited with Juni down at Ho'o'kena at Lenda Hand's house, or in the cafes and restaurants in Kailua Kona, where Juni often entertains.

Besides being a Paniolo, Juni is also a recording artist, a painter, entertainer and writer. He plays the guitar and sings traditional and modern Hawai'ian songs. Juni said one time, "Well, if you really want to know about a cowboy's cowboy, then you should know

 about my father, Alfred Medeiros. And he is still alive." For years he was the foreman of the McCandless Ranch in South Kona. He and a band of cowboys, including his young son, Juni, took on the job of lassoing and castrating wild bulls, which were wily and dangerous. When they did this job, they were putting their life on the line. Juni's father was in the rodeo too and was known as a top roper. Alfred Medeiros and some other relatives are enshrined in the Paniolo Hall of Fame in the Paniolo Museum in Waimea.

We passed green fields on the east and wet side of Waimea and drove down to the end of a tree-lined country road. The ranch gate at the end of the road was the entrance to Juni's ranch. Clustered near the gate was a whole herd of cattle that started bawling with excitement as Juni approached. With the grace of an acrobat Juni popped over the gate and entered into the midst of the herd. He was talking to all of them, and they were mooing back. It seemed obvious that they all were happy to see each other.

### A Plan to Visit the Hilo Side

PAUL AND I WERE BACK AT PALEAKU PEACE GARDENS and woke up in our tent to the sounds of birds announcing the morning at the break of dawn. The large tree sprawling above us was full of Mynah birds singing and squawking, and it was no longer possible to sleep. Several times during the night they all squawked in unison if we as much as turned over in our outdoor bed. They were very keen to the slightest sound and the whole flock would go off, in synchrony. Actually it didn't bother us at all. It was part of the ambiance, just as the roosters were. The roosters of Painted Church road crowed any time of the night, not just at dawn. And when one rooster would go off, all the roosters in the neighborhood would go off, as a crowing chorus. Again, after living here a while, none of this local sound track bothered anyone.

Today we planned to drive up to Waimea to have lunch with Kapua. Paul drove the jeep and was grateful that we didn't have to pay for a rental car. As we approached Waimea, I pointed out Mauna Kea, the mountain sacred to the Hawai'ian people. This morning the summit was shrouded in clouds. We had the car radio on, and Brother IZ was singing "Somewhere over the rainbow." As he sang, a double rainbow appeared in the clouds. "Now this is Hawai'ian magic!" I said. Paul agreed and we sang along with Brother IZ. I chuckled to myself as I remembered Aka's words about singing, "Some people are just car and shower singers." Then she would laugh one of her robust, belly shaking laughs. "If someone wants to be happy, they should sing happy songs for at least an hour a day." She did this, and I know, as I stayed at her house later in 2012, along with Anni McCann and two of Aka's sisters, Kela and Kalehua, and her daughter Suzy and granddaughter, Lauae, and took part in this family karaoke chorus.

### *Paul Meets My "Big Brother," Kapua Edyson Ching (son of Eddy)*

PAUL HAD NEVER MET KAPUA BEFORE, but he was aware that Kapua had been like a big brother and protector to me during this year. He was eager to meet this Hawai'ian man. Later we planned to go to the Hilo side to visit Kumu Dane Silva and the warm ponds. We met Kapua in a Waimea restaurant for lunch.

Kapua laughed and treated Paul to one Hawai'ian joke after another. Paul was not used to this totally hang loose humor and seemed a little overwhelmed by the parade of jokes. Later, driving to the Hilo side, I explained again to Paul how very kind and helpful Kapua had been to me, even helping me move twice.

We were heading towards Akaka Falls on the Hamakua coast when the car suddenly sputtered and lurched and came to a stop. We walked to a little gas station nearby and two local boys towed the jeep to their small garage. It turned out to be a bad alternator. We were stuck, as they would have to go elsewhere to get a new one. They drove us to Honaka'a where we stayed overnight in an old rustic hotel from the 1800s, while they worked on the jeep. We paid top *haole* prices for the car repair, since we were so far away from services.

Staying in Honaka'a was interesting, as it is the town closest to the Waipio Valley. The town was mainly for locals, not having resorts like tourist towns such as Keauhou and Kailua, or the North Kona Coast. Honaka'a had been a sugar town hosting Hamakua Sugar Co. from 1873-1994. There had been many sugar fields and companies on the Big Island, but by the 1990s they were gone. We had some delicious malasadas and coffee for breakfast. These donut-like delights are often filled with different types of fillings and sprinkled with sugar. The poi was my favorite. Paul liked the cream fillings. This treat, loved by Hawai'ians, originated with the Portuguese immigrants. The alternator problem was especially annoying to Paul because he felt we had been overcharged. "We would have never paid this much at home," he said. "I know," I said, "but everything is different here. These people are struggling financially themselves, especially after the 9/11 events. It has put so many local people out of work or severely compromised financially." After this reminder, Paul agreed with me, as he is a generous person, and especially after we saw the repairman's three small children playing in the shop. However, Paul was calculating how many more books he'd have to sell to cover the cost, which was still less than a car rental!

Planes had now begun to fly and tourists were visiting the islands again, but not in high numbers as before. People all around the world had a little trepidation about traveling on planes and were just watching and waiting to see if any more airliners would be used as lethal weapons. I had been living here in the post 9/11 climate for quite a few months now and understood how it affected this island and the economy of the local people.

Since we were so close to the Waipio Valley, we drove to the over-look point. Down below was a long expanse of black sand beach and palm trees, and a valley filled with Taro patches. What a beautiful gem this valley was, stretched out below us. But we weren't going down into it today, as we already had Aka's promise to take us there during the coming week. Now we were even more excited about having this trip and the ceremony that Aka had promised us. The jeep was running smoothly now and our breakdown and unexpected expense was forgotten as we looked at the beautiful coastal scenery . . . the ocean was sometimes close and at other times at a distance. We drove down three deep ravines that had streams running down them into the ocean. At one time, railroad trestles had crossed these ravines during the heyday of the sugar cane plantations. Tsunamis had destroyed the train trestles and as a result the railroad came to an end. The scenery was supremely beautiful on this crystal clear sunny day.

### *Akaka Falls*

AFTER PULLING OFF THE ROAD AND DRIVING a few miles up to Akaka Falls, we took a short walk down the steps to follow a path flanked with huge bamboo groves, tropical plants, and ferns on all sides, to the look-out for observing the gushing Akaka Falls. The negative ions from the spray hit our faces, and rainbows laced the falls, as soft sunlight fell upon its whiteness like a long bridal veil. At the parking lot there were some local people selling beautiful art work. I spoke with them and found out that one of them was a member of the Akaka family. I thought of Auntie Fern and her shop at Kealakekua Bay next to the Heiau. As spiritual guardians of certain places, selling arts and crafts is a way of keeping a protective eye on a sacred location and fulfilling the *kuleana* (spiritual duty) that is passed from one generation to another.

After visiting the falls and Hilo, I wanted to show Paul where I had lived. So we drove to Hawai'ian Paradise Park, which is on the way to Pahoa. We drove slowly down the red dirt road to the house and paused at the driveway entrance so I could show him the house and adjoining cottage. All the fruit and avocado trees were at a bit of a distance from the road. I laughed and told Paul that this was the place that we joked was our home in the witness protection program. Paul laughed and said, "Well, this is remote enough to be a good location for it." We didn't feel like barging in on my former landlady without notice, so we continued on our way.

We then drove a few miles down to the end of Hawai'ian Paradise Park to the rocky shoreline and the cliffs. I showed Paul the house overlooking the ocean where I attended the shamanic drumming circles. Then we went to a place nearby where I had watched the local boys and men fishing and collecting *opihi* from the wet rocks. We parked and walked to the lava cliffs overlooking the ocean where the waves were breaking hard against the shore. We walked hand in hand watching our feet carefully on the somewhat uneven lava rock. This is where I had come to play my Native American cedar flute and where Rika and I had come to practice Hawai'ian chants. I shared these memories with Paul. Even though it was only a few months ago, so much had happened, both internally and externally, that it felt like a long time ago. I didn't feel like quite the same person, and I felt deeply nostalgic sharing these memories. Paul was mesmerized watching the waves and the white spray leaping high above the waves each time they broke on the rocks. "I can see why you love living here. I wish there was a way our whole family could move over here. But we are too rooted on our property, and I am quite a way from retirement," he said wistfully.

We tried to visit Kumu Dane Silva, as Paul had heard so much about him, but he wasn't home. At Pahoa, we stopped at the health food store where I had first met Douglas. We got picnic supplies to take down to the warm pond where Rika and I had enjoyed so many times together. Now I would be able to show Paul the way we took turns, holding each other's heads gently, with a plastic noodle float under the knees. Then gently and slowly we took turns moving each other through the warm water. It was a total surrender. The thermally fed warm pond was constantly being refreshed by waves that would tumble over the stone levy at the east edge of the large pond. When I got Paul into the water, I placed a noodle under his knees and held the occipital area at the back of his head. The water came up to the top of my shoulders so I could easily stand up in the pond. I told him to close his eyes and just become empty and relaxed. With a deep sigh or two later, he was "there." It was far better than a *samadhi* tank. He said he became "nobody" in these waters . . . warmed by the volcano Goddess, Kupuna Pele. Later Paul said, "It was not as vigorous or dizzying as Watsu, but felt much more like the smoothness and deep relaxation of Lomilomi massage or a great session of meditation."

Later we drove down the Red Road to Kalapana where Uncle Robert had his compound which was also a center for the Hawai'ian sovereignty movement. Later I met Uncle Robert's partner, Koko, a woman of amazing talents. She was also mentioned earlier as a friend of Mayumi Oda and is an excellent artist herself. A Hawai'ian flag danced in the breezes near Uncle's garden of indigenous Hawai'ian plants. As we walked on the lava pathway out to the beach, I told Paul the story of Douglas conducting a memorial

UNCLE ROBERT AND KOKO

service here for a family of total strangers who had just lost their mother. Yards and yards of black lava had changed the landscape of this beach, which was once right in front of Uncle Robert's house. Now the water was much farther away than it was before the lava flowed and created new land. The lava flow also covered the road that once continued on to the south. The community, under Uncle Robert's leadership, physically moved the local Catholic Church to higher ground and out of harm's way, as the lava would have engulfed and burned it. You never know what will happen next, when you're living on a live volcano. Paul said he would like to meet

Douglas, so we decided to stop by his treehouse to see if he was home.


## A Last Visit with Douglas


I HAD REALIZED SOME MONTHS AGO that Douglas was a secret yogi. His renunciation came naturally to him. His happiness came from within. He had no attachment to things. My former landlady felt he was a flaming hippy, and sadly, she never gave herself the chance to get to know him. He never mentioned having any gurus or spiritual teachers. If he did, the topic never came up. When we were together, we shared the present moment. He did recognize that he had the awakened *kundalini* that some yogis in India and Tibet have activated through meditation, visualization, chanting and breathing practices. Douglas was very much like many of the yogis I had read about in India. He had renounced the world, had inner peace and magical qualities, and supreme kindness towards others. It always felt peaceful to be around him. Douglas had no post office box, no car, no bank account, no phone and no money. He traded his hand-hewn musical instruments and wooden spoons with the Pahoa health food store for food. He didn't eat very much. He never claimed to be anything at all. In fact, he didn't talk much. And he was completely unpretentious. I wanted Paul to meet him.

As luck would have it, he was at home when we arrived. We were invited to climb the ladder up into his tree-house. There we sat on wooden, hand-hewn stools. Conversation took place with Paul doing most of the talking and Douglas listening attentively. I spoke up to share with Paul the way Douglas made coffee every morning for the homeless people who lived in the forest nearby. He collected the coffee from wild coffee bushes and hand-roasted them in a large black iron skillet over his campfire. He had a hand coffee grinder and made campfire coffee in percolators. I had not yet shared with Paul the stories about the trip to Green Lake and the White Dragon.

I felt terribly sad, sitting there, feeling that I would never see Douglas again. My eyes gazed around the tiny tree-house, first landing on the hand-carving tools and some half-finished musical instruments placed carefully on the bench. Clothing and a hat hung from two hooks. The sadness became deeper until I had a physical ache in my heart. He had such a profound effect on me during my early months here. It was also rare for me to feel like he had become a spiritual brother in just a few months' time. Douglas didn't write letters, so we would not stay in touch after I went home. But I would be eternally grateful to him, as he had taught me a lot by his example. I felt he was someone I had known in the past, as a fellow spiritual seeker, in another lifetime, possibly in India or Tibet. "*Mahalo* Douglas, I wish you all good things. You're a magic man! *A hui hou!* (Until we meet again!)"

### The Huli Huli Chicken Man

SOMEWHERE ON THE ISLAND you may come upon the *Huli Huli* chicken man. Paul and I found him on this trip around the island. The first sign may be smoke and an aroma of barbeque, and then a truck with a trailer, which has been transformed into a big rotisserie barbeque on wheels. Turning spits of *Huli Huli* chicken roast as they

turn round and round over hot coals. This is the most delicious roast chicken ever, never too dry, never undercooked, and basted with *Huli Huli* sauce. The kids or *keiki* of the *Huli Huli* chicken man sell home-made pickles of daikon radishes and sometimes homemade *kimchee* (hot spiced, pickled cabbage). Little tan faces with big eyes and black hair would hold out a jar of pickles or kimchee, asking for you to buy. How could you resist these adorable children helping with the family business? Mom or grandma, at home, had made the kimchee and the pickles and the children were helping, too. This is *Ohana.* Everyone helps.

### A Visit to Wood Valley Meditation Center

ON THE WAY BACK TO HONAUNAU and Paleaku Gardens, we drove to Wood Valley Meditation Center, which is named Nechung Dorje Drayang Ling. Originally in 1902 it was a Buddhist temple for Japanese immigrants who worked in the Ka'u sugar plantations and factory. It was relocated in Ka'u, up on a *mauka* area above the town of Pahala, in order to be saved from floods. It had been restored and redecorated and is now a beautiful Tibetan Buddhist temple for meditation and retreats. The grounds of the retreat center are both beautiful and quiet with a tangible atmosphere of compassion and peace. We had been here once before and had met Marya and Michael Schwabe who came to the Center in 1973 and have stayed as temple directors ever since. Being close to His Holiness the 14th Dalai Lama, they went to India every year to partake in his teachings. Both of them studied written and spoken Tibetan, and Marya has often acted as a translator for visiting Tibetan Lamas who do not speak English.

Nechung Rinpoche was their personal teacher and he came often to conduct retreats until his death in 1983. Over the years more

than fifty different lamas have taught at the center, and His Holiness the Dalai Lama visited twice. On the first visit in 1980 he dedicated the new temple. On His Holiness the Dalai Lama's second visit, over three thousand, five hundred people came to listen to his talk which was given from the temple veranda.

In more recent years Marya and Michael helped find the reincarnation of their former teacher in Chinese occupied Tibet. In spite of many challenges, they were able to get this eight-year-old boy out of Tibet and into India with the blessings of his parents and teachers. The young Nechung Rinpoche then studied in Tibetan Buddhist monasteries in India and is now (as of this writing) about thirty years old. With the completion of his monastic training he will be coming to visit Nechung Dorje Drayang Ling regularly. This beautiful land and retreat center has been offered to him as his second home, in Hawai'i. After this visit we drove the rest of the way around the island to return to Honaunau and our sweet tent which was erected on a platform in Paleaku Gardens.

*{At a later date, in 2018 or 2019 we were honored to meet Nechung Rinpoche for a tea and talk at Paleaku Peace Gardens. Besides enjoying the tea party and talk by Rinpoche, it was delightful to spend time with Marya Schwabe, Barbara DeFranco, Mayumi Oda and other friends.}*

NECHUNG RINPOCHE AND
BARBARA DEFRANCO

NANCY, MARYA SCHWABE, MAYUMI ODA

# PILGRIMAGES WITH AKA

## The Waipio Valley

AKA HAD PLANNED TO TAKE PAUL AND I to the Waipio Valley for a long time. "Waipio is sometimes called *wahi pana,* which means a place of spiritual power. Paul can't miss this. He'll never be the same after being there, and I have a surprise for both of you," Aka said. She laughed in secret delight, as she visualized her surprise. The day had finally come. Paul was here now, and we had the day planned. She said she was going to take us to the "*Po,*" the head of the valley. It is only accessible by unlocking a locked gate at the farthest end of the valley, below the cliffs and waterfalls. She held up the key, to show me, with a glint in her eyes. "Here is the key to the *Po,*" she said. She told us that it took a four-wheel drive to go down the very steep hill that descends into the valley. "If you don't have a four-wheel drive, you have to take a horse or mule down . . . or walk. It's VERY steep." Aka drove the jeep and Paul was in the front seat, next to her, and I was in the back. As we climbed into the hill and cattle country near Waimea we suddenly saw a rainbow appear, and Aka broke into song singing IZ's song, "Somewhere over the Rainbow." The rainbow appeared close to the same place where Paul and I had seen one a few days before. "Ahhh, it's God's promise! We are going to have a blessed trip today," she said.

When we got to Waimea, we went to the KTA grocery store. It was still early enough to get poi malasadas and butter rolls. "The buttah rolls always sell out early and you have to be the early bird to get them," Aka said. The sun was still low in the sky and we loaded our cooler up with picnic goodies from the deli counter. "We need to have some good grinds with us for this trip today. We are going to work up an appetite." As we drove, I asked Aka what the words "*holoholo*" meant to her. I often heard local people saying to each other that they were going "*holoholo.*" I figured it meant they were going on a little trip. Aka had always reminded me to keep a diary, and to write in it every day, and she especially urged me to record our talks. I had eventually named my diary "my holoholo diary." Sometimes after a visit with her, she asked me to go home and write down our conversation in my diary. I had assumed *holoholo* meant going somewhere without a destination. Aka was amused at that in the past, but we had never really discussed the actual meaning of *holoholo*.

She laughed and said, "Have you heard the expression, 'a *holoholo* man'?" I said that I hadn't. She said, "Well that's just a local expression for a man who is going fishing or a fisherman. You know,

'a *holoholo* man'. My sister Kalehua has a son who is a *holoholo* man. He brings her fish and she loves it. And her husband Pancho knows how to cook 'em up. He's an awesome chef. When you love fish and grew up on fish, you have to make sure you have a friend who is a *holoholo* man! Wanda's husband, Uncle Jerry loves fish too! Miloli'i, in South Kona, is still a traditional fishing village. My sister Kela spends a lot of time down there because she has family and friends there. Ma and her brother spent time there with an auntie for a while, when they were just little kids. Her own mother, my grandmuddah, was working in Oahu for the police department at the time. So she needed someone to take care of the kids."

I thought about Auntie Mona Kehele's stories about living in Miloli'i and wondered if Auntie Fern and Auntie Mona had lived there at the same time.

"Ho'okena village used to be a traditional fishing village too. Now the village has changed and many visitors camp at Ho'okena beach," Aka said. "It no longer has quite the same old South Kona vibe. You know da kine that goes there, or camps there: some locals, but a lot of tourists. Most of them are very respectful of the beach and campground. To the right of the beach is a locked gate that protects the Hawai'ian people who live along that north side of the beach from unwanted tourists or visitors. It is not a good idea to trespass there as you would get stink eye and maybe some *pilikea* (trouble) from some watch dogs. They're not all on chains. There are a number of local people who live in little houses and beach shacks along that shoreline. Towards the end of the houses are some relics of an ancient woman's village where women gave birth." I told Aka that Paul and I had been invited there one time by our friend, Lenda Hand, who lived at the end of this stretch of beach. She had shown us the "birthing well."

She continued, "There is also an ancient pathway that goes north and leads to the City of Refuge, Pu'uhonua o Honaunau. There are stories about ancient people running for their lives on this path to reach safety in the City of Refuge, before being caught by those pursuing them. The dolphin swimmers usually look for the dolphins at K Bay first, early in the morning. If

LENDA HAND

they're not there, they drive south, to Two Step at Honaunau Bay and check it out. If the dolphins aren't there, they usually find them at the south end of Ho'okena beach. The poor dolphins are just trying to find a quiet place to sleep after fishing in the ocean all night.

"But back to *holoholo*!" Aka said, "What it actually means is 'going somewhere without knowing where you are going, or where you're going to end up.' Like your journey here, Nancy. You've been going *holoholo* ever since you got here. You just headed out and didn't know where you were going to end up! And you just let the magic, the guidance, and the lessons happen, especially under the tutelage of Kupuna Pele." At this she broke into a big, long and loud belly laugh. "In our family we call her Kupuna Pele, but many people call her Tutu Pele. Going *holoholo* usually has no agenda, at least not one that you can understand. But if you are under her guidance, you will go through a purification that's not always so easy. And sometimes it is not so fun," Aka said, turning around and looking at me with an arched eyebrow.

Aka continued, "Do you remember how some people call the Big Island the 'dirty laundry island'?" I said, "Yes, and I guess I've been at the wash house scrubbing myself this whole time." Aka and Paul laughed. Then Aka said, with a laugh, "On the spin cycle, sistah!" I thought about the hard times here, and the deep loneliness and the tears that I experienced at times. And I also thought of how not having a home of my own had made me feel insecure. Barbara had "offset" my feeling of insecurity by always offering me her hospitality at Paleaku Gardens.

There had been many extremes for me, but they had been changing me internally and had made my mind lighter and more subtle. So many things that used to bother me seemed petty and unimportant now. The mind had wonderful feelings of spaciousness so much more of the time. Disturbing thoughts and feelings evaporated when I sat gazing at the ocean or meditating with closed eyes. I noticed that the daily meditations had deepened as well. I had been gifted with some supreme guides too. As I thought of each one of them, as their faces appeared in my mind, I dispatched a big *Aloha*-filled *Mahalo nui loa* (thank you very much) out to each of them on the coconut wireless. Each person that I encountered was a gift and a teacher in one way or another. Aka continued her discussion of *holoholo*. "Going *holoholo*, you go with the flow, and your guidance takes you to where you're meant to end up, or to the people you're meant to meet. Or it may take you to the *Huli Huli* chicken man!" Aka said, laughing. She knew that I loved the barbeque chicken that came off the rotating spit of the *Huli Huli* chicken man.

Now we went back to the discussion about where the dolphin swimmers find the dolphins. I concurred with Aka, as I had seen dolphins at all three places we mentioned. They come in to sandy-bottomed bays around sunrise exhausted after a night of fishing. The sandy bottoms help them see predators, and bays are calm for a good day's sleep. They are resting in the day time and sleep one hemisphere of the brain at a time, as they need to come up for air every few minutes. When I was swimming at Two Step, a favorite place of mine at Honaunau Bay, I was often surprised by encountering the dolphins while I was snorkeling out in the bay. They sometimes came up next to me, without me expecting them or looking for them. Sometimes they swam around the bay, as a synchronized pod, power swimming right by you at an amazing speed. What was more amazing is that they managed not to crash into you. Now that is how I had come to think about dolphin swimming. If they find you, or encounter you naturally, it seems all right for me to swim next to them or above them. But I did not believe in chasing them. As time went by, I decided that I didn't need dolphin swims to connect with their energy anymore. "Armchair surfing" is a term I came up with while writing the *Guide to the Dolphin Divination Cards*. You can sit on shore, or sit in your armchair, hundreds or thousands of miles away from them, and connect with their healing energy in a peaceful and meditative state.

Our food and drinks were in the cooler on ice. This *holoholo* conversation took place as we drove through the green and wet side of Waimea, past the stand of tall eucalyptus trees to the east of Waimea, and then down through the green hills close to the Hamakua Coast on the eastern side of the island. We just couldn't wait! We got into that box of malasadas and started eating them in the car. Paul laughed and passed us wipes for our sticky fingers. We drove through the historic little town of Honaka'a, which, like many towns on the Big Island, had been a "sugar" town during the plantation era.

We stopped at the Waipio Valley Overlook and gazed down upon its wide black sand beach. The name Waipio means "curved water," and was on the north part of the Hamakua coast. The waves were rolling onto the beach. The ocean stretched out far to the north with no land in sight. The valley, which was dotted with *taro* patches, emanated a certain magical aura. The sun was shining and the air smelled sweet. Old Hawai'i and the old ones were still here. After all, another name for the valley is "The Valley of the Kings." Aka told us that King Kamehameha I had been hidden here when he was a young child and that it had been the home to ancient royalty and gifted healers and *kahunas*.

No corporation was going to ruin this sacred place with condos and tourist hotels. Today it looked like a patchwork quilt of taro fields, little wooden houses, and local farmers who planted and tended their Taro patches. Many of these *taro* roots would be pounded into *poi*. As we drove down the very steep, narrow road that led to the valley floor, I thought back to times in high school when I rode the roller coaster and wondered if I would fall out of my seat during the steep downhill run. The road "seemed" straight down and it was a little scary. When we arrived on the valley floor, Aka drove the jeep right into the river, which was shallow enough to ford. We went over rocks and rushing bubbling water. The jeep came through once again, just as it had when Kapua drove it through a rough lava field.

We parked and got out and went for a walk around the little wooden houses that sat beside taro fields, with the green *taro* leaves waving in the breeze. Below in the mud the tuber was growing, which would become the island delicacy of local people – *poi*. Aka seemed to know most of the farmers. She called out, "Aloha Uncle!

Howzit?" Or "Aloha Auntie, howzit? Your patch is looking so beautiful!" She stopped to chat, as if it was her old neighborhood. Aka told us that the root of the Taro is called *oha*. It could be boiled and eaten, or pounded into poi.

Then we got back into the car and followed a road that went back, deep into the valley, which was much more shaded than the *taro* fields. When we came to a gate, she pulled out the key and opened the lock and then re-locked it after we had passed through. It was like a jungle here at the "*Po*" (head), as Aka called the head of the valley with the waterfalls dancing down from the tops of the cliffs. The waterfalls fed the river which was icy cold. I remembered that Kumu Dane had told me that his mother's ancestral home was up above the Waipio Valley. What amazing energy Dane's family was blessed with, living in the atmosphere of the Waipio Valley.

### The Ceremony of the Po at Waipio Valley

WHEN AKA STOPPED AND PARKED THE JEEP, we got out and went to the bank of the river. She told us that we were going to have a purification ceremony, and that we were also to be born anew for the renewal and next stage of our relationship. In a sense, it was to be "a kind of baptism," she said. At the *Po* (head) of the valley was a beautiful waterfall named Hiilawe Falls. This was the largest waterfall in the valley. We had our bathing suits on under our clothes, so we got ready to get in the water, one at a time.

She said, once we were in the river, we were to *kapu wai*. This is a ritual of purification. We would be totally immersing ourselves under water five times. Aka said, "No cheating . . . all the way under . . . every hair on our heads needs to go under the water and get wet." We were to think of purifying ourselves, becoming newly born, in purity and goodness, leaving no traces of our old selves. Old pain, regrets and resentments towards each other, would be washed out to sea and transmuted. Toxic patterns from our ancestral lines would be lifted out of us and cleansed too. Aka was very serious! She was in her ceremonial mode, and her *tutus* and *Ke Akua* would be helping too.

As each of us did this ritual, she resumed chanting, and her voice sounded different than at other times I had listened to her chant. It felt as if we were back in time undergoing an ancient ritual . . . as if unseen spirits were blessing us. I remember Aka's words. She had told us that we would never be the same again. She told us we would be better, purer, cleaner, more loving, more patient . . . and expunged from any painful actions or memories from the past. It would now be our job to maintain these qualities in our daily life. After the ceremony was over, we got out of the water and wrapped ourselves in our beach towels, looking for a sunny place to dry off. Then Aka took off her *lava lava* (sarong) and slippahs and got into the water and completely dunked herself five times, all the while chanting between immersions. After she got out, water droplets reflecting rainbow colors, stuck to her hair. We stood in the sun drying ourselves, trying not to let our teeth chatter. This is one of those moments in time that one never forgets . . . the cold water, the warm sun, the reverberations of a chant, and rainbow-colored droplets of water in Aka's salt and pepper, fly-away hair.

"So this is the *Po* (the head) of this sacred valley," Aka said. "Many things have taken place here in the past," she said in her velvety soft voice. "Royalty and chiefs had ceremonies here, some similar to the one we just did. This is a blessed place, and I called upon these ancestors and great ones to come to you, from spirit, to give you their blessings. Who knows," she said, "you may have connections to this place from another time. You may have thought I was exaggerating when I said you would never be the same. But it's the truth. You will see. You will never forget this place, and all the power that is here to invoke, if it is done with the proper protocol and by someone who is connected to the ancient history of this place." We were deeply touched and appreciative and gave Aka and the ancestral spirits our sincere *mahalo*.


### The Picnic on Waipio Beach


WE WERE BACK IN THE JEEP and locking the gate to the *Po* behind us. We drove down close to the beach and got out our picnic cooler and drinks. The beach was beautiful, but we knew that there were strong currents here, so it would be best to just enjoy the beach and not swim. Aka began to talk about her children while we spread out the meal on a blanket. "My kids would love this picnic. If they weren't in school today, we could have brought them along. We'd have two in the back with Nancy and one curled up in the way-back. You know all of my kids are gifted. They all have a destiny with helping people in some way, shape, or form. All of my kids will have children, and our family line will carry on into the future. Lilinoe already has one child, Shai-Shai. Our blood line brings through gifted people who will help to preserve our culture and our spirituality. We open up to it when we feel comfortable, or when the time feels right. Even having the gift of being a receiver may be intimidating. They do not have to accept the gift until the right time comes. It's not easy being so sensitive and living in this world with jobs, rent money, car problems, and all the energy that children need."

We pulled out the butter rolls and barbequed meat, the potato/macaroni salad, pickles, avocado and chips, and some cooked purple/blue sweet potatoes that Aka had cooked up before leaving home. We laid out on our beach towels and ate while we mused and closed our eyes and listened to the surf breaking at the edge of the beach. Everything was so delicious. I was glad that we didn't have butter rolls at home because I could get addicted to them! There was a lot of food left over and we told Aka to take it all home to her kids.

I felt as if my energy was becoming more and more spread out and diffuse. There was an ecstatic floating feeling that took me off into a meditative state. Lying on our backs, we watched the clouds scud across the sky, changing shapes, in this timeless moment. I suddenly said to Paul and Aka that there was a convocation of clouds taking place overhead. Paul said it was a short convocation as the clouds started drifting apart. Paul looked more relaxed than I'd seen him look in a long time. He too had been watching the sky. On and off, he closed his eyes. Suddenly we noticed two white birds circling overhead, spiraling on the air currents. Aka told us it was an auspicious sign to see these birds, especially after a ceremony.

After an hour or so of relaxing this way, Aka reminded us that we were going to visit Mayumi Oda later in the afternoon, so we needed to get going back to Kona. She wanted to bring Paul and I to see Mayumi at her retreat center in Kealakekua, which is named "Gingerhill Farms." Paul and I were both looking forward to seeing "Mayu" too, as Aka sometimes called her. I had already met Mayumi before, but Paul hadn't. While driving back to Kealakekua, Aka told us that Mayumi was "one of her very dearest friends, evah!" Aka was also very close with Mayumi's two sons.

As we drove onto the property of Gingerhill Farms, I wondered how many people have parking lots lined with banana trees. And these were those sweet little bananas that Mayumi frequently shared with guests. When we arrived, we were welcomed by a smiling Mayumi! She was slim, with short dark hair, and she wore white yoga pants and a flowing white shirt. On another day we would be invited to come back to visit her art studio and be mesmerized by her large thangka paintings of Goddesses. World-wide art critics had named Mayumi Oda "the Japanese Matisse." Mayumi offered us tea and some of the most delicious soup we have ever tasted. It was a home-grown cream of butternut squash soup with turmeric and the most delicate herbal flavorings.

The sun was sinking low in the sky, over the ocean, sending beautiful shafts of golden light into the living room where we were sitting. Aka and Mayumi were lit up, looking like two illuminated Goddesses. There had been a mythic quality in the time in Waipio Valley today, and it carried over to our visit with Mayumi and her home that overlooked the ocean. Aka told us that introducing her good friends to each other is one of her greatest pleasures. "It is all part of weaving the web of life," she said. Mayumi's house shimmered with spiritual energy, not unlike the energy that we had just experienced in the Waipio Valley. And a most delightful day ended in such a delightful way. *Mahalo nui loa, Ke Akua*, Aka and Mayumi.

### Moving Again

PAUL AND I HAD MANY LONG TALKS during his visit. I made a firm decision to come home in a few more months. He was really happy about it. Our relationship was renewed, partly because we had both done such intensive, inner work during this time of living apart. I

413

missed the family. However, Paul thought it would be nice if I would accept some finances from him so I could just spend the last two or three months relaxing, without having to have a job or a

"work/trade." That sounded wonderful to me! To be able to go to the ocean and swim every day was my idea of total relaxation and enjoyment. This would be the vacation segment of the trip. Up until now I had been busy much of the time with part-time jobs. Paul had shared this idea with Aka, and she agreed that this would be a good chance to integrate the experience of this year.

The next day Aka arrived at Paleaku Gardens and asked Paul and I to come with her. She was excited and began to tell us about two friends of hers that had a nice house with a view of K Bay. They were looking for a third roommate. The rent would be very reasonable. She drove us to the house and we met Bill Bothell, who rented this three-bedroom one-story house. The other roommate was a young Japanese lady named Rinko. I can't help but smile when I think of these two people, who were soon to become good friends. We talked to Barbara about the plan and she was fine with it, saying that I could come back anytime. I enjoyed doing work trades with Barbara because gardening and landscaping on a beautiful piece of land with the many shrines is a real blessing.

Barbara and I sometimes smiled over how we both had life-sized statues of Padmasambhava on our properties. Ours was sculpted by the revered Tibetan lama, Chagdud Tulku Rinpoche. Barbara's statue was sculpted by the joint efforts of two other great Tibetan Lamas: Lama Tharchin Rinpoche and Lama Thinley Norbu Rinpoche, who was the son of His Holiness Dudjom Rinpoche. All three of these lamas were from the Nyingmapa school of Tibetan Buddhism. Paleaku Gardens held part of my heart, and Barbara would always be a spiritual sister. I felt I would return sometime in the future. I believed in inter-religious harmony and felt at home with these shrines that honored all of the world's great religions.

414

## ANOTHER MOVE TO CAPTAIN COOK

### A House above Kealakekua Bay

THE MOVING DAY WAS SIMPLE, as by this time I had very few things. Paul helped me pack the jeep and then we drove to the town of Captain Cook and down a steep hill into a little neighborhood of houses surrounded by coffee plants. Before the houses were built, the hillside had been a Kona coffee farm, the richest and most delicious coffee ever. The coffee plants were flowering with white flowers that smelled like gardenias. It was March now, and by April the flowers would be gone and little green coffee beans would start to appear where the dried flowers fell off. As the beans matured, they would turn into shiny red berries and then be ready to be picked. Who would think that the coffee plant would have such sweet flowers? I thought about Auntie Mona Kahele and wondered how she felt when the Hawai'ian name of *Kuapehu*, for this town, was changed to Captain Cook? From my conversations with her I knew that she wanted the old names to remain or be restored.

The house was a simple, but clean, one-story house with a nice lanai which overlooked Kealakekua Bay. The beautiful bay was stretched out below . . . Kealakekua, Pathway to the Gods. There below us was one of the most beautiful bays in all of the Hawai'ian islands. It was the bedroom and sanctuary for the spinner dolphins and the nursery for their babies. Dolphins, being mammals, did not hatch from eggs, but had live births like whales and humans. This would prove to be an awesome lanai for watching the sunsets and looking for that rare green flash that sometimes appears as the sun is setting.

Bill Bothell is a counselor for troubled youth who also does "harm reduction" counseling for youth with drug problems. He is tall, thin and muscular, and has the weathered tan of a surfer. And he is a surfer! I found out that he still surfed in his late fifties. We talked and got acquainted, and I learned that he grew up on Oahu as a *haole* but had become such a local boy that he spoke pidgin English and hung out with local people. He was an advocate for keeping the Hawai'ian culture alive. He was friendly and relaxed and showed me my room.

The aroma of the coffee flowers came drifting in my screened windows smelling like gardenias. Coffee starts, originally brought from Brazil in about 1829, would develop into the famous Kona coffee. At first it was the Japanese farmers who planted the coffee, but merchant Henry Greenwell established Kona Coffee as "a brand." The fertile soil on the slopes of Hualalai and Mauna Loa volcanoes made the perfect terrain to grow one of the most delicious coffees in the world. After the red coffee berries were picked, mules carried the bags of coffee down the slopes to the various mills where it was sun dried, sorted, and roasted. I was amused when I found out that these mules were called "Kona Nightingales" due to the loud braying of their voices. By 1899 three million coffee trees were planted in the region. What had once been the breadfruit belt now is the coffee belt of South Kona.

Rinko is a pretty Japanese lady in her early forties. She laughs a lot, and I was soon to learn that she had an uproarious sense of humor. I was surprised when she told me why she had come to Hawai'i. She was an industrial engineer in Japan. She made a lot of money, but the job had long hours and great demands. All the stress of the job made her exhausted. She said it was out of desperation and fear of a nervous breakdown that had caused her to come to Hawai'i for a long leave from work. She felt that she would learn to relax by swimming with the dolphins. When she learned that I had created the *Dolphin Divination Cards* and the *Guidebook*, she was so excited as she was already familiar with the cards and book. "Why are they not in Japanese?" she asked. I told her that they had gone into five languages but had not been translated into Japanese yet. So she asked me for a reading and I told her that sometime later we could do that. I was to learn that Bill and Rinko liked to swim early every morning. They wanted to be in the bay when the dolphins came in from their night fishing in the open ocean. I was invited to join them about seven a.m. to swim out into Kealakekua Bay. Paul liked both Bill and Rinko and thought it was a nice household for me to share for the next two or three months. Paul was already counting the days we still had, before he would have to leave for home. Before our trip to the volcano with Aka, we went up north to do a little more sightseeing before his departure.

## Some Thoughts on Meditation

DURING PAUL'S VISIT WE STOPPED in various beautiful places to meditate, side by side. Beaches, mountain tops, jungles, Paleaku Peace Gardens, and the warm ponds were all places we meditated together. It seems that in meditation we can be released from our small self, from the litany of concerns, plans and thoughts relating to everyday life. This also helps clear the chatter and clutter of the ceaselessly thinking mind. Here, in nature and in places of silence, and letting go of everything, we can just breathe and relax. There is a deep merging with everything, and paradoxically, nothing at the same time. If one has the luxury of sitting in nature, one can spread out and expand one's energies, feeling a part of everything, and at the same time feeling the relief of becoming nothing.

In this state humility is born, sensing the smallness of the individual self. What can be discovered is the large Self, which is part of the collective, without ego. When we have those moments and glimpses of shedding our ego, we are released from the bondage of borders, languages, and races. "We are all one people, turning round and round, rotating on this Mother Earth," said Western Shoshone spiritual leader, Corbin Harney. And meditation is not limited to sitting on a cushion with a mantra and prayer beads. It is universal and can happen in dozens of different ways. My new roommate Bill found it in surfing. Some find it in running and sports and refer to it as being "in the zone." Each individual finds this state of peace and clarity in their own unique way. It can be a flash, a moment, or a longer length of time. It doesn't matter. It is that soul refresher! It is renewal. It is the emptying out of the past with our exhalation, and the newness and connection to everything that can be born within us, with each incoming breath. I used to coach my massage clients with their breathing when they were on my massage table. I would say, "Exhale the old, used up, dirty *chi*, and inhale rainbow light and circulate it from head to toe."

### On Our Way to the Volcano

VERY SOON PAUL WOULD BE FLYING HOME to California. There were so many things to share with him and so little time. Today was the day we would go to the volcano and pay our respects and thanks to Kupuna Pele, the Goddess of the Volcano. Aka told us that many people call her Tutu Pele, but in her family they call her Kupuna Pele. Her sister Kalehua told me the same thing. "Some think she's a mythological figure," Aka said, "but to me she is real! I think of her as one of those beings who can go in and out of form, manifesting and dissolving and re-manifesting. She reigns over the Big Island, and woe be it to anyone who disrespects or harms the island. There are many ways one can be corrected." I always like to think of what Aka taught me about correction versus punishment. Tutu or Kupuna Pele is a mistress of purification, humility, and respect.

Aka has many, many friends, and I am sure each one of them has their own favorite stories of their connection to her. Her friends range from movie stars and famous musicians and artists, to healers of various kinds, and to simple everyday people with a desire to "open up, and grow their spirituality." Her friends live all over the world. She treats everyone the same. I have been lucky enough to know her *ohana* and some of her local friends, as well as some of her friends from Europe and Japan. The Big Island is an island hub, equidistant between east and west in the Pacific, and a destination for world-wide visitors. Aka has met with many of them. They have all enjoyed her company, teaching stories, her wise counsel, and her Aloha, each in their own unique way. Some visitors attended her workshops and retreats as well.

The visitors come for the weather, the beaches, the snorkeling and diving. They come for the *na'ia* (dolphins), and some come to learn *Lomilomi* massage from authentic *Kumus* (teachers), like Auntie Margaret Machado and Kumu Dane Silva. Visitors come to enjoy the *hula*, slack key guitar, and the *luaus*. They come to see the volcano, the waterfalls, the flowers, the *heiaus*, the *kohola* (humpback whales) and manta rays. But whether they know it or not, they come for the *Aloha* that permeates the atmosphere and emanates from so many of the local people. It is food and nourishment for the heart and soul. They take the *Aloha* home to their own country and they always remember it. Those who have met Aka never forget her either. She has been many things to many people, as she treats each person as the unique person that they are. Her wisdom, love, humor, and hugs are dispensed freely. She rarely even remembers what she has said to anyone, as she keeps her mind clear in the present moment.

I remember seeing pictures of Aka in Japan holding a big sign saying, "Free Hugs." Her hugs were very popular there! One of Aka's Japanese friends giggled as she told me about a short little Japanese man whose head was buried between her two generous breasts during a long hug. I'll bet he never forgot that hug. One of Aka's jokes was her saying: "Don't mistake my *Aloha* for flirting." Aka doesn't hold on to or necessarily remember advice, guid-ance, or teachings that she has shared with people. Her words are like the breeze. They come and they go.  They are always fresh. One time she laughed and told me that her "real job was sharing *Aloha* and being an ambassador for this beautiful island. And my kids, too, will have the same job, each in their own unique way."

{*Years later, she was to bring several of her Japanese friends – Toshi Suzuki (Koamaikai), Tomoe, Tomoka, and Saraspea Yuka -- to our land in Nevada City for a retreat.*}

### Giving Aloha from the Heart

AS PAUL, AKA AND I WERE DRIVING from Kona towards the Volcano, Aka talked about some things she learned from her grandmother. You know, she said in a soft voice, when I was a little girl, I asked my grandmother, "Why did Captain Cook have to come here? That was the beginning of losing our land and our culture. That was the beginning of smallpox and diseases that killed so many of our people." Her grandmother said to her, "Well 'beybey,' how else would people in this world learn about *Aloha*?"

Aka went on to point to her belly and said, "This is the center, the *na'au* where our guidance comes into us, those gut level feelings and intuitions that warn us or give us information. She laughed and said the *piko* was the belly button. Then it goes up to the head to be processed, and then we give out love and *aloha* from our heart. There are those who have come to our islands to learn about our spirituality. Some have written about it and then even taught it. But they weren't always correct in their understanding. For us, the heart is for giving love to our Ohana, to those who are connected to us by blood or by heart, and then to all those friends we haven't met yet. Then it goes to the Mother Earth and all her beings, and then to the whole Universe, and to our star brothers and sisters in the Pleiades and other galaxies. Our Aloha is given from our heart to all these beings."

Aka had gotten up early and gone up the mountain to pick flowers and herbs to make a *haku po'o lei* (a crown *lei*) and flower offerings to Kupuna Pele. She told us that she knew of a special picnic spot where we would make the *leis* before going to the Volcano.

420

## A Visit to South Point

AS WE APPROACHED THE SIGN THAT POINTED to South Point (*Ka Lae*), we made an "on the spot decision" to make a quick drive down to the shoreline to make prayers. The road was very bumpy in places, and when we got there, we noticed a row of windmills turning in the winds. There was such a strong wind outside Paul had to hang onto his hat when we got out of the jeep. As we walked to the shore line, Aka told us that this is where many of the voyaging canoes set sail and departed the Big Island in the distant past. "This is the very south end of our Island chain and it was always considered especially sacred. It is like a rift in time. A lei line passes through it. It is especially powerful. There are *ku'ula* stones, monuments to plentiful fishing, and there are *heiaus* here and other remnants of the past too. This land was always thought to be the land of the volcano goddess, Pele," Aka said. Then she pointed to an area to the northwest and told us that there was a remote beach there, that she and her sisters and brothers visited when they were kids. "The road to get there is very difficult so very few people know about it. But there are awesome coconut palms there."

I knew the Green Sand Beach, composed of volcanic green olivine was close by, and that the semi-precious gemstone, peridot, existed on this island as a result of volcanic activity. I had never been there, but my son James had, and said it was gorgeous. We all stood on the shore and looked to the south. "Tahiti is about a thousand miles from here, right out there," Aka said, pointing towards the south. The ocean was very blue this day, and with the winds there were little whitecaps appearing and disappearing on the surface of the ocean. The vast blue ocean stretched out to the horizon and beyond.

### Continental Soil

"THERE IS CONTINENTAL SOIL HERE AT SOUTH POINT," Aka said. "Generally it is thought that the Hawai'ian islands are relatively new, made up of lava flows from many volcanoes, but there is more to the story. Geologists came to South Point here on the Big Island

and were drilling some very deep core samples. I happened to come down here one day when they were drilling. They date the arrival of the Tahitians at about twelve hundred A.D., but our oral history contains stories of our ancestors living here long before their arrival. These geologists acted amazed that they had found continental soil under some of the layers of lava in their core samples. I said to them, "Brothers, welcome to the land of Mu. Here you will find remnants of this ancient continent. You have many more things to discover, but this is a good beginning. You are standing on ancient land and I personally welcome you . . . with my Alohaaaaaa!" And she gave one of her famous belly laughs, reminiscent of a child laughing with delight.

## *Voyaging*

AS WE WALKED TO THE SHORELINE, Aka told us that this is where many of the voyaging canoes set sail for long-distance journeys in the ancient past. "The *Hokule'a*, our first replica voyaging canoe, sailed to Tahiti in 1976, with no instruments or navigational tools. The name *Hokule'a* means 'star of gladness,' and it is Arcturus, the zenith star, that passes directly over the island of Hawai'i.

NAINOA THOMPSON WITH BRUCE BLANKENSHIP,
POLYNESIAN VOYAGING SOCIETY

"Can you feel how strong the wind is?" Aka wet her finger and held it up to the wind. "You've heard about the wind gourds right?" I told her that I had. "Well, a specialized *kahuna* could gain control of the winds. They used the wind gourd as a focal point.

"Mau Piailug, who was schooled in ancient canoe navigation, grew up in Sataval, Micronesia. He came to Hawai'i to train the first Hawai'ian crew in ancient navigation, and went with them on their first long voyage to Tahiti. Voyaging long distances across the ocean had been common in these islands in our past, but there were no living people here who remembered the navigating skills or the building of the voyaging canoes. These skills had been lost for more than several generations.

"Herb Kane, the famous Hawai'ian artist who lives here in Kona, studied drawings in the Bishop Museum in Honolulu and rock petroglyphs of the old canoes. These studies led him to make drawings and schematics for building a new one. The Hokule'a was built by Hawai'ians in the old way. Mau's Hawai'ian students were eager to learn, especially Nainoa Thompson, who trained as the first Hawai'ian navigator. He spent days in the planetarium studying the stars and constellations.

"There were challenges on this first voyage to Tahiti, but the crew was eventually successful in arriving safely in Tahiti! They were celebrated with huge crowds, cheers, music, leis, and feasting, when the Hokule'a sailed into the harbor in Tahiti. A different crew took the canoe back to Hawai'i. Mau did not accompany the crew on the trip back to Hawai'i. He disliked the dissension that had been caused by six of the crew members on the voyage from Hawai'i to Tahiti. But Nainoa Thompson and the others in the new crew were able to navigate the Hokule'a back to Hawai'i without Mau. This voyage proved to the world that cross-oceanic travel had been possible many hundreds of years ago, with the double-hulled voyaging canoes of our ancestors. This first voyage excited other island peoples to build voyaging canoes of their own. It was the beginning of a re-awakening of the trans-oceanic canoe culture."

This subject had always excited and thrilled me and I never tired of hearing more about it. I was grateful to Kumu Dane for introducing me to some of the Makali'i crew members of the Big Island's voyaging canoe. When I was at Clay Bertelmann's house for the second visit, I met a group of Maori people from Atearoa (New Zealand) who were training on the Makali'i in preparation for building and sailing their own canoe in Atearoa.

Aka and I had often talked about voyaging and had imagined sailing across the ocean in a double-hulled sailing canoe. I can remember her saying, "Can you imagine weaving two tightly woven pandanus-leaf sails? It would be a lot of work, but oh, how beautiful they would be in the winds." Aka had brought her *pu* with her and she lifted it to her lips and blew a long, sonorous note. Then she began her prayer, which was for our journey today, for our families and friends – "those connected to us by blood or by heart – for the well-being of the island, and for peace and goodness in the world." Then she chanted an old *mele* (song). She looked at us and said, "We need to put the vibrancy of our prayers and our *meles* into the air so it can travel on the wind." When the prayer was finished, she said wistfully, "If only everyone could just live Aloha." We both silently nodded our heads. After the prayer and song, she showed us some petroglyphs, and also a large hole filled with deep water. She called it a *Mo'o Puka*. "The *mo'o* are the guardians of the water," she said. In the past Aka and some of her friends from Europe and Japan had jumped into it, testing their courage. It was a long jump down before one would hit the water. For anyone afraid of heights it could be a little intimidating. That would be me.

### Na'alehu

WE STOPPED IN THE KA'U DISTRICT in the town of Na'alehu, to get some of their famous chocolate chip banana bread from a little grocery store. It was so delicious that we devoured half of the loaf right outside the store. There was also a big bakery, named Punalu'u Bake Shop, that was a favorite destination for tour buses, as they had pastries, fresh "out of the oven" bread, and hot coffee. This part of the Big Island was very local and there were no tourist hotels anywhere. It felt peaceful, with the old island vibe. In a few short blocks we walked past the local school, a retired movie theater, a few churches, and an outside market. A young man was making and selling glasses of fresh squeezed orange juice from his own orchard.

We each savored a large glass. The young man and his wife had bought a ranch with an old orange grove and had brought it back to life. We had never tasted such refreshing orange juice. Paul started quoting the poet, Rainer Maria Rilke, and said we needed to "dance the taste of the orange." Other local people had booths selling tropical fruits, vegetables, arts and crafts, and hand-sewn clothing. After browsing the booths, we got back into the jeep and continued on our way. A few miles beyond Na'alehu we passed fields of grazing cattle on the left side of the road. On the right, grassy slopes gradually dropped down several miles to the ocean.

## Paniolos

As WE DROVE BY THESE FIELDS EAST OF NA'ALEHU, I remembered one very special sunset evening from a few months back. When I drove by these fields, I saw a whole family on horseback driving their cattle. With the golden glow of sunset illuminating this Paniolo family, I just had to stop on the side of the road to take a mental snapshot. There was grandma and grandpa, parents, children and maybe grandchildren, too, on horseback, gilded in gold light, driving their cattle into another field. I will always remember this beautiful sight.

Years later, a local woman sat next to me on an inter-island flight from Oahu to the Big Island. This lovely Hawai'ian woman started talking with me and told me that she grew up in Ka'u and was raised in a *paniolo* family. As it turned out, she was part of this particular *paniolo* family and had probably been in my 2001 "mental snapshot." She laughed and said, "That could be me . . . and my horse . . . and my Ohana."

## Making Leis and Ho'okupu's (Offerings)

We PASSED THE TURNOFF TO THE BLACK SAND BEACH of Punalu'u and continued on to the area where we were going to make *leis* and flower offerings. Aka pulled off the main road and drove down a little dirt trail until we came to a remote picnic table and sat down in the middle of a forest of trees. Aka unloaded all her flowers, ferns,

425

and greens that were going to make up the *Haku po'o lei,* the necklace *leis,* and *Ho'okupus* (offerings) that we were going to offer to Kupuna Pele at the Volcano. With everything spread out on the table, we began to learn how to place a flower or leaf and then wrap the lash around it to hold it in place. Then another flower or leaf or fern was

placed, and the lashing wrapped around that one, and so forth, until there was a band of lashed flowers, leaves, and ferns tightly woven together. When done correctly, the lashing didn't show, only the flowers, ferns and leaves. As she was the ceremonial person, she fastened it and put it on her head for us to see the perfect fit. She looked like a queen smiling at us. Then she took it off, saving it for later.

Paul and I had made more conventional *leis* that were worn as a necklace of flowers. We had fumbling fingers, having never done this before. The skill and speed of Aka's fingers making this *haku lei* or *lei po'o* (flower wreath for the head) was testament to how many times she had done it since childhood. Later, as I got to know her sisters, Wanda, Kalehua and Kela, I saw that they were equally fast when making several varieties of leis, wreaths and flower arrangements. I felt very awkward, struggling with this art, as I had not grown up with tropical flowers and Ti leaves. But then Aka told us it was not about the skill, but the intent of making this offering to Kupuna Pele, as an offering from the heart.

As we sat at the picnic table, we pulled out our picnic and ate our sandwiches and fruit and finished the chocolate chip banana

bread. We had wrapped fruit up in Ti leaf packets, tied with strands of Ti leaves, and adorned with flowers on top. These offerings were called *Ho'okupu*. I knew that some *haoles* offered gin or pork, and I asked Aka if those were traditional offerings. "Well, the most important thing is that you offer with your heart," she said, not really answering my question. It was almost dusk now, and we left the picnic table under the trees and got into the jeep. Now, we were off to the volcano which was not far away.

### Arriving at Volcanoes National Park

ARRIVING AT THE RANGER STATION of Hawai'I Volcanoes National Park, the ranger just waved us through as she recognized Aka with a *"shaka"* and an "Aloha, Cuz." Looking into the jeep she saw that we had *ho'okupu* offerings. It was almost dark, but we could see the width and depth of the caldera. It looked like a moon-scape below us, with the central portion of the caldera holding a lava lake with flames coming up out of it. There was no doubt that this was a live volcano . . . unpredictable . . . and liable to change at any time. Geologists kept a close watch on it and had instruments to monitor it. Or it could erupt, sending flames, plumes of gasses, smoke, and boulders of lava, high up into the sky. It had happened before and, no doubt, it would happen again. When we drove to the place along the rim of the caldera where we would have our ceremony, Aka parked the jeep and we got out carrying our offerings, while Aka carried her *Pu* (bamboo instrument). There was a fenced sidewalk leading to the edge of the caldera. We were grateful for the fence as, without it, it would be easy to fall down in the dark into the long and wide caldera.

The shadowy dusk had morphed into night now. That is how Aka had planned it, so we could easily see the orange light dancing above the fiery caldera. We watched as it took an uncanny, ever-changing shape of a woman dancing. Aka said softly, "See Kupuna Pele, how she is dancing for us? Auntie Io introduced us to Kupuna Pele a long time ago. The volcano Goddess embodied Auntie Io and spoke to us. She is very real to me." The fiery orange light kept moving and swaying and changing shape every few seconds. Aka, in her soft voice, kept telling Kupuna Pele how beautiful she was. Watching the tall dancing Goddess's constantly changing and undulating golden, orange form was mesmerizing. Paul and I felt as if we were entering a mystical state.

### The Ceremony at the Volcano

AKA HAD HER *HAKU PO'O LEI* ON HER HEAD when we arrived, and she began by blowing some long tones on her pu. Then she said some prayers to Kupuna Pele and began to chant in the Hawai'ian language. Her chants went on for a long time, and it seemed to both Paul and I that we had slipped back through a time warp into an ancient past. She invited us to chant with her. Aka took the *haku po'o lei* from her head and tossed it into the caldera with an offering prayer. Then we tossed our offerings over the edge to the caldera with silent prayers. Aka began to chant again and her voice sounded ancient this time with a lilting calling. It became very low for some of the tones and fluctuated as she ascended and descended the scales. We could feel the vibrancy of the chant in the air. We too felt as ancient as these chants. All this felt so familiar. Had we done this before? After a while Aka finished her chant and said to us, "Do you remember? Do you remember that we have done this before, a long, long time ago?" "Yes," we both said automatically, without even thinking about our answer.

### Human Manifestations of Kupuna Pele

"YOU KNOW," AKA SAID, "Kupuna Pele has been known to manifest herself as a human being a number of different times. Herb Kane has written about it. There are many substantiated stories of her showing herself as an ordinary person.  She has been known to manifest herself as a very old lady with a little white dog, or as a beautiful young woman with a red dress and long black hair. She has been known to hitch-hike by the side of the road with her little dog. Herb Kane records a story of a person who picked them up to give them a ride. She and her dog got into the back seat. There were no stops. When the driver looked around into the back seat, a little later, both the woman and the dog were gone. There are a lot of interesting things that happen on this island that are, what you might say, 'out of the ordinary'." And Aka winked at me and laughed one of her deep laughs that comes from the belly, or as she would say, the na'au.

"I believe *Kupuna Pele* can go in and out of physical manifestation. Very, very high beings, from all cultures in this world, are able to do this. Some people think these things defy the laws of time and space. It comes from a very high level of consciousness and mastery. But this is part of the great mystery of 'so called' miraculous things that appear to us that are unexplainable, at least at this time: visions, remote viewing, bi-locating, apparitions, and miraculous healings. Divine forces are involved, as they join with the prayer person and their consciousness to create these blessings. Certain highly evolved beings can do these things and see things that aren't ordinarily seen. And then there are ordinary people who are sometimes graced with some extraordinary experiences as a glimpse into worlds beyond the ordinary."

At that moment there was such a flare of the volcano's fiery mist that we could see each other's faces in the dark. She stopped and looked at me, with a knowing look. Then she continued, "These glimpses can encourage a person to go farther and deeper in raising their awareness and consciousness. First, it may be gifted as a glimpse. Then in order to have more sustainable experiences, one has to earn them. There is so much that we ordinary human beings do not understand. Someday there may be advanced science that can explain these things. For one thing I am quite sure that it has to do with the manipulation of energy, the power of thought, as well as the activation of the invisible human anatomy. A person who has purified their inner channels may manifest something with just a thought. Only good things should be manifested, and that is why our purification process is so important. If these gifts are active in a person, we believe it is important that they are always used for good. Everything must be *pono* (right or good). And we must always remember to be humble. We are small, still imperfect reflections of the 'Man in White', the Elohim, and the greatest benevolent force of all, our creator, *Ke Akua*." There was no pidgin English in this talk.

# ~Mission Aloha~

## The Foundation: Aloha
## The Method: Ho'oponopono
## The Goal: Peace

Who was this woman? I wondered. There are so many aspects of her. I remembered how she always told me that her *tutus* would perch on her head and speak through her. Some of what we were hearing could be a gift from her *tutus*. There were local people who had no idea who this little child had become, who they once knew as "little Aka." Some remembered her swimming at Kealakekua Bay when she was just a small girl. Others remembered her wilder days, as a teen, and had her fixed in time. Some of them remember those youthful years, when she went to AA and worked the program. She was always very frank about this period of her life. She said that AA had been a wonderful program for herself and many others. "Sensitives often try to shut down their extreme sensitivity and raw energy with drugs and alcohol. But that always does more harm than good. And then the only solution is recovery and learning tools to cope with being so wide open and sensitive." I chimed in by saying, "When I am experiencing extreme sensitivity, I say that I feel unzipped."

Aka gave a low chuckle at that and then continued. "But no matter how long it takes for someone's destiny to become manifest, one must always remember that the potential for higher realization is within all of us." The prophesies at Aka's birth, of her being a *Kapu* child (a specially blessed and sacred child), had come to fruition, even more fully in the more recent years. The famous *hula* dancer, Aka's auntie Iolani Luahine had welcomed her birth into this world with a *maile lei*, a *hula* dance, and a chant in Kaiser Hospital in Honolulu.

International visitors sought Aka out when they came to Hawai'i. Before long, in the following years, Aka would be invited to share her teaching of *Aloha* and *Ho'o'ponopono* at the Jung Institute outside of Zurich, Switzerland, and in Russia, Japan, and several European countries. Within a few years "Mission Aloha" would be launched. We realized how blessed we were to be her close friends.

Aka continued to speak, "All these abilities are mysterious gifts that certain people have mastered. Our *Kahuna* (priests and priestesses) know the same spiritual sciences as the Tibetan and Indian Yogis and the Native Medicine Peoples of this world. They don't announce themselves. They just quietly do their work of healing and helping, with humility. In Hawai'i's past there were a very few who were adept at harming others. They were called *ana ana* (dark arts) practitioners. The same principles that are used for good can also be used to harm. It all depends on the motivation. This has been phased out in today's culture, but my grandmother and great grandmother knew about them. You know, this world is a world of light and dark." There was a long pause and the three of us were silent for a long time. Paul and I just leaned our arms on the railing and watched the ever moving and changing misty orange shape dancing in the caldera.

Aka began speaking again, "These gifted beings who do good are not afraid of death, as they already realize that there is no death, at least not in the ultimate sense. We all shed this body at some point, but our spirit lives on. We keep migrating in different forms. There are so many wonderful realms to explore, when our time comes. Remember how Jesus said, 'In my Father's house, there are many mansions.'" Aka had given us so much to ponder on this dark night above the caldera. It seemed like we leaned against the railing for a long, long time watching the dance of the flames, the shadows, and the golden orange reflections in the mist, and of that fire burning in the crater of this live volcano called Kilauea, the home of Kupuna Pele.

### The Steam Vents

AFTER LEAVING THE VIEWING AREA OF THE CRATER, we got in the jeep and drove the short distance to the steam vents. We stood by the vents as the warm steam bathed us, puffing out waves of soft liquid air wafting over us. Between the puffs of steam, we began to shiver. And then a delightful series of steam puffs would moisten our skin and clothes. This was blissful for all of us. We stayed here for a long time. My strongest memory of this is that Paul felt totally out of his body after being in the hot steam. He was glad he didn't have to drive, as he said he wouldn't be able to. It was a perfect ending to a most wonderful day.

## Paul and I Reflect

THE TIME WITH PAUL HAD FLOWN BY SO QUICKLY. It was time now for him to get on a plane and go back to life in Nevada City, back to the long hours at Blue Dolphin Press and Blue Dolphin Publishing, back to the adult children, back to the land and the old farm house in the forest. It seemed so far away from this island and the blue water that surrounds it.

There was a lot to process from all the things we had done together just in the last day, and the effect on us, from the ceremonies we had participated in with Aka and meeting Mayumi. Paul said to me upon waking up in the morning, "I feel so clean. I feel like we really did get purified by Kupuna Pele during the ceremony at the volcano. And in the Waipio Valley I feel like I got in touch with my ancient past and feel more like this is just one stop in the road, amidst many, that stretch out behind us and ahead of us." We were listening to a beautiful instrumental by Keola Beamer, and his dream guitar, on the radio. How sweet Hawai'ian music is.

I told Paul that I felt very much the same way about the ceremony in the Waipio Valley. I was going to take him to the airport in a few hours, so we talked about what he was going to do when he got home, and also about my return home a month or two later. He told me that he was grateful to have gotten a taste of what I had been experiencing here on the island, and how the island itself and the local people had contributed to a transformation he was feeling and that he said that he could see in me.

I was more relaxed after these months here on the Big Island. I had developed a trust that everything that happened was for a reason and a purpose: for learning or being able to help in some way, for purification of blind spots and limitations, humbling the ego, and to see beyond the limits of what we call ordinary reality. And of course, most important was the greater opening of the heart and the growing of Aloha. Forgiveness, tolerance, patience, humility, and a connection with nature merged with the open-heartedness that made up true Aloha. I had been the grateful recipient of this true Aloha from many local people. Once Aka asked her grandmother why Captain Cook had to come here in the first place? Her grandmother said, "How else were the people in the world ever going to learn about Aloha?" She had told me this before, but this phrase often went through my mind.

Paul said he felt like he was going to take this "hang loose" relaxed attitude back to his work. He and I had been to Hawai'i with our family for a one- or two-week vacation almost every year since the mid-'80s. Each time he felt the relaxed island energy and did his best to bring it home with him. But the mainland has a different vibration, and island energy is hard to maintain in the density of the mainland. He said, "This spaciousness that I am feeling inside will clear my energy of the collective congestion when I get back home."

A publishing business is one of multi-tasking, juggling multiple jobs, trouble shooting, long hours, and talking to people all day. Dozens of new manuscripts are submitted each day. They have to be looked at and evaluated. Letters have to be written. Proofreading has to be done and phone calls answered. Some authors submit manuscripts with letters claiming that their book is going to be a best seller and will make us millions. That is always a red flag for us! That type of author will be predictably demanding, time consuming, and will end up being angry at us, when their book proves NOT to be a best seller. We had learned this in the past. How does one hang loose in a hectic printing and publishing business?

It was off to the airport now with Paul's suitcase in the back of the jeep. There were gifts inside that we had chosen for the family back home. There was organic Kona coffee and Macadamia nuts too, and some "Local" slippahs. Paul was driving and we were quiet as we drove to the airport. Part of me wanted to get on the plane with him. But, I also wanted a little more time here. Both of us liked the changes that we saw in each other. I was so happy that Paul had so many glimpses of what I had been experiencing. Later I came to see that this time renewed our relationship and in future years it continued to rise to higher octaves of peace and happiness. Aka had told us that the ceremonies in the Waipio Valley, and at the volcano would change us forever. She said we would never be the same. Now, twenty years later I know how very true her words were. How could we ever thank Aka enough for the journeys and ceremonies that she had shared with us? Little did we know then that Aka would come to our home many times in the future and that we would be able to reciprocate her hospitality.

## THE LAST PART OF THE JOURNEY

### *Life Has a Mirror-Like Quality*

FOR SEVERAL MONTHS I HAD BEEN FEELING HAPPY and relaxed much of the time. Somehow surrendering to the healing energies of this island had brought me through the washing machine (on the spin cycle), and now my once dirty laundry was on the clothes line in the sun, fluttering in the breeze. I now understood why the locals often laughed and called the Big Island "the dirty laundry island." Without a doubt there would be future heartaches, growth and challenges, but I now had such a different viewpoint about them.

The dolphins had taught me by swimming with them, but more recently from a distance, while "arm chair" surfing. And it wasn't only the dolphins that had helped with this cleansing. There were numerous people who had blessed me, either kindly or harshly, according to what was needed, in the moment. The mirror had been held up to me in numerous ways. The island itself, the precious *Aina* (land), and all the layers of history here, had been a part of the blessing as well. Those who had been harsh gave me a lesson of humility and compassion. I had also tried to embody and integrate the Eastern teaching of, "Praise or blame, it's all the same."

Then I remembered the teaching from Ven. Geshe Thubten Phelgye and other Tibetan Lamas of doing analytical meditation in order to grow and do better. In this practice we observe ourselves carefully and are not afraid to look for and find our faults in order to correct them. As Geshe Phelgye always says, "We need to move from being 'me, my' people to being 'we, us' people." He suggested that we do a private inventory of our daily thoughts and behavior at the end of each day and ask ourselves, "How did we do today?"

I do not believe that the dolphins and whales are bound by time and space, and I knew I could connect with their healing energy back in the mountains of California. All it would take is going into a state of meditation, beyond thought, and inviting their presence and energy. And it would not be a one-way street. I would tell them how much I love them, how beautiful they are, and how I pray for their safety, peace, and well-being, and for their babies and unborn as well.

I will never forget one particular day. I was having a hard time thinking about leaving the island and going home. I was filled with sadness, doubts of all kinds, and a heavy feeling in my heart. Auntie Fern and Aka had taught me that when faced with a day like this, we can do things to change the energy, from negative to positive. We are not condemned to having a bad day. The first step was kicking the *akole* (butt) of self-pity.

On this particular day I could hear my inner voice telling me to "Go wash dos buggahs off." So I went down to "Two Step" at Honaunau Bay and found a parking place right away. I laid my towel out on the smooth rippled black lava rock and laid face down in the sun. The temperature in the high 70s F was perfect. The body did not need to expand with too much heat or contract with cold and chill. The sun warmed my back and I found myself breathing deeper and deeper and releasing whatever unnamed debris was clogging up my inner channels. It was hard to discern whether it was personal or collective. After a while I got up and walked across the lava and sat on the two lava steps that most snorkelers use, and glided into the water. I swam out past the shallow coral reef filled with colorful fish, past the rocks on the sandy bottom that spelled ALOHA, and then into the deeper water where lavender fountains of light seemed to come up from the depths like flowers.

All of a sudden I found myself in the midst of a pod of dolphins. One particular dolphin left the pod to sonar my chest. I felt something being extracted, energetically. I continued to swim and they were all around me and gliding below me, as a synchronized group. Then they would come up to the surface again, to breathe and dip and dive before doing another deep dive.

I was on the surface with my mask and snorkel. Every now and then this one particular dolphin would break away from the pod to swim next to me, eye to eye. In this moment, eye to eye with the dolphin, I saw the mirror-like quality of the encounter. We were two beings in two different kinds of body suits, reflecting back and forth to each other. "Salt water, sonar and sun," the dolphin seemed to say to me, wordlessly, "will clear the channels and bring you joy." At that, the dolphin flipped out of the water, jettisoned up into the air and was spinning above me as a flash of silver.

Life is not determined by the outer circumstances which are in constant flux and duality, the mirror and mirrored. Life and peace and happiness are determined by the inner attitude of peace, humility, and generosity . . . and an attitude of compassion for all beings. I thought of Uncle Lanakila Brandt telling a few of us that a friend of his described Aloha as "inner paradise." In a millisecond these truths seemed to come to me, in a flash, from this particular dolphin. Whether they truly came from the dolphin or my inner self didn't matter. What mattered was that in this beautiful water sanctuary these truths resonated deep within me, finding a home, in a different way than I had ever realized them before. I was hooked!

Getting out of the water later, I shook the droplets off like a dog and stood in the warm sun gazing out to the part of the bay where I had just been. The feeling of champagne bubbles all through my body gave rise to a feeling of effervescent joy. Here I had a demonstration of how a sad or dark mood can change quite quickly into brilliant happiness and freedom.

### Swimming Above Giant Groupers

ON ANOTHER DAY WHILE SNORKELING far out in Honaunau Bay, I found myself looking down, quite a few feet under the surface, to a group of huge fish that were cruising below me. At first I thought it was a pod of small whales. They seemed to be at least eight feet long and several feet wide. There were about seven or eight of them. Then I saw their faces, which looked prehistoric to me. I don't know if they knew I was above them, but I had a strong instinct to "get out of there." I had never been afraid of sharks or of swimming way out in the bay, but these huge fish set off an alarm within me. Without splashing, I turned around and swam back to shore and got out of the water.

Sometimes I watched Wayne Leslie bring his fishing boat out of the water at the boat ramp at Honaunau Bay and then trailer it back home to Napo'opo'o, where the Leslie family has lived for at least several generations. He mainly fishes *opelo* (mackerel) and makes his nets in the old traditional way. He is one of the last of the traditional fishermen. I looked around to see if he was here today, but he wasn't. As such an experienced fisherman, surely he would know what type of fish I had seen.

Over a number of months, I tried to identify these fish and had no luck. At first some people thought they were large tuna, but the faces and heads didn't match what I saw. No one that I talked to seemed to know what they were. Aka and I got on the computer and looked at pictures of possibilities, and we finally decided together that they were possibly Giant Groupers or Goliath Groupers. I have heard that they have a huge vacuum within, when they open their large mouths. Maybe that is why I turned back to shore so quickly. I have since found out that, if this is what they were, there are only rare sightings of these huge fish in the Hawai'ian islands.


### My New Roommates


IT DIDN'T TAKE LONG BEFORE Rinko and Bill and I got to be good friends. Rinko brought numerous Japanese lady friends to our house for Dolphin Card readings. Bill was so easy going that he never minded if we had a group of ladies in the living room or out on the *lanai* (porch). Sometimes he joined us, and his light-hearted sense of humor fit right in with the rest of the group. I never accepted cash donations from the girls for the readings. I simply enjoyed their delightful company and the discussions that would take place after the card readings. I always told them that the reading was to be interactive, with their participation. I also told them that I was not a fortune teller and did not make predictions. The cards could be a "mind mirror" which could act synchronistically with what was going on in their life. They, themselves, could explore the possible meaning of the cards with me and the guidance that they presented. It was a great way to get people to open up about deep and meaningful issues and concerns in a space that felt safe to them. When interpreting the cards, it's fun to think like a dolphin. I realized, once again, that the cards were often a catalyst and ice breaker for really deep discussions within a group.

I was to learn that Bill and Rinko liked to swim early every morning. I was invited to join them about 7 a.m. to swim out into Kealakekua Bay. Paul liked both Bill and Rinko and thought it was a nice household for me to share for the next two or three months.


## Surf's Up...


MY ROOMMATE, BILL, IS A SURFER. He grew up in Oahu and learned to ride the big waves when he was young. Often we would see Bill tie his surfboard to the top of his car and take off for a favorite beach. Just as people would check where the dolphins were on a given day, surfers would communicate with each other about where the best waves were! I never learned to surf, so I don't know much about the form or size of waves or the terms that surfers use with each other that describe the many different types of waves. I do know that those who surf absolutely love it and spend a lot of time in the water. I often watched them at Kahalu'u Beach Park, which is a favorite surf spot in Kona. I loved watching them paddle out lying on their board and then turn around and wait for the right wave to ride. In an instant they would go from a prone position to kneeling and then to standing, one foot in front of the other. Then they either ride the wave in to shore very skillfully, or if not, wipe out.

Another surf spot is Magic Sands Beach on Ali'i Drive between Kailua-Kona and Keauhou. There is a white sand beach there and quite a strong surf break. In some weather all the sand disappears to reveal black lava rock. But then the white sand can wash back in again with a change in the weather or currents. Another favorite spot on the Big Island is on the Hilo side: It is Pohoiki, the shore line at Isaac Hale Beach Park. Here there could be twenty-foot waves at times. However, like many other special places, Pohoiki was wiped out by the lava flow from the 2018 eruption of the volcano. Today, post 2018, it is the newest black sand beach on the Big Island. The old boat ramp has been destroyed and near it is a warm thermal pool. There are four other small warm pools of various temperatures that recently appeared along this new beach. Always best to test the water for temperature first and to never go in with open sores.

Duke Kahanamoku was an iconic Hawai'ian surfer. He was born when Hawai'i was still a kingdom. His *papa nui koa* (surfboard) was made of wood and was sixteen feet long. Besides surfing he was a champion swimmer who set records in competitions world-wide. He rescued so many drowning people that it led to hiring lifeguards at many of Hawai'i's public beaches. I remembered seeing a statue of him at Newport Beach in California. There are two other statues of him on the islands. He had a big charismatic smile and was called "The Ambassador of Aloha." He often entertained tourists with his surfing tricks, such as carrying a lady on his shoulders while riding a wave.

Today, most surfboards are made of fiberglass and have a rudder. When the first foreign ships arrived on the shores of the Hawai'ian islands, the sailors were shocked to see men and women, of all classes and ages, "surf riding" on wooden boards. The wooden surfboards could be anywhere from six to sixteen feet long. It is said that Polynesian people have enjoyed this sport for centuries. I found it amusing to read a diary entry from one of the earliest visitors, in the 1800's, proclaiming that Hawai'ians were "amphibious human beings."

### *"Eddie Would Go"*

THE DUKE WAS THE HERO of young Eddie Aikau who became an impressive surfer of the pipeline at Waimea Bay on the North Shore of Oahu. He became a big-wave star having no problem with twenty- or thirty-foot waves. Like his hero Duke, Eddie rescued endless numbers of drowning people, and finally he was able to win the Duke Kahanamoku Invitational Surfing Championship. The biggest thrill for him was to meet his hero shortly before the Duke passed away. In 1978 Eddie joined the voyagers and began a sail on

440

the Hokule'a. Leaving on March 17th in very strong winds and rough swells, the Hokule'a capsized about twelves miles out from Hawai'ian shores. As the crew clung to the floating hulls, Eddie volunteered to paddle the ten or twelve miles to shore for help, with his surfboard. Even after extensive searches Eddie was never seen again. The next day an overhead plane spotted the canoe, and the rest of the crew was rescued after twenty hours. In Eddie's memory each year there is an Eddie Aikau Big Wave Invitational Surf Contest. Eddie's kind and brave nature is memorialized in the phrase, "Eddie Would Go."

## Harvesting a Tree

IN ANCIENT HAWAI'I, TREES WERE CONSIDERED SACRED and were treated as such. When a tree was about to be cut down, prayers and chants were performed at the base of the tree, thanking it for giving up its sacred *uhane* (soul) and gifting the wood for canoes, surfboards, and other items. Food offerings were made and later, food was left on the stump of the tree as a thank you. A wooden surfboard had a special place in a Hawai'ian *hale* (house) as the wood still carried the *uhane* or soul of the tree. The wooden canoes for fishing and the double-hulled voyaging canoes were also revered for the same reason.

## The King Kamehameha Bulls and Juni's Paniolo Family

PAUL AND I LOVE OUR FRIEND, JUNI MEDEIROS, who comes from a *Paniolo* family. We originally met him at Lenda Hand's house in Ho'okena. So I shared a little of the story of Juni and his family with Aka and her family. The Medeiros family had originated in Portugal and had become a famous family of *paniolos* (Hawai'ian cowboys) who worked on the large McCandless Ranch in South Kona. Our friend Juni roped the fierce, strong and wily King Kamehameha bulls when he was only a young teen-ager.

These cattle had originally been a gift that Captain George Vancouver brought by ship to Hawai'i as a gift for King

Kamehameha I. The King made it *kapu* (forbidden) to kill these cattle, so they were set loose to wander and breed freely. Before long there were thousands of them. Being wild, they had become dangerous and had become a big menace for the roadways, the people, their crops and gardens.

The King Kamehameha bulls needed to be castrated in

ARTWORK BY JUNI MEDEIROS

order to stop the uncontrolled breeding. Juni said that, when he was a little older, he could throw a lasso sixty feet. "It is such a dangerous job!" Juni said. He told us that he had "to rope 'em, tie 'em, cut 'em and finally, let 'em go." He often had to hide behind a tree when he cut them loose, or he could have been gored to death. It is a dangerous job riding a horse over mountainous terrain with under-brush that often hides big lava rocks, lava tubes, and caves. The bulls are especially clever at trying to dump a Hawai'ian cowboy and his horse into a lava tube. And there are stories about that very thing, and the near impossible rescues.

Juni's father, Alfred Medeiros, was the foreman of the McCandless Ranch in South Kona and he was a strict boss to his son, Juni, and the band of *paniolos* that rode with him. He had to be strict, as this was a job where life and death hung in the mix. Alfred Medeiros and several of Juni's uncles have their photographs featured in the Cowboy Hall of Fame in the Paniolo Museum on the Parker Ranch located in the "up country" town of Waimea. I hope that someday Juni will be inducted into the Cowboy Hall of Fame too, and have his picture next to his father and uncles. Rodeos sprung up in Hawai'i as the *paniolo* culture grew. There are still rodeos today, with riding and roping competitions. I said to Juni one time, "Ride 'em high. Ride 'em low, but don't put 'em away wet." Juni laughed with his habitual good humor. A cowboy's horse, whether in Hawai'i, or anywhere else, is a cowboy's best friend. Auntie Fern had known the Medeiros men when she was a young woman. She smiled as I mentioned them. I knew from their pictures that the Medeiros men were especially handsome.

### South Kona: Kimura's, the Manago Hotel, Ma's Kava Shop, Teshima's, and the Aloha Theatre

FIVE CLASSIC KONA DESTINATIONS that I love are Ma's Kava Shop, Kimura's fabric store, Teshima's Japanese restaurant, and the Aloha Theatre in Kealakekua, and the Manago Hotel in Captain Cook. Teshima's Japanese restaurant is a friendly place with delicious food that first opened in the nineteen fifties. I always love seeing Grandma Teshima who is close to one hundred years old and still greeting the customers. (Grandma Teshima passed away at one hundred and six years old, a testimony to her good food and kind disposition.)

Both of these towns have a good old Kona vibe. Driving on the belt road I sometimes went to the Manago Hotel for dinner. Their pork chops and gravy are delicious and famous with the locals. This affordable and clean hotel is popular with local people as well as travelers. The hotel has been here for about a hundred years. It was started by the Manago family and is still run by descendants of the original Manago family.

Ma's Kava shop in Kealakekua has the type of *kava* that can numb the tongue and create a pleasant but mildly altered state. In pre-colonial times the *Ali'i* (chiefs) would include this drink in their ceremonies. Ma's also sells *kava* powder. Ma was an iconic figure in South Kona. She's passed on now, but the family continues the business. Locals bring their own half coconut shell for their kava. One lazy afternoon Kapua and I were doing errands and he suggested that we drop in to Ma's for a shell of kava. In this small shop, we ran into an old friend from California named Lenda Hand.

It was great to see her after a number of years. She knew my family back home, and she invited us down to visit her house among the locals, which was located right on the beach in Ho'okena. The harmonies that occur on the Big Island never cease to be amazing.

On rainy days I loved going to Kimura's fabric store, which is right next door to Oshima's grocery, to immerse myself in the huge selection of Hawai'ian, tropical, and Asian prints. This magical store was opened in 1926. It is always a happy place to be and, for as long as I can remember, Mrs. Kimura herself was always there to measure and cut the fabric off the bolt with such kindness and a smile. When I wanted to make a *lava lava* or get a gift for my daughter, Stacy, this is where I went.

The Aloha Theater may have echos of theater, *hula* and music groups hovering in its last-century atmosphere. It has hosted all kinds of entertainment for over eighty years. I enjoyed some *hula* performances as well as a classical music concert here. This is a South Kona favorite for good local entertainment. Of all the places that I lived on the Big Island, I think South Kona is my most favorite location.

### A Visit to Antonio Grafilo

MANY PEOPLE HAD MENTIONED A MAN NAMED Antonio Grafilo. He lived on the Kona side with his wife, and he had a background working with psychiatric patients on the mainland. He was also alleged, by several friends, to be clairvoyant. In semi-retirement he sometimes did counseling sessions with people which were drawn to him for his highly developed intuition. Kapua had suggested that I have a session with him before going home. So I made the appointment and found him to be a friendly older man with warmth in his eyes. I believe he told me that he was part Hawai'ian and part Filipino. I felt comfortable with him right away. As he knew nothing about me, I thought his reading would be interesting. I told him that I had been here on the Big Island for almost a year and that I had a home and family in California. From there he began to speak and amazed me with the accuracy of his intuition. He detailed some events in my life that no one else knew. I was impressed with the details that he intuited. In summary he tracked my journey and what I had learned both at home and especially here.

But the part of the reading that stands out most strongly for me are the words:

"You have been one of the rare persons who has lived through a 'Reincarnation Drama'." I was shocked at hearing these words and wanted to know what he meant. He went on to say, "You had a Native American teacher and now she has been reborn as your granddaughter." This was shocking coming from a total stranger. He went on to say that it was time for me to return home soon, as it would be important for me to have a relationship with my granddaughter and my grandson.

I left Antonio's feeling that I had had another confirmation of what I already thought could possibly be true. Lilliana would not be like Grandma Eunice in her new life. She would explore different directions and manifest herself uniquely, as the present times require. She might carry over the power and "knowing" of her previous life, but not the life style. For her, it would be a clean slate. She would write her own script.


### Flashback: Pondering Cultures and Remembering Times with Grandma Eunice Silva, a Newe Western Shoshone Medicine Woman

MY MIND WOULD OFTEN THINK BACK ON TIMES I spent with the Native American people out on the Nevada desert. This land was called *Newe Segobia* in the Shoshone native tongue, and their name was the *Newe* people. But in more recent years they were called the Western

Shoshone people, and their territory covered most of Nevada and parts of California and Idaho. There were things about the *kupuna* (elders) in Hawai'i that reminded me of the elders in the Western

Shoshone tribe. Grandma Eunice Silva was 111 years old when she passed away. She was a famous Western Shoshone medicine woman who was born behind a sage brush and who lived most of her life on the reservation in Battle Mountain, Nevada. We were blessed to have learned from her the last ten years, or so, of her long life. Her brother, Doc Blossom was also a famous healer and medicine man and was one

EUNICE, CORBIN, AND FLORENCE

of Corbin Harney's medicine and plant teachers.

Our granddaughter, Lilliana, and our grandson, Doc, had not been born behind a sage brush out in the Nevada desert near Silver Creek as Eunice had, but in a hospital in Sacramento, California in 1999 and 2001. Lilliana lived with modern conveniences and would become familiar with technology. She would have a college education. Instead of riding a horse, she would drive a car. She would be a totally different incarnation, but perhaps with the same soul that cared for others and was wise, extraordinarily sensitive, intelligent, and strong. She was born as a triple fire sign (Aries, Aries and Leo), and our astrologer friend said she had the chart of someone who could run the United Nations.

As Doc grew and matured he also took a great interest in his Native American bloodline. He knew that his name, Doc, was given after his great grand uncle, Doc Blossom. In time he would learn the songs and traditional ways of the Western Shoshone.

As I contemplate Grandma Eunice, I remember her wizened face, her white hair, and her eyes which were as sharp as an eagle's. I remember her walking along slowly, pushing her walker on the desert's sandy earth, moving between sagebrush bushes, avoiding the holes made by badgers, ground hogs, and gophers. She came to the breakfast tent and tables as the announcement was being made by one of the younger medicine people, "Elders first." Eunice said that you had to keep moving no matter what, or you would lose the use of your legs. "If you stop moving," she said, "you will soon be under the ground."

Eunice and Florence were cousins and had known each other all of their lives. They had both been two of Corbin Harney's medicine teachers when he was a young man, and they still liked to tease him, playfully referring to him, as "a boy." Eunice and Florence had run sweat lodges together and they had doctored people for many, many years. Both of them were way over one hundred. Their minds were sharp and clear. There was no sign of dementia with either one of them. They both chuckled when they told me stories of the old days when they were young women. From time to time they went gambling, and woe be it to any white man who made any racist or depraved remarks to them about being Indian squaws. They both told me that they were very strong and they would give "this kinda man a dirty lickin'."

Grandma Florence was over a hundred years old too, and she winced as she walked along slowly, with her *boto* (walking stick, healing staff), as her knees were painful and swollen. "I knew it would come to this," she said, with a slight smile crossing her face. These two *hoobeejos* (old ladies) had seen a lot of life together. Now, at their advanced age, they had clear minds unscathed by dementia. Their bodies may have hurt them some, but they still slept on the ground, in a tent, just as they had when they were young girls. They had to keep the sacred grounds alive by keeping the ceremonies alive, they said, and they would attend the seasonal ceremonies until their dying day.

Breakfast was made over the open fire on a grill and it was always good. Everyone attending the ceremony had contributed to the food teepee. The smell of hot coffee, hot cakes, bacon, eggs, and potatoes and onions frying made you hungry in the icy cold morning of the Nevada desert. By ten o clock it would be getting warm and by midday it would be hot. The fire for the morning sweat lodge was roaring and the lava rocks were heating up under the teepee-shaped burning logs. The morning ceremony had already taken place, in the canyon at dawn . . . a circle of people praying around a fire below the ancient cliffs of the canyon. Some years there had been more than fifty people that attended. Other years the circles were smaller. Prayers were said and songs were sung and everyone danced in a circle, just as generations of Shoshone people had done before.

It was very cold as the sun hadn't risen in the canyon yet. As we snuggled in our sleeping bags, inside our tents, we could hear a pack of coyotes singing eerily, in the distance, just as the morning star faded into dawn's early light. As dawn had begun to break, Corbin would start the beat of his drum to awaken everyone still sleeping. He had already made the coffee. People began to emerge from their tents, teepees, and vans to make their way to the out-houses. Then after pouring a cup of coffee, they would walk single file on the narrow path that entered the canyon. After rounding a curve, at the base of the Eagle Rock the long and deep canyon appeared. A patch of nettles and multi-colored moss and lichen were growing at the foot of the Eagle Rock. The people walked into the canyon, wrapped in jackets, scarves, gloves, and hats. Clouds of vapor encircled their heads as their breath met the icy cold air.

Dancing in a circle helped to warm everyone up. Corbin kept the beat with his drum. After a few rounds of dancing and singing, the elder ladies stood up carefully and gave everyone their prayers and blessings in their Shoshone language. Corbin passed a can of tobacco around the circle and everyone took a pinch of it. Then Corbin stood and gave his prayer in his native tongue. Next everyone went, one at a time, to stand next to the fire, to offer their tobacco and a prayer. Some did it silently. Some did it with tears over the loss or illness of a loved one. Others had long orational prayers in their own language. Every one of them was beautiful. Every prayer was sacred and rose up on smoke or on the wings of eagles. There were almost always eagles circling over this sacred canyon.

Shoshone people had prayed in this place for many hundreds and perhaps thousands of years. The bones of their people were hidden in caves here and under big piles of rocks. This was a sacred burial ground. Eunice said, "My mother and my mother's mother are buried here. Their songs still echo off the canyon walls." There were two chairs set up at the west side of the circle for the two most elder medicine people, Eunice Silva and Florence Vega. They were helped to their chairs by their two grandsons, Rudy and Gani, and then wrapped in Pendleton blankets. Corbin stood beside them, wearing a turquoise-colored down jacket, trimmed in purple. Corbin Harney was in his seventies. He led the ceremony and walked around the circle, towards the end, with his two eagle feather fans, blessing each person before the circle closed for the morning. He would gaze at you with rather entranced eyes and wave the two eagle feather fans up and down gracefully, with a silent prayer. The breeze from the fans would encircle you and bless you. "Be sure to get some of those ashes from the fire before you leave," he said. "The ash is sacred, and you can put it in water and drink it as a medicine, or you can bless yourself with it, or make a medicine with it for someone at home."

Eunice had a sweat lodge in her back yard and ran sweat every week. She doctored people in the sweat lodge and often made herbal teas that were her own proprietary formulas of desert herbs and roots. Doc Blossom, Eunice's brother, was also an Indian doctor and was one of Corbin's spiritual teachers. The two of them would ride horseback over the rolling sagebrush hills out into the sacred canyon from Battle Mountain, Nevada. It was a long ride . . . but a beautiful one, and when it rained on them, the aroma of wet sage was pleasantly intoxicating. Besides being an Indian doctor, Eunice was also a laundress and ironing lady for "white people." She once said to me in her unique accent, with her low gravelly voice, "I don't like white people. But I like you." She paused for a long time and then said, "You see, you and I were sisters in another life. I remember you, and that's why I'm teaching you."

## The Boto (Healing Staff, in Western Shoshone)

MY SON-IN-LAW, RUDY, WHO IS GRANDMA EUNICE'S grandson, has a photo of Eunice and Florence with their *botos* (staffs, in the Western Shoshone language) walking across the desert, on a day that they were digging roots and collecting herbs. Eunice showed me that her *boto* was made of a straight elderberry branch, which was hollow in the middle. She said it was not only a cane, but a medicine staff. She showed me how she would have a sick person lay down, and she would put the *boto* on various parts of their body and blow on them through the hollow branch with her prayer-laden breath.

Another time Eunice and her young friend, Fred, took me in his pickup truck up onto Stevens Mountain (outside of Battle

EUNICE AND FLORENCE

Mountain) so she could show me the large Elderberry tree where she and Grandma Florence collected their *botos*. She said, "This is a sacred *"Goonigep"* *ah boto* (elderberry tree), and if you want to have a *boto* someday, you will know where to come. Be sure to pray first and make an offering if you cut a branch. When gathering or digging a healing plant or root," Eunice said, "you've got to pray for it first or 'it won't heal nothin'. You've got to talk to the plant and tell it, who it is for, and what kind of sickness that it needs to cure. You need to leave an offering too. If you don't have tobacco or a quarter, you can always offer a hair from your head."

## Grandma Eunice: "I wasn't always a good woman"

I REMEMBER EUNICE'S TEARS ONE DAY as I was braiding her white hair and massaging her hands. She had her head down and tears were rolling down the gentle folds of her century-old cheeks. "I was not always a good woman," she said. And she cried. I tried to console her, telling her that she had gone to Washington D.C. as an activist for her people, to protect their rights and their burial grounds, and that she had helped heal so many people from cancer and other illnesses. I told her that she had raised a family too: Edna, Cecelia, Aloisa, and Mary Ann. She continued to cry as she said, "I wasn't always a good woman."

She talked about drinking a bottle of whiskey every day, in her younger years, and how her husband Mike had to do her chores for her, sometimes, when she had been drinking. Her husband, Mike Silva, had been born in New Mexico and worked as a buckaroo on a ranch close to Battle Mountain and Argenta, Nevada. I thought to myself, 'Gifted people often have trouble living with their extreme sensitivity and their gift, and often turn to alcohol to ease raw, intense feelings.' Eunice dried her tears with a Kleenex that I handed to her, and spoke about the day when she realized she had to give up drinking. She told her husband, "Mike, don't buy my bottle today." He didn't, and she told me that she never had another drink again, after drinking a whole lot of whiskey for such a long time. Mike was so happy that he picked her up in his arms and twirled her around and around with joy. She smiled through her tears, as she reminisced about this memory of her husband, Mike, joyfully twirling her around and around and around.

One of the difficult things about having such a long life is that your husband, friends, and acquaintances usually die before you. She told me one day that everyone she used to know was "under the ground," except for her cousin Florence. "It took the tribe all these years to finally get around to making me a ramp. The tribe has money for elders, but they don't always use it for elders." We were sitting on the porch of her house on the reservation, which was located on the western edge of Battle Mountain. This was the Battle Mountain

Indian Colony, called the Western Shoshone Te-Moak band. It was established in 1917. Battle Mountain was also the original home of the Tosawi (Tosa wihi) White Knife Shoshone. Eunice waved her hand in a sweeping motion across the colony of Native American homes and the nearby town and said, "All the people here and in the town are gone now. They are all under the ground. All the people that I remember are under the ground." Two tears rolled down her cheeks and I took her hand in mine. I tried to imagine what that would feel like.

### Grandma Eunice's Great Grandchildren

ONE DAY, GRANDMA EUNICE SHOWED ME A PHOTO of her multi-racial great grandchildren . . . rows of them, like a school picture, with every kind of color and ethnicity. "These are all my kids. Look at my kids – little Mexican kids, little Black kids, little Puerto Rican kids, little Japanese kids, little Indian kids, and little White kids. These are all my kids." She looked wistfully at the photograph of the several rows of over thirty diverse looking children. "This is how the world's gonna be. All kinds of kids," she said. Lilliana was one of those great grandchildren, but she hadn't been born yet, at the time that group photo had been taken. She was born in 1999, three years after Grandma Eunice passed away. And Doc hadn't been born yet either. He arrived a little over two years after Lilliana in 2001.

Our daughter and son-in-law had taken Lilliana to the Western Shoshone sacred grounds from the time she was a baby. I can remember a time when Lilliana was confused by her feelings. She could talk now and express her feelings. She told me that every time she came to the Rock Creek Canyon that she felt strange and couldn't understand why. She said she felt she had been here a long time ago, but didn't know why she felt that way. Her father, Rudy, was Grandma Eunice's grandson and Lilliana was Grandma Eunice's great granddaughter. Grandma Eunice had died three years before Lilliana was born. The day she died soft snow fell slowly to the ground and two eagles circled overhead. As was the custom, Eunice's coffin was placed in the back of a pickup truck, after resting in her closed coffin for three days in the colony community center.

452

At least three people sat with the body, in shifts throughout the three days. Fred Badman came through several times a day to smudge the room with the smoke of sacred Juniper needles. Several young men, including her grandsons, got in the back of the truck to hold the coffin steady. Then the procession began to the little Indian graveyard out in the middle of the sagebrush desert. There was a dusting of snow on the mountain tops that surrounded this high plateau. The air was cold and fresh. We all stood around Grandma Eunice's grave site as she was buried. Water and dried sagebrush was sprinkled on top of the coffin. Dried sagebrush was smoking in

an abalone shell. The young warriors stood tall, in a line, and sang a rousing Sundance song that brought tears to everyone's eyes. A great woman had gone home.

I will never forget the time that I took Lilliana across the creek that meandered through the canyon at the Sacred Grounds. It was an area where the creek bank had a seasonal flood zone of very smooth, small stones. Grandma Eunice had sent me to this location some years' before, to find a smooth, round, white stone for my medicine bag. She told me that this place was where ancient Shoshone people had gone to find stones like this, for their medicine bags. It took nearly an hour to drive to Rock Creek Canyon from Battle Mountain, Nevada. Part of the road was a washboard gravel road that passed some large ranches that grew green fields of alfalfa, and grazed cattle. But the last part was a bumpy, dirt road that was best driven with a four-wheel drive vehicle. Sometimes free-range cattle were in the road or along the sides grazing on sagebrush and desert plants. Sprawling sagebrush grew everywhere, leaning into the narrow road. One had to drive very slowly and carefully to avoid bottoming out or getting their vehicle scratched from the sharp sagebrush branches. The gently rolling hills were dotted with sagebrush, filling the air with a lovely fragrance.

As one approaches the end of the road, one can see part of the canyon wall with complex rock patterns that were ever changing, as the light and shadow changed. Towards the end of the day the canyon wall was bathed in golden sunlight. Within the rock formations were the shapes of buffalo, bear, a man and a woman, and many other natural stone images. At the entrance to the canyon is a large stone formation, at least thirty feet tall that looks like the head of an eagle. For centuries Shoshone people have done their vision quest atop this Eagle Rock and their Shoshone ancestors had gazed upon these same natural stone "bas relief sculptures" on the side of the cliff. This place had been a ceremonial ground for many centuries.

EAGLE ROCK AT ROCK CREEK CANYON

A beautiful creek meandered through the canyon, and at the north end there was a heart-shaped pool that had always been called the "holy water." It was for ceremonial bathing and was not meant to be used as a swimming hole. Along the edges grew abundant and beautiful watercress. Swallows flew in and out of their homes on the canyon walls and eagles often circled overhead, soaring on thermals high above us.

## *Déjà Vue*

OUR DAUGHTER AND SON-IN-LAW were at the sacred Shoshone grounds with Lilliana and Doc. Lil was about four years old at the time. Doc was still very little. Lil had long, dark wavy hair and big brown eyes. She was a beautiful child, and each time we were together was precious to me. I asked Lil if she wanted to go for a walk with me to find a stone for my medicine bag. She was eager to come along, so we walked, hand in hand, across a shallow part of the stream. When we climbed up onto the embankment, Lilliana looked at the dry bed of smooth stones and then looked up at me quizzically and asked, "Grandma, what does it mean when you think you have seen something before? Or done something before, but you know you didn't?" I said, "Oh Lilliana, there is a name for that. It is called *déjà vu*." "Oh *déjà vu*," she said . . . "there's a word for this feeling?" I said, "Yes, it's a French word, but that's what it means. It means you feel like you've already seen it before or have already done it before." She seemed happy to know that there was something that described the strange feeling she was experiencing.

If this is true, what did she carry forth from Eunice, if indeed she had been *her* in the past? I could see in her a power and an acute knowing, kindness, and intuition. She was a keen observer and she didn't miss anything. When she was very little, she enjoyed having me show her herbs that are used for medicine. But I don't think she wanted to be a *"hoobeejoe"* (old lady) living on a reservation out in the Nevada desert again, running sweat lodges, digging herbs, and doctoring sick people. I am sure that she will manifest herself uniquely as her new self. She may or may not be the reincarnation of Grandma Eunice. In a way, it really doesn't matter, and the synchronicities that were experienced may mean nothing. Lilliana may never be able to relate to reincarnation stories and may never believe that she had lived before as a Shoshone medicine woman, who happened to be her great grandmother. I wouldn't expect her to believe it, and I hope that she is not bothered by my writing about it and suggesting it as a possibility. I would never try to impose this belief on her. She is free to be herself. When we are born, we have a clean slate to create a new destiny. But sometimes the cast of characters in one's life may feel very familiar.

Yes, Antonio, I will go home to enjoy the family, and I will be a grandmother to my grandchildren. I will bring Aloha home with me. *"Aloha"* will greet *"Shundahai,"* a Western Shoshone greeting that means just about the very same thing.

HAVING THIS CLAIRVOYANT READING with Antonio had taken me back to many memories and flashbacks about my relationship with Grandma Eunice Silva, during the last eight years of her life. She had taught me a great deal. She taught me to sit with her in silence, sometimes for hours, before she was ready to share stories. Traditional Native American people do not feel the need to fill the space with conversation when two people are together. The silence with her took me to deep places inside myself and led me to a special kind of communing with her. One day she said, "Our families are coming together again." This was before we knew that our daughter would meet and marry her grandson. Once, while sitting under the spring-green leaf canopy of our old walnut trees, she said, "You have a lot of medicines growing here, on this land." She mentioned some particular plants that were growing at least two acres away, down near our garden. She seemed to be able to send a part of her spirit out to look around, even though she was confined to walking with a walker at her advanced age. She was subtle and never flaunted her gifts.

Another time while she and her younger friend and helper, Fred Badman, were visiting us from Battle Mountain, I got a very urgent type of impulse to go to the fabric store and get certain colors of fabric and thread. I was not someone gifted with sewing, so I knew it wasn't for me. The urgent feeling wouldn't go away. Finally, I got in the car and went to buy the fabric and thread in these particular colors. By the time I got home, I knew I was supposed to give the fabric and thread to Eunice. She laughed her deep, gravelly voiced laugh and said, "Well, now I see that we can talk without words." She went on to tell me that she was going to make medicine tobacco ties for her sweat lodge. I immediately thought of all the times she had me sit with her in the silence. I wondered if there was a medicine way that she was able to link our minds together, telepathically. Without knowing the physics or mechanics of it, I noticed that from this time forward we were telepathically connected. This telepathic connection became especially strong right after her death and for three years afterward. Then it stopped, right when Lilliana was born.

# LIVING IN SOUTH KONA

## Aka, Telepathy, and my Childhood

NOW, YEARS LATER, I HAD THIS SAME KIND of telepathic relationship with Aka. We never talked about it, but there were numerous instances when we read each other's minds or asked for help in various ways, without talking. One time her car had broken down. I drove to the spot where she was . . . and picked her up. We never even talked about it. Once she told me that telepathy was one of the ways island people talk to each other: "mind to mind, heart to heart." She said her *tutus*, in the spirit world, talked to her in this way all the time. When she got silent, closed her eyes and listened, she would later say, "They were perching on my head, and had to tell me something." Or she would say, "Tutu was sitting on me." This was never treated as anything out of the ordinary. Later I was to discover that her mother, siblings, and children were all like this too. Telepathy was "quite ordinary" in Aka's *ohana* (family) and many other island *ohanas*. They all receive telepathic wise counsel and premonitions. Growing up, I was sometimes confused by what was being said to me out loud and what I felt was "thought" about me silently. This was very confusing, and I didn't have the tools to deal with what was sometimes, for me, a double message. I didn't know then, that I was often getting clear messages. It took many years to trust my inner voice. And even then there is always a chance of being mistaken.

When my mother was in her nineties, she confided to me that I irritated her when I was young because I dared to be a free spirit

457

and had too much energy for her. Now she wished that she had been able to feel freer herself. She was gifted with an intuitive and emotional nature. She loved books, family history, nutritional health, and stories. She sewed many of our clothes for us when we were young. She could also knit the most beautiful Afghans and sweaters with complex patterns. She was very social, active in the church, and volunteered in many organizations. She had healing abilities and studied to be a nurse, but the world she lived in stifled her to some extent. After her four children had left home, she took a Trager healing training. She bought a massage table and, when she gave me a treatment one time, I knew then that she had very good healing energy in her hands.

My father was an extraordinarily smart and kind man and had great integrity. His temperament was logical and linear. He was a natural born leader in school, overseas while in the Air Force during World War II, in his business life, and as a community leader. He was a chemical engineer in charge of three hundred physicists and other chemical engineers. He loved tennis, fishing, and backpacking in remote mountains. Nature was where he felt very spiritually connected, and he was a "foodie" long before that expression was popular. Although my parents traveled all around the world after my father retired, my mother took two trips without him. In mid-life my mother took two spiritual journeys with her church group: one to Great Britain and one to Egypt. She had some extraordinary experiences on both trips. In her later years she published several books of her poetry and taught a poetry class. I was proud of her and happy that she was able to express her sensitivity in this way. My mother was telepathic too, often calling me when I needed her counsel.


## Ho'o'mana and Communing with Nature

"WE NEED TO KEEP OUR MINDS FREE OF WORRY and all useless distracting thoughts," Aka said to me one day. She continued, "Then we can become aligned with guidance and mind to mind connections. When we are quiet, we can learn to hear nature speak to us. The trees talk, and so do the plants. People think that rocks are not alive, but they are! These *pohaku* (stones) have been sacred to us here in Hawai'i for generations. In the old days there were some stones that were considered sacred and powerful. They were protected and revered. A sacred stone would be placed on top of a *heiau* or in other places."

{*Marza Millar Allen had a home on the Big Island which Aka cared for when Marza was away. As an herbalist and rock person, Marza also has a strong connection to the sacred stones of Hawai'i.*}

"When Christian missionaries came to Hawai'i, they didn't understand our spiritual traditions and thought they were evil. But God created nature, and the Hawai'ian religion was totally based around the natural world. As more and more Hawai'ians were baptized as Christians, the climate became ripe to ban the old religion. The *tiki* statues and artifacts were banned and destroyed. Some of the power stones had to be buried or put in the ocean to protect them."

We sat quietly for a while as I absorbed what she had just said. "Nature speaks to us the quieter we get inside." Aka would often say to me, as a reminder, "Stay clear. Do not become distracted." Now I more deeply understand her constant prayers of appreciation, telling trees, birds, flowers and plants how beautiful they are. Not only did she pray and thank them, but she sang to them too.

One time she said to me, "Put the vibrancy of the *pule* (prayer) and *mele* (song) into the air and onto the wind." The sacred connection with the natural world, and not allowing ourselves to be distracted, helps us access and increase our *mana*. *Mana* is 'spiritual power', and *Ho'o* means 'to make'. So the practice of *Ho'o' mana* is the generation of spiritual power. Alignment and communication with the natural world does this and helps us to be in harmony with positive manifestations and success in whatever positive goals we wish to achieve. In these positive prayerful ways there is no lack in this universe. So much is possible when we open ourselves to the abundance of *Ke Akua*." *Mahalo lui noa,* Aka, I thought, for sharing these precious teachings.

### Remembering a Conversation with Auntie Fern

I HAD MET AKA IN THE YEAR 2000 in a grocery store, but I had known her mother, Auntie Fern, for many years. Sometimes Auntie Fern and I would talk about the spirit world, the ancestors and guides that help us from the heavens, and the dark ones who tend to bring interference or misfortune to us. She always said a prayer when she sensed something troublesome. She would rebuke any dark forces by saying this prayer or variations of
it: "*Ke Akua*, I rebuke this one (or ones) who seeks to diminish the light – bind em, lock 'em up, and *Ke Akua*, you do with them, as you see fit. *Mahalo nui loa, Ke Akua,* for your many blessings."

I had a lot of questions for her, and one of them was how beings in the spirit world can tell who on earth is a receiver? And how do they recognize receivers from the perspective of the heavens? And how are they able to intervene for a person here on Earth from the spirit world? "First of all," she said, "you have to know how to be quiet and listen, or you will not get the message at all, or you won't get it right. So you have to clear your mind of all the *pilikia* (trouble). You can't be thinking bad things about anyone. You can't be worrying. You have to be clean and *pono* (good) in your life, and most important, you have to be *pono* (righteous) with 'the man in white'."

And I said, "And you have to keep washing dos buggahs off?" She gave me a look that said, 'Don't be a smart alec.' "Oh, *Kala Mai* (I'm sorry)," I said.

Then we sat quietly for a little while. She picked up her ukulele and started strumming a song, but this time she didn't sing. I thought, "Oh I blew it, trying to be funny. And now she isn't going to answer the question." After what seemed like a long time of her strumming and both of us sitting in silence, she began to talk. "From the heavens receivers are easy to spot. They have a cone of light coming from the top of their heads. The widest part of the cone is on top . . . and it narrows down as it comes into the top of the head. Dark or trouble making spirits can never connect through this cone of light." She had continued to strum on her ukulele softly, as she talked. "Sometimes you may hear a high pitched tone in one of your ears, too." At this point she struck a high-pitched note on her ukulele, for emphasis. "Sometimes that means someone is trying to get your attention, and you should listen. Or maybe something is wrong with your ears!" she said, giving me a stern look, over the top of her glasses, with one eyebrow arched.

"Sometimes you feel energy or tingling coming into the top of your head." I knew what she was talking about, as I call it a "light shower." Auntie Fern continued, "You might even jump when that *puka* (hole or opening) is first being opened. Some people never feel any 'presshah,' as their *puka* is already open. My daughtah, Aka, is wide open." She made a gesture with her arms spread out wide. She laughed and said, "Sometimes the *tutus* are standing in line to talk to her. But she knows how to open and close the *puka*. You have to be *akamai* (smart) about when to open the door and when to close the door."

I could tell that this conversation was over, as Auntie Fern turned her attention to her little dog, Pule, who was running in circles around her and looking for attention. She opened a bottle of water and began to drink, and she offered one to me. Then she put some water in a little bowl for Pule too. I thanked her, and she said with a stern look, "Now, you be careful!"

I thought that maybe she found me annoying at times. She said she would help me with being a "receiver," and she did. Many times when I visited her in past years, she shared a little at a time about it. I was reassured, over the years, as our friendship endured. You had to be really respectful of Auntie Fern, or she would either ignore you or get very serious and stern with you. And then again there was her smiling face, her laughter, and her strumming and singing. She was full of *mana* and full of *Aloha*. Her own *ohana* was the recipient of her greatest love and devotion. But with those loved ones, she was strict. She had to be tough, to make spirit warriors out of them.

### *Dolphin Card Readings*

I WAS HOME ALONE RELISHING some quiet time and reading. I sat on the lanai looking down at Kealakekua Bay and wondered how the dolphins were doing today. Rinko was off with her Japanese girl-friends, and Bill was taking one of his young clients surfing. I thought that winning a troubled teen-aged boy's trust, on surfboards, was a wonderful way to begin therapy. Bill was intuitive and innovative as a therapist. Most of all, he was compassionate. Rinko had asked me if she could bring her Japanese girlfriends over for Dolphin Card Readings sometime soon, and I said, "Yes!" Her English was quite good and she would be the translator.

I had done Dolphin card readings recently at the Avocado Festival which was held in the Amy Greenwell Ethno-Botanical Gardens. My table was right behind Auntie Fern's booth, where she was selling jewelry with her daughter, Kalehua. She often looked

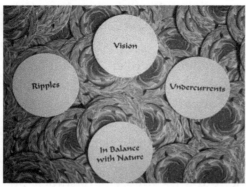

back at me with a big smile as she saw that I was busy doing readings. These were "cold" readings, as I didn't know the people who sat down at my table.

Things just "came to me" and I had learned to trust that they would turn out to be accurate. I felt a kind of joyful, detached energy when I was doing readings, and I finally came to understand that something else happened when I was in this setting. For one, my heart opened to the person sitting across from me. Then some kind of clairvoyance switched on. I guess this is me being "a receiver." My unspoken wish and prayer was always to be able to help and uplift the person. It was gratifying for me to see people walk away with a smile and a positive "aha" for their life. Best of all, Aka's sister Kalehua sat down with me for a reading. Things just came to me in a rush, along with a tingling feeling on the top of my head. Auntie Fern turned around from her jewelry table and smiled. I knew "they" were perching on my head, and Auntie Fern knew it too. The things that were said to Kalehua seemed to ring true to her and added to her understanding of a situation in her life. I found out later that Auntie Fern had been the one who encouraged her daughter to sit down with me for a reading.

Japanese girls would frequently approach me at the beach for dolphin card readings too. Most of them didn't know me but had heard that I had created the cards and the *Guidebook*. It was fun to interact with them, and they always wanted to know why the cards

BILL, NANCY, ANDRE, RINKO

and book had not been translated into Japanese and sold in Japan. They were translated into three other languages, but not Japanese (as yet!). Rinko's friends often came over to the house, and Bill and I enjoyed having them visit. Sometimes we all cooked dinner together. Bill and I are big fans of Japanese food and especially homemade *sushi*. Sometimes we would be joined by Mike Tomson, from back home, and his new sweetheart, Jeannette. I had my massage table set up in my room, and if someone was hurting, I would just have them get up on the table for a mini *lomi*. I can remember one time when Mike hurt his neck and I was able to relieve his pain. One time both Jeannette and I teamed up and both massaged Mike. Silently I thanked Kumu Dane Silva, as I learned a lot from him about how to treat neck problems when he relieved me of my stiff neck, months earlier. Rinko and I had become good friends already, and somehow we always ended up laughing together. She had such a delightful sense of humor. Because of that humor I planned to play a harmless, but fun, practical joke on her and her friends.

### A Fun Ceremony

WHEN MY ROOMMATE RINKO BROUGHT A GROUP of her Japanese lady friends over to visit, they had asked me if I had experienced a Japanese Tea Ceremony. I told them that I had. Feeling some mischief coming on, I told them that we had a tradition at home that was not exactly a tea ceremony, but it was a "graham cracker and milk ceremony." They were all curious and begged me to introduce them to it.

So one day I bought graham crackers and milk and had Rinko invite her friends over to our house. There were about five Japanese girls. I told them that they would each be given a glass of milk and a package of graham crackers, and it would be a dipping contest. Four graham crackers, held together, would be dipped into the glass of milk to get soggy and then quickly taken out, and eaten, before they broke off and fell into the milk. This was a little tradition that our family had at home. One of us would always lose their crackers into the milk. It was usually me. But Paul never did. To my amazement these girls got the hang of it right away and not one of them lost their crackers in the milk. We all had a good laugh while doing this, and it seems that no one in the group was lactose intolerant. What made me laugh the most was that they wondered if they could find graham crackers to buy in Japan. They wanted to have their friends at home try it.

## Sympathetic Joy

ONE DAY IN THE LATE AFTERNOON Mike Tomson called me from a restaurant in Kailua Kona. He reported to me that he and Jeanette were eating wonderful platters of *sushi*. He described the deliciousness of each type of *sushi* roll. In the past I would have been a little annoyed, thinking that I was being teased with something that I loved, but was not being offered. Later he told me that he wasn't teasing but just sharing. Then suddenly, before I could even get a little envious or annoyed, I remembered the Buddhist teaching of "Sympathetic Joy." This is an attitude or feeling of genuinely delighting in the happiness or good fortune of others. And the emphasis is on "genuinely." It also helps us let go of the "me, my" grasping of our own ego, and the wish to have something for ourselves that someone else has. I found that I had sincerely felt happy for them. My craving for *sushi* had gone away almost immediately. I basked in a happy feeling about their relationship and their wonderful *sushi* dinner.

After we hung up from this phone call, there was a knock at the door. I opened the door and it was the Japanese woman who lived next door. She had never visited before, but we had waved to each other when we were out in our yards. She was holding a large platter of assorted *sushi*. She said, "I just had relatives over today and I had all this *sushi* left over and hoped you might like it. I made it all myself." "Oh, yes," I said, "I love *sushi*. Thank you so much. I will surely enjoy it." There was enough to save some for Bill and Rinko. She gave me the platter and excused herself, saying that she had to clean up from her party. I laughed to myself at this harmony and was once again amazed at how the universe works.

## Another Harmony

THE JEEP WOULDN'T START ONE MORNING. It had gas. The battery was charged, clean and hooked up, but it just wouldn't turn over. Instead of getting frustrated I decided to sit on the *lanai* (porch), meditate, and generate the feelings that the problem was already fixed. This visualization did not include taking the car to the shop and having a big bill. As I sat on the *lanai*, a car pulled into our driveway. Out popped a friend named Terry. I enjoyed talking with him down at K Bay from time to time. His sudden appearance was a surprise. He said, "Wow, so this is where you live. I recognized your jeep parked in the front of the house. I've never driven down this street before. Actually I was wondering why I was driving down a street with such a steep hill. What a coincidence!" he said.

He came up on the *lanai* and joined Rinko and I. We offered him coffee and we three chatted for a while. Terry admired the view of the bay, so far below us, from this high perch. Well, the other coincidence is that Terry is a mechanic. He offered to look under the hood of the Jeep, and within a few minutes the jeep started up and was running just fine. I don't remember just what he did, but he was an "angel in skin" for me on this morning. I thanked him profusely and offered him some cash, but he refused. "It was my good deed for the day. I try to do at least one a day," he said. "Thank you, Terry! I will always remember your kindness and your good deeds."

### A Tiger Shark as a Family Aumakua

IN TRADITIONAL HAWAI'IAN FAMILIES there are *Aumakuas*, ancestral clans or spirit animal guardians, much like the traditional Native American, totem animal, spirit helper, tradition. Some people say the *Aumakua* is the higher self. One family that I met had the *manu* (Tiger Shark) as their *Aumakua*. A young girl in this family was gifted as a shark communicator. She had certain methods of calling a particular tiger shark. It would come to her into the waters of a shallow cove. Then the whole family would walk into the water and remove barnacles from the shark's body. The family member who described this to me said it was "shark *Lomilomi*," and apparently the shark loved it. I never saw this ritual myself, but these were honest people. They just never wanted any "on lookers" coming to the cove to watch, and for this reason, I honor their privacy. I thought to myself, a pig that gave *lomilomi* massage and a shark that received *lomilomi* massage. Only in Hawai'i.

## Looking for Auntie Margaret in Ke'ei with Mariah Dodd

KE'EI IS THE LITTLE FISHING VILLAGE where Auntie Margaret and her husband Dan Machado lived. Auntie Margaret was world famous as a teacher of Lomilomi massage and the healing arts. Aspiring healers from all over the world came to Hawai'i to take her training. Two quotes from Auntie Margaret that I had always loved are, "I just love the person and God does the rest. Lomilomi is a praying work." She also has said, "Lomilomi is the spirit of Aloha flowing through the one that gives and the one that receives."

During her lifetime she was given the honor of being named a National Living Treasure for her contribution in the field of Hawai'ian *Lomilomi* massage and healing. Ke'ei is on the south side of Kealakekua Bay and is rather forbidding to tourists . . . as a four-wheel drive vehicle is needed for the bumpy, rutted road. Many of the locals in this little village and their ancestors have lived there for a number of generations and they prefer their privacy. However, if one is unobtrusive and respectful, it is just fine to visit the beach and shoreline there. It is a rather rocky shoreline with a little beach, but the view is beautiful, out over the ocean. Taking a short walk to the south, one passes a big covered structure. I believe that it was used either by the Boy Scouts or the Y.M.C.A. Walking farther to the ocean on the north side of the village is an ocean pond that is walled off by rock walls like a swimming pool with waves tumbling over the top of the walls. I never did find out what this pool was for, or why or when it was built. I could not figure out if it was very old or relatively new, or why there were small circular holes drilled into the lava stone around the edges of it. I would like to know more about this. I wondered if there was an awning put up over this pool of ocean water.

Auntie Margaret's classes focused on the teaching of *Lomilomi* massage and, most importantly, how the practitioner is to massage the body with unconditional love. But in addition to the massage training, Auntie Margaret was famous for guiding her students to do the salt water cleanse. "The Cleanse" included drinking diluted ocean salt water and almost no food. Everyone at Auntie's classes would have their own bucket for elimination. "The Cleanse" was geared to clean out old debris from the intestinal tract, which was based on the belief that most illnesses start in the intestines. People claimed to feel rejuvenated and energized after this "clean out" that could last anywhere from three to ten days. There is also a steam room in Auntie's backyard which was a preliminary to giving or receiving massage. Auntie Angeline, on the island of Kau'ai, had a steam room too. The steam was neither too cold or too hot but just temperate.

Mariah and I went to Ke'ei hoping to see Auntie Margaret and take a steam bath. But after going to the door of her house we found out that she wasn't home and that the steam room wasn't open for visitors either. I had spoken to Auntie on the phone, but I had not been able to take her classes. She had had an accident boarding an airplane which left her with lifelong injuries. But the injuries never stopped her from teaching. So Mariah and I went to the little patch of beach across from Auntie's house. We waded out in the water and sat in the tide pools, making sure not to sit on, or step on, any sea urchins, as they have long, sharp spikes. One time with Aka's sister, Kalehua, I accidentally stepped on a sea urchin while swimming with her at Spencer Beach. The sting was very painful. Kalehua told me to *shishi* (pee) on the puncture and the pain would go away. And like many folk medicine remedies, it worked.

This beach was rocky if you were going to get into the water to snorkel, but I heard that the snorkeling was good. However, if the water was choppy, it could be a little difficult to get out. But this was one of those relaxing afternoons in which we just chatted lazily, about relationships, children, and our spiritual paths, and then drifted off into dreamy reveries. From time to time we went in and out of the water to cool off from the warm sun. Tall coconut palms, set back a little way from the beach, waved their fronds gracefully in the warm afternoon breezes. What a quiet place. There was almost no one around, but a few children playing in the water with their dog and two old men, out near Limukoko point, who were fishing from the shoreline. Mariah had lived on this island for a while now. She had ended her marriage not long before, but was not disabled by it. If anything, she seemed relaxed and empowered. She is a beautiful, talented woman who, as a former mainlander, had the deep bronze tan of a local. It was easy and enjoyable to talk to her and to hear her life story. I was grateful for women friends who were willing to share their journey of self-discovery with me. I realized that many women who were between fifty and sixty years old were becoming ripe with experience and wisdom.

### Uncle Abel and Uncle Moses

I HAD HEARD ABOUT THE ICONIC UNCLES for a long time, from both Aka and her mother, Auntie Fern. Uncle Abel Simeona and Uncle Moses were legendary on this island and were known as healers, musicians and activists in the Hawai'ian Sovereignty movement. Uncle Moses lived in South Kona. The two uncles were older men, and Aka's mother Auntie Fern showed me a photo of her singing with them. Uncle Abel dressed in a *lava lava* wrapped around his waist and was either bare-chested or had a T-shirt on top. This thin elder had long flowing grey hair, a grey beard, and flashing eyes that could be angry or soft and kind. Uncle Abel spent a lot of time on his land which was near the Black Sands Beach of Punalu'u. When the government tried to take his land away, he waged a peaceful but powerful protest which claimed his sovereignty rights. He had posters and signs, and crowds of protesters gathered when the government officials tried to tag his land.

He said he had the names of all of the individuals who lived in this *Alapu'aha* (ancient district) and that all of them had families that had lived there for generations. Therefore, there was no way that Uncle Abel, his neighbors and followers were going to give up their land that bureaucrats of the state of Hawai'i wanted for their own purposes.

"There is no way that you are going home to California without first meeting my two uncles . . . Uncle Abel and Uncle Moses," Aka said to me one day. So we set off in the jeep for another excursion. We stopped in Na'alehu for coffee and had a conversation about some of the *kapus* in the old culture. "Men and women were not allowed to eat together," Aka said. "And during the Mahahiki season, the royalty walked around the whole island on the King's Trail going clockwise. They started and finished this procession at

469

Hikiau Heiau. They felt that the right side of their body should always be facing the mountains. Commoners were never to cast their shadow on royalty or *Ali'i*. That was a major *kapu* and could be punished by death. Protocols were very, very important in the old culture," Aka said.

I wondered if it was thought that a shadow carried a vibration that a person of a lower class could hurt the *mana* of the *Ali'i nui*? After finishing our coffee, we drove on and found the two uncles in Whittington Beach Park, not far from South Point. The park was pretty with lawns and picnic tables close to a pond and a beach on the shoreline. Most tourists passed by the exit to this park, so it was a nice, quiet place for the uncles to "hang out." We had brought a picnic to share with them. There were hugs and *honis* (nose to nose, sharing breath) when we met them, followed by the picnic. I wondered if Uncle Abel got enough to eat. Unlike many Hawai'ians, he was very thin. Uncle Moses was quieter and a little heavier. He had a mysterious presence, as if he were hiding his power, so that it would not be noticed. But when the ukuleles came out and they started singing harmonies, Aka joined in and it was a choir of wonderful Hawai'ian *meles* (songs). Together their music was pure joy, and I was so grateful that Aka had taken me to meet them and to hear their wonderful singing.

### Aka's "Downloads" Give Me a Silent Confirmation

WE LEFT THE PARK and began heading back to Kona. As we approached the exit to South Point, Aka asked me if I had time to take a side trip. "Of course, I am free today to do whatever," I said. Aka laughed and said, "I never go anywhere I don't want to go. I give up my power if I do anything I don't want to do. When I leave home, I put my feet on the Earth and say, how can I help today?" So off we went down the bumpy road to South Point, passing the giant row of wind-farm towers. Once we were on the shoreline, we blew our *pu*'s and chanted a chant that Aka had taught me. Feeling very still inside, I felt Aka was about to share something very important.

She began talking about the ancient continent of Mu and how we were standing on a remnant of it right now. "So much of it is

470

under the ocean and yet to be discovered," Aka said. "You and I were together here on Mu, so very long ago. There were even dragons that flew around Mu blessing the land. Very few people would even believe any of this. But I know you can." She looked at me with a long, knowing look. Now I would be going home with a confirmation of what seemed so hard to believe, even after having the experience. However, it took several more years before I was to tell her about the experience that Douglas and I had with the White Dragon. He and I had agreed to keep it a secret for a while.

Aka continued, "When the waters started rising fifty to eighty thousand years ago, our people left in huge waves of migration from the motherland of Mu. We originally came from the stars. We had our covenants and agreements. I am so honored to stand here today as a descendant of families who were left behind, who never made the migration. We still live on what are the remnants of Mu, these Hawai'ian islands.

"You have been brought back here, Nancy, as your soul was once here, long ago. This is the beginning of the red road. This is Kane. This is Pele. This is Hina, grandmother moon. There were grids that existed here, as it was an advanced high-tech society that pre-dated the ancient continent of Atlantis. This knowledge has been passed down through stories and chants for thousands of years from one generation to another. This continent of Lemuria was called Mu or Mo'o. There were even good dragons on Mu and now their only visible remnants are the tiny dragon-like lizards that we call *mo'o* or geckos. Those little lizards that we see today are what we have to remind us of the mighty blessing dragons of old.

"People like you and I, Nancy, are human lightning rods and body dowsers. Ley lines and vortexes have a powerful effect on our human consciousness. Our bodies can find and recognize these special places. We get a current through our bodies or we get a downloading or downfusing from the celestials. Or we may get that tingling in our body that I call chicken skin and you call goose bumps. Our bodies find things and places that we need to find, and we recognize the power spots or the people that we are meant to meet. Partly it is the awakened fire within that rises up from our body and lights it up with spiritual light. Our *kahuna nui* knew about the secrets of this energy. It was used to heal and to give wise counsel.

"But if the motivation was dark, this same energy could be used to hurt. We called people like this *'ana ana'* practitioners. They could literally pray someone to death. I actually saw this happen to someone when I was very young. This is the misuse of a God-given gift. In our tradition, the one learning from the *kupunas* and *kahunas* are watched carefully, and they don't receive the teachings if their motivations are selfish or mean.

"In the ancient times of Lemuria, people could shift from a physical body to a light, vibrational body, just like the dragons and other wonderful creatures," Aka said. "Some of the star beings as well as their ships are able to make these shifts too. There are portals in various places on the Earth where our galactic visitors can shift in and out of what we call physical reality. Kealakekua Bay is one of these portals. I have seen the ships there many times. They have connections with the dolphins and whales too.

"When I told you that 'this' was your home, I was not referring to Hawai'i today, but to the older continent of Mu. We are in for a change in the coming years, and sometimes change is uncomfortable. We need to get ready for more big changes. Our bodies are being adjusted to receive more. We are all getting pumped out. We have to clean out the cobwebs. We are like babies being squeezed out of the womb and birth canal . . . out of the darkness of our Mama's bellies, into the light. We will all need to step out of our comfort zones. My wing span keeps expanding, and so can yours, as we enter the space as butterflies."

Aka continued this serious talk without a bit of pidgin English. "Love, peace and harmony prevailed on Mu. We could live that way now, but so many people are bonded to negativity. I am here with a *kuleana* (spiritual responsibility) to teach these things. That is the goal of Ho'o'ponopono. I was born to help heal the pain that people carry inside that keeps them from being able to love and live Aloha."

I listened carefully. A place within me that always wondered, now felt a silent confirmation. I had never mentioned the experience with the White Dragon to anyone, and I didn't tell Aka for several more years. But somehow I felt that she already knew.

## A Healing Ritual Led by Uncle Abel

I CANNOT FAIL TO OMIT A MOST EXTRAORDINARY experience that we had with Uncle Abel. I am choosing to go out of order here, and recount something that actually happened in 2012. It is the only time that I jump ahead in this diary. A group of Aka's European and Japanese friends came to the Big Island to participate in a retreat with Aka. I seem to recall that there were twenty people or more. One day, Aka announced that we would have a special guest. It turned out to be no other than Uncle Abel. The retreat was held at Ahhh Paradise, a wonderful inn located on a beautiful fruit and coffee farm near Middle Ke'ei and Painted Church Roads. Our host, Miles Mulcahy, later became a good friend. I had seen both Uncle Abel's angry, flashing eyes and strong rhetoric in a stand-off with officials of the state of Hawai'i, and I had seen him singing soft and passionate Hawai'ian songs.

But I could never have anticipated the way he manifested himself in a situation which called for  healing. Uncle Abel came to the group to speak about healing and Hawai'ian herbs. After speaking for a while, he became aware that a young Japanese man in the group was suffering from the pain of advanced cancer. His wife had brought him to the Big Island from Japan, seeking healing.

Uncle Abel spontaneously decided that we would do a group healing for this man. He arranged everyone in a long line. Each person had their right hand on the right shoulder of the person in front of them. We were to generate prayers, healing energy, and love inside of ourselves to send up the line to the sick man. Uncle Abel placed himself at the very back end of the line. The person in the front of the line had their hand on the man seeking healing.

Then Uncle Abel began a long and profound Hawai'ian healing prayer and chant as he generated healing energy that passed through everybody in the line and ended, eventually, with the man. His chanting voice was deep and powerful! The energy that was passing through all of us was so strong that it almost made us fall over. Each one of us tried to do our part in this group healing, generating healing energy and Aloha. The Japanese man said he felt it very strongly, and when the healing was over, he lay down in a pile of big pillows that were on the floor. He felt very weak but happy, and he said the pain was gone.

We found out later that his late stage cancer had been healed and that there were a few years that he was completely cancer free. A few years later I heard that the cancer had come back and he passed away. The blessing of this healing gave him a life extension. Uncle Abel was more than an activist, a cultural expert, and a musician. He was also a healer, and he allowed all of us to participate in the healing.

### A Big Island Camping Trip

AKA AND HER FAMILY WERE PLANNING a camping trip near Ke'ei, on a bluff over the water. I felt very happy to be invited to what would turn out to be a very large group of grandmas, aunties, uncles and many nieces, nephews and cousins. I believe there were over fifty people there, and I had never met most of them before. I knew Aka's mother, sisters and children, but the others were new to me. Aka and Auntie Fern introduced me to a lot of them and then, as there was so much going on, I was left to introduce myself to the rest of the family.

When I was young, we had been on a lot of camping trips with my parents and my brother, Scott, and my sister Lacey. Our sister Debbie was born later, when I was sixteen. Our parents took us to Yosemite, Lake Tahoe, Echo Lake, and the Desolation Wilderness many times. We camped in our big old Army tent, and we kids learned to hike with a backpack on our backs and fish for trout. Our dad bought each of us our own fishing pole, reel, and spool of line.

He gave us Panther Martin lures, and, oh yes, the floats and sinkers too. But I had never gone camping in the tropics with a big family like Aka's *ohana*.

When I got there, I parked and carried my coconut cream cake to the area where the family was placing all the food. The men and some of the boys were fishing from the edge of the bluff. Sometimes when a big wave rolled in, it would splash up high, reaching the top of the lava bluff and get them wet. But they didn't care, as they were having so much fun. I noticed that they kept fishing after the sun set, after dusk, and into the night. The sound of the surf was ever present, beating out a strong rhythm on the rocks, rolling in and then pulling back out . . . to repeat this rhythm, over and over. There is something so soothing about the rhythm of the waves.

There were loud shouts of excitement each time one of the men yelled out "fish on." After they "got one," they put it into one of the many buckets. Some of the relatives were building a big campfire when I arrived. They had gathered wood and surrounded the fire with large rocks. There was a kind of flat lava platform of the smooth *pahoe hoe* (smooth rippled, ropelike) lava. I watched as the teen-agers, children and adults laid out their blankets, pillows and quilts.

By the time everyone was done with the blankets, there was no lava left to be seen, but only a massive patch work of blankets and quilts that covered every square inch. I laid out my sleeping bag and pillow too, as we all wanted this to be done before dark. The teen-agers were grouped together, dozens of cousins, chattering and giggling the way teen-agers do. Some of these relatives hadn't seen each other for a long time. But there was no lack of talking, laughing and story-telling. Grandma Fern or Auntie Fern, as I call her, was strumming her

COUSIN PUNA KIHOI AND AUNTIE FERN

475

ukulele and singing songs. I never tired of hearing her sing her large repertoire of Hawai'ian songs. I imagined that she might think of her husband, Mahoe, sometimes, because earlier in life, they were both entertainers in the hotels for *luaus* and special events. He had passed away quite a long time ago, but I felt sure that she missed him.

I always admire the talent in this family. Aka joined in, singing with her beautiful voice. There were many more musicians in this group. Some of the fishermen morphed into singers and guitar players later in the evening. Aka told me that almost every Hawai'ian is musical in some way, shape, or form. Music is key to the culture and so is story-telling, which is called *mo'olelo*.

Someone asked if Uncle Abel Simeona and Uncle Moses would be coming. Unfortunately, the two elders could not come this time. I would have liked to hear them sing and play with Auntie Fern.

When Auntie Fern took a rest from singing and strumming, she motioned for me to come over to sit with her. I perched myself on a large rock. "I read your book, you know," she said. She was referring to *A Guide to the Dolphin Divination Cards*. "Yes, I read it all the way through, every page." I was surprised and had even

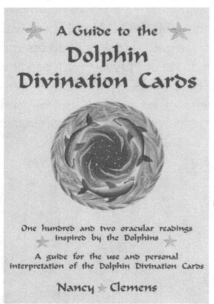

One hundred and two oracular readings inspired by the Dolphins

A guide for the use and personal interpretation of the Dolphin Divination Cards

Nancy ✷ Clemens

forgotten that I had given her a deck of the cards and the book a few weeks before. "You know, I really liked it," she said. "Oh, thank you, Auntie, that means a great deal to me, especially coming from you," I said.

I told her that I was going to turn my Hawai'i diary from this year into a book someday. I asked her, "Do you mind if I include you in my book? I may also come out with a second edition of *A Guide to the Dolphin Divination Cards*. I would like to include you and Aka in those books. I will send you

copies of the parts where I mention you. That way you can decide if you want those parts included or changed in some way."

She said emphatically, "Oh no, that will not be necessary. You can write anything you want about me. I don't need to see it ahead of time. I totally trust whatever you write about me." Aka was standing there listening to our conversation and she added, "The same goes for me, sistah. You just write it."

"Can I say that you have done a lot of genealogy?" I asked Auntie Fern. "Of course, Auntie." You should learn to do the genealogy of your own family." "I will, when I get home," I said. She had suggested this to me several times during this year. I don't think she had ever called me "auntie" before. It sounded nice.

A little later in the evening Auntie Fern started talking about her own genealogy research, sharing it with some of the children and teenagers. I pulled my sleeping bag up next to the fire to listen to the story of so many generations of Hawai'ians. I learned that the family was descended from Prince Kuhio, and that on the Pule side of the family they were related to King Kamehameha the First. Aka had shared a lot of this with me earlier, but Auntie went into much more detail. There were ancestors from the northwest Native American tribes near Seattle, and even a Scandinavian ancestor was in the mix. By now there was a large group listening to Auntie Fern's stories of ancestors and historical lore.

At a later date Aka's older sister, Kela, told me of a time in the mid-seventies when their father, Mahoe William Pule, had been chosen as *mo'i* (king) for Aloha Week in Oahu. He reigned for a whole year. There was a ceremony and he had a court with a Queen and princes and princesses and Kahili bearers. He wore the cape and the large curved hat on his head, looking so much like King Kamehameha the First. A new Aloha Week court was chosen each year.

MAHOE PULE

Aka joined in and spoke about what she had learned from her maternal grandmother, Matilda Makekau, and her great grandmother and aunties (Auntie Helen and Auntie Rosalie) who had lived in both Oahu, Molokai, and Napo'opo'o village, so very close to Kealakekua Bay and the Hikiau Heiau. Aka said, "I learned Ho'o'ponpono from them and I attended many sessions, which are honored with the greatest confidentiality. These ceremonies are all about making everything *pono* (right) with ourselves, others, the spiritual world and *Ke Akua*." She made a point to say it went way beyond mediation. She continued, "It is a spiritual process to bring things back to love, peace, and harmony between people or families at odds with each other. It restores balance and goodness. Each session begins with a prayer and an invocation to the ancestors and to God. A true practitioner must be apprenticed to older and experienced spiritual practitioners for a long time. Just as people can't become an 'instant coffee' medicine man, no one can take a seminar or read a book and then set themselves up as a practitioner of Ho'o'ponopono. This is not the authentic way. The practice becomes diluted or altered if people do this. It is a very long process of spiritual purification, and readiness by birth, that qualifies a practitioner of Ho'o'ponopono. It has a lot to do with being connected to the blessings that come from the ancestors and those 'upstairs'." I saw some of the young people listening attentively. Maybe a few of them would later ask Aka to train them someday.

Before Captain Cook's arrival, some of their ancestors had lived in this village which was only a few yards back from the beach at Kealakekua Bay. It had been one of the largest villages on the island, and had a famous fish pond where fish were raised for food. Members of the royal family and *Ali'i* (aristocratic people) lived here, as well as common people. King Kamehameha I was young at the time, but he was there on the beach with the villagers when Captain Cook first arrived.

Today the beach of Kealakekua Bay is filled with large boulders, and it takes some nimble footwork to walk over them before getting into the water. But when Aka was a child, it was a beach of sand which was in front of and facing the side of their family *heiau*. Hikiau Heiau is a tall, rectangular platform temple of carefully placed lava rocks. I believe I remember Aka saying that this temple of stone was at least one thousand years old. It is possible that it was re-built in the 1700s. Auntie Fern and family members had done repairs on the *heiau* some years before, lifting heavy rocks back into place. The family had continued to do traditional seasonal ceremonies on top of the Heiau wearing flower leis and ceremonial garb. Conch shells and *pu*'s were blown to open the ceremonies.

Hikiau Heiau is dedicated to the God Lono, the God of nature, fertility, agriculture, rain, and peace. Lono also reigned over the several winter months of the *Mahahiki* season. When the rising of the *Makali'i* (the Pleiades star cluster) in the east syncs with the setting sun in the west, it signals the beginning of the Hawaiian new year and the *Mahahiki* season. The circumambulation of the island that took place at the opening of the Makahiki season began and ended at Hikiau Heiau. This season lasted for about four months and traditionally was a time of feasting, music, dancing, games, sports, and relaxation. Large work projects ceased. When Captain Cook sailed his schooner into Kealakekua Bay in January, 1778, the *Mahahiki* season was in full swing. The Native Hawai'ians thought that he was the legendary, red-headed God, Lono, as some say that Captain Cook had red hair. The white rectangular sails of his schooner looked like the rectangular white Lono banner, which was carried at the front of a procession that circled the island on the King's Trail.

The villagers welcomed Captain Cook and his crew with feasts, provisions, and great hospitality. Before long some of the women developed syphilis and other venereal diseases that they contracted from the sailors. The crew did some other disrespectful things and broke local *kapu*s. The chiefs and local population became angry. The final straw occurred when Captain Cook attempted to kidnap  Kalani'opu'u, the ruling chief of the Island of Hawai'i. It was the year 1779 when the loyal subjects of the chief killed Captain Cook.

Today, there is a white obelisk monument on the west side of Kealakekua Bay which is the alleged spot where Captain Cook was killed. The Ka'awaloa hiking trail goes from up high on Na'apo'po road all the way down to the monument. It is about four miles both ways. Many people love this hike. After hiking downhill to the bay, people often enjoy a refreshing swim and excellent snorkeling. The uphill hike is hot and challenging and requires lots of drinking water!

Captain Cook's visit was the first visit from the outside "civilized" world. Before long, many sailing ships came to all of the Hawai'ian islands. Diseases, that the Hawai'ian people had never known, wiped out a huge number of the Native population. Smallpox, cholera, leprosy, and all the venereal diseases were responsible for thousands of deaths of the *kanaka* (the people) all across the islands. Leprosy (Hansen's disease) was brought to the islands in the 1850s and was widespread just ten years later.

Father Damian, a Roman Catholic priest, founded and tended a leper colony on the island of Molokai. In the 1800s, the crews of the sailing ships brought mumps, measles, and whooping cough to the native population. The Hawai'ians had never had these European diseases before, so they had no immunity to them.

A great deal of history has taken place at the site of this *heiau* and old village site, Luali'iloa (the ancient Ali'i fishpond), and Kealakekua Bay. Today, there is only the slightest marshy remnant of this beautiful fish pond and the once clear, white sand beach is covered with lava boulders. Kamehameha I had a thatched *hale* in a row of houses that belonged to other chiefs and members of the royal family. Their homes were behind the fishpond. Later when the Greenwell family transported their cattle out of Kealakekua Bay by ship, the cattle used the fishpond for a watering hole and further damaged it. There has been recent talk about restoring this Ali'i fish pond to its former use and beauty, but I wonder if it will ever happen. Maybe someday this beautiful beach will be clear of boulders again. A tidal wave brought them in, and someday another tidal wave could take them out. Sitting at this place, as I often did, I found it amazing to visualize and contemplate the daily village life and the adventures of these ancient peoples.

"Sailors" was a word that came to my mind. Once the sailing vessels started coming, the bloodlines of native Hawai'ians started getting mixed with the Europeans and the Asians. People who lived in the Azores islands, off the coast of Portugal, sailed around the horn of South America to immigrate to Hawai'i. After these ships refueled supplies and water in Peru, the ships would set sail for the Big Island. Many of these islanders from the Azores and Portugal arrived in the late 1800s and settled on the Hamakua Coast. They brought farming, ranching skills, and the slack key guitar. It has been said that many of the Portuguese immigrants worked in the sugar industry, and that some of them were put in managerial positions and often were in charge of the Asians who worked in the fields and mills.

We all began talking about the Paniolo culture. It began with several Spanish-Mexican and Portuguese cowboys who came to the islands. They were invited to teach the Hawai'ians how to raise cattle, as well as develop riding and roping skills. The Paniolo culture is also renowned for its music. The slack key guitar developed when the foreign cowboys came to Hawai'i. Over a period of time Hawai'ian Paniolo songs have become famous. Many Paniolos have a voice and a guitar in addition to their horse, riding, and roping skills. Music and grub around a campfire was often what happened at the end of a hard riding day.

Everyone around our campfire chimed in, singing a few of the old Paniolo songs. Aka's large *ohana* and I were all around a beautiful campfire and had our bedrolls laid out, but the horses were missing. When the Portuguese came, they not only contributed to the Paniolo culture of cowboys and cattle ranching, but they brought their delicious doughnut-like *malasadas* and Portuguese sausages.

Soon some of the teen-agers began to share about the voyaging canoes. Some of the young people had training on the replica voyaging canoe, Makali'i, which literally means "little eyes" and refers to the star cluster, Pleiades. They shared what it was like for them to learn about the star compass, and the exercise of mapping out the stars in the sand on the beach, and then later to have the excitement of sailing up and down the western coastline of the Big Island. Since they were fledgling sailors, accompanied by older, more experienced sailors, the double-hulled sailing canoe didn't venture far from the coast.

481

Ordinarily the Makali'i was docked in Kawaihae and they would sail from there, down the west coast to Miloli'i, and then back again to dock at Kawaihae. Each student kept a log of what they

THE HOKULE'A ARRIVING IN TAHITI

learned about voyaging and the times they spent sailing. A student who had already completed the program would become a personal mentor to a new student entering the program. I remembered reading the book about the *Kon Tiki* by Thor Heyerdahl when I was a teen-ager. His raft traveled from Peru to the Polynesias in his attempt to prove that ancient peoples had long-distance ocean travel. Even then I thought there were missing pieces to the pan-oceanic travel mystery. How my brother and sisters and I would have loved this kind of learning in our school days. It was great hearing from the Hawai'ian youth about the way their time sailing the Makali'i opened their curiosity about many other aspects of their culture.

Oral history tells that the voyaging canoes of the Hawai'ian islands had reached other continents, including the North American shoreline, long before the arrival of Captain Cook. And it is speculated that some Hawai'ians intermarried with Native American tribes a long time ago. Modern day DNA testing reveals this. Even today there are mixed-race people in California who are descendants from both Hawai'ian and Native American people. In the 1800s, during the California Gold Rush, ships arrived in San Francisco from Hawai'i bringing Hawai'ian men who came to work in the gold fields. Up in the northwest, John Kalama from Maui became a famous jack of all trades who married a Native American woman. Today there is a town in the state of Washington named Kalama. Many descendants of John Kalama honor their mixed-race Hawai'ian/Native American blood.

California has some Hawai'ian place names that go back to these days too, such as Kanaka Creek. Owyhee is a town in northwest Nevada and is the home of Shoshone-Paiute tribes and a reservation called The Duck Valley Indian Reservation. Later, in the history of Hawai'ian immigration, Chinese and Japanese people arrived. Then the Filipino people arrived. These immigrants often worked in the sugar plantations, pineapple fields, mills, and factories.

As it was getting late, some people were getting ready to go to sleep in their bedrolls and blankets. Sticks and small logs were added to the campfire from time to time. There was the soft background sound of giggling and hushed whispers coming from teen-agers sharing secrets with each other, cozy in their bedrolls. One of the aunties said to them as it got later: *"Moe, Moe"* (sleep, sleep).

The stars were bright this night, and I gazed at the twinkling stars, planets, and distant galaxies overhead. How gorgeous this sky is on a dark night and especially to the accompaniment of the waves which were slapping against the rocks below our camp. I thought of the voyagers who depended on the location of stars and constellations to navigate their long-distance, double-hulled canoes. The ancestors did not feel very far away.

The fire felt warm, as the evening cooled off, and I found myself lulled to sleep in the middle of Auntie's Fern's and Aka's talks. The breezes were soft and they kept the fire going, which crackled and hissed each time a breeze swept over it. I half awoke a few times during the latter part of the evening to hear a soft, sweet jam session of Hawai'ian guitars and voices singing. The constellations overhead had changed positions. *Moe, moe,* I thought to myself. Then with the greatest contentment I drifted back to sleep.

### A Morning Talk with Aka

As I WAS WAKING UP IN THE MORNING, Aka asked me, "Did you sleep well, sistah Nancy?" I stretched as I got out of my sleeping bag and told her that I had the best sleep "evah"! We sat down together on rocks while we drank the coffee that she brought over from the make-shift camp kitchen. "I made your coffee just the way you like it," Aka said. The leftovers from dinner were packed in ice chests that were being hauled off to the cars in the parking area. "Sure you're not hungry, sistah? . . . there are lots of grindz left over. I saved you some of my chicken long rice." I laughed and said to her, in her own pidgin, "Dinnah was so ono last night dat it broke dah mouth." When it's really good, it breaks the mouth. It was true! I had one of the sweetest sleeps of my whole life on this camping trip. The true Aloha in this family had filled me, top to bottom, with love and sweetness. I thought to myself, "How kind they had been to invite me, 'on-e *haole'*, the name I sometimes used jokingly to refer to myself." There was always a friendly chuckle or smile when I said that. Hawai'ians seem to love it when people poke fun at themselves.

Aka said, "There are lots of leftovers if you want to take some with you, but your cake is gone." The family was packing up and

getting ready to leave. Some of them would have fish dinners tonight from last night's catch. The *ohana* was saying *Aloha* and *a hui hou* to each other and giving each other those big Hawai'ian hugs that had to "last all day." "*A Hui Hou*, uncle! Aloha, auntie. See you, cuz! Take care, brah"! I loved hearing them speak with a smattering of Hawai'ian and pidgin.

After talking lazily with Aka, as we drank a big cup of pure Kona coffee, she said to me that it was time for me to go home now, like "really home" to California. I asked her why she felt I should leave. I had wanted to stay longer. She said, "Look how you had such a good sleep. Do you know why you cuddled up next to the fire near Ma, and had such a good sleep?" I gave her several reasons. She said, "Yes, all that, but the real reason is that you were surrounded by family, and you really miss that family love that you have back home. They miss you too. It's time now. Ma and I noticed it and we both agree."

Aka paused again to say *"A hui hou"* and to hug some more relatives who were leaving. I wished them a good day also and told them how glad I was to meet them. They smiled back at me and some of them gave me a hug. This Aloha spirit warms the heart.

As they faded into the distance carrying their bedding, coolers, and fish buckets, Aka began talking to me again. "You can come back and visit us and this *aina* anytime you want to, but it is time to go home now." I silently pondered what she had just said, and then said to her, "Okay, I guess you and your Ma are right." I trusted their guidance. But it will be so hard to leave this beautiful *aina* and the people it had birthed.

### A Sweet and Savory Parting Story

ONE DAY SHORTLY BEFORE GOING HOME, Aka suggested that we go on a shopping trip to Kailua Kona. I picked her up and we drove "downtown." After parking we visited some thrift stores and the outdoor market. "No need to buy new. I always find the best clothes in the thrift stores. But you have to wash and purify them all when you get home. You know, dah buggahs. Sometimes I find really awesome vintage shirts. You know da kine, the Aloha shirts with the bamboo buttons. The Aloha shirts have been around for a long time. It's always like a treasure hunt," Aka said.

She and I had already shopped, and we each had a bag of treasures. Later I was curious about the history of the Aloha shirts and it seems the prototype shirt came out in 1932. Others came out in 1936 and were made by the Kahala Shirt Company. Most of the images on those early shirts were hula girls, palm trees and outrigger canoes. Tourists were coming to Honolulu on ships in those days.

At the outdoor market Aka and I bought baby coconuts which were opened for us by the vendor. The coconut water and soft gel-like meat was delicious and refreshing on this warm day. Everywhere we went, people recognized Aka and greeted her with hugs and *honis* or *shakas*.

As we walked by the Hulihe'e Palace on Ali'i drive, Aka asked me if I had ever been inside. I told her that I hadn't. But I had come with friends to a gathering on the lawn outside the palace, which was called *Kona Kai Opua*. Once a month *hula* and *mele* performances took place there. It ended with everyone singing the rousing and emotional Hawai'ian anthem. The palace had been a summer vacation home for King Kalakaua and his family. "The king's family would come here to chillax. Now it's a museum with artifacts and belongings from King Kalakaua and his Queen consort, Kapi'olani. Auntie Io worked here too, back in the day, as a curator. The Koa wood furniture and décor are very Victorian and so beautiful," Aka said.

Makuaikaua Church, the oldest church in all of the Hawai'ian islands, was across the street. I had already visited this old church. Then we walked around in the areas where the tourists usually go, looking at the trinkets, jewelry, and clothing in the little shops.

"Have you ever been to Chubby's?" Aka asked. The name "Chubby's" made me laugh and I thought she was joking. "Oh no," she said, "Ma just loves it and it's a favorite of our family." "What do they have?" I asked. "All *kine*," she said. "They have chicken fried steak with mashed potatoes and gravy, fried chicken, pot roast and best of all is their ox tail soup. It's so *da kine!*" she said licking her lips.

"And they give those 'at home' beeg portions too!" Then she giggled and said, "It's kind of a local secret. Most tourists would have a hard time finding it."

So I drove, while she directed me through a labyrinth of streets in downtown Kailua Kona, until we pulled up in front of a bowling alley. "Chubby's is in here," she said. As we came through the door we were greeted with the loud sounds of arcade games and bowling balls knocking down pins. On one side of the bowling lanes we found the restaurant. We both ordered the ox tail soup. "My grandmother used to make this soup," I said, and this soup is as delicious as hers! Each big bowl was big enough to feed at least two people. Aka wasn't kidding about large portions. What a big lunch, I thought. I told Aka I would need a nap, as I was getting chubbier by the minute. So she suggested we go over to the beach that was next to the King Kamehameha Hotel. Right on the edge of the bay is the Heiau and the traditional thatched *hale* which was the home of King Kamehameha I, his family and retinue.

## *On the King's Beach*

AKA AND I WERE SITTING ON THE BEACH and she said, "Can you go back in time and just imagine what this spot looked like when Kamekameha the Great and his family lived here? Can you see all the *koa* wood canoes that were on the bay?" I told her I could imagine it. She said that was the first step. "If we could just lift all the veils, imagine what we might be able to see. We might be able to see the

HULIHE'E PALACE

king and queen. It's a lot like going back in a time machine. I don't tell many people, but I travel back a lot." Aka sighed and reached out her hands in a greeting to the unseen world.

I remembered a story Kapua had once told me. The Queen Lili'uokalani Canoe Race was started on September 2, 1972. Paddlers would come to compete from all around the world. The long race of eighteen miles went to Pu'uhonua o Honaunau. One year, back in the nineteen seventies or eighties, Tutu Clara Manase prayed over the Keaou Honaunau canoe club and other Big Island teams in this very bay. As the canoes were about to begin their race, someone took a Polaroid picture of her praying over the regatta. A ghost image of Queen Lili'uokalani, the last monarch of the Hawai'ian kingdom, appeared in the picture. I never saw it, but according to Kapua, a lot of people did see it and were amazed. I asked Aka if she had seen the picture. Aka smiled and with a faraway look in her eyes said, "Someday people will be able to lift the veils, and see so much that we ordinarily don't see. This picture and others like it give only a glimpse." She turned towards me with the biggest childlike smile. I felt the *mana* that she shared through her smile, traveling up and down my whole body, like waves of bliss. I was going to miss her.

### Leave Nothing Behind but Footprints

AS I WAS PACKING MY SUITCASE and preparing to go back to California, I surveyed the items I had picked up along the way, and decided to have a "give away." The massage table had already been shipped to California. I took my bamboo bookcase up to Auntie Janice at Super J's. I gave my camping equipment and books to Aka. Some other items were given to Auntie Fern. There were other things too that I gave away, leaving me with just my *pu* and suitcase to take home on the plane. I traveled back in memory to the time that Douglas and I picked up trash at Punalu'u Black Sand Beach in the rain. He mentioned that we had cleaned up the whole beach and *heiau* area so well that all we were leaving behind were our footprints in the sand. And they, too, would be washed away by the rain.

### Behind the Clouds the Sun is Always Shining

AS I THOUGHT ABOUT GOING BACK TO CALIFORNIA, and the journey I had been on for almost a year, I pondered the changes I had been through. While living on the Hilo side, soon after my arrival, I had felt so terribly lonely and uncertain about my relationship back home. There were times when I cried and felt lost. I reviewed my entire life many times, examining influences, trends, and tendencies. On the inner level, I slowly changed. Over these months my true self was gradually revealed to me.

There was a lot of letting go, forgiveness, and just learning to live in the present moment. Influences from childhood and ancestral lines had created overlays that cast shadows over my true Self. When they are observed impartially and gradually let go, we feel more spacious inside. Many obscurations were shed while swimming in the ocean or meditating in nature's beauty. It's no wonder that so many people never really come to know their true essence, because of all the layers and programs, weighing them down. Not everyone has help in the ways that I did. My heart was bursting with gratitude for all the local friends and teachers who gave me their *kokua* (help). What is it to be a "natural human"? I had wondered. This question led me gradually to the discovery of myself as a "natural human." Blessed individuals from indigenous cultures like the Tibetans, Native Americans, and Hawai'ians had been guides.

By sharing this very intimate diary of my year on my own, I hope that others will receive at least a glimmer of the love and inspirations which I was blessed to receive. Oddly enough I felt most like a natural human when I was close to the dolphins and whales, either in or out of the water. I wished to help protect these beautiful sea creatures from the growing impact of humans in their own natural habitat. With some suggestions from Auntie Fern and Aka, I developed a way to commune with them, out of the water, which I came to call "armchair surfing."

I realized that there are many people and props in life that help form our self-image and create our feeling of security, connection, and well-being. Conversely, they can also infuse us with anxiety, resentment, feelings of inferiority, guilt, and insecurity. We are so often defined by being someone's spouse, someone's parent or child, the student or friend of so and so. But who are we when we stand alone?

Our self-image defines us by our work, family, friends, reputation, talents, appearance, home and interests. We rarely realize how much all of these things give us a sense of confidence, security, identity, and belonging. But these very things can layer us in such a way that our true essential nature is hidden, even from ourselves.

The outer world that is ultimately temporary and always changing helps to uphold us and keeps us from thinking about our ultimate destination. As we all have differing belief systems about death, it remains a great mystery. Death can be seen as the shedding of this physical body, to either go on into a next life, to abide in the heavens, or to disappear into oblivion. And then there are those who don't know and don't venture to guess. Our beliefs about death, of either being a continuation or oblivion, depend on beliefs taught by religions, parents, books, or those beliefs we come to on our own.

Some people have had "after-life" experiences while still in their physical bodies. And for those people there is a conviction of an after-life and a continuation of consciousness. As His Holiness the Dalai Lama says, we must all have long-range thinking, in the sense that our actions, our compassion and wisdom, or the lack of same, create the circumstances for the next life.

Our self-image is a security net that holds us and keeps us from falling into uncharted waters. But when we strip all our securities away, we are left with our raw selves, our feelings, our memories, our fears, our ethics and morals, and most of all, our consciousness. Pure consciousness, a tamed ego, compassion and wisdom are the states yogis hope to achieve when they isolate themselves in a remote retreat hut or cave. But I was not a yogi. I was just someone who wanted to make progress on the path and contribute something positive.

It was not easy to be stripped of so much, so abruptly, and by choice. This is what I came to call, "taking it raw," with no drugs or alcohol to soothe these raw feelings, with no family to give love, conversation or daily drama, and only occasional phone calls from family and friends back home.

And at times there had been tears, regrets, and fleeting

feelings of being lost in a vast ocean. There were times, when I first arrived, that I felt like the last survivor on an ocean-going double-hulled canoe, bobbing up and down in the doldrums. But that would change, as everything is always changing. As nature has taught us, behind the clouds the sun is always shining. Clouds and storms pass and the nourishing and warming rays of the sun appear again, and sunbeams stream down upon us, to warm and uplift our spirits.

I was no longer afraid when I went into the no-thing-ness in meditation, or in waking states. It no longer mattered if someone liked me or not, or didn't understand me. Egos are insidious and tricky, but a few of my layers had been shed in humility and tears. I had also been nourished by old and new friends here on the island, and the Aloha they had shared and infused into me. I had come to feel peace and a quiet joy. Hearts, like flowers, can be a bud or in full bloom with love, or at some stage in between. My heart was much more open now than it was when I arrived.

With deep relaxation, an open heart, and a wish for all beings to have peace and happiness, harmonies and synchronicities seemed to be a greater part of everyday life. How grateful I am to have been on this sacred island. This was Kupuna Pele's island, where I had seen her dance in orange light, in her volcanic crater, against a night sky, and where on another day she manifested the most glorious rainbow, arching like a curved multi-colored bridge over her crater. I felt cleansed, peaceful, and happy. Most of all I was so grateful. *Mahalo nui loa!*

The jeep was on its way home now on a Matson's Line ship. It left as it had come. It had allowed me to have many adventures and survived some rough treatment. It circled the island many times and visited the Waipio Valley, the Volcano, and remote beaches. It had transported moving boxes, cleaning supplies, beach gear, and a number of friends.

I had my plane ticket and a ride to the airport. There were gifts in my bags for the family back home. An inter-island flight would take me to Honolulu before boarding a plane to Sacramento. Soon I would be wrapped in Paul's arms and giving big hugs to my children and grandchildren. It was time to say goodbye or *"A Hui hou"* ('til me meet again) to my island friends and to this beautiful *Aina*.

491

By sharing this very intimate diary, I hope that others will receive at least a glimmer and an infusion of the inspirations which I was blessed to receive. As Aka always said to me, "If you receive a blessing, the way of Aloha is to share it, in some way, shape or form." And this is why I decided to finally share *My Holoholo Diary*.

As I climbed the steps of the portable staircase up into the plane, I made one last glance, *mauka*, to the hills above the airport. Dark clouds hung over them. The palm trees at the airport were swaying in the sunshine and breeze. Tears began to roll down my cheeks. As the plane took off, taxiing down the runway, the sun was shrouded by passing clouds. Soon the angle changed, and the sun broke out from behind the clouds and shone brightly on the water below, forming little glints of sparkling light on the whitecaps.

Aka had stood beside me a few moments earlier and had enfolded me in one of her big Aloha hugs, and said, "Don't cry sistah, you will come back, and I will come over to visit you in California too. Think of me when you see 11:11 on your clock. I will be winking at you. When I come to your place, you can take me to all *your* magic spots." She said, "We will have *ohana* all over the world."

And she did come . . . many times over the next twelve years, and she named our land . . . "Mission Aloha, Nevada City."


## EKOLU MEA NUI
### by Robert J.K. Nawahine

| | |
|---|---|
| Ekolu mea nui ma ka honua | Three great things on Earth |
| O ka mana'o 'i' 'o ka mana'o lana | Faith, hope, and love |
| A me ke aloha ke aloha ka i 'oi 'a'e | The greatest is love |
| Pomaika'i na mea apau | All things are blessed |
| Pomaika'i na mea apau | All things are blessed |


## THE END

*A Hui Hou Kakou*
(Until We Meet Again)

# Afterword

AUNTIE AKA ESTABLISHED MISSION ALOHA with the intent of bringing peace to humanity through the ancient practice of Ho'o'ponopono. The focus of Mission Aloha is to share this Hawai'ian wisdom and spread Aloha (love, compassion, kindness, forgiveness and humility) around the world. Ho'o'ponopono is *Akua's la'au* (Father in heaven's medicine). The ability to make all things right, to bring balance and harmony back to share with the world, and with *Akua's* blessing, Mission Aloha began.

A copy of the last letter Aka wrote to me, on May 16, 2014:

*Aloha Nancy…*

*Awesome Sista … I am actually flying in to Cali on the 12-13 (of June) and then leaving out of San Francisco to Italy on the 16-17th … that's a tentative date because I haven't locked in our tickets yet. But that is the plan because we have to be in Sardinia on the 21-22 to do my first wkshop. Then we jump back on the ferry to go to Livorna . . . back to Lucca for a couple days (3) then off to Bled, Slovenia for another wkshop, then off to Graz, Austria for another wkshop, then off to Vienna for another wkshop, then off to the C.J. Jung Institute in Kusnacht, Switzerland (the Gold Coast on Lake Zurich) for a 5 day wkshop, then off to Germany for a Ho'o'ponopono conference. Then down to Lustenau, Austria for my last wkshop … then drive back to Italy for 3 more days and then fly back to Cali first part of August. Can you give me a lomilomi when I get to California? And then leave for Oahu and then, after two days, to speak at the young adults' conference at Brigham Young University. And then Wanda wants me to do an open house meeting there and then home to Kona to sleep for a week.*

*Whewwwwwwww! … I am tired already!! Anyways . . .*

*Love ya,     aka*

After her last workshop in Austria, Aka returned to Italy, where she suddenly passed away. She was but 50 years old and is deeply missed by her children, Ohana, and her worldwide friends. She, and her mother Fern, will not be forgotten.

Harriet Haleaka ("Aka") Iolani Pule
Born September 7, 1964 in Honolulu
Passed Away August 11, 2014 in Lucca, Italy

# APPENDIX

*A PRAYER BY HALEAKA IOLANI PULE (AKA) as she addressed the State Legislature of Hawai'i, around 2012 or 2013. Transcribed from a video on YouTube filmed by Haleaka's sister, Wanda Puaainahau Iokia.*

*Blessing Prayer: In this house I offer a Pule, which is also our family name: It is a great honor to be here and I thank you. I would like to share just a few words that I learned from my Ohana. Ho'o'ponopono is the most beautiful gift the people of Hawai'i have gifted to the world. This "awareness" of our symbiotic relationship with the universe around us is how we relate and how the universe around us relates to us. Our "acknowledgment" of that symbiotic relationship, in all that we do and all that we say, reflects that relationship. And our "activation" of that relationship is important, not just thinking about it, but doing something with it and for it.*

*Ke Akua, in this place that you have created here . . . this Earth that we call home, we ask for your presence with us here today, and your guidance in all that we do. We ask for your protection. We ask that you soften and open the hearts of those that are here, all of us who are gathered here, for you are the Creator of all life on this planet, in this universe, and all the universes that exist alongside of us. We are here to continue to honor you, and to acknowledge this in all that we do and all that we say. We ask you to open the way. Guide us to all that we need to be guided to. Allow us to reflect this, in every step that we make, every breath that we take, and every word that we share.*

*Ke Akua, we thank you for this beautiful home that we have here in Hawai'i. We are so blessed to know it. Forgive us for forgetting sometimes just how blessed we are. But also, Mahalo for the ability to go out and Aloha all of our loved ones, even those that we don't know. We Aloha everybody that is here. Mahalo for giving us the ability to share, to open our hearts, to open our arms, to open our homes and to share that which may be needed. We ask that we continue to be of highest service to you in all ways. Allow us to see things through your eyes. Allow us to get out of our own way, not reflecting all the hurt of the pain that we have had in our past. We ask that we continue to be of service to all of those that need to be served here . . . all of life. We humbly ask these things.*

*With this prayer, I give each and everyone of you a lei, and I place this lei upon your shoulders . . . as every flower represents the people of Hawai'i. May you wear it proudly.*

*ALOHA!*

*"In our Ohana (family), we know what we're here to do. We're here to kokua (help), share, and contribute positively to this world." -- Aka*

# Glossary

| | |
|---|---|
| 'ae | yes |
| A hui hou | good bye, until I see you again, see you later |
| Aha aha | humble |
| Aha | needlefish |
| Aina | Hawai'ian ancestral land |
| Akamai | smart |
| Akua | God |
| Akualele | fireballs |
| Alapua'a | wedge-shaped regions, mauka to makai |
| Ali'i | aristocrat, royalty, chief |
| Aloha | hello and goodbye, infused with love |
| Aloha'oe | "Farewell to Thee" song written by Queen Lili'uokalani |
| Aloha kakahiaka | good morning |
| Aloha kakou | Aloha to all |
| Ama | single outrigger canoe |
| Anuenue | rainbow |
| Aumakua | spirit helper, personal or family God (shark, owl, plants, rocks) |
| | |
| Haku Po lei | head crown of flowers and greens |
| Halau | space used for canoe making or *hula* dance |
| Hale | house |
| Hana hana | crafts, work |
| Hanai | informal adoption |
| Haole | white person |
| Hau'oli Hanau | Happy Birthday |
| Hoku | star |
| Holoholo | going wandering, a fisherman |
| Honu | sea turtle |

| | |
|---|---|
| Honua | earth, or turtle |
| Ho'okupu | offering |
| Ho'omana | to draw upon, carry, manifest and give spiritual power |
| Ho'oponopono | making right, method to restore harmony and balance |
| Huaka' i po | night marchers |
| Hula | graceful dance, ancient or modern |
| Hula noho | seated hula dance |
| | |
| Ikaika | strong |
| Ili | little |
| Ili Ili | water-worn pebbles; two pebbles were used in each hand in certain hula dances |
| Imu | earth oven |
| Iwi | bones (pronounced 'ivi') |
| | |
| Kai | ocean |
| Kahuna | priest or priestess, expert in certain skill |
| Kahuna ha ha lomilomi | diagnostician in healing and massage |
| Kala mai ia u | pardon me, forgive me |
| Kala'au | clicking sticks used in sitting hula. |
| Kalekona | dragon |
| Kalohe | mistakes |
| Kama aina | person who has lived in Hawai'i for a long time |
| Kanaka | the people |
| Kanaka Maoli | the name of the Hawai'ian people |
| Kane | man |
| Kauna | hidden or secret meaning |
| Keiki | children |
| Ki'i | Ancient tiki carved of wood or stone (once believed to have supernatural power) |
| Kina ole | doing the right thing |
| Ko | sugarcane |
| Koa | warrior, wood |
| Kohola | whale |
| Koko | blood |
| Kokua | to help |
| Kolohe | mischief, rascal |
| Kuleana | spiritual duty, responsibility |
| Kumu | teacher |
| Kumu Honua | first man |

| | |
|---|---|
| Kupuna | elder |
| Kupuna kane | grandfather |
| Kupuna wahine | grandmother |
| Ku'ula | stone monuments for plentiful fishing |
| | |
| La | sun |
| La'au lapa'au | herbal medicine (practitioner) |
| Lani | sky |
| Lei | necklace of flowers |
| Li'ili'i | small |
| Lolo | crazy |
| Lokahi | living in harmony |
| Luau | feast |
| | |
| Mahalo | thank you |
| Mahalo nui loa | thank you very much |
| Mahina | moon |
| Maile Lei | an honoring lei from greens |
| Makai | by the sea |
| Makali'i | Arturus (guiding star for navigators) |
| Make | dead |
| Malama | care for, protect |
| Malama Honua | to take care of the Earth |
| Mana | spiritual energy, power |
| Manao | ideas, thoughts |
| Mauka | uphill |
| Mele Kalikimaki | Merry Christmas |
| Menehune | legendary little people, who work at night |
| Mo'o | lizard, dragon |
| Mo'olelo | story or myth |
| Mo'opuna | grandchild |
| | |
| Na'ia | dolphin |
| Na'au | heart, belly |
| Niele | nosy |
| Ninipoo | baby |
| Noa | freedom |
| Noho | seated hula dance |
| | |
| Okie | cut |
| Okole | butt, behind |
| Olahe Lua | Hawai'ian martial arts |

| | |
|---|---|
| Ono | delicious |
| O'oe pu | you're welcome |
| Opae | shrimp |
| Opala | trash, garbage |
| Opelo | mackerel fish |
| Opu | belly |
| | |
| Pau | finished, empty |
| Pau hana | finished work |
| Piko | belly button, umbilical cord |
| Pilikia | trouble |
| Pleiades | star cluster |
| Pu'eo | owl |
| Puhaku | stone |
| Puhi | eel |
| Puka | hole |
| | |
| Ukana | luggage, baggage |
| | |
| Wa'a | canoe ('w' pronounced 'v') |
| Wa'a kaulua | Polynesian double-hulled voyaging canoe |
| Wahine | woman |

## List of Photos and Illustrations

Cover Art.........."Aka" by Mayumi Oda

Mayumi Oda lives at Gingerhill Farms, in Kealakekua, Hawai'i. She leads retreats there with people from all over the world, guiding them in meditation, gardening, cooking and art. Mayumi is a prolific, world-renowned artist and is often referred to as the "Matisse of Japan." She is especially known for her large Goddess Thangkas. Mayumi is also the author of several books: SARASWATI'S GIFT. The life of a Modern, Buddhist Revolutionary; DIVINE GARDENS: Mayumi Oda and the San Francisco Zen Center; MERCIFUL SEA: 45 Years of Serigraphs; and most recently a deck of Goddess Oracle Cards: GODDESS ORACLE DECK OF KEALAKEKUA. Gichlees: high quality fine art archival pigment prints of Mayumi Oda's art are also available. Website: https://mayumioda.net

Painting of Uncle Robert, p. 184, photo of Palm Trees, p. 372, and photo of Sunset, p. 374, by Koko Momi Kawauchi Johnson

Koko Johnson resides on the island of Molokai, Hawai'i, and enjoys painting, cooking, and gardening. She is proactively involved in the "Aloha Aina" Movement for protecting Hawai'i's culture and land.

Keoua Honaunau Canoe Club and Hale, poster by Carol Tredway, p. 380

Drawing of cowboy and lassoo by Juni Medeiros, p. 442

Juni is a true Paniolo from the famous Medeiros family of South Kona. He worked with his father Alfred Medeiros and band of cowboys for the McCandless Ranch when he was a young man. He is also a writer, artist, recording artist, and well-known musician.

Most of the photos were taken by Nancy, Paul, and Aka's Ohana, unless otherwise noted or unknown. Murals by Herb Kane were photographed on location by the author.

506

## *About the Author*

NANCY CLEMENS WROTE *MY HOLOHOLO DIARY* about a retreat year that took place in 2001-2002 on the Big Island of Hawai'i. It was written from her diary, letters, notes and memory. Nancy lives in Nevada City, California with her life partner, Paul Clemens, on ten beautiful acres of forest and meadows. They have five adult children and four grandchildren. She is an herbalist and gardener, growing her own herbs and flowers for tinctures and salves. She has immersed herself in the Tibetan, Native American and Hawai'ian cultures and is an environmental activist for the dolphins, whales, and their ocean home. For many years the Clemens family opened their home and land to spiritual teachers of many traditions, with Nancy as the event coordinator for these many rustic retreats.

Nancy is also the creator of the *Dolphin Divination Cards* and the author of *A Guide to the Dolphin Divination Cards*. She believes in citizen diplomacy and welcomes letters from friends everywhere in the world.

Correspondence letters may be addressed to
ncnancyclemens@gmail.com
Please also see   www.dolphindivinations.com

## My Holoholo Diary Summary

Loving Hawai'i and having repetitive dreams of the Volcano Goddess, Kupuna Pele, brought Nancy to take a mid-life journey to the Big Island of Hawai'i. With her partner Paul's agreement, she embarked on what she calls "a sabbatical between being a mother and a grandmother."

*My Holoholo Diary* records her adventures, mystical experiences, and challenges while living in the Hawai'ian culture. Nancy's colorful stories bring local Hawai'ian people "to life" with their pidgin English, native wisdom, humor, and warm Aloha.

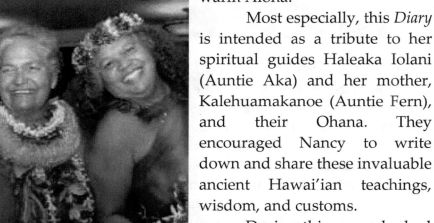

Most especially, this *Diary* is intended as a tribute to her spiritual guides Haleaka Iolani (Auntie Aka) and her mother, Kalehuamakanoe (Auntie Fern), and their Ohana. They encouraged Nancy to write down and share these invaluable ancient Hawai'ian teachings, wisdom, and customs.

During this year, she had valuable training in *Lomilomi* massage and the principles of *Ho'o'ponopono*, met sovereignty activists, and a captain and crew members of the trans-oceanic voyaging canoes.

Nancy shares some almost-unbelievable supernatural experiences she had and the ways they catalyzed a change in her world view. As many *kahunas* say, including Aka and her mother, "Imagine what we could see if we could lift the veils."

Having come many times before to the Big Island on vacation with her family, this time she arrived alone, six days before the New York Twin Towers attack on 9/11, 2001. She immediately witnessed the Island of Hawai'i come together as a community, as people lost their jobs, due to the shutdown of airports and the sudden halt in tourism. She joined the local people as they met to dialogue, to problem-solve, and renew the old self-sustaining ways of their ancestors, and to *kokua* (help) each other.

Her *Diary* sometimes reads like a travel guide as she lived in four different parts of the island, and is full of stories of her jobs and colorful local people, who shared culture, humor, music, feasts, and stories with her. They took her on treks to sacred sites and brought old Hawai'i alive through sharing family stories, history, ceremonies, hula and chants. Many stories illustrate the impact of colonization on Hawai'i.

Lyrical passages in this very intimate diary record her ongoing inner journey of initial loneliness, doubts about this journey, purification, mystical experiences, spiritual opening, and change. Aka and her mother, Auntie Fern, offer guidance and teachings about how to function as a "receiver" in this world.

As the creator of the *Dolphin Divination Cards* and *A Guide to the Dolphin Divination Cards*, Nancy eventually became an advocate of "armchair surfing" to help protect the well-being of the dolphins.

She hopes that, through these stories and teachings, others will receive an infusion of the Aloha and inspiration she was blessed to receive from so many local people. As Auntie Aka always said to her, "If you receive a blessing, the way of Aloha is to share it, in some way, shape or form."

## Praise for My HoloHolo Diary

"Aloha, Nancy!

"I'm grateful and honored to receive your writings of experiences you've had with my mother, my sister, my ohana, my home. How wonderful it is to also read about our culture, traditions, beliefs, and our home Hawai'i. Your "journal" becomes a valuable addition to "my story" which will be passed on to the generations that follow... Mahalo Ke Akua.

"Mahalo nui loa! Malama pono a hui hou."

*– Wanda Puaainahau Kamau'u Iokia, eldest child of Auntie Fern Pule, and Aka's sister*

"I remember when my mom first introduced me to you, asking me if I wanted to go with her to Captain Cook, where you were sharing a booth with my sister, Haleaka. You were like ohana to me, and that was 2009. Your talents and gifts were familiar to me, so I could trust you wholeheartedly, and still (2023) love you, Nancy."

*– Kalehua (Fern) Cardenas, second daughter of Auntie Fern, and Aka's sister*

"I love your book. It brings back a lot of fond memories and I'm holding it forever it my heart."

*– Sarah Kela Pule, daughter of Auntie Fern and Aka's sister*

"I absolutely love your book, Auntie. It brought happy tears to my eyes. It helps bring back what had been gone for so long."

*– Suzy Kalehuamakanoe Reed, daughter of Aka and granddaughter of Auntie Fern*

510

"Nancy Clemens's latest book, *My Holoholo Diary*, will take you with her on a Spiritual Journey to the Big Island of Hawai'i. You will experience sacred places & humble people she meets along the way. Nancy beautifully recounts their wisdom & culture, honoring all Life & Spirit Realms. With each chapter her Storytelling awakens many deeply felt emotions with heartfelt compassion, inspiring one's own life."

*– Roberta Bloom, massage therapist*

"*My Holoholo Diary* is like a true Hawaiian *'aha'aina* or *lu'au*! Nancy has cooked up a richly flavored, deeply nourishing feast of experiences. She uses some mysterious, mystical ingredients and many unexpected blends of sweet, sour, and spicy. Prepared with great love and respect for traditional Hawaiian culture, this book shares the true story of her teachers and their wisdom."

*– Joan Schleicher, Anodos Foundation*

"These reflections, memories and stories are woven with a perspective that allows us all an intimate opportunity to perceive the union of realities in the human experience, Hawaiian legacy, and the craft of the written word. I would read this book for your own good!"

*– Stan Padilla, artist, indigenous educator and cultural activist*

アカにハグされて涙を流さなかった人はいませんでした。彼女は愛そのもの。

混迷の時代、今こそ アカ (ハワイ島 第44代カフナ・ヌイ ハリアカ イオラニ プレ) の叡智が必要です。是非彼女の愛そして叡智を受け取ってください。

"No one cried while being hugged by AKA. She is love. In times of turmoil, we need the wisdom of AKA (Haleaka Iolani Pule, the 44th Kahuna Nui on the island of Hawai'i). Please receive her love and wisdom. – ALOHA"

*– Toshi Koamaikai Suzuki, Aka's close friend and organizer for her teachings in Japan*

"私と同じ質のヒーラーだよ"と言われて
初めて"ありのまま私"を
認めてくれた
私の大切な"オハナ"Aka♡

"Aka told me that 'You are the same type of healer as me.'
It was the first time for me to be accepted as I am.
My precious 'Ohana' Aka♥"

– (Tomoka) Jasmine

ブレス店で突然全身に"稲妻が⚡"　『アカの写真』に感激、この人
に絶対逢いたい、ついにハワイ島に❣
アカの『大きなハグ◎』『自然との調和』決して忘れません♥

"Suddenly, a lightning came through all my body when I
saw Aka in a photo at a stone shop in Japan. I was deeply
impressed by the photo and strongly hoped to meet her. My dream
has come true on the island of Hawai'i. I never forget Aka's big hug
& her harmony with nature."

– (Toshiaki) Frank

アカから繰り返し貰った言葉、無条件の愛♥
アカの美しいピンクトパーズと共に私のハートにいつもあります

"Aka gave me the word 'Unconditional Love♥'repeatedly.
It is always in my heart with the beautiful pink topaz from Aka♥"

– Atsuko

"I can hear Aka's voice through your words. I feel Aka is
sharing with us 'from above'. Nancy, you are an amazing story
teller and writer with deep insight, wisdom and passion."

– Rika Soeda Bilan, Lomilomi massage therapist and
Japanese translator, Big Island of Hawai'i

"So many thanks for writing this book. When I read the text,
I was completely back in Hawai'i and felt all that you wrote, which
took me to the places we were with Aka and the time I spent with
her. God bless you."

– Gerda Fochs, Medical Administration and European
organizer for Aka, Switzerland

"Being with Aka was like a never-ending Aloha bath. Your book reveals Aka's legacy to all readers and all of us who had the grace to be with her. Your words bring me back to the times I was with Aka, listening to her prayers and singing and her wisdom that poured out of her deep state of being ONE with all."
  – *Heidi Oberli, European organizer and translator for Aka's workshops and private sessions for five years; Cranio-Samvahan systemic therapist*

"When I visited Hawai'i for my 75th birthday, Nancy arranged for Aka to do a ceremony for me. The ceremony was extra-special, as Aka called in the whales who joined us just off-shore! I so loved meeting Aka! "
  – *Helen McDonald, revered elder and mentor*

"What a wonderful work you have done. Each line brings back memories of being with Aka. Sentence by sentence I am on the spot with you, experiencing the stories directly!
  – *Christa Bauer, Hawai'i Spirit, Lomilomi trainer, and organizer of Aka's workshops in Austria*

"Aloha. Nancy's personal journey of self-discovery, as she manages her daily adventures on the Moku O Keawe, the Big Island of Hawai'i, is a beautiful, expansive tale that captures the every nuance and challenges of the good, the bad, and the ugly. A great personal memoir and quest for the 'unholy grail'. With much love and laughter,"
  – *E. Kapua Ching, "a fellow FACK KOW WEE"*

"Through Nancy's magical, divine eyes, her experience and view are egoless, pure Aloha. Her stories will bring us right there, in the moment, to enchanting Hawai'i and its people."
  – *Koko Momo Kawauchi Johnson, artist, Hawai'ian activist, and chef, Molokai, Hawai'i*

"Aloha, Nancy Clemens is a beautiful person and author. She embraces the people and culture of Aloha. It is an honor to be at the same table with her."

*— Juni Medeiros, Paniolo cowboy, musician, and artist, Big Island of Hawai'i*

"I loved listening to Paul read some of the stories out loud. Nancy's path is amazing and full of Aloha every blessed step of the way."

*— Lenda Hand, Big Island of Hawai'i*

"This is one of the more beautifully written books we have ever published. Nancy not only writes with heart, but exhibits here her great love for all people and cultures, and a sincere desire to share the insights she has gained from her mentors. Enjoy her exhilarating and very personal trip to Hawai'i from your armchair (or your bed!). Her journey will uplift your life, too, for the better."

*— Paul Clemens, publisher, Blue Dolphin Publishing, and author's best friend and life-long partner*

DOLPHIN CARD: "A WHALE OF A TALE"